W9-ADP-835

ANCESTORS' BROCADES

THE LITERARY DEBUT OF

EMILY DICKINSON

————o🝔o————

Other books by Millicent Todd Bingham

ANCESTORS' BROCADES

THE LITERARY DEBUT OF
EMILY DICKINSON

BY

MILLICENT TODD BINGHAM

. . . but truth like ancestors' brocades can stand alone
—EMILY DICKINSON

NEW YORK AND LONDON
HARPER & BROTHERS PUBLISHERS

1945

This book is complete and unabridged
in contents, and is manufactured in strict
conformity with Government regulations
for saving paper.

To the memory of

my mother

Mabel Loomis Todd

PREFACE

EMILY DICKINSON died in 1886. Her poems, except for a few which appeared anonymously, were not published during her lifetime. Her "literary début," as my mother called it, took place four years after her death. By 1896 three volumes containing 449 poems, edited by my mother, Mabel Loomis Todd and Thomas Wentworth Higginson, had been published by Roberts Brothers, Boston. One hundred and two additional poems had been included in two volumes of letters edited by my mother, and four other poems had appeared in magazines but not in any of the books. This makes a total of 555 poems which, ten years after Emily's death, had appeared in print. At this point publication stopped. The literary début was apparently over.

It was not until 1932 that I asked my mother to tell me what happened. She agreed to do so. But it would take a long time, she said, to explain it all.

As a beginning, she read to me during that summer the passages in her journals and diaries (1886 to 1896, inclusive) which referred to her editing of the manuscripts. We also read letters she had received from Colonel Higginson and from Thomas Niles of Roberts Brothers, from William Austin Dickinson and Lavinia Norcross Dickinson, Emily's brother and sister, as well as letters from friends and admirers of the poems. I copied the letters. I copied extracts from the diaries and journals, a preliminary choice of excerpts, on each of which, and on each letter as we read them aloud, I jotted down my mother's comments. The pile of manuscript was accumulating fast. I was in the midst of putting the documents in order, preparatory to going over with her the raw material of this book when without warning, on the fourteenth of October, 1932, she died. The task of completion was left to me alone.

After a few months' delay I returned to the manuscripts. First I tried to summarize them, to write an account of the original editing based on the letters and excerpts I had copied. The gist of the correspondence, journals, and diaries, I thought, would make a more readable narrative than the documents themselves. But I soon found that no paraphrase would do. To trace versions, to determine reasons for textual alterations, and to settle other debatable points, access to primary sources was indispensable. And the letters at least must be reproduced with all their imperfections even to lapses and colloquialisms, because my original aim was to provide accurate sources of information for future editors of Emily's poems. Nothing more.

In carrying out this purpose I have followed my mother's expressed wishes in all ways but one. In that respect this book is different from what it would have been had she lived to finish it.

When I first began, I thought my task was to give an account of complicated literary work successfully accomplished, one of interest chiefly to the student. But I soon realized that that narrative was only surface deploying. Something was going on beneath the surface. I must find out what it was. In trying to do so I was confronted with a dilemma.

At the request of William Austin Dickinson the name of his wife, Susan Huntington Gilbert Dickinson, had been omitted from the 1894 volume of Emily's letters. My mother respected his wishes. She asked me to do likewise—to make no reference to Mrs. Dickinson in this book. Family feuds were, in my mother's opinion, irrelevant. I tried to comply with her request. But it has been impossible. If this book is to contain a true account of the literary début of Emily Dickinson I cannot leave out any facts pertinent to it of which I am aware. The day for that is past.

My first draft was finished in 1935. I wanted to publish it then, but decided against it as Susan's daughter was still living, and the book is frank. In some respects the delay has been fortunate. For in the interim many letters addressed to the publishers not only by Colonel Higginson and my mother but also by Austin and Lavinia Dickinson have come to light. They complete one phase of the story, many of them being replies to letters from Mr. Niles already in my possession.

PREFACE

Emily Dickinson's family is now extinct. The story of the first editing of her poems and letters can be published for what it is— an episode in American literary history. Facts no longer need to be glossed over or evaded. Passions have been quieted and "truth like ancestors' brocades can stand alone."

M.T.B.

Washington, D.C.
October, 1944

CONTENTS

xi

Appendices

ILLUSTRATIONS

Plates

Facsimile Reproductions

ANCESTORS' BROCADES

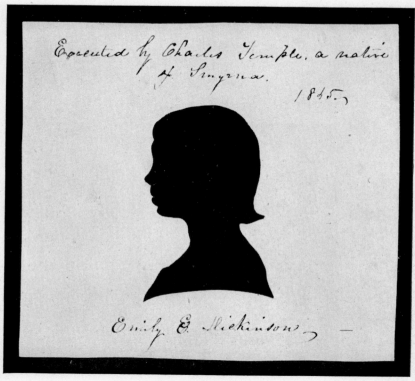

PLATE I

Earliest known likeness of Emily Dickinson

PLATE II

The Dickinson Homestead

From a photograph first used as frontispiece of *Letters of Emily Dickinson*, 1894, Vol. II.

PLATE III

Mabel Loomis Todd as Emily Dickinson knew her in 1882

PLATE IV

Cast of "A Fair Barbarian" "A. B. Frost, Mrs. Leslie and members of the Salmagundi Club

PLATE V
David Peck Todd about 1890

PLATE VI

William Austin Dickinson about 1890

PLATE VII

Thomas Wentworth Higginson and his daughter Margaret in 1885

PLATE VIII

Thomas Niles about 1890

PLATE IX

POEMS, first edition of first volume, 1890

PLATE X
Susan Huntington Gilbert Dickinson in 1897

PLATE XI
Edward Dickinson
Father of Emily Dickinson
Described by Colonel Higginson as
"thin, dry, and speechless"

PLATE XII

Discarded sketch of Emily Dickinson drawn in 1893

PLATE XIII

Child portrait of Emily Dickinson
Frontispiece of *Letters of Emily Dickinson*, 1894, Vol. I

PLATE XIV

Mabel Loomis Todd in Japan in 1896

PLATE XV

Emily Dickinson from a daguerreotype about 1848

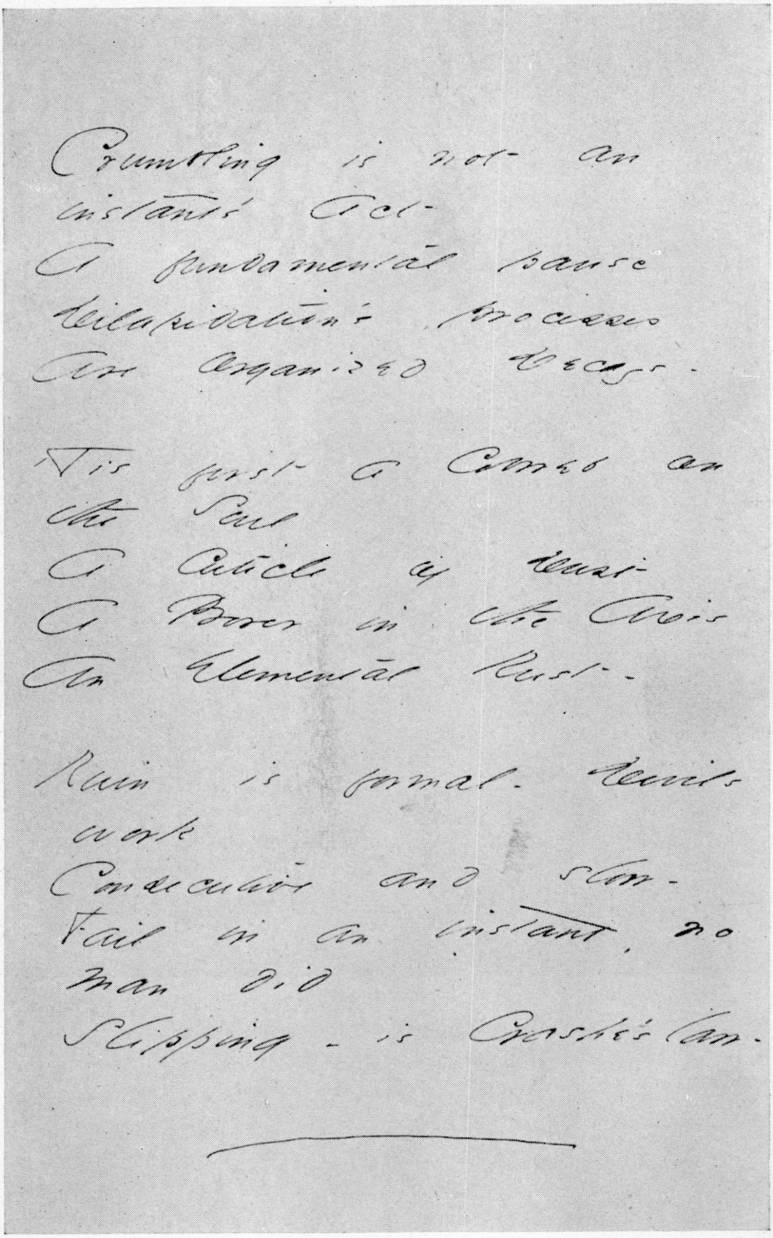

Crumbling is not an
instant's Act
A fundamental pause
Dilapidation's processes
Are organized Decays.

'Tis first a Cobweb on
the Soul
A Cuticle of Dust
A Borer in the Axis
An Elemental Rust –

Ruin is formal – Devil's
work
Consecutive and slow –
Fail in an instant, no
man did
Slipping – is Crashe's law.

PLATE XVI

Poem in Emily Dickinson's handwriting of the late 1860's

Prologue

We must be careful what we say.
No bird resumes its egg.

EMILY DICKINSON has always been shrouded in mystery. Curiosity has been playing about her ever since the first little volume of poems appeared in 1890, four and one-half years after her death. Even before that, in the town in which she lived she had become a legendary figure. The neighbors whispered about her. She stayed always at home, in her father's house, and saw no one. Was it not, someone asked, because she had been disappointed in love? Soon the form of the question changed: "She was disappointed in love, wasn't she?" From this it was but a step to omitting the question. Such was a plausible explanation of her behavior; but if true, who was the man? No one could identify him.

The enigma was not disposed of by her death. It merely took a different form. She had written poems, it seemed. Hundreds of them had been discovered by her sister Lavinia. This was a surprise. Though it was common knowledge that Emily had now and again sent little poems to her friends, her sister and housemate had never been aware of the extent of the activity to which it now appeared she had devoted her life.

Lavinia found a way to begin publishing the poems. There was no mystery about that. "Two of her friends" did the necessary work. Three little books were launched, and more were on the ways. All was going well when suddenly work stopped. No more poems appeared. One of the editors had stated in print that only a fraction of them had been published. The public, as Lavinia put it, "demanded more of her." Why, then, should the issuing of the small volumes have ceased in 1896 with the appearance of the Third Series? For the reader there was no answer. Whatever the cause, a "hermetic stone" had sealed another mystery.

PROLOGUE

For half a century curiosity has spent itself in two directions. If the topic, "Who was Emily's lover?" began to pall, it has been equally enticing and equally unrewarding to ask, "Why, after a generation has passed, do so many of her poems still remain unpublished?" Sometimes the question has taken more pointed form. Why have small collections of hitherto unpublished poems edited by Emily's niece appeared intermittently, each with an explanatory preface that explained nothing? Why the delay? And why the change of editors? As each successive volume came out, reviewers hammered away at the same questions. But so far no answers have been forthcoming.

Why Emily Dickinson chose to retire from the world will remain a matter for speculation. But the intermittent publication of the poems need be a mystery no longer. It can now be disposed of by a matter-of-fact well-documented narrative.

An account of the literary labors preceding the publication of the poetry and letters has historic value. It gives to the reader a glimpse of the task of editing troublesome manuscripts—glimpses also of a poet's workshop. But the story would be a mere collector's item were it not for the fact that interwoven with it is a drama of elemental intensity—a clash of conflicting personalities so insistent and so prolonged that no account of the literary activity can be extricated from the emotional strain in the midst of which it took place. The objective factual account of the literary début of Emily Dickinson is inseparable from the characters and interrelationships of the persons who were closest to it, but who in some cases were obstacles to bringing it about. How such a situation could have arisen it is hoped this book may serve to disclose.

Personalities—very positive, all of them—throw light upon the mystery, from the determination and tenacity of purpose of one woman which touched off the sequence of events, to a legal decree based on personalities rather than on evidence at the end. All of which goes to show how subservient are judgment and reason to the deeper drives of human nature.

CHAPTER I

Dramatis Personae

That sacred closet when you sweep
Entitled "Memory,"
Select a reverential broom
And do it silently.[1]

DEEP in rural Massachusetts the town of Amherst with its two colleges lies on a westward-facing slope above the fertile valley of the Connecticut River. Beyond that broad valley on the west is the faint blue outline of the Berkshire hills. Toward the north rises the rugged mountain-mass of the Toby range—still forest-covered, still concealing deep, cool ravines and mysterious waterfalls where ornithologists look for the Louisiana water thrush and botanists seek out the yellow lady's-slipper in hidden places. The near-by Pelham hills hem in Amherst on the east, with open spaces and habitations among the wooded slopes. Toward the south their level summits subside in a depression where roads and railroads converge. To the right of the gap the bold dark profile of the Holyoke range fills the southern horizon from Norwottock to Mount Tom, an abrupt peak standing out against the far-away Berkshires.

Thus is the span of Amherst vision completed, "a landscape not too great to suffocate the eye." It is a well-defined world, far enough removed from the centers of action, one might think, to satisfy those who wish for quiet—to be alone with books and thoughts in the midst of natural beauty.

During the eighties and nineties Amherst was not, however, the altogether peaceful haven its surroundings would lead one to expect.

[1] Except where otherwise indicated, the lines at the beginning of each chapter are taken from hitherto unpublished poems by Emily Dickinson.

1

In 1881 my father and mother, aged twenty-six and twenty-four, respectively, had come from Washington to live in Amherst. My mother's first impression of the town is given in her own words:

The college, town and general life of Amherst were decidedly different in the early eighties from those in 1930. People at that time were more absorbed in the severities of living than in its gayeties. The faculty were mostly elderly men, their wives estimable ladies of quiet tastes, dressing in dark colors, having their supper at six o'clock, not playing cards, nor dancing, nor doing any of those things which I had been taught in Washington were a part of a lady's equipment; and my first thoughts on entering this somewhat peculiar environment were somewhat amazed, even troubled. Of course they were all courteous, called duly upon this young woman whose husband, notwithstanding his youth, had acquired a reputation for his scientific papers at the Observatory in Washington and for his observations of the sun's eclipse in Dallas, Texas, where he had been sent in charge of the Government expedition when only three years out of college. He was bent on making the little observatory of his Alma Mater as noteworthy as possible.

My own opinion is that they did not wholly approve of me. The students were beginning their "promenades" and some fraternity dances, and they seemed delighted to have a member of the faculty for a chaperon, one who could also dance!

One lady, wife of an older professor, told me when I was about starting my own housekeeping in the D.K.E. mansion,[2] that my bill for shades would be almost too high for a young professor to stand. "But I'm not going to have any shades," I replied with mischief intent. The good lady evidently thinking me crazy, looked at me with amazement for a moment, while I explained that the thin silk curtains I was getting were quite as opaque as shades and far prettier. Evidently a completely new idea to her, and one requiring quite an expenditure of thought. But at all events, she meant well and kindly, and I was grateful.

I soon saw that my life in the New England college town was not to be wholly circumscribed by the orthodox ideas of the majority of the faculty.

[2] "The D.K.E. mansion" was a gaunt wooden house with a tall square tower. It stood in a grove of ancient oaks at the top of the hill behind the Dickinson houses. We lived in it for a year or two before the time when this narrative begins. Later it became the fraternity house alluded to.

The two Dickinson houses, beneath tall trees, stood side by side at a distance of a few hundred feet upon a strip of land bordering Main Street. A dense evergreen hedge was hemmed in by a fence in which there was a front gate for each house with a carriage gate between. Through the gates one caught a glimpse of clumps of rhododendron and other exotic shrubs which blossomed flamboyantly in early summer.

The house of William Austin Dickinson was a smooth, wooden, tan-colored building with a square tower, of the mid-Victorian black-walnut era. It exhaled the decorum of the eighteen-fifties. A walk of granite slabs led up to a few granite steps and again up to a few more toward the massive front door. I can say no more about that house, as I cannot remember ever having entered it. If I was obliged to walk along that part of Main Street, I kept my eyes straight to the front and hurried as fast as I could until I was safely past.

The other Dickinson house, the "homestead" where Emily and Lavinia lived, had been built by their grandfather, Samuel Fowler Dickinson, in 1813. A substantial brick structure with a cupola, it was painted yellow with white trimmings and dark-green blinds. On each side of the swinging front gate stood a giant pine, the gnarled roots of which spread out beneath the hedge and under the gravel walk outside. Here they suddenly reached light and air where the road-level had been cut down ten feet or so to temper the grade of Main Street. A flight of granite blocks spanned this abrupt slope from street to sidewalk leading up to the front gate. I never used that gate, but another, a little to the right, also opening on a walk of granite slabs which led past the conservatory around to the back porch. In the barn beyond lived Tom, the highstepping sorrel horse, and Stephen who took care of him. The fenced-in hedge continued along down Main Street, concealing from passers-by the garden which lay beyond. There were no houses behind the barn, none behind the garden; only a grove of giant oaks on higher ground (Plate II).

On the lower side of Main Street opposite the entire length of the Dickinson property there were but three buildings: opposite Austin's house the granite-built First Congregational, usually called the "Village" Church, the construction of which he had supervised, and two houses. For the rest, there was only an open field, the "meadow" across which Emily's gaze had wandered down toward a little brook at the far end. Beyond the meadow, pied with daisies in early June, the Dickinsons might, through partly closed blinds, look across to the blue hills of Belchertown, where Pelham and Holyoke ranges blend in a depression in the sky line. Halfway across his meadow—for in the eighties he owned it all—Austin Dickinson had, in 1886, cut a street, or rather a private road with square cobblestone posts at the lower entrance. The first house on this new street was built by my parents in 1887—a Queen Anne house, painted red with green trimmings, a shingled second story and an arched porch over the entrance. Our only neighbors were the Reverend Dr. Dwight W. Marsh, a white-bearded retired missionary and his wife. Their missionary son, an only child, was usually absent. The meadow was dotted with rare trees planted by Mr. Dickinson. One great maple with low-swinging boughs above the dell at the back made an ideal play world for a child.

What of the family living in the Queen Anne house?

My gifted, vivid young mother, Mabel Loomis Todd, had been brought up in Washington among distinguished scientists and men of letters. Her father, Eben Jenks Loomis, was an astronomer at the United States Naval Observatory. He was also a poet and a student of nature, a friend of Asa Gray, Henry Thoreau, and Walt Whitman. He was tall and straight with dark eyes, white hair and beard, and the quick, straight step of an Indian. Her mother was a lady of the old school whose father, the Reverend John Wilder, had been the Trinitarian (Orthodox) minister in Concord during Transcendentalist days. The high-bred grandmother, Mary Wales Fobes Wilder, in whose veins the blood of the Pilgrim Fathers was blended with sweetness and light, lived part of the time in Washington with her daughter, and part of the time with us until her death in 1893—her deft fingers usually fashioning lacy objects to my childish amazement and delight (Plate III).

The first Washington home of the Loomises had been in Georgetown, where Mabel attended Miss Lipscomb's School, learning the accomplishments of the well-bred young lady of the seventies. For two winters also she had studied at the New

England Conservatory of Music in Boston. At the time when she arrived in Amherst, she was the most accomplished pianist in the vicinity. She was the soprano in the quartet of the Village Church and the soloist in cantatas given by local talent, as it was called. At our house musical students of the college met to play string quartets or to sing to her accompaniment. In dramatics she was the heroine. A photograph of the cast of *A Fair Barbarian*—a play which focused the histrionic talents of Amherst in 1883, one to which Emily refers in an unpublished letter—shows Mrs. Todd in the title rôle. She painted, too, the flowers of the countryside—dainty conscientious little studies. One of joe-pye weed with a balancing butterfly was chosen, as much because of its beauty as because of its fidelity to nature, by Samuel H. Scudder for the cover design of his monumental twelve-volume work, *The Butterflies of the Eastern United States and Canada, with Special Reference to New England*. She painted friezes in the Queen Anne house, dogwood blossoms against a copper background in one room, magnolia tops against a summer sky in another.

My father, David Peck Todd, a graduate of Amherst College in the class of 1875, had returned, after several years' training under Simon Newcomb at the United States Naval Observatory in Washington, as Instructor in Astronomy and Director of the Observatory. He was a quiet young man, reserved and dignified, more interested in his stars and telescopes than in the society of human beings. In the *Fair Barbarian* picture he sits beside and a little behind his wife (Plate IV).

The other member of the family was myself, the solemn child with the "deep eyes, every day more fathomless," to whom Emily once referred.

Such, with a Negro servant, was the youthful family in the Queen Anne house at the foot of the meadow.

What of the occupants of the two big houses up on Main Street?

Let us for a moment return to a time before my remembrance, before Emily's death in 1886, and read my mother's impressions of Mr. Dickinson and his family, contemporaries of her own parents:

When Mr. and Mrs. Austin Dickinson called upon me as they did shortly after my arrival in Amherst, I was much impressed with both. He was the leading lawyer of the region and Treasurer of the College, a truly regal man, tall, slender and magnificent in bearing, and she well dressed with an India shawl over her shoulders which became her dark beauty.

I should interpolate before going further that of all the Dickinsons Austin's wife, or "Sue," as she was usually called, was the first to take up the young couple from Washington, quick to see that they were out of the ordinary. For a time she considered them her special protégés. They, in turn, were much flattered, since Squire Dickinson's handsome wife—of "lordly bearing and obscure parentage to which she never referred"—posed as social arbiter of the town.

My mother's description of Mr. Dickinson continues:

His eyes were blue. With strong features, his face was shaved except for small burnsides. His hands were white and strong. His voice was a deep bass that boomed so it scared people to death. He was as much a poet as she [Emily]. Only his genius did not flower in verse or rhyme, but rather in an intense and cultivated knowledge of nature, in a passionate joy in the landscapes to be seen from many a hilltop near Amherst, and in the multitude of trees and blossoming shrubs all about him.

Soon after our arrival I began to hear about a remarkable sister of Austin's who never went out and saw no one who called. I heard of her also through others in town who seemed to resent somewhat her refusal to see themselves who had known her in earlier years. Then came a note from this mysterious Emily's housemate, her sister Lavinia, demanding that I call at once, with my husband. I went to the ancestral mansion in which the two lived a few days later.

And then began the series of picturesque encounters which made life in Amherst far from commonplace to me. Lavinia was a brilliant exponent of ancient wit and comment not involving any superfluous love for one's fellow man. . . . I could not help a liking for the fierce denunciations which sprung forth from Vinnie's nimble tongue. Her two passions were cats and her sister Emily. Her wrath over any person, child or grown-up, who attempted to molest her cats was only equalled by one trying to impose upon Emily, whom she was vigorously alert to protect.

"Miss Vinnie," as she was known in Amherst, soon began to send little notes[3] to my mother requesting her to call.

DEAR FRIEND
Will you do me the favor to come down to me, with Mr Todd, this evening for even a few minutes talk? There are fresh whips "on ice" waiting your disposal & rose buds longing for your hands? If I go to you, I may encounter strangers. I shall be ready from 8 to 12 P.M. to see you. No harm shall overtake you, please say yes.

Lovingly
VINNIE D.

DEAR MABEL
Can't you come down & talk with me a while *This* evening? I will provide escort for return home. Please come to the kitchen door. I shall look for you about 7 1/2.

My mother often visited at the home of her parents. Some of Miss Vinnie's early letters sent to her while there have been preserved.

[*Envelope addressed to Mrs D. P. Todd, 1413 College Hill Terrace, Washington, D.C.*]

April 30th [1883]

MY DEAR FRIEND
Your welcome letter reached me about 10 days ago. Thank you for loving words. I wish I could join you in your lovely rambles. I know what Washington is in spring time. I should love to be anywhere with you for your nature rests & delights me. I'm surprised at my missing you so much, for I have seen you only a little. It's too bad that prudence exiles you from so many friends. I think if the real reason of your absence was known, there would be great indignation. I hope the days bring peace to you & that is healing. You are blessed with so many sweet tastes that *all* joy cannot be shut away from you. That is

[3] Letters and other documents quoted in this volume are printed with all their inaccuracies exactly as written, or as nearly so as they can be reproduced in print.

a triumphant comfort! Is n't [it]? I've seen your companion [Mr. Todd] once. I should be glad to lessen his loneliness in any way in my power. His "silent partnership" must be exasperating.

The days are beautiful but so sorrowful without my sweet Mother. I'm so glad you saw her dear face & *she* heard your bird voice. She was so fond of every bird & flower & so full of pity for every grief. Keep fast hold of your parents, for the world will always be strange & homesick without their affection.

Thank you for remembering the little jar. I shall feel honored by any decoration you choose, when you come again. The Indian pipes [panel painted by my mother for Emily] are admired anew every day by lovers of art. Thank you for your charming picture. It only needs your voice to be you.

I hope you are stronger every day. Write to me when you are inclined & be sure I'm Faithful & true

VINNIE D.

In this letter Miss Vinnie refers to the death of her mother. Mrs. Edward Dickinson had been an invalid ever since my parents arrived in Amherst. She died on November 14, 1882. The following excerpts from my mother's notes give the setting for an oft-repeated anecdote.

Their mother, quiet gentle little lady, died without causing a perceptible ripple on the surface of anyone's life or giving concern to any of her family. Emily once said of her that "she does not care for thought." Austin told us that her chief claim to attention had been her constant attempts to bring something to any caller which he or she could possibly require. Her continual questionings had almost exhausted their patience. "Won't you have this or that to make you more comfortable?" or "Can't I bring you another chair?" Such questions were the basis of her poor little attempts to make anyone within her circle happier, which failed sadly, as she never seemed to realize.

One day Emily was holding a very high and intellectual conversation with ——— where they were quite above the mundane plane. Mrs. Dickinson had fussed in and out many times to see if they needed anything, and at last she bustled in, just at some fine climax of the talk, and asked if ———'s feet were not cold, wouldn't she like to come in the kitchen and warm them? Emily gave up in despair at that. "Wouldn't you like to have the Declaration of Independence read, or the Lord's prayer repeated," and she went on with a long list of unspeakably funny things to be done.

Well, she departed this life with little ostentation, and life flowed on as before.

Emily referred to her mother's death as "unobtrusive." And yet that it moved her profoundly is shown in the following letter[4] to a cousin, Miss Harriet Austin Dickinson.

DEAR FRIEND,

I want to thank you for the tenderness to Vinnie, who has been Soldier and Angel too since our Parents died, and only carries a "drawn Sword" in behalf of Eden—the "Cherubim" her criterion. I am glad that you have your mother with you—forgive a pang of covetousness that I have not my own—a sacred place for envy—and you have, I believe, one sister the most, bereaving me again. Mother—Brother—Sister! "What a Triumvirate"!

But Yesterday, and those three Wealths were actually mine! With sorrowing gluttony I look away from your's. Thanking you again for the affection for Vinnie,

HER SISTER—

I am especially glad to have this letter as it reveals Emily's brooding tenderness for her younger sister. Usually she spoke of the practical side of Miss Vinnie's nature and her preoccupation with household tasks. This letter suggests that "specially close" relation to which Miss Vinnie so often referred and around which she built her life. Two more letters from Miss Vinnie follow:

[*Envelope addressed to Mrs D. P. Todd, 1413 College Hill Terrace, Washington, D.C.*]

December 27th [1883]

MY DEAR MABEL

I was delighted to hear from you.

I miss you every day & your companion also, whom I consider *gold* in character.

Winter is here & Sunday was a dreadful day for gloom & cold.

---

[4] This note was sent to me by Miss Harriet Dickinson's nephew, Wallace Huntington Keep, to whom I am indebted for permission to print it.

How I did wish you were in reach of my summons. Austin is oppressed by these "glad days" & I hardly know how I shall cheer him so many weeks without you to help him. Write to him often. I have almost forgotten how joy feels, anxiety for others beside my own sorrow has for the time hidden all light.[5] "Without hope" is a doomed thought. I'm glad your journey was safe. What joy to be with a real Father & Mother. I rejoice you have such a possession. I know what Washington life is & sometimes I wonder if *I* could be whirled into forgetfulness by social excitement. Pardon my way of talking & make no allusion to it when you reply as your letters are read by more than me. I hope you will be well & absorb all the pleasure that comes to you.

Dear love for you & your companion. Kind remembrance for your household in whom I feel a real interest. Write when you can & believe me

Faithfully
LAVINIA

Emilies love
Box 207

[*Envelope addressed to Mrs D. P. Todd, 1413 College Hill Terrace, Washington, D.C.*]

Monday
[*February 5, 1884*]

DEAR MABEL

Your kind note was welcome & I hasten to say a word to catch you before your journey.

I'm glad you have had a satisfactory winter (I wish I had). I shall rejoice to see you here again & I think all your friends will endorse this sentiment. Austin says tell Mr Todd to purchase 8 chairs to match in *color* light oak. I still envy your possession of Father & Mother. Realize the joy to the full for memory is poor substitute for reality. I *know* what *each* means.

The sleighing has been fine & I ride sometimes with Austin. "Tom" whirls us over the white country at a flying pace. I always think of you & wish you could share this pleasure.

Remember me cordially to your parents whose faces attract

[5] Their nephew, little Thomas Gilbert Dickinson, died of a fever on Oct. 5, 1883. Although the date of Gilbert's birth on his gravestone is Aug. 1, 1876, the town records give his age at the time of his death as eight years, two months, five days, which would place his birth a year earlier.

me deeply. I hope I shall know them some time. My love for
Mr Todd & your gentle Grandmother & kisses for Millicent &
her Mother. Emilies love.

> Good bye till you come.
> VINNIE

Miss Vinnie was much attached to my father, whom she
described as "a very true & noble nature." She depended on him,
too, in all sorts of practical ways. He kept her clocks in running
order, including the one on which Emily learned to tell time.
I very well remember how he used to sit in Miss Vinnie's dining-
room for hours at a time with the entrails of a clock scattered
about on the table before him (Plate V).

If she wished to make a call, he usually accompanied her.
One request from her reads as follows:

> Will Mr Todd call to take me to see Miss Kellogg *this* evening
> & ascertain beforehand if she will let us in.

> Most *humbly*
> LAVINIA

On this occasion Miss Kellogg, temporarily in Amherst, replied that she could not receive them, concluding her letter with
the words

> You and Vinnie must not be again "*furious*" with your poor
> sick friend.

> Cordially
> ANNA M. KELLOGG

Sometimes my father escorted Miss Vinnie out of town. Mrs.
George C. Pearl of Haverhill, Massachusetts, recalls their presence at the funeral of her uncle, Sidney Turner, at Norwich,
Connecticut, in 1892. (Mrs. Annie Holland Howe, daughter of
J. G. Holland, told me that Miss Vinnie "could have more
adventures going from Amherst to Springfield than most people
going to Europe.")

My mother's narrative continues:

Austin was delighted to have me know his two sisters. For Vinnie he seemed to have a half humorous, half-absurd feeling not to be compared to his real attachment to Emily. She to him was the embodiment of family devotion. Her curious leaving of outer life never seemed unnatural to him. He told me about her girlhood and her normal blossoming and gradual retirement, and her few love affairs. Her life was perfectly natural. All the village gossip merely amused him. . . .

I went abroad one summer. That really seemed to bring grief to Emily, who, despite her intimate poems upon "Teneriffe, receding mountain," Tunis only "an easy morning's ride," and other remote regions, seemed to feel that a European summer was always danger to her dear friends. . . .

Emily's notes to me became personal and affectionate, and although our interviews were chiefly confined to conversations between the brilliantly lighted drawing-room where I sat and the dusky hall just outside where she always remained, I grew very familiar with her voice, its vaguely surprised note dominant. I usually sang to her for an hour or more, playing afterward selections from Beethoven and Bach or Scarlatti, which she admired almost extravagantly. . . . Dressed always in white, her presence was like an inhabitant of some other sphere alighting temporarily on this lovely planet.

In May, 1886, the visits with the eerie presence, the invisible voice, the phantom in the enchanted corridor, came to a sudden end. Emily was ill.

A few entries in my mother's diary sum up the final chapter:

May 13

Emily sick. I went over there after dinner. No change.

May 14

Went over to Vinnie's at 11.30. No change, only greater weakness. . . . To Vinnie's again on our return, about 6. Still unconscious, & losing constantly. Mr. Dickinson in the evening—for about an hour. He is terribly oppressed.

May 15

Note early—only "a little nearer the great event.". . . Vinnie's at 12.20. All hope given up, of course. Early dinner. Painted dogwood on board until toward five. Then to Mrs. Hills' for an errand. Then to Vinnie's. Emily just leaving. A few very sad minutes there. . . . Across at 8.45. Emily died about six. . . . To bed before ten, full of grief.

May 19

Dull morning. . . . Mr. Dickinson came in with his hands full of apple-blossoms to tell me his final arrangements for the afternoon. Did various things until 3.30. Then David came & we went across to Emily's funeral. The most deliciously brilliant sunny afternoon. Simple "services." Col. Higginson read Emily Brontë's poem on Immortality. Then we all walked quietly across the sunny fields, full of innocents & buttercups to the cemetery.

One who watched the funeral procession as it passed slowly through the blossoming fields—"while bluebirds and orioles were singing ecstatically and apple-blossoms were filling the air with delicious odors"—remembers only how small the coffin was.

Through those old grounds of memory
The sauntering alone
Is a divine intemperance
A prudent man would shun.

It was not Emily, however, but her closest relatives who fashioned the pattern of my life. The harsh qualities of her father which had passed her by had settled upon her sister Lavinia.

There she sat in her apple-green kitchen, or on the sheltered back porch, an uncompromising, slender little figure in a black cashmere dress made in the style of the sixties. The knife-pleatings which adorned it fascinated me. Her sour, shriveled face with its long nose was wrinkled like a witch of the fairytale, her hands twisted and knotted like the faggots in the wood box. But her hair, her marvelous dark hair streaked with gray, seemed to concentrate all the juices of her wizened body—heavy, luxuriant, the focus of interest in her person. Sometimes it was tied in a sort of bowknot on the back of her head, held fast by two large pins shoved in from either side. But often she sat there with it hanging, while with her gnarled hands, outspread fingers rigidly extended, she thrust through it slowly, caressing it from root to farthest tip. Pussy sat near by washing her face, and fat Maggie billowed about the kitchen as Miss Vinnie sat slowly combing her hair with her knotty fingers. Any tradition which pictures her as a mild, sweet New England spinster will be dissipated, I think, during the course of this narrative.

Sometimes she would open the door into the dining-room, windows always shut, inner blinds so nearly closed that the pattern of the dark-blue china on the sideboard could hardly be distinguished—the design an old-fashioned ship in a strange harbor, called "The Landing of Lafayette." If I tiptoed in, it was to receive an apple, perhaps, but I had to go far away to eat it for Miss Vinnie could not bear the sound of crunching.

Oftener, when the dining-room door opened, there sat Mr Dickinson. I cannot remember that he ever addressed a word to me except "Hello, child!" A spare, lean man sitting rigidly erect in his chair, his face, clean shaven except for red side whiskers, was without a smile. I could not have guessed how he would look if he should smile. It would not have occurred to me to try to guess. A shock of fine, silky, coppery hair stood out in an aureole about his granitic face. This was Squire Dickinson, tall form faultlessly dressed, with high collar and long gold chain, his slender feet in soft kid shoes of curious square cut. Austere and haughty, yes; but to me just the somewhat terrifying center of the universe—though why he was I could not have said. When he came to see us, he put on a brown velvet cap which he kept in our music case. He knew all about a wood fire, just where to put a bright coal on top of two smoldering logs to pull the flame up through. One did not venture to touch the fire in his presence, but one might brush the hearth (Plate VI).

Who were the members of his household living in the square house with the tower—the family in the forbidding house behind the hedge next to Miss Vinnie's? To meet one of *them* on the street—there were three in all, his wife, his son, and daughter—benumbed the day. That they could be human beings, made of flesh and blood, never occurred to me. They were a race apart. To make any connection between the velvet-capped man sitting at our fireside or in Miss Vinnie's dining-room and the blight which fell upon me from a chance encounter with any member of his family was beyond my power or my wish to do. I accepted the situation. Although I never heard, or overheard, one of them referred to by anybody, I would have run a mile rather than risk meeting any one of the three face to face. A bolt from heaven would have been no surprise to me if anyone had dared to speak their names aloud. But no one ever did.

CHAPTER II

Preliminaries

The poets light but lamps,
Themselves go out;
The wicks they stimulate,
If vital light

Inhere as do the suns,
Each age a lens
Disseminating their
Circumference.

BETWEEN the date of Emily's[1] death and the time when Thomas Wentworth Higginson was first consulted about the poems, three and one-half years elapsed—from May, 1886, through November, 1889. For the most part the account of that period can be given in my mother's words. Some of it is taken from the source books, her diaries and journals. The little diaries give a day-by-day record of events. The occasional entries in the large journals, supplementing the diaries, touch on things that lay beneath the surface. Part of the story is taken from an early draft of "Emily Dickinson's Literary Début," an article in *Harper's Magazine* for March, 1930; part is taken from her account of the editing of Emily's manuscripts, written in the nineties, and part from her comments made to me verbally as we went over her diaries and journals together in the summer of 1932. My mother says:

Shortly after Emily's death her sister Lavinia came to me actually trembling with excitement. She had discovered a veritable treasure—a box full of Emily's poems which she had had no instructions to destroy. She had already burned without exami-

---

[1] Emily Dickinson was referred to as "Emily" by her contemporaries—by those who did not know her as well as by those who did. This implied no intimacy, if anything, rather the opposite—a detached deference.

nation hundreds of manuscripts and letters to Emily, many of them from nationally known persons, thus, she believed, carrying out her sister's wishes, without really intelligent discrimination. Later she bitterly regretted such inordinate haste. But these poems, she told me, must be printed at once. Would I send them to some printer—as she innocently called them—which was the best one, and how quickly could the poems appear?

Having already had some experience with publishers, I told her that no one would attempt to read the poems in Emily's own peculiar handwriting, much less judge them; that they would all have to be copied, and then be passed upon like any other production, from the commercial standpoint of the publishing business, and that certainly not less than a year must elapse before they could possibly be brought out. Her despair was pathetic. "But they are Emily's poems!" she urged piteously, as if that explained everything.

I asked her how many there were, but that she could not tell. She showed me the manuscripts and there were over sixty little "volumes," each composed of four or five sheets of note paper tied together with twine. In this box she discovered eight or nine hundred poems tied up in this way. They looked almost hopeless from a printer's point of view. The handwriting consisted of styles of three periods, absolutely different one from another. All were written in a hand which to most persons is exceedingly difficult to read, and many words were liable to be widely misconstrued. The poems were written on both sides of the paper, interlined, altered and the number of suggested changes was baffling. Almost every page had a number of crosses [before] many of the words. Each cross referred to a choice of several words at the bottom of the page which the author had thought equally good, and quite as expressive of her meaning as the word actually employed in the text. There was nothing whatever to indicate which word was supposed to fit into which place. The crosses were all alike. As there were frequently several sets of such changes on a page, no guide to assist in choosing could be relied upon except a sense of the working of the author's peculiar mind, by which the most characteristic word should be retained from the choice of several which she had indicated. It was of course necessary if anything were to be done about publishing the poems that they should be clearly and carefully copied and edited in copying, by choosing always the best of the author's own suggested changes, and putting the poems into such shape that they could be submitted to a publisher and easily read by him. The mere copying, I estimated if pursued for four hours each morning, would occupy two or three years, and if time was used in carefully selecting the most characteristic of her own suggested alterations, might take much longer.

Actually, several months elapsed before I began the work. During that time Vinnie was trying to secure help elsewhere.

That is all my mother says about that.

In point of fact, Miss Vinnie had first taken the box of poems to Mrs. Austin Dickinson who professed great admiration of Emily's work. Miss Vinnie asked her to do the necessary copying and editing. That she refused we know from Miss Vinnie herself, who described her efforts in a letter to Colonel Higginson on December 23, 1890, shortly after the publication of the first volume of poems. The complete text of the letter is given on pages 87-88. A sentence or two will suffice here.

If you knew my disappointed endeavors for 2 years before Mrs. Todd & yourself came to my rescue, you would realize my gratitude to you both. Mrs. Dickinson was enthusiastic for a while, then indifferent & later utterly discouraging. . . . But for Mrs. Todd & yourself, the "poems" would die in the box where they were found.

Discouraged in her first attempt at publication, Miss Vinnie next wrote, my mother says,

to Colonel Higginson, to whom Emily had been for more than twenty years in the habit of turning for literary advice, to ask whether he would be willing to see the poems through the press. He wrote that he was extremely busy, and that the confused manuscripts presented nearly insuperable obstacles to reading and judging such quantities of poems. Though he admired the singular talent of Emily Dickinson, he hardly thought enough could be found to make an even semi-conventional volume. He told her that if this tangle of literary wheat and chaff could be put in easy shape for consideration, he would be glad to go over it carefully. Otherwise he could not give the necessary time.

Meanwhile, Lavinia continued to urge me throughout the

same period of time to undertake the work. She came frequently to our house, almost always late at night begging me vehemently to begin, only *begin* on the poems. One winter evening she arrived just before midnight. She was more than ever certain that I *must* undertake it. I knew that once begun, they would take most of my time until they should be in shape to submit to a publisher. Lavinia almost went on her knees to me that night, and it hurt me to see her so intensely in earnest over what might prove disappointing. But at last I did promise to put the poems in shape, try to find a publisher, and to begin the very next day.

And I did so, in spite of the fact that both Lavinia's brother and my husband expressed themselves as hoping I would not undertake a piece of work which would certainly require years to finish.

Those nocturnal visits were part of Miss Vinnie's "pattern," as the phrase goes nowadays. It was a habit to which we were all accustomed, one which, though sometimes inconvenient, we were obliged to accept. She merely disliked having her movements known to her neighbors and so made her calls after dark.

In the little back parlor of the Queen Anne house with its blazing fire and its magnolia branches flowering against a summer sky, beside the window which opened toward the big maple tree overshadowing the dell there was usually a fever of work in progress. My mother sat at one desk, my father at another, correcting proof, or writing in large ledgers. Had I looked over their shoulders, the chances were that I should have seen sheets of Emily's picturesque manuscript spread out before them. Such was the focused interest of our family in that topic that even I was sometimes called in to help with the endless task of copying. The other day, among the hundreds of copied poems, I came across a group in my own childish hand. Initiation into the vagaries of Emily's handwriting is one of the earliest rites that I can recall.

In the spring of 1887 [my mother continues] my husband received an appointment as Chief of the United States Eclipse Expedition to Japan, to observe the total eclipse of the sun on August nineteenth. Although we had just completed our new house in the meadow facing Lavinia's, and were not at all inclined to leave it, the appointment was a great honor and we could not refuse. Accordingly, we left Amherst on June eighth for Vancouver, by way of the recently completed Canadian Pacific Railway, and did not return to Amherst until the thirteenth of October.

The following letter from Miss Vinnie was received in Japan:

[*Envelope missing*]

July 16th [1887]

MY DEAR MABEL

I hope you are very well & enjoying your new & interesting experience.

I miss you very much & feel there is one less to help me in emergency. So far as we have tracked you everything seems bright. Your pretty home is a constant picture—its lawn as green as mine & the trees all thriving.

Mrs Marsh finds it quite convenient! I know you will see wonderful things. I should like to join you in shopping trips. You are fast taking in the entire world. I wonder *where* the next freak of the sun will lead you! I hope Mr Todd is sound again. [He had had a brief illness just before leaving.] Your friends here are so glad of this rest for you. I expect you will have a regal visit & every kindness. If you can *easily* bring home some little thing not costing over a dollar [for] me to give Maggie & Stephen, perhaps a silk handkerchief—I should be grateful—but don't trouble about it. I almost feel as if you were in my closet, some of your dresses having decided to spend the summer with me. Maggie has made some royal currant jelly for you. It is sealed & awaiting your mouth.

Stephen is to be married in 2 weeks. My dear little tabby pussy is dead & I really pine for her sweet little ways. It's hardly safe to love anything.

With warm love for you both I will leave you for this time. Keep well & dont forget

LAVINIA

Maggie & Stephen wish to be remembered to you both.

Miss Vinnie's request for "some little thing" for Maggie and Stephen, her servants, was a familiar one. Indeed, my mother seldom went to Boston without making some purchase for Miss Vinnie, whose interest in tangible objects and their money equivalent was a dominant characteristic.[2]

In November, 1887, after her return from Japan, my mother's diary indicates that she had already begun to copy the poems. She says:

. . . As I have said, Vinnie called the little fascicles "volumes." . . . As they were copied, I took them over to her and we read them together. If the meaning of any was in doubt, she would

[2] Two notes, both postmarked Apr. 14, 1884, refer to such an errand. My mother explained that Miss Vinnie had admired a cloak of hers and wanted one like it.

[*On the envelope, addressed to Mrs D. P. Todd, Boston, Mass., the letter head of the Parker House, Boston, Mass., was pasted in the lower left corner, the stamp in the lower right*]

Monday A.M.

DEAR MABEL

Your promp[t]ness is angelic. I will take the [$]16.25 or 16.45 as this may be. Austin will pay the amount when he sees you. Could you get 2 like the 16.25 if I should want? after seeing mine or would it be too late & how early in the Fall are "bargains" made? You need not trouble to write again unless a postal to assure me you have received these words. Austin can bring the box with him, so it can be packed ready for the journey. I appreciate your kindness in a way that my future conduct will show! I rejoice in all your happy time. Love for Mr Todd & yourself. Should you see in windows, blue cups for baking custards, please ask the price & tell me when you come. Don't allow my wants to burden you in the least.

Gratefully
VINNIE

16.25—16.45

Monday

DEAR MABEL

I answered your kind letter this *noon*, requesting you to purchase the 16.25 cloak. Lest it fail to reach you, I repeat the wish for the 16.25 cloak.

VINNIE

After 1887 the trip to Boston became less difficult, for the Central Massachusetts, a bucolic little railroad connecting Boston with Northampton by way of Amherst, was opened in December of that year. It ran through lovely country but not one large town and was scorned by our affluent friends. They compared the trip from Amherst to Boston, a distance of ninety-seven miles, to a trip at sea. But my mother enjoyed the three- to four-hour journey, often bouncing along on the milk train which left Amherst long before light on winter mornings.

try to remember the circumstances under which the poem might have been written. But she worked in a vague sort of way, most exasperating to me.

During the month of September, 1888, I went to the seashore for a brief holiday before the beginning of the college year, much to Vinnie's regret. She deplored the interruption of work on the poems. While gone, I received from her the following letter.

[*Envelope postmarked "Brattleboro & Palmer. . . , Sep. 11, 1888"*]

Tuesday

DEAR MABEL

Thank you for longed wished seeds & papers & letter—

I'm rejoiced you are thriving on sea charms.

It seems very strange never to see "Aunt Todd or Uncle David" "going out & in before us"

Stephen's going seems like a fresh death in the house, he is associated with so much that was precious—

I may want to ask an errand or two when you are in Boston. Will you have any time there? I shall send a letter to the Parker House for you—

I should like to join hands with you in the "surf." 'Twas a delight in early days—A saddle horse & the sea were the only playthings I valued! Remember me warmly to your kindred whom I hope to meet by & by & be sure I miss you & "Uncle David." Pussies send love & are pretty well—pears are awaiting the knife & kettle. Stay longer if you fatten in strength & then be ready for poems!

Lovingly
LAVINIA

The fantastic appearance of Miss Vinnie's handwriting is due in part to the fact that she refused to wear glasses. She would not capitulate to age. And so her writing, never clear, became more and more illegible. The half-formed letters sometimes overlap. They are so misshapen that a key is needed to decipher the text: "would," for instance, looks as if written "whuld," and one is led not without reason to doubt her spelling. She almost never wrote out the word "and," but used instead a hieroglyph which began as an "&," turned into a loop, then subsided into a dash with a quirk at one end. Fortunately, however, the mannerisms

Letter from Lavinia Norcross Dickinson to Mabel Loomis Todd
September 11, 1888

like a fresh
death in the
house, he is
associated with
so much that
was precious,—
I may want
to ask and expound
up me when you
are in Boston,
While you have
any time There
I shall send
a letter to the
Parker House
for you.
I should like

to join hands
with you in
the "duff". Truly
a delight in
early days —
a double hustle
to the dock were
the only play
things I knew,
Remember me
warmly to
young Kindled
Whom I hope
to meet by &
by & be Sure
I miss you.
& "Uncle David"

Pretties and lace & are pretty
well - peas are awaiting
the knife & kettle. Stay
longer if you
& waken in strength
& there be ready
for poems!

Lovingly

Lavinia

are more or less uniform. Once a code is established the script becomes clear.

Miss Vinnie had her own ideas about punctuation. She seldom made a paragraph, placing the most incongruous ideas in juxtaposition so that one is led without a break from pathos to grotesquerie. While dashes usually replaced commas and periods, she sometimes did use commas, but instead of periods. With numbers, an apostrophe took the place of a period between digits, although she dispensed with apostrophes where required, as in the case of possessives. If space was lacking at the end of a line, a question mark was cut in two, the upper part of it placed above the final letter of the last word, the lower part below; and when a word was divided, the hyphen was put not at the end of the first, but at the beginning of the second line.

Envelopes were usually addressed by herself in ink, even though the letter was written in pencil. But sometimes she followed Emily's example, pasting on the envelope a printed address cut from a newspaper or from hotel stationery. The stamp was placed in the lower corner of the envelope, sometimes at the right, more commonly at the left.

Miss Vinnie's fading eyesight had another disadvantage. It was becoming impossible for her to read, which would have been a greater hardship for one who "cared for thought." In later years her chief reliance upon the printed page was placed in *The Springfield Republican*. Every morning as the retinue of cats performed their ablutions she would sit in the kitchen while Maggie read it aloud to her.

I regret that I have been unable to find a picture of Miss Vinnie in her later years.[3] A few snapshots are known to have been taken of her in garden clothes with a "pussy" on her shoulder, but although I have made inquiries about each one—several persons having been so kind as to go through their garrets at my insistence—the search has been fruitless. As a partial substitute I offer the following reminiscences of Wallace Huntington Keep, a young cousin of the Dickinsons who graduated from Amherst College with the class of 1894. On his arrival

[3] The only known picture of Lavinia Dickinson was made in her girlhood.

in September, 1890, he was taken by his mother to call on Miss
Vinnie. He says:

I can remember how deeply I was impressed by "Vinnie"—as
Mother addressed her affectionately—by her unkempt hair and
lack of style and by her mobile face and fascinating talk.

We had arrived about eleven in the forenoon intending to
stay for only a half hour, but Lavinia insisted that we must stay
to lunch so we did; but the dainty lunch proved to be for the
two ladies *only!* Her maid of many years, Maggie, had set the
table for two and before they were seated I was assigned to a
seat not far from the table where I could *see* what they were
eating and be heard if necessary. . . . Nary a bite to eat nor a sip
to drink was offered me! . . . I longed to have a taste of the
good things, but the best Lavinia would do was to ask me to
come *after* I had had my supper the next Saturday evening
and she would give me some apples and pears. Just why she
chose to discriminate so painfully against me and my youthful
appetite I could not understand. . . .

Well, on that first Saturday evening, lonesome and homesick
at being separated so far from Mother's apron strings I went
to Lavinia's kitchen door and received a cordial welcome; and
for an hour she entertained me with her quaint style of conversation. Her chief topic concerned my boarding place and if
I was getting "good nourishing meals." . . . When on later
weekly visits her anxiety regarding my meals grew to be somewhat monotonous and insincere I would think up in advance
some fresh adverse criticisms respecting either the quantity or
the quality of the food that was furnished me at my boarding
place in order to secretly enjoy and be amused by the varied
looks of distress or horror or despair that would be pictured
in her features.

When my hour was up she would address her many cats that
were ranged about the floor of her large kitchen, calling each
one by his or her own pet name, and opening the door leading
to the cellar stairs she invited certain of the cats to precede her
and then, with her lighted candle in one hand and a large
basket in the other she started down the stairs followed by all
the remaining cats. As I recall these felines now it seems to me
there were from eight to ten of them, perhaps a dozen though
I doubt whether there could have been. At any rate it was an
impressive procession and all the way down the stairs she kept

up a constant conversation with them and through the big
cellar until her voice and footsteps were too distant to be longer
heard and the only sound in that big house was the tick-tocking
of the kitchen clock. After an interval of possibly five minutes I
began to hear her footsteps and voice again and these growing
louder told me she was on the way up the cellar stairs. The
same two or three cats that preceded her downstairs preceded
her on the climb up and finally all the felines were back and
Lavinia laid down her candle and heavy basket of fruit. She
would never permit me to accompany her to the fruit cellar
or carry the basket when it was loaded. I kept up those weekly
and fruit-ful Saturday evening visits all Freshman and Sopho-
more years.

On one occasion in spring when the day was still bright she
took me through her house and with great solemnity showed
me Emily's room. How I wish I could remember all that Vinnie
would tell me of her sister! . . .

The cats were Miss Vinnie's closest companions after Emily's
death—her "pussies" whose wants were commands. She used
to say "pussy wishes" this or that. Her friend Miss Buffum told
me that "one day Vinnie's cat brought in a Wilson thrush, and
when I expostulated, she said, 'You must blame the Creator.' "

Emily had tolerated the cats up to a certain point, for Vinnie
had been surrounded with them from childhood. But it is difficult to love birds and cats with equal fervor, and Emily agreed
with Miss Buffum:

> His bill is locked, his eye estranged,
> His feathers wilted low,
> The claws that clung, like lifeless gloves
> Indifferent hanging now;
>
> The joy that in his happy throat
> Was waiting to be poured,
> Gored through and through with death. To be
> Assassin of a bird
>
> Resembles to my outraged mind
> The firing in heaven
> On angels, squandering for you
> Their miracles of tune.

Next to her "pussies" Miss Vinnie loved her garden, an enthusiasm Emily shared. Some of her most characteristic notes refer to it, this for instance—long weeks of care distilled in a few words: "Your sweet beneficence of bulbs I return as flowers." Miss Vinnie gave the garden her personal attention and was always alert to protect it from harm. The first killing frost of autumn Emily called "a visitor in marl" (incorrectly printed "a visitor in March" in the current edition[4] of her poems). Of this visitor she says:

> But whom his fingers touched,
> And where his feet have run,
> And whatsoever mouth he kissed
> Is as it had not been.

Miss Vinnie used the same figure of speech in a letter to my mother, September 25, 1883: "I smell a frost coming, so I must prepare my garden for avoiding his kisses."

The Dickinson way of speech was contagious. Even Maggie, enclosing her card in a gift to my mother, expressed her admiration in extravaganza:

Visiting card of Miss Margaret M. Maher, Lavinia Dickinson's servant "Maggie," sent with flowers to Mrs. Todd

Beginning with the year 1889 work on the poems progressed at a more rapid rate, though still not fast enough to suit Miss Vinnie who, my mother continues,

was feverishly anxious to have the copying and arranging proceed as swiftly as possible. Frequently she came by night to our

[4] The current edition of the collected poems, bearing on the title-page the name of Martha Dickinson Bianchi as editor, will be referred to hereafter as "the current edition."

house and urged me to work faster, telling me that Emily's especial friends were dying so rapidly that she feared there would be no one left to welcome them [the poems] even if they did see the light of print. She begged me to work on them every possible moment, adding that if it were really tiring (which she could not imagine) she would give me a strengthening drink once in a while if I would only come for it. And indeed several times I did stop work long enough to run over to the old, ancestral mansion across the meadow, to take a milk and egg and whiskey combination most delicious.[5]

. . . . The poems were having a wonderful effect on me, mentally and spiritually. They seemed to open the door into a wider universe than the little sphere surrounding me which so often hurt and compressed me—and they helped me nobly through a very trying time. Their sadness and hopelessness was so much bitterer than mine that

> I was helped
> As if a kingdom cared.

Most of them I came to know lovingly by heart, and I was strengthened and uplifted. I felt their genius, and I knew the book would succeed. No one else had faith in them—except Vinnie, and hers was a blind sort of faith, not in the least from any literary appreciation of their power. . . . It was during the year 1889 that I tried to get a copyist [Miss Graves, later Mrs. Houghton, of Amherst] to help me. But it took more time to strike out rejected words and arrange the chosen phrases for her, and then to correct the strange mistakes made in the copy, than to do the whole thing myself. So I gave up trying to secure help and continued to do it all.

The pile of copied poems was growing larger. By this time it was more than three years since Emily's death, and there were several hundred in shape for judgment. The time was drawing near when they could be shown to Colonel Higginson. Meantime Lavinia had been discovering more and more poems which

[5] "We used to spend hours and hours," my father told me, "just looking at the poems. Vinnie would bring over a basketful which she would dump on the floor in front of the fireplace in the back parlor at night. After your mother had finished copying them, I compared them with the originals and then she went all over them again. It took hours and hours of my time."

Emily had herself never copied, scraps merely. They were written on margins of newspapers, on grocers' brown paper bags, on backs of envelopes, or other homely medium, and some of the finest were among them. These there was no time to copy. Though Lavinia had known that Emily had been in the habit of sending poems to her friends, she had not known that she had been in the habit of writing others. Indeed, Lavinia had not even known that she had copied poems in the little "volumes." So this ever increasing quantity filled her with amazement.

Meantime, my husband was planning another expedition. This one being also under the auspices of the Government, the U.S.S. *Pensacola* had been detailed by the Navy Department to him as Chief of the Expedition to observe the total eclipse of the sun in West Africa on December 22, 1889. As the *Pensacola* was a combatant vessel, however, women were not allowed, and I was left behind. My husband sailed on October sixteenth for Saint Paul de Loanda, Portuguese West Africa.[6] On October twenty-fifth I left Amherst for Boston where, with my mother, my grandmother and my little daughter I was to spend the winter, returning at intervals to Amherst to give lessons in painting and singing. On these visits I always lunched with Lavinia, and curious lunches they were! A small table was set for me in the dining-room, where I ate alone. Lavinia herself waited upon me, while a gallery of cats solemnly looked on.

Soon after I reached Boston I tried to see Colonel Higginson, at first without success. Lavinia's eagerness to hear his verdict is shown in her letters to me. The first was received about two weeks after my arrival.

[*Envelope missing*]

November 5th [1889]

MY DEAR MABEL

I hope you are comfortably settled at last. I think you have had a cruel experience. I hope you are well & will enjoy many luxuries. I miss you & Mr Todd more even than I expected. I wish you might have stayed in your lovely home.

I suppose you received Col. Higginson's reply. Should you find convenient time before you come again, perhaps you would

---

[6] Eben J. Loomis, *An Eclipse Party in Africa*. Boston: Roberts Brothers, 1896. My grandfather was official historian of the expedition.

copy the few originals that we selected the last time we separated the *printed* [typed] from the *written*. I would rather *they* should not be out of *your* hands. In case you copy these, please bring the original with you. Pardon if I ask too much. I shall rejoice to see you hurrying along as of old. My chrysanthemums are glorious—*they* miss you. I shall be eager to hear about Col. Higginson & your meeting.

Love for you & Mrs Andrews[7]
Faithfully
LAVINIA

My mother was ready to accept as final Colonel Higginson's judgment regarding the poems. Though a lesser figure he had been coeval with the greatest and that sufficed. There was but one questioning voice. My grandfather, whose contemporary he was, had his doubts. Himself a poet as well as a man of science, he had explored with Henry Thoreau the woods and fields of Concord. He had walked in the Shenandoah Valley with Walt Whitman when the latter was a government clerk in Washington and he himself was computing stellar distances and planetary perturbations. Against such a background the attainments of Thomas Wentworth Higginson did not loom large. He admired Mr. Higginson's courtesy and gentle breeding, and he cast an understanding if reserved eye toward many of his reforms and enthusiasms. That he was equipped to appraise obscure works of genius, however, my grandfather questioned. But his dissenting opinion was expressed with no particular emphasis and to Colonel Higginson the poems went (Plate VII).

All could not be taken to him, of course. So, from the vast conglomerate of poems in all stages of completion, a residue had been sifted through screens of varying sizes. Those which Emily had copied into the little "volumes" were finished poems. Others, though rough in form, contained breath-taking thoughts. Still others had merely the glint of an idea, jotted down for future use.

My mother says:

---

[7] The wife of John A. Andrews, a Boston merchant, who lived in the Hotel Kensington at the corner of Boylston and Exeter Streets.

I selected from among the hundreds of copied poems about two hundred of the most characteristic, most different from the mediocre verse being put forth in papers and magazines. Armed with what seemed to me the most remarkable poems written within recent years, I went to Cambridge to interrogate Mr. Higginson.

On November sixth he returned the visit.

Colonel Higginson came [the diary says]. He staid an hour or more, and we examined the poems and discussed the best way of editing them. . . .

Colonel Higginson asked me, in order to save his time, for he was not well, to classify the poems into three sections, A, B, and C. He suggested putting all the best ones, and my own favorites, into a class marked *A*—not only those of most original thought, but expressed in the best form. The next choice, *B*, those with striking ideas, but with too many of her peculiarities of construction to be used unaltered for the public, and *C*, those I considered too obscure or too irregular in form for public use, however brilliant and suggestive. During the next ten days I worked on the final arrangement and my copying of the poems, and on November fifteenth I went to Amherst, and as usual lunched with Vinnie. These lunches throughout the winter were devoted to discussion of the poems.

On November seventeenth my mother "finished final re-reading of the poems and prepared them for Mr. Higginson." This preliminary choice was sent to him on the eighteenth. He mentions them in his diary for the first time on November 20, 1889. A few days later he wrote the following letter, of which only the two opening sentences have been published.[8]

Cambridge
November 25, 1889

MY DEAR MRS. TODD

I can't tell you how much I am enjoying the poems. There are many new to me which take my breath away & which also have *form* beyond most of those I have seen before. That one

[8] Mary Thacher Higginson, *Thomas Wentworth Higginson, the Story of His Life*. Boston: Houghton Mifflin Company, 1914, p. 368.

descriptive of the shipwreck for instance! ["Glee! the great storm is over!"] My confidence in their *availability* is greatly increased & it is fortunate there are so many because it is obviously impossible to print all & this leaves the way open for careful selection. I have to proceed slowly, being busy in other ways; have gone through about half your "A" section, rejecting some (provisionally) & dividing the rest into three headings (provisional also)

1. Life
2. Nature
3. Time, Death and Eternity

Perhaps you can suggest more subdivisions. The plates will cost rather less than $1 per page & there can often be two poems on a page—rarely more than one; say $230 for 250 pp. including 300 poems. Would that satisfy Miss Lavinia?

> Ever cordially
> T. W. HIGGINSON

Nearly a month elapsed before the next word came from him.

> Cambridge
> *Dec.* 19, 1889

DEAR MRS. TODD
I am at work with many interruptions on those poems; have gone through *B* & transferred about 20 to *A* (we *must* have that burglary ["I know some lonely houses off the road"]—the most nearly objective thing she wrote). *C* I have not touched.

> Ever cordially
> T. W. HIGGINSON

And so we come to 1890, the year in which the first tentative little volume of the poems of Emily Dickinson was to appear.

Miss Mary A. Jordan, Professor of English at Smith College, 1884-1921, referred to Mrs. Todd's task as one of "creative editing." Whether or not the term is appropriate will appear if, while Colonel Higginson is occupied with the poems from among which he is selecting enough for a volume, we go back and examine a few of the obstacles which had been disposed of before they came to his attention.

CHAPTER III

Creative Editing

They have a little odor that to me
Is metre, nay, 'tis poesy,
And spiciest at fading, indicate
A habit of a laureate.

SOME of the difficulties which confronted Mrs. Todd in her task of copying the manuscript poems have already been touched upon. Problems connected with editing the letters will be discussed in later chapters. A few of these were mentioned in the Introduction to *Letters of Emily Dickinson*, first published in 1894 and reissued, with additions, by Harper & Brothers in 1931.[1] In this chapter I wish to amplify some of the more urgent points at issue in 1890, particularly those which perplexed my mother.

The copyist-editor encountered a wide range of difficulties. First, deciphering the manuscript was a task in itself. It is easy to misread Emily's handwriting. Though it can be roughly divided into three periods, gradations from one period into the next provide a number of variants. But, to borrow an alien word, if norms of each period are compared they bear little

[1] Books relating to Emily Dickinson brought out by Mrs. Todd:
Poems by Emily Dickinson, edited by two of her friends, Mabel Loomis Todd and T. W. Higginson. Boston: Roberts Brothers, 1890. Hereafter referred to as "*Poems*, 1890."
Poems by Emily Dickinson, Second Series, edited by two of her friends, T. W. Higginson and Mabel Loomis Todd. Boston: Roberts Brothers, 1891. Hereafter referred to as "*Poems*, Second Series."
Poems by Emily Dickinson, Third Series, edited by Mabel Loomis Todd. Boston: Roberts Brothers, 1896. Hereafter referred to as "*Poems*, Third Series."
Letters of Emily Dickinson, edited by Mabel Loomis Todd. Boston: Roberts Brothers, 1894. Hereafter referred to as "*Letters*, 1894."
Letters of Emily Dickinson, edited by Mabel Loomis Todd, new and enlarged edition. New York: Harper & Brothers, 1931. Hereafter referred to as "*Letters*, 1931."

resemblance one to another. The earliest hand, though micro-scopic, is legible; but few poems were written in that hand. Although the writing grows progressively more difficult to read, once the key is discovered uncertainties disappear. This is due to the fact that the writing of each period is consistent, so that within a given period a *b* is always a *b* and an *f* an *f*, even if to an unaccustomed eye neither looks much like the specified letter. The evolution of the handwriting of Emily Dickinson, the mere mechanics of it, apart from the importance attaching to it as a means of determining approximate dates of composition, will one day provide an interesting study. (See facsimile, Plate **XVI.**)

Once the handwriting had been mastered, editing began. For, in copying, it was often necessary to choose one word from among many alternatives—a point which should be emphasized, since the form in which we know many of the poems is due to this original selection.

It was not always easy. My mother says:

In one copy of the well-known poem on "The Humming Bird" which she [Emily] had sent to me, and which is one of the very few named by herself, she offered four alternative words in the line, "With a revolving wheel," which is the way it is left in her own copy. At the bottom of the page is written, "with a delusive, dissembling, dissolving, renewing wheel." But in this case as in many others I retained the word she evidently pre-ferred, using it in her own final copy. In the many poems where several words were offered for choice, it often seemed as if those suggested were only to make her meaning clearer, more unmis-takable, and almost never to smooth rhyme or rhythm.

Emily never made a final choice in the last stanza of "The Bible is an untold volume"—a poem entitled by her "Diagnosis of the Bible by a Boy"—which reads in manuscript

> Had but the tale a thrilling (typic, hearty, bonnie,
> breathless, spacious, tropic, warbling, ardent,
> friendly, magic, pungent, winning, mellow) teller
> All the boys would come—
> Orpheus' sermon captivated,
> It did not condemn.

But in a draft of "The Preacher" Emily underlined the words she preferred.

> He preached *upon* (about) breadth till *it argued him*
>   (we knew he was) narrow—
> The broad are too broad to define;
> And of truth until it proclaimed him a liar—
> The truth never flaunted a sign.
>
> Simplicity fled from his counterfeit presence
> As gold the (a) pyrites would shun.
> What confusion would cover the innocent Jesus
> To meet (at meeting) so *religiou*s (enabled, accomplished,
>   discerning, accoutred, established, conclusive) a man!

I present these documents with hesitation on two accounts. First, I question whether it is fair to give so intimate a glimpse of Emily's workshop, even though she once acknowledged to Colonel Higginson that "for several years my lexicon was my only companion." Second, I do not wish to imply that she never finished a poem. In the majority of those she herself wrote in the little fascicles no alternatives were suggested. The fact remains, however, that the present form of many poems was determined by the first copyist. When a systematic study of my mother's editing is made, the reasons governing her choice among alternate readings should be investigated. Some of these considerations will be referred to later in the correspondence between Colonel Higginson and Mrs. Todd.

Emily placed a great responsibility upon her editors by leaving to them so often the choice of a key word. For it authorized them to color her thought with their taste. Obliged so often to make a choice, they might be tempted to go further, to *change* a word to fit their own preference—a dangerous leeway, for the thought is timeless while taste may change. It is well to bear this in mind in connection with the efforts of both Mr. Higginson and Mrs. Todd to make Emily's poems rhyme. Her apparent indifference to it bothered them. In the nineties rhyme, particularly in a lyric, was the first necessity—as now it appears to be the last. Here is an example of the kind of thing they felt called upon to do:

> That is solemn we have ended,
> Be it but a play,
> Or a glee among the garret[s],
> Or a holiday,
>
> Or a leaving home; or later,
> Parting with a world
> We have understood, for better
> Yet to be explained.

That is the poem as it reads in manuscript. As printed, the last line reads, "Still it be unfurled."

Textual changes ranged all the way from altering a word to make a rhyme, or to conform to the rules of grammar, to leaving out entire stanzas. In the famous poem, "Arcturus is his other name," the second stanza was omitted:

> I slew a worm the other day,
> A savan[t] passing by
> Murmured, "Resurgam! Centipede!"
> "Oh, Lord, how frail are we!"

While omitting a stanza might sometimes improve a poem, it was more often a mistake.

Other editorial decisions incidental to copying were not so much matters of taste as of typographical convention. Emily's habits with regard to punctuation were individual to say the least. The editors decided that her way of beginning important words with capitals would not convey in print the nuance of emphasis intended. Capitals must be used sparingly if at all. Another pet device, that of underscoring for emphasis, would look exaggerated as italics on the printed page. Superfluous quotation marks, too, were scattered through the poems. Were they intended as guideposts, the editors questioned, if the strangeness of a word was considered too shocking? Or did Emily use them because she wanted to reassure the reader that she meant what she said? However that might be, the poems usually lost nothing by the omission. Decisions such as these were quickly made. But other vagaries were not so easily disposed of. As Emily grew older, she dispensed with punctuation more and more until at last she was using dashes for the most part, with an occasional comma or period. What should be done about those dashes? To what conventional forms did they most closely correspond?

Questions like these were inseparable from those of verse form—length of line, division into stanzas, and so on. Though the quatrain was Emily's preference, it was by no means the only form she used. And she often wrote but three or four words to the line, so that a capitalized word might be mistaken for the first word of another line. This matter of length of line was not unimportant to her. In a letter to Colonel Higginson she says (referring to a poem which had been incorrectly printed, one of the few published during her lifetime), "It was . . . defeated, too, of the third line by the punctuation. The third and fourth were one."[2] But her spendthrift use of capital letters often makes it difficult to tell where Emily did intend that the lines should begin.

Though most questions of this sort had been settled by my mother previous to November, 1889, when she first took the poems to Colonel Higginson, debatable points were marked for later discussion with him, textual changes in particular. If there was any doubt as to the *meaning* of a poem or of a phrase, it was usually Colonel Higginson who raised the question and Mrs. Todd who offered the explanation—a fact worth noting in view of his greater age and experience. (See "tare," pages 142 and 146.)

Though both editors considered it necessary at times to smooth the poems off, they preferred to make as few changes as possible—to leave a poem as Emily wrote it. But they knew that if she was to be read at all, she must be presented in a form not too disturbing to the reader of the nineties, who might be discouraged if a poem did not fit an accustomed mold. Eccentricities of grammar and spelling, too, might so prejudice a critic that he would dismiss the poems after one glance. So a good many changes were made.

Habitual mistakes in spelling were corrected: "woe" for "wo," "veil" for "vail," "bouquet" for "boquet," "peninsula" for "peninsular," and so on. The editors also agreed to correct lapses

---

[2] *Letters*, 1931, p. 282.

such as "her's," "it's," and "your's," even if sanctioned by the King James's Version of the Bible.

Again, Emily misspelled or misused certain geographical names—"Vevay" and "Saint" Domingo, for example—errors easy to correct. But who would wish to change the mythical locality "Himmaleh," which stood for distance and altitude and unapproachable majesty, into an authentic range of mountains bounding India on the north? She leaned most heavily upon that "trusty" word during the sixties.

When it came to bad grammar, however, there was room for difference of opinion. Emily used "him" for "he" and "her" for "she":

> Had nature an Iscariot,
> That mushroom, it is him.

And the poem beginning, "Her little parasol to lift," ends with the lines,

> Content if nature's drawer
> Present me from sepulchral crease
> As blemishless as her.

This mistake also was current in New England.

Colonel Higginson usually stood for correct usage. And yet he it was who preferred "lain" when "laid" was correct. Emily always misused that past participle. She even seems to fondle the word. An unpublished poem begins:

> Lain in nature, so suffice us
> The enchantless pod
> When we advertise existence
> For the missing seed. . . .

My mother particularly disliked this mistake. In her letter of December 29, 1890, to Colonel Higginson she asks, "And do you think it best to leave the ungrammatical use of *lain* instead of *laid*, in 'When one who died for truth was lain'?" As Colonel Higginson preferred "lain," it so appeared.[3] But his preference

---

[3] See his own misuse of "laid" in a letter on p. 309.

was often challenged, not only in the poem, "I died for beauty," but in others as well. Each time the word appeared it gave rise to argument and each time he prevailed. Even outsiders protested. The following letter was received from one of the joint principals of a school for girls. Across the top of this letter Colonel Higginson wrote in pencil, "I have discouraged this."

> Dana Hall
> Wellesley, Mass.
> *February* 22, 1891

Col. T. W. Higginson
DEAR SIR

Would it be an "impertinence"—to borrow your own word—to ask if one change might not be made in the next edition of Emily Dickinson's Poems?

On page 119, in the line, "When one who died for truth was *lain*," could not *laid* be substituted without harming the poem? The poem on the following page has the same error in the last stanza, but an amendation would be more troublesome there.[4] To most of the educated people of New England, the confusion of *lie* & *lay* is condoned with some difficulty, and the writer of this note is the more sensitive, perhaps, with regard to a grammatical error of this nature, from the fact of her having known Miss Dickinson, and also in her having the most unspeakable delight in her poems.

Trusting that I have not troubled you by my suggestion, I am,

> Very truly yours,
> JULIA A. EASTMAN

Professor Whicher of Amherst College has suggested that Emily's grammatical errors are mostly traceable to the fact that she followed current *spoken* usage, a point which will reward further investigation.[5] For the first editors the perennial uncer-

---

[4] Entitled by Colonel Higginson, "Troubled about Many Things," the last line of this poem, "How many times these low feet staggered," reads, "Indolent housewife, in daisies lain!"—*Poems*, 1890, p. 120

[5] George F. Whicher, *This Was a Poet*. New York: Charles Scribner's Sons, 1938. In this scholarly volume some of the points referred to in the present chapter, completed before Mr. Whicher's book appeared, are treated at length. Many niceties brought out by him, though important to scholars, do not belong here. I have tried to confine myself to questions of policy which concerned the editors in the nineties.

tainty was: which are mistakes and which are intentional irregularities with a definite function to perform.

Grammatical vagaries were not so troublesome as Emily's idiosyncrasies, most of them trivial but distinctive, such as using "of" for "by,"

> A clover's simple fame
> Remembered of the cow,

and her chaos of singulars and plurals. "We cannot put ourself away," printed "ourselves" in the poem, "I tie my hat," is an example of a frequently recurring mannerism. In "I died for beauty," the seventh line, "And I for truth, the two are one," reads in manuscript, "And I for truth, themself are one." Emily persistently used a plural verb with a singular subject, as in the poem, "Air has no residence, no neighbor," which ends

> Ethereal guest at e'en an outcast's pillow,
> Essential host in life's faint, wailing inn,
> Later than light thy consciousness accost me,
> Till it depart, convoying mine.

To change the verbs to "accosts" and "departs" would defeat not only the meaning but the Miltonic surge of sound. This "mistake," my mother thought, was deliberate, as Emily's use of "be" for "is" was deliberate,

> Menagerie to me
> My neighbor be.

Though these peculiarities were mere elision, they gave rise to much discussion half a century ago. Emily's grammatical irresponsibility is well summed up in a line of an unpublished poem, "This chasm, sweet, upon my life," which reads "Ourself am lying straight wherein."

The subject of textual changes and the reasons for them includes not only those made by the editors, however. Emily herself sometimes altered her manuscripts. This topic offers both a perplexing dilemma and an enticing field of investigation for future scholars. It opens the way to the whole matter of versions, of which in her handwriting there are sometimes as many as half a dozen of a single poem. In order to trace its evolution the penmanship is of course the best guide. A manuscript of the sixties may be corrected in writing of the eighties. For finished poems—those copied by Emily in the little "volumes" of eight or ten sheets of letter paper—in some cases both the draft and the copy (in which alternative words may still remain) have been preserved. She further confused the issue by sometimes enclosing in a letter a poem which had been composed much earlier—as shown by the fact that copies of it exist in the writing of both periods. Only by comparing as many as possible in Emily's own handwriting can the preferred form, the form in which she finally left a poem, be determined with certainty.

But there is yet another complication. In some instances, although the writing of both versions is of approximately the same date, they may not agree, making it difficult if not impossible to say which was "the original" version. The question may even arise as to what constitutes a separate version. Two poems sometimes differ by only a word. In a second copy of "Who robbed the woods," the pronoun "who" reads "I" throughout the poem. Sometimes a change of punctuation gives a twist to the thought. Sometimes a line, an entire stanza, or series of stanzas is added to a quatrain which can stand alone, as in this unpublished poem:

> I heard as if I had no ear
> Until a vital word
> Came all the way from life to me,
> And then I knew I heard.
>
> I saw as if my eye were on
> Another, till a thing—
> And now I know 'twas light because
> It fitted them—came in.
>
> I dwelt as if myself were out,
> My body but within,
> Until a might detected me
> And set my kernel in.

And spirit turned unto the dust,
"Old friend, thou knowest me,"
And time went out to tell the news
And met eternity.

With only slight changes Emily used the final stanza elsewhere as a complete poem:

The spirit said unto the dust,
"Old friend, thou knewest me,"
And time went out to tell the news
Unto eternity.

On the other hand, some versions are different enough to constitute separate poems.

The multiplicity of versions is partly due to the fact that Emily used her poems for different purposes. She often sent to a friend a stanza—or just a line—from a longer poem. She altered a word to fit a case. "Going to him, happy letter," reads in a different copy, "Going to her, happy letter." In *Poems*, Third Series, page 109, we find

Not knowing when the dawn will come
I open every door;
Or has it feathers like a bird,
Or billows like a shore?

After hearing of the death of Helen Hunt Jackson, Emily sent the same poem to Colonel Higginson, changing it to read

Not knowing when herself may come
I open every door.
Or has she feathers, like a bird,
Or billows, like a shore.[6]

Here is an unpublished love poem:

One thing of thee I covet,
The power to forget,

[6] *Letters*, 1931, p. 320.

> The pathos of the avarice
> Defrays the dross of it.
>
> One thing of thee I borrow
> And promise to return,
> The booty and the sorrow
> Thy sweetness to have known.

With the stanzas inverted, and a few slight changes, the poem served to thank Colonel Higginson for a book.[7]

Out of all the conflicting difficulties loomed one perpetual problem, a decision which confronted my mother afresh with each poem—should it be published or not? Just how much shock, of form or of content, could the reader absorb? Irregularities of usage and roughnesses of expression now accepted as part of Emily's technique, many readers thought merely grotesque half a century ago. Such things must not be permitted to subject her to ridicule, of course. But, my mother told me, technical correctness seemed to her beside the point. She always doubted whether the poetry should be judged by such a standard. For instance, should a poem be rejected because it was rough when an inner spark might hold enough power to change the course of a life? Should it be discarded if it contained a word not in the dictionary? Emily could invent a word if there was none to suit her need, as in "Size circumscribes," two lines of which read

> The giant tolerates no gnat
> Because of *gianture*.

When Emily Dickinson was unknown, her acceptance by the literary world problematical, such decisions were weighty. The poems chosen to introduce her must not be too queer. The editors never ceased to feel handicapped by this limitation.

Further discussion of editorial problems is not within the scope of this chapter. For the present, enough has perhaps been said to suggest what Professor Jordan meant by "creative editing."

[7] *Letters*, 1931, p. 313.

CHAPTER IV

The Poems Reach the Printer

Unproved is much we know,
Unknown the worst we fear.

As THE new year opened, the year 1890, my mother, my grandmother, my great-grandmother, and I were still in Boston during
the absence of my father and my grandfather in Africa.

For several weeks Colonel Higginson had been examining
the poems—edited, copied, and classified—which my mother had
taken to him in November. Throughout this time Miss Vinnie
kept writing to my mother. Her letters, addressed to "Mrs. Prof.
David Todd, 124 Boylston Street,[1] Boston, Mass.," reveal her
impatience for his verdict.

January 3ʳᵈ [1890]

My Dear Mabel

I'm so grieved you should have had such a hard time. You
didn't deserve it. I should have sent loving messages to you by
Austin had I known he was going to Boston. I fail to see *how*
the "African Expedition" has (so far) been sanctified to *you*.
My *native* views of *sky work* is not abated! I do hope there'll be
no more briers in *your* part! The poetic breaking of gay bottles
is hardly ratified on your side! But that you know *how* to *find*
the sweet in every bitter flavor I should be more anxious.

Your gift was the most *vital* of my Xmas courtesies. Thank
you again for always thinking of me in some pretty way. I dare
say you may not have seen Col. Higginson yet. Your lunch will
be all waiting when you come. It seems a long time since you
were seated at *your* little table with a pussy by your side.

Love for your household & Mrs Andrews & yourself.

Lavinia

Maggie is charmed with her dress & sends gratitude

[1] In 1890 the house on Boylston Street bearing this number stood opposite
the Arlington Street Church.

I asked my mother to tell me more about the "little table." She explained that

Vinnie didn't keep house at all. Maggie went out every day at two o'clock [to her house below the railroad track] and came back to sleep. Vinnie did not sit down at a table. When she invited me to lunch she brought me my things on a little table in the dining-room, just inside the kitchen door. She never joined me. She never gave me coffee, nor milk, but sandwiches and a cream whip with a piece of cake which was very nicely made.

She used to dress herself up in the most horrible things you ever saw and go out into the garden.

Miss Vinnie's next letter came a month later:

February 6th [1890]

DEAR MABEL

I enclose a note that discourages me, please return it when you come. I hope you are well & not taxing your strength too much. I hope Mrs Andrews reception was a success. I sent a letter to her which I hope she has.

Have you seen engravings & "*spotted*" any?

Mrs *Lawrence* is very ill & in great danger. I do little but visit homes where sickness reigns. Take care of yourself & believe me lovingly

LAVINIA

[*Enclosed in the same envelope*]

February 6th

Mrs Lawrence died, yesterday P.M. I was fond of her & shall miss her. What can Mr Hills do without her? I pity him so.[2]

LAVINIA

Nearly three months had elapsed since the poems had been put in Colonel Higginson's hands. "We had hoped," my mother said, "that the enthusiasm he had expressed to me in November

---

[2] Leonard Dwight Hills, friend and neighbor, later became Miss Vinnie's business adviser. Mrs. Lawrence was his housekeeper. His estate was separated from the Dickinson property by a lane, now called Triangle Street.

might have led him to communicate with us sooner. Lavinia's impatience at his silence was mounting every day." This impatience was aggravated by the fact that my mother was soon to leave for a long-planned visit in Chicago.

Feb. 27th

MY DEAR MABEL

I was disappointed not to receive any message from you by Austin. I hoped to know if you had any word from Col. Higginson. I wouldn't *ask*. I trust you will call upon him before you leave Boston. You are acting *for* me & I'm quite sure you will not be refused admission. You need not trouble to *answer* these words. I know you are brim full of sweet & I'm glad of it.

Lovingly
LAVINIA

March 4th [1890]

MY DEAR MABEL

Your letter dated 28th & mailed March 2, reached me *this* morning. I wish you had told me before & then I should have asked you to go *to him* without farther notice. If *possible* can you call *tomorrow*? You are acting for me & *not* yourself. I can't believe he has gotten any word from *you*. I wrote him you would call upon *him* & maybe he expects you whenever you are ready to do so. It is a great disappointment & surprise that this *delay* must be. I *now* regret the poems are in his hands.

Perhaps you can't see him at this late hour, but I wish 'twas possible.

The "Town Meeting" was one of the Devils Choicest. The mob had their own way & the vilest mouths were hurled at every white man. Respectable persons fled the place lest their souls be soiled beyond water. The Indian described the first steam engine as "Hell in harness." The above occasion was the same place "bare backed"!

I shant kill you if you dont find our friend but I shall wish.

Lovingly
LAVINIA

In spite of Lavinia's commands [my mother continued] I was obliged to leave Boston before another meeting with Colonel Higginson could be arranged. My little daughter and I left for

Chicago on March twelfth. We remained there two months, returning to Amherst on the fifteenth of May. My husband returned from Africa shortly thereafter.

During her absence in Chicago, the following letters were exchanged:

[*Envelope addressed to Mrs. M. L. Todd, Care Mrs. A. L. (L. A.) Coonley, 391 La Salle Avenue, Chicago, Illinois*]

April 16ᵗʰ [1890]

My Dear Mabel

I was glad to hear from you & glad you are reasonably well. I hope your lunch was satisfactory. It seems very strange not to see you for so long a time. I trust your Western experience will be a pleasure to remember even if you tire (sometimes) of *all* social life. Work is luxury when one is in condition for it. Company manners would soon end my bodily career! I enclose a note from Col. Higginson. I replied at once telling him I would forward his words to you. I told him I thought you could not attend to *your part* of the poems till you returned to Boston. I should not think it *wise* to send them so far, even if you had time & I know you have not. I like his classification. I asked *him* to write the paper for the "Century" magazine if he thought it desirable. How does the suggestion strike you?

When are you coming home? I hear many pleasant words said of you. The Hyacinths are in their glory. Sorry you can't share them. Maggie thanks you for thinking of her. Get all the rest you can. I shall rejoice to welcome you home again. Love for Millicent & her Mother.

Faithfully

Lavinia

I shall want the 5 volumes [fascicles] I have to go to Col. Higginson with you.

The enclosed letter from Colonel Higginson ran as follows:

Cambridge
Apr. 8, 1890

Dear Miss Lavinia

I have selected & arranged about 200 poems, classified as follows

Life	44
Love	23
Nature	60
Time & Eternity	72

199

Now I should be glad to have Mrs. Todd go over them again. What is her present address? She was going to Chicago.

I think these will do to begin with. Then, if you wish, others may follow. The best way to prepare the way for them will be for some one to write a paper, perhaps for the "Century" magazine, with some specimens.

Ever cordially
T. W. Higginson

My mother continues:

Soon after my return from Chicago I received a letter from Colonel Higginson asking me to come to see him. I met him in Cambridge on May thirtieth and arranged about taking the poems to Roberts Brothers [3 Somerset Street, Boston].[3] The head of the firm was Thomas Niles, Jr., a bachelor and an urbane, cultivated gentleman [Plate VIII]. He had written to Emily several times it seemed, and had received remarkable letters from her, all of which he later sent me. But to publish her "lucubrations" had always seemed to him "most undesirable." Still, he would look them over, give them to a reader for the house, and let us know as soon as he received the verdict.

Unfortunately, on the occasion of my first visit [May thirty-first] Mr. Niles was ill, and I was obliged to leave the precious little package, asking that he communicate with Mr. Higginson as soon as he had had the opportunity to read the poems.

[3] My father told me that Colonel Higginson first recommended the poems to Houghton Mifflin Company for publication, as he was one of their readers at the time. They decided against it. The poems, they said, were much too queer—the rhymes were all wrong. They thought that Higginson must be losing his mind to recommend such stuff.

"Next," said my father, "we thought of Roberts Brothers. Being a reader for Houghton Mifflin, Colonel Higginson did not want to ask another Boston publisher to bring out a book which they had turned down." This may explain why it was Mrs. Todd rather than Colonel Higginson who first took the poems to Mr. Niles.

During the week following, Professor Todd went to see Mr. Niles. I quote my father's words:[4] "Mr. Niles was accustomed to use his own judgment in literary matters. We thought he would be especially interested in Emily's poetry as he had had some correspondence with her about 'Success,' published anonymously in his *Masque of Poets*. But he was scared to death about printing the poems! He suggested a hectograph edition of five hundred copies. He said he would himself pay for such an edition. I said, either the poems should be properly printed in the best possible dress or not at all and walked out. Later he came around to my way of thinking."

On the twelfth of June my mother received a letter from Colonel Higginson enclosing one from Mr. Niles, as well as a report from the poet Arlo Bates, to whom Emily's poems had been sent by Mr. Niles for appraisal. Mr. Bates's report follows, then the letter from Mr. Niles to Colonel Higginson in which the report was enclosed, and finally Colonel Higginson's letter to Mrs. Todd.

There is hardly one of these poems which does not bear marks of unusual and remarkable talent; there is hardly one of them which is not marked by an extraordinary crudity of workmanship. The author was a person of power which came very near to that indefinable quality which we call genius. She never learned her art, and constantly one is impelled to wonder and to pity at the same time. Had she published, and been forced by ambition and perhaps by need into learning the technical part of her art, she would have stood at the head of American singers. As it is she has put upon paper what reminded her of a mood or an emotion, and in nine cases out of ten she has not got enough down to convey the intelligence of her mood to any but the most sympathetic and poetical. There are some poems in the book, however, that are so royally good, and so many that to the poetical will be immensely suggestive, that it seems a pity not to have at least a small edition.

It seems to me, with all due deference to those who did it, that

---

[4] The part played by my father, especially in seeing the poems through the press, has hitherto been overlooked. For several years he gave a good deal of time to the work—to proofreading in particular. "We made independent lists of the ratings, A, B, and C, and then compared them," he told me, adding that "we used to sit up all night to read the proof."

the work of exclusion, that most ungrateful task, has not been pushed far enough. The "cold permanence of print" would put a different color on many of these. It would seem to me best to make a selection, and have it edited with a good deal of care. There should be few changes as possible, but some are absolutely necessary, while there is not the slightest pretence of anything it is fair to call punctuation. I have taken the trouble to number the poems, and these are those which I should include.

[Here follows a list of numbers with comments. Unfortunately, since his numbering of the poems has not been preserved, those approved or condemned by him cannot, with one or two exceptions, be identified.]

I have been through the poems twice, pretty carefully. Some that I have included I have chosen for the enticing charm of a single phrase as I suppose the original selectors may have done. I think the force of the volume, it being understood just what it is would carry it farther than most volumes of verse go nowadays. Its faults are colossal, but it has the real stuff in no stinted quantities. I have cut it just about one half. The religious poems are the weakest and least original, but their very conventions make them the best for the closing section as they are put. I do not think the volume would make a tremendous stir. I do think it would be a distinct success of esteem.

ARLO BATES

I do not know that you wish to show this to Col. Higginson, but I have no objection if you do.[5]

Arlington
June 10/90

DEAR MR HIGGINSON

It has always seemed to me that it would be unwise to perpetuate Miss Dickinson's poems. They are quite as remarkable for defects as for beauties & are generally devoid of true poetical qualities. If, however, Miss Dickinson will pay for the plates, we will publish from them at our expense a small ed, say 500, which shall be exempt from copyright, all future issues to be subject to 15% copyright on the retail price of all sold.

[5] In view of Mr. Bates's estimate of Emily's poems it is well to recall his own standing as a poet at that time. A review of his book, *The Poet and His Self* (1891), in the *Boston Herald* contained these words: Arlo Bates "gives greater promise of high and enduring power than almost any other American poet of our own generation."

I enclose Mr Arlo Bates' criticism, not, however, for any other purpose than to shew you the opinion of a poet who is not apt to be optimistic.

I have had an opportunity to read the poems while confined to the house, & if Miss Dickinson wishes us to publish them if she will notify Messrs. Roberts Bros to that effect, they will forward the MSS either to her or to you as she may direct.

> Yours very truly
> THOMAS NILES

T. W. Higginson, Esq.

> Cambridge
> *June* 11, 1890

DEAR MRS. TODD

I think Mr. Bates's criticisms excellent. Niles will send you the poems & please revise with these criticisms & then return to me. I'll send you the *rejected* by express. My address will be Dublin, N.H., after Friday.

> Yrs. ever
> T. W. HIGGINSON

P.S. I have told N. that you will probably approve his offer.

The effect produced by these communications is told in my mother's words. The reader should bear in mind, however, that in spite of her "fury" Miss Vinnie accepted Mr. Niles's offer.

The fury of Vinnie over these mild descriptions of her beloved sister's extraordinary writing might, I suppose, be imagined, although she had no real literary appreciation of Emily's verses. But they were Emily's. To her loyal mind that sufficed. Vinnie was inarticulate with rage. She swept away the entire publishing profession in her wrath. I half agreed with her, though the comments of publisher and critic were perhaps as complimentary as we ought to have expected. But at the time the opinions of both Mr. Niles and Mr. Bates were disappointing. Besides, in connection with his criticism, Mr. Bates had cut the number of poems practically in half, leaving out the most striking of the two hundred submitted, among them, "I died for beauty," "Safe in their alabaster chambers," and "How many times these low feet staggered." Of course I could not bear that, and I put back about twenty of his "discarded" ones. Of these I wrote to Mr. Higginson in detail.

Mrs. Todd's letters to Colonel Higginson at this time have not been preserved, but his replies follow:

Dublin, N. H.
July 3, 1890

MY DEAR MRS. TODD

I have gone nearly through the poems numbering & rubbing out pencil marks. My opinion of Mr. Bates has gone down greatly, for he certainly wished to leave out several of the best. In all cases I have agreed with you & kept the poems. I am sorry you did not use an *eraser* for dashes, etc., instead of crossing out, which disfigures the MS & is less desirable for the printers. If I had a copyist at hand I would have some of them copied, but I can't give so much time to it. I shall copy a few & put in *Century* if they will take them—with a comment. I shall send to Niles tomorrow, but without my little preface, which will perhaps be identical with what I put in *Century*.

Cordially yours
T. W. HIGGINSON

Dublin, N. H.
July 6, 1890

DEAR MRS. TODD

I find with dismay that the beautiful "I shall know why, when time is over" has been left out. How could you acquiesce? Please send it to me *at once* as I have put it in from memory & inaccurately into the MS & also into my *Century* paper which I have just sent off. Do you think it would be wrong for me to keep whatever compensation I get from the *Century* or elsewhere, in view of the time I have given?

Poems given as samples
Glee, the great storm
I never saw a moor
Soul wilt thou toss again
'Tis so much joy
Of all the sounds
This is my letter
This is the land the sunset washes

Almost! [Within my reach]
Delayed till [she had ceased to know]
How many times these low feet
Departed to the judgment
Safe in their alabaster chambers   (both versions)[6]
I shall know why

> Ever cordially
> T. W. HIGGINSON

> Dublin, N. H.
> *July* 14, 1890

DEAR MRS. TODD

I have today sent the MS. to Niles—115 in all. I enclose three finally omitted. I have said "Time and Eternity" for the last heading. I thought your emendation "put on" to the first line of that verse in "Indian Summer" ["These are the days when birds come back," *Poems*, 1890, page 100] better than the substitute verse. Nothing final from Gilder.[7]

> Ever yrs.
> T. W. HIGGINSON

[6] A version of this poem had appeared in *The Springfield Republican*, (date undetermined) without the third stanza:

The Sleeping

Safe in their alabaster chambers,
Untouched by morning,
    And untouched by noon,
Sleep the meek members of the Resurrection,
    Rafter of satin, and roof of stone.

Light laughs the breeze
In her castle above them,
    Babbles the bee in a stolid ear,
Pipe the sweet birds in ignorant cadences:
    Ah! what sagacity perished here!

Pelham Hill, June, 1861

With the exception of a youthful valentine also printed in *The Republican*, Feb. 20, 1852, this poem appears to be the first known published poem by Emily Dickinson.

[7] Richard Watson Gilder, editor of *The Century*.

"There were two or three matters of editorial policy," my mother wrote, "on which Colonel Higginson and I did not agree." Differences of opinion, however, did not ruffle the cordiality of their relationship. The editors' courtesy to one another seems never to have flagged. She continues:

During all this time we were discussing at intervals the question of naming the poems, and of the changes either of us might wish to make, independent of her [Emily's] own multitudinous corrections and suggestions. But upon this subject we never wholly agreed, Colonel Higginson looking at it more in the light of the reading public as well as of the publishers, while I, with fewer books and articles to my credit than my much older co-worker [Mr. Higginson was born in 1823], was exceedingly loath to assign titles to any of them which might not be unmistakably indicated in the poem itself. I had found, I believe, ten altogether to which she herself had given names. After much consideration between us he yielded a good many titles of his own pleasant devising, and we kept them unnamed, I in turn giving way to those titles which were distinctly indicated. . . . I protested against such as seemed to me inappropriate, "A Prayer of the Lowly," for the poem beginning, "I meant to have but modest needs," for instance, so it appeared in the Second Series [page 34] entitled, "A Prayer."

He put the title "A World Well Lost" to a little poem beginning

> I lost a world the other day.
> Has anybody found?

thereby to my mind entirely misrepresenting the thought.[8] He suggested "At Home" as a title for

> The bee is not afraid of me,
> I know the butterfly,

whereas the gist of that poem lies in the last two lines, which "At Home" never touched. And one more title I had to strike out because it did not apply, "In The Wood," beginning

[8] Mrs. Todd compromised on "Lost," the title under which it appeared in *Poems*, 1890, p. 148.

> A little road not made of man,
> Enabled of the eye,
> Accessible to thill of bee,
> Or cart of butterfly,

for it is not a wood-road intended, but that airy highway whereon bee and butterfly pursue their invisible business.

In general, I objected to titles in the Latin language, although of course Latin names came naturally to an educated man of that time. But to me "Astra Castra," "Numen Lumen," and "Resurgam" sounded stilted when used with the poems of Emily Dickinson. [Compare "Emigravit," page 114] . . . I wrote to him hinting that Lavinia also preferred to leave the titles out, except such as Emily herself had given, to which he replied: "Of course Miss D's wishes would have been consulted about titles, had they been known in time, but probably the early sheets are now printed."

Actual changes in the poems themselves were even harder to settle. I agreed to a few of decided improvement, where by altering the succession of words, perhaps, a good rhyme might result,[9] but even these seemed to me questionable; however, a few went in, only one, I believe, against which I did protest—the last line of the poem on the grass:

> The grass so little has to do
> I wish I were a hay,

wrote Emily. The quaintness of the article really appealed to me, but my trusted collaborator was decided on that line. "It cannot go in so," he exclaimed, "everybody would say that *hay* is a collective noun requiring the definite article. Nobody can call it *a* hay!" So I retired, feeling that of course he was right with regard to the public. But I have always had a sneaking desire to see a change back to the original version![10]

[9] Denis Wortman, in *The Christian Intelligencer*, May 27, 1891, gives examples of offensive wayward rhymes. He says, "What shall one say of rhyming 'tell' with 'still,' 'arm' with 'exclaim,' 'own' with 'young,' 'pearl' with 'alcohol'? all of which are fair examples of many instances." Denis Wortman and Colonel Higginson were not alone in their attitude. As anticipated, lack of rhyme in Emily's poems proved to be a first obstacle to other literary craftsmen—to Thomas Bailey Aldrich and Nathan Haskell Dole among others.

[10] Printed "the hay" in 1890, it reads "a hay" in the current edition.

Miss Vinnie was by this time in a frenzy of excitement, not only because the poems were actually soon to appear, but because of opposition in the family. Without at this time going further into the matter of her relationship to her brother's wife —whom she called "the Old Scratch,"—it is at present enough to say that they were at swords' points. My mother described to me one typical episode. It seems that in the spring of 1890, without asking Miss Vinnie's permission, a fact soon to be discovered by her,

Sue had sent [Emily's] poem, "There came a day at summer's full," to *Scribner's Magazine*. It appeared in the August [1890] number. Several things connected with it enfuriated Vinnie. In the first place, Sue had no right to send the poem to a magazine. (See footnote 11, page 149.) Lavinia regarded herself as the sole proprietor of Emily's poems, and that she only had the right to dispose of them. In the second place, Sue kept the money she received for the poem instead of turning it over to Lavinia. . . . In the third place, to quote from my diary, "There was a ridiculous mistake, printing *sail* for *soul*."[11] [To Lavinia a mistake in reading Emily's manuscript was *lèse majesté*.]

[11] The editors wished to use this poem in the forthcoming volume. But as it had been sent to the magazine by Sue, neither Lavinia nor my mother was willing to write for permission to reprint it. Colonel Higginson agreed to do so. Sue is the "sister" referred to in Mr. Burlingame's reply.

Charles Scribner's Sons
Publishers
743-745 Broadway
New York

Sept. 26, 1890

DEAR COL. HIGGINSON

There will certainly be no objection to the use of Miss Dickinson's poem in the collection, but on the contrary we shall have a great deal of pleasure in seeing our choice confirmed by its inclusion in those of her writings put into permanent form.

I can't account for the misprint; the copy (in her sister's hand) seemed perfectly clear "sail," for it attracted my attention at the time to what seemed a bold if not obscure figure; and her sister saw a proof in which it so stood. I am bound to confess too that in spite of my doubts the notion of a sail passing a solstice did not seem to me as much among the impossible metaphors as perhaps it should have done, & therefore I followed the question no further after the proof was passed. . . .

Sincerely yours,
E. L. BURLINGAME

As the date of publication drew nearer, and it seemed that the poems were actually to appear [my mother continued], Vinnie became terrified. She feared lest Sue should get wind of the fact —that I had completed the task which she had failed to do. The consequences Vinnie dared not face. . . . She was in a panic, and wished to have Colonel Higginson assume the entire responsibility for the publication of the poems. She wished not only to disguise her own connection with the undertaking, but to eliminate me as well. On July fourteenth she sent the following letter to Colonel Higginson. He, gentle, kindly man, was oblivious of the antagonism between Sue and Lavinia, as well as of Lavinia's state of panic. He sent the first half of the letter to me to decipher, as he could not read the key-word! That word was "co-worker." That letter was the first inkling I had that she feared to have my name appear on the title-page.

July 14th [1890]

My Dear Friend

I wish to express my gratitude for the progress of the dear poems, but you will forgive a little disappointment at the small number accepted. If all *your* choice had been received I should have been quite satisfied. The *rules* of printing are new to *me* & *seem* in many cases to destroy the grace of the thought but of course this can't be helped, I suppose.

'Twould be a pleasure to me to see a copy of your introduction before the printer has it, if not too much trouble.

I'm glad you are to attract attention to the book, by an article in the "Century." The poem so long watched for in the "Scribner," will appear in August number.

I dare say you are aware our *"co-worker"* is to be "sub rosa," for reasons you may understand.

[Remainder of letter missing]

The envelope addressed to "Mrs. Mabel Todd Loomis" was postmarked West Peterborough, N.H., July 18, 1890. On this letter is a pencil query by Colonel Higginson, "Can you interpret the words underscored?" He was, as I have said, unaware of the sulphurous family situation, the nature of which, however, was

---

The steps taken to rectify this error are described on p. 149. The word was corrected in the volume of poems which appeared in November, 1890, but in the current edition it has been changed back to the form in which it originally appeared in *Scribner's Magazine*.

gradually beginning to dawn upon him. My mother explained the foregoing letter to me in these words, which I reproduce without alteration:

Vinnie did not want my name on the book because she didn't want Sue to know that I had anything to do with it. Sue would have annihilated her if she could. They hated each other black and blue. She was scared to death of Sue, though she talked awfully about her. If I could begin to tell you what she said about Sue it would take the whole day.

I asked Mr. Higginson what we should do about this, a species of treachery beyond my imagining. He tossed it off airily. "Nothing is going to be done about so foolish a request," he answered. "It does not amount to anything."

Though I was hurt and disgusted, naturally, I tried to control my indignation. I continued to work on the poems as if nothing had happened.

On July thirtieth I received the first proof of the book, and on August first went to Boston to see Mr. Niles.

As a result of this interview, Mr. Niles forwarded to my mother on August fifth not only all his letters from Emily but also the poems she had sent him.

My mother gave the month of August to reading proof and to comparing each printed poem with the original manuscript. Meanwhile, Colonel Higginson had been working over his article for *The Century*, part of which was to serve as a preface to the volume of poems. This he sent to Amherst with the accompanying note:

DEAR MRS. TODD

I send this preface for your criticism & Miss Lavinia's too, if you think well of it. I did not at first put in the *personal* paragraph & shld. like as well to strike it out—let Miss L. decide—unless you can for her. If you have improvements to suggest (as I hope you have) send it back to me, otherwise send to publisher.

Yrs. ever
T. W. HIGGINSON

Dublin, N. H.
Aug. 26, 1890

P.S. *I* should prefer, instead of the preface, to put in the good sketch of E.D. by her sister-in-law from Spr. Republican.

This postscript galvanized Lavinia. She lacked words sufficiently emphatic with which to repudiate the idea.

Poor Mr. Higginson! He could not yet entirely grasp the situation. He had begun innocently enough by trying to make the Dickinson women pull together, or, if not that, at least to show one another some consideration. But after burning his fingers several times he at last saw his folly, exclaiming as he withdrew, "It is hard to steer safely among Dickinsons!"

Mrs. Todd called Colonel Higginson's preface "very good and tasteful." She returned it to him on August thirtieth, sending off to the printer the final galley proofs of the rest of the book on the same day. The plate proofs of "poems, 32-78" were returned on September third, and she then went "to Vinnie's to compare originals."

I have said that changes in the manuscripts were often suggested by Colonel Higginson to make the poems conform more closely to conventional standards. But it is worth noting that, in the following letter, almost in spite of himself he seems to be falling under their spell.

Aug. 26, 1890

Dear Mrs. Todd

On pp. 128, 129, 148 I have made conjectural changes not sustained by MS. Please rub out if you don't approve!

How wonderfully strong are some of these later ones! Surely they must find readers.

Correct my preface freely
T.W.H.

Alas, these are all. I am sorry to stop revising.[12]

The fact that the poems were actually in print acted upon Lavinia like an elixir. Her dejection, her fears even, were vanishing. The diary says on September eighth, "Vinnie came over, & spent the evening here. She was even brilliantly entertaining."

The next letter from Colonel Higginson contains an astonishing query. He could not recall whether he had seen Emily once

---

[12] In a letter written to his sister on Aug. 28, 1890, he referred to "the poems of Emily Dickinson which I am editing—very remarkable though odd."—No. 1203 in T.W.H. collection of manuscripts in the Harvard College Library

or twice! Had she indeed made an indelible impression upon him?

> Dublin, N. H.
> *Sept.* 12, 1890

DEAR MRS. TODD

I have the proof of my preface. Will you please go at once to Miss Lavinia & ask if I was at their house *once* or *twice*. I have printed it *once*, but I have a vague impression that I made a second visit, in Emily's lifetime. If it was *twice*, please write at once to A. W. Stevens, University Press, Cambridge, & he will correct. Let me know also.[13]

Again; in my preface I speak of the *editors* & it seems to me better that we should both sign it; will you not? Your name should appear somewhere. Or we might say on the title-page "edited by" both of us. Perhaps that would look too heavy for so small a book. Tell me what you think as I must send title p. at once.

> Yrs ever
> T. W. HIGGINSON

He soon thought better of his suggestion that they both sign the preface, following up his letter with a post card, the printed heading of which, as on many others, reads, "Massachusetts Military and Naval History, 25 Buckingham Street, Cambridge, Mass."

> Dublin, N. H.
> *Sept.* 17, 1890

I thought afterwards that it would not do for you to sign the preface, as I give personal experience. So I hv put on the title-page

> Edited by two of her friends
> Mabel Loomis Todd & T. W. Higginson

> In haste
> T.W.H.

It is proper that yr name shld come first as you did the hardest part of the work.

[13] For an account of Colonel Higginson's two visits to Emily, see *Letters*, 1931, pp. 284-289 and 291.

How the Indian pipe (*Monotropa uniflora*), later accepted as the symbol of Emily Dickinson, came to be put on the cover of the first volume is explained by my mother.

Wishing, in the winter of 1882, to send Emily Dickinson a little remembrance, by a happy thought I painted for her a group of those weird, strange but perfect flowers of shade and silence, the *Monotropa*, or Indian pipe. She sent me at once the following note:

DEAR FRIEND

That without suspecting it you should send me the preferred flower of life, seems almost supernatural, and the sweet glee that I felt at meeting it I could confide to none. I still cherish the clutch with which I bore it from the ground when a wondering child, an unearthly booty, and maturity only enhances mystery, never decreases it. To duplicate the vision is almost more amazing, for God's unique capacity is too surprising to surprise. I know not how to thank you. We do not thank the rainbow, although its trophy is a snare.

To give delight is hallowed—perhaps the toil of angels, whose avocations are concealed. . . .

With joy,
E. DICKINSON

When the first volume of her poems was ready for publication and a design was needed for the cover, nothing seemed so singularly appropriate as these spectral blossoms, and the design was actually cut from the original painting [a little panel] which had stood in Emily's room during the last few years of her life.

Mrs. Todd had written Colonel Higginson that she had shown some of the forthcoming poems to William Dean Howells, an old friend of our family, and that he was "immensely enthusiastic," offering to write an article about them for *Harper's Magazine*. Colonel Higginson replied as follows:

Dublin, N. H.
Sept. 19, 1890

DEAR MRS. TODD

I finally put both our names on preface. What you say about Howells is interesting but he is a dangerous friend, often praising so whimsically (e.g. that turgid & imitative Cawein) that his praise rouses opposition as much as sympathy—but these are risks that we must take. I do all the poetry for the *Nation* & will write to the *Critic*, where they are disposed to be fair, though a little in what Howells calls the "Manhattan-cockney vein." Their poetry is often done by Jas. H. Morse or Alice W. Rollins, both of whom are appreciative & not truculent. Do not trust too much in H[owells]'s predictions of a sale; I do not expect this; but feel like you increased confidence in the real power thro' this intimacy which editing gives. I am disappointed at the delay in my paper in *Christian Union*, but daily expect proof. The Indian pipe would be admirable, on the whole, perhaps not *too* uncanny; only this morning Benson, the landscape painter, asked me if it was not a fungus.

Ever cordially
T. W. Higginson

Colonel Higginson's article, "An Open Portfolio"—a study of Emily's poems with selections from the forthcoming volume—had been written for *The Century*. But he explained that as "the *Century* could not print in season," the article would appear in the *Christian Union* (September 25, 1890). Lavinia expressed her appreciation in a letter to him.

October 9th [1890]

My Dear Friend

I have waited to thank you for your most satisfactory article in the "Christian Union", because our *mutual friend* thought you were not at home & I didn't know where else to direct. I am delighted with your introduction & more grateful than I can tell that the one wish of my heart has begun to be gratefied. I was not expecting the notice so early, when a friend put it in my hand, the first Saturday of its print. I trust you are well & your household. I hope I shall see you again, some day. I could tell you some facts that might amaze you. With the deepest gratitude to you for your beautiful labors, I am

Heartily
Lavinia Dickinson

The day following, Mr. Dickinson also expressed his approval.

Amherst *October* 10th 1890

My dear Col Higginson

It is inexcusable that I have not sooner acknowledged, in even the briefest manner, my appreciation of your notice of my sister and her work in "the Christian Union" of week before last. It has been because while not quite up to my usual strength I have been pressed by a variety of duties to it's limit, and so have put this off for a little better time, which has not come. I do not take the paper. My attention was called to the article by a neighbor, who does, and in whose copy I read it, and I at once ordered a dozen copies from the office, but having been away the last few days, have only just received them.

It struck me, as I read, that you had hit and revealed her exactly, and with great skill, taste, and good judgement. I do not see how she could have been brought before the world, if she were to be brought at all, more aptly and more favorably, and if the little volume meets with any success, I shall attribute it in the main to the labor of love which you and Mrs Todd have given to it, and of which I shall have something more to say hereafter.

Whether it was, on the whole, advisable to publish is yet with me, a question, but my Sister Vin, whose knowledge of what is, or has been, outside of her dooryard is bounded by the number of her callers, who had no comprehension of her sister, yet believed her a shining genius, was determined to have some of her writing where it could be read of all men, and she is expecting to become famous herself thereby, and now we shall see.

For myself and for the present, my warmest thanks for the interest you have shown in Emily, and in what she wrote, for the time without stint you have spent in reading and sifting it, and for your public indorsement of its quality.

Yours, very sincerely
W A Dickinson[14]

The book was nearing completion. The final set of plate proofs including the table of contents was sent on September

[14] This letter is one of four from the Dickinsons kindly presented to me by Dr. J. Dellinger Barney after the death of his wife, Margaret Higginson Barney, Colonel Higginson's only child. Unless otherwise specified, letters addressed to Colonel Higginson are in the Galatea Collection of the Manuscript Division of the Boston Public Library, Boston, Massachusetts, to which my thanks are due for permission to print. Letters addressed to my mother are in my possession.

twenty-fourth. Mr. Niles wrote, "When we receive these back, the book will be ready to be printed." All proofs were returned by both editors on the following day.

As we were reading these letters together, I asked my mother at this point whether a contract had been signed. "No," she said, "up to that time there had been no mention of a contract. Vinnie was unused to business dealings and had never heard of such a thing until I mentioned it to her. She had about as much knowledge of business as a Maltese pussy cat." Mr. Niles was the first to bring up the matter.

Boston
Sept 30, 1890

DEAR MRS TODD

I suppose we ought to have a contract for the Dickinson poems. In whose name shall we make it out?

Yours truly
THOˢ NILES

Mrs. Todd replied that inasmuch as Miss Dickinson was to pay for the plates the contract should be made out in her name.

Boston
Oct 4, 1890

DEAR MRS TODD

I send the contracts, made out to Miss Dickinson wh. if she approves she can sign & return us one.

I cannot tell the cost of the plates yet, but will send the bill as soon as we get it from the printer.

The book is printing and the design for cover is being made. We hope to publish Nov. 1ˢᵗ.

Yours very truly
THOˢ NILES

On October seventh my mother took "the copyright contracts" to Lavinia for her signature. Only a few final details remained.

Boston
Oct 10, 1890

DEAR MRS TODD

I mail the design for side of Miss Dickinson's Poems. I propose to stamp it in silver on white cloth and have a gray or drab cloth for the back & strip on the side.

It strikes me it will look very modest & unobtrusive in silver whereas in gold it would look *heavy* & glaring.

> Yours truly
> THOˢ NILES

> Boston
> *Oct* 15, 189

MY DEAR MRS TODD

Mʳ Howells called upon me yesterday for a copy of Miss Dick inson's poems wh. I gave him (folded of course). He had no recd. the copy wh. I had sent to him c/o Harpers. I have give folded copies to Miss Gilder of The Critic, to Mr Parsons of The Tribune, N.Y., & to the Book Buyer.[15]

I have two folded copies wh. I can send to you, or I will ma them to addresses wh. you may furnish.[16]

We shall not probably receive bound copies for a week of more.

> Yours very truly
> THOˢ NILES

My mother's narrative continues:

This folded but unbound copy of the poems reached me o October twentieth. On October twenty-first appears the followir laconic entry in my diary: "Later to Vinnie's. Showed her tl book." I cannot remember that she made much comment. SI merely assumed that Emily would be, if known, the greate poet in the world.

She was at this time pressing me to write an article for tl *Independent*, a journal of importance, the editor of which, D William Hayes Ward, a graduate of Amherst College, was friend of hers. I did as she requested, and on October twent fourth wrote, "I finished and sent an article on Emily to tl *Independent*."

[15] Notices in the above papers appeared as follows: *The New York Tribu* Nov. 15, 1890, and Jan. 4, 1891; *The Bookbuyer*, December, 1890; *The Cri* Dec. 13, 1890.

[16] One of the folded copies was given to Mrs. "Helen" Whitman, p sumably Mrs. Henry Whitman of Mount Vernon Street, a "focal pers ality" of Boston; the other was sent to Mrs. Todd. On October eighth, she for review had also been sent to Richard Henry Stoddard and to Nath Haskell Dole.

We were almost holding our breath, waiting for a first glimpse
the bound volume. It did not appear on November first as
anned, but we did not have to wait many days before we had a
finite promise from Mr. Niles.

Boston
Nov 5, 1890

:AR MRS TODD
We shall publish the poems on the 12ᵗʰ. I shall send you some
pies as soon as the books come in from the binder.

Yours truly
THOˢ NILES

Two days later six copies were sent to Mrs. Todd. The entry
the diary on November eighth was merely: "Emily's volume
ne—complete, binding, design, all." "The sense of actually
lding it in our hands," my mother told me, "was one of ex-
ation." The book was put on the market on Wednesday,
ovember twelfth.

A great calm seems to have enveloped them all—an oppressive
iet, like the eye of the storm.[17]

[17] The little 16ᵐᵒ volume (Plate IX) measuring approximately five by seven
hes, was bound in white, with a "drab" back and overlapping narrow
p of the same color on both covers edged by a wavy gold line. Though
book had a gilt top, and though the title and name of the author
re also stamped in gold, the design of Indian pipes was in silver—as Mr.
es said, to make it look more "modest and unobtrusive." Mrs. Todd
led: "The gray, white and silver of the first edition thus, by happy
uition, expressed somewhat of Emily's 'cool and nun-like personality,'
one of her critics afterwards (perhaps mistakenly) described her."
he dainty binding, devised partly with this symbolism in mind, partly in
hope of beguiling Christmas shoppers into buying the book for the
uty of its cover, was protected not only by a plain jacket but also by a
ny white pasteboard box made to fit. The price was $1.50. The heavy
ndered paper on which it was printed made the book of 152 pages (116
ems) seem larger than it was. The first edition consisted of 480 copies. See
pendix III.

CHAPTER V

The "Auction"

To earn it by disdaining
Is fame's consummate fee.

THE world's verdict regarding the poems of Emily Dickins
was awaited with trepidation by her sponsors—by sister an
editors alike. Their suspense was as breathless as if they had n
felt sure that the poems were works of genius. In the end,
course, the poetry would find its level and be recognized f
what they knew it was. But meanwhile, what would the criti
say? Would they read the book through to the end, or wou
they be so offended by the lack of form, of rhyme in particula
that they would condemn it before they had finished readin
The poems might very well be doomed to oblivion before d
criminating readers had had an opportunity to know of the
existence.

Was this anxiety a reflection of Emily's own attitude whi
made her refuse to publish? Why indeed had she refused? S
knew the worth of her poems. *She did not ask Lavinia to destr*
them. But she realized only too well that they were as foreign
Victorian standards as she herself was foreign to her place an
time. "All men say 'What?' to me," she exclaimed in an ear
letter,[1] acknowledging the futility of trying to make hers
understood. Not that Emily had not tried to obtain an expe
appraisal of her work when in the spring of 1862 she ask
Colonel Higginson for his opinion.[2] It was not fear of critici
which restrained her, for that she courted. She took anoth
tentative step two years later, when she gave the poem "M
Sabbath" to her Sweetser cousins for their paper, *The Rou*

[1] *Letters*, 1931, p. 278.
[2] *Ibid.*, p. 272.

70

Table. It was published on March 12, 1864.[3] One has only to read other verses in that periodical to realize that Emily's poetry was as foreign to current taste as "firmament to fin." Here are a few typical first lines: "What though my locks be gray, Jeanette," and "The drooping willows whisper soft, the rushes murmur low," and this introduction of a "Sonnet to Shakespeare"

> Coruscant Presence, who dost ever shine
> Unbodied benefaction on the blest.

Might it have been the reception given to "My Sabbath" which

[3] Bibliographies of the poems of Emily Dickinson have overlooked the first appearance of this much quoted poem, "Some keep the Sabbath going to church," printed in Vol. I, No. 13, p. 195, of *The Round Table*, a weekly newspaper published in New York by her cousins, Henry E. and Charles M. Sweetser. Appearing every Saturday, this paper was "A Review of Politics, Finance, Literature, Society and Art," "A Weekly Record of the Notable, the Useful and the Tasteful." Under the title, "My Sabbath," the poem appeared anonymously as did the other poems published during Emily's lifetime.

Besides being a first edition, *The Round Table* version is of interest on at least three other counts. First, the title was given by Emily herself. She called it "My Sabbath." In *Poems*, 1890, it appears on p. 74 under Colonel Higginson's title, "A Service of Song." Second, this version shows that the quatrain was the form in which Emily cast the poem. In 1890, it was printed in the same form, though without indented second and fourth lines. The punctuation too, though conventional, differs slightly from that in the 90 volume. Third, there is one difference in wording in the two versions: "going," in the next to the last line, reads "getting" in the 1890 volume—a change in meaning the authorization for which will be established when the original manuscript, or manuscripts, become available.

As printed in *The Round Table* the poem reads:

My Sabbath

> Some keep the Sabbath going to church,
> I keep it staying at home,
> With a bobolink for a chorister,
> And an orchard for a dome.
>
> Some keep the Sabbath in surplice,
> I just wear my wings,
> And instead of tolling the bell for church,
> Our little sexton sings.
>
> God preaches—a noted clergyman,
> And the sermon is never long;
> So instead of going to heaven at last,
> I'm going all along.

convinced Emily that it was useless to attempt to gain a hearing
In any event, after that she withdrew, declaring that "publicatio
is the auction of the mind of man."

I venture the suggestion that some such attitude as the abo
may have carried over to her editors—uncertainty not as to th
value of the poems but as to the competence of the critics. Th
one thing that my mother at least seems never to have doubte
was the correctness of her own estimate of Emily's poetry.

On the day of publication Colonel Higginson wrote to M
Todd.

> Cambridge
> *Nov.* 12, 18

DEAR MRS. TODD

I am distressed exceedingly to find that among E.D.'s countl
letters there are poems as good as any we printed—one on t
Blue Jay ["No brigadier throughout the year"], one on t
Humming Bird ["A route of evanescence"], etc. This shows
must have another volume by and by & this must include pr
from her letters, often quite as marvellous as her poetry. Howe
is doing missionary work in private & that lovely child Mildr
[Howells] selected as her chief favorite, today in talking with
your favorite about the two who died & talked between t
tombs ["I died for beauty"]. I have written to Roberts for t
sheets, which I have not seen, though [Nathan Haskell] Dole a
others have.

> Ever cordially
> T. W. HIGGINSON

P.S. Books just arrived—bound. I am *astounded* in looki
through. How could we ever have doubted about them.[4]

Newspapers absorbed the first shock of publication. A revi
in *The Springfield Republican*, Sunday, November 16, 18
had particular importance in Amherst since that paper mold
opinion throughout western Massachusetts. Recognizing Emi
"wilfulness of intonation," the writer nevertheless suggested
analogy with the poetry of Emerson, calling her "transcenden
ist by native essence" since "her intuitions were her reasor

[4] Part of this letter was published in *Letters and Journals of Tho
Wentworth Higginson*. Boston: Houghton Mifflin Company, 1921, p. 331.

On the whole, he thought, this was "an uncommon book," one which, furthermore, without the author's seclusion, could never have been written. And he added, "That it should have a large public is not to be expected," but "those who are fit will read."[5]

One of the first enthusiasts was a literary cleric, the Reverend John W. Chadwick, part of whose letter is quoted below.

> 626 Carlton Avenue
> Brooklyn, N. Y.
> *Nov.* 20th 1890

MY DEAR MR. HIGGINSON

I wish to thank you for the wonderful book of poems, Miss Dickinson's. What lines & phrases & words & thoughts & fancies & imaginations!

May I use two, pp. 48 & 60, in a little compilation I am intending? If you say yes I'll make it all right with Niles.

I've had "A Service of Song," p. 74, in my head for more than 20 years, ever since it came out in the *Round Table*. Are there two forms or have I misremembered! My memory is "With singing birds for choristers," & for the last stanza

> "God preaches in this way to me
> A sermon in a song," &c.

> Yours very truly,
> JOHN W. CHADWICK

What *do* you make out of XII, p. 25? How tantalizing & fascinating it is! ["I asked no other thing."]

On December fourth, Mr. Chadwick again wrote to Mr. Higginson about the poems. "I have since read them all over three or four times," he said, "& like them better every time."

On Sunday, November twenty-third, several notices appeared, including one by Arlo Bates in the *Boston Courier*.

[5] Colonel Higginson and Mrs. Todd were curious about the authorship of this unsigned review. Though Frank B. Sanborn of Concord was at the time contributor to *The Republican*, the writer proved to be Charles Goodrich Whiting, the literary editor.

It is seldom that the reviewer is called upon to notice a boo
so remarkable as the "Poems" of Miss Emily Dickinson. . . . It
so wholly without the pale of conventional criticism, that it
necessary at the start to declare the grounds upon which it is
be judged as if it were a new species of art. . . .

With regard to "My Sabbath," Mr. Bates queries, "Could an
thing be more delightfully pagan, or worse in workmanship
and concludes:

Had Miss Dickinson possessed the aptitude and the will to lea
technical skill, she would have enriched the language with lyri
which would have endured to the end of time, it might well b
As it is, she has put upon paper things which will delight tl
few, but which will hold their place on sufferance, and as showi
what she might have been rather than for what she was. Tl
book gives us keen delight, but it is delight mingled with regi
equally keen for what it fails to be.

In the Boston *Sunday Herald*, November 23, 1890, Loui
Chandler Moulton voiced a similar opinion.

Madder rhymes one has seldom seen—scornful disregard
poetic technique could hardly go farther—and yet there is abo
the book a fascination, a power, a vision that enthralls you, ai
draws you back to it again and again. Not to have published
would have been a serious loss to the world. . . . I have read tl
book twice through already. I foresee that I shall read it sco
of times more. It enthralls me and will not let me go.[6]

6 From Mrs. Todd's journal, Nov. 30, 1890:
I had a long talk with Arlo Bates at a musical at Dr. Mixter's.
shows his limitations closely at hand, but he is refined and gentlemar
and he began at once about the poems. His review in the *Bost*
Courier, however, is not nearly so strong and appreciative as M
Moulton's in the Sunday *Herald*.
Dear Mr. Howells! [William Dean Howells was also a guest.] W
all his immense success as a novelist, he is as simple as a child, and swe
natured and cordial. So lovely to me, and so helpful about my stories
He thinks the *Poems* simply marvelous. I asked him last summer if
would not review them, and he said he should like to. He has writ
a lovely article, of which he kindly sent me the proof, for the Janu
Editor's Study. Almost the most appreciative of all.

On the same date, November 23, 1890, the *Boston Budget* published a review by Lilian Whiting, one which concludes:

> They are poems of such extraordinary intensity, insight and vividness, and an almost equally startling disregard of poetic laws, that the reader will find himself pursuing almost a new language, and perhaps speculating curiously as to what results would have been insured had the author subjected herself to careful study of poetic ideals—had she learned to chip and polish the marble.

In the issue of November twenty-seventh, *Life* prints a review by "Droch" (Robert Bridges), who calls the poems "intensely ethical." He suggests that

> the love poems are written in the attitude of a worshipper and not of a lover—and the exaggeration is often of a kind that is saved from being absurd by its sincerity. It is not passion, but fervid loyalty that is depicted—and the chill of intellectual monasticism is in it.

Thus within two weeks after publication the keynote had been struck regarding the nature of Emily Dickinson's attitude toward romantic love.[7]

From the letters received by my mother at this time, I have chosen one.

The Reverend Dr. E. Winchester Donald was a graduate of Amherst College in the class of 1869. In 1890, he was Rector of the Church of the Ascension, Fifth Avenue at Tenth Street, New York. Well known for his impressive presence and for the beauty of his voice and speech, which added distinction to the performance of his priestly duties, he was a brilliant, elegant, if somewhat irascible man of the world, as rigid in his requirements for dishes served at his table as any French gourmet. After the consecration of Phillips Brooks as Bishop of Massachusetts in 1891, Dr. Donald succeeded him as Rector of Trinity Church in the City of Boston, a post which he held until his death on August 6, 1904. With his family he used to spend the summer in Amherst,

---

[7] Eighteen days after the book appeared, and before notices had begun to come in large numbers, my mother wrote in her journal an account of the launching of the poems, published in full in Appendix I.

often renting the Sweetser house in the grove of oak trees at the top of the hill behind Mr. Dickinson's.

Ascension Rectory
7 West 10th Street

MY DEAR MRS TODD:

I opened the *Poems* this evening at ten o'clock: it is now long past midnight: I have read them, every one, and I shall read some of them again before I sleep. I own that you had roused my curiosity and, by one or two quotations, raised my expectations, but who could have imagined—never having known her, or for that matter having known her—that, all unknown to the thousands who have passed her silent house eager only not to miss a train,[8] there was a mind & imagination that could tell them more of nature and the mysteries of life than the combined wisdom of the College. "Wisdom is justified by her children." Yes! but so often wisdom is childless. There is a keen condemnation and, in some sort, a shame upon us—upon me at least & others—that we should have been so unsensitive as not to have felt, through silence and invisibleness, the presence of one who was reading the inner life of bee, grass & sky—the secrets of the most passionate lives of men & women.

Mr Higginson figures badly, in my judgment: his preface is a bit of brutal impertinence. I shall tear it out of a copy I mean to put into the hand of a dear friend. Beside his clumsy pedantry, how gentle, pathetic, tender, and sufficient is her own *Prelude*. My God! What a bloodless tragedy must have been enacted behind those doors—that innocent hedge:

> A fever in these pages burns
> Beneath the calm they feign;
> A wounded human spirit turns
> Here, on its bed of pain.

Beneath the blythest lines, the most dainty & jocund of her verses

> There sobs I know not what ground tone
> Of human agony.

[8] The tracks of the Central Vermont Railroad, the only one in Amherst during Emily's lifetime, crossed Main Street not far beyond the Dickinson property.

I wonder what these poems will effect—I dont care what is *said* of them by the wise or the foolish—Higginson's screed is not promising, is it?

One other thing: was the inexorable cost of all this illumination her seclusion renunciation & ache? Would John Baptist be forerunner without the years in the desert, the locusts and all that? Is the nun's self-effacement, her veil and her virginity, the explanation of her unquestioned power? We cannot wear lace and pearls—go often to town & the play, be experts in salads beers and truffles, know what to do with our hands—and expect either to see heaven or to have anyone believe we have seen it.

Her "Calvaries of Love" surely have brought, ere this, the grand recompense to her poor, rich, suffering, victorious soul.

> If I can stop one heart from breaking
> I shall not live in vain
> If I can ease one life the aching
> Or cool one pain

I testify that she did 'not live in vain'—even as I thank you for your part in bringing to the light a hidden treasure; and to thank you is really the reason that I am writing.

Yours very sincerely
E. WINCHESTER DONALD

Dec. 8 or 9 (just as you like) 1890

On December eleventh, a long review of the book appeared in *The Independent.* The article received much attention, not only because of the standing of that journal, but because the author was thought to be Professor Maurice Thompson, who had "a reputation for letters that grew to be the most commanding of his generation in the middle West" (to quote the *Dictionary of American Biography*). "So far as technical execution is concerned," the reviewer said, "the author invented her poetic idiom. . . . It is the delirium of a sane mind poised on a very serious basis of living and thinking." So far, so good. He admits that the poems bear the stamp of genius but states categorically that "There are a few serious misprints in the volume. On page 9 read *sate* for *state*; on page 105 for *satin* read *Latin,* and (probably) *tunnelled* for *funnelled*." By these comments he forfeited his right to consideration as a critic sensitive to the "mind" of Emily Dickinson. The "misprints" are italicized.

> It goads me, like the goblin bee,
> That will not *state* its sting.

This is the final stanza of the poem beginning, "If you were coming in the fall." (A year later this word was still a debatable point.)

The second "misprint" he found in the poem about the hemlock, beginning

> I think the hemlock likes to stand
> Upon a marge of snow,

the final stanza of which reads,

> To *satin* races he is nought;
> But children on the Don
> Beneath his tabernacles play,
> And Dnieper wrestlers run.

My mother's comment on this was:

"To satin races he is nought." Ah ha! gloated this critic, there is a mistake! For he thought that Emily must have meant, as well as written, "Latin" races! . . . If any of them had studied Emily as I had, they would have known that to use the phrase "Latin races" would have been as impossible for her as to refer to "Nordic facial characteristics" or to "Aramaic culture." She was never pedantic.

The reviewer's final query had reference to the third line of

> I went to thank her,
> But she slept;
> Her bed a *funnelled* stone.

On the very day this review appeared [my mother continues], Mr. Niles wrote to me about it,[9] disturbed that mistakes so flagrant should have been found in a book which had received such unremitting care in editing. I explained to him that the verses were right as they stood.

Both editors were so much troubled by the allegations in *The Independent* even though false that Colonel Higginson wrote asking his friend Maurice Thompson whether he was indeed the author of the review in question:

> Bay Saint Louis
> Mississippi
> 27 *December* 1890

My dear Colonel Higginson

Must I confess that I am almost mean enough to wince at having to say that I did *not* write the review of Emily Dickinson's poems.

About that time I was taking up my winter stakes and fixing myself and family here for the cold season; so fortunately the book fell into better hands. I am glad of it; for while I appreciate the fine originality of the poems and honor the forthright sincerity of expression that marks them as coming from a strong, independent soul, I should not have probably appraised them as highly as did the writer of the notice. They seem to me so good that the finish ought to have been better. The rhyme should have been abandoned wholly or it should have been perfect— likewise the metre. The first stanza of the "*Humming Bird*"[10] is a surprise of the true lyrical sort; but the second reflects back badly on the sheen of its predecessor. Pardon me for saying that Miss Dickinson's verse suggests to me a superb brain that has

9

> Boston
> *December* 11, 1890

Dear Mrs Todd

What do you say to the closing ¶ of the Independent's notice.
The book is out of print for the moment, but we hope to get in the 2ᵈ Ed. in a day or two.

> Yours truly
> Thoˢ Niles

10 The reference to this poem is mysterious, inasmuch as it was not published until October, 1891, in Mr. Higginson's *Atlantic* article.

suffered some obscure lesion which now and again prevents the
filling out of a thought—as if a cog slipped in some fine wheel
just at the point of consummation. I admit the fascination of
the defect, but I cannot make it out to be equal to the beautiful
grace of genius. Go read again Keats's *Ode to a Nightingale*
and see how the divine touch brings out the wonder of perfect
form, while the heavenly vision is molded to the measure of
perfect music!

As regards the influence that most affected Miss Dickinson's
method of expression, it is clear to me that Emerson is the name
of it. She has his curious scorn of continuity and his way of
appearing ignorant of absurd discords, setting them just where
the finest accord is imperatively demanded. The surprise of this,
I repeat, has its fascination, but it is fleeting—gives place at once
to regret. Miss Dickinson is "suggestiferous," as one at my elbow
remarks, she flashes like the revolving light on Point Mariann
yonder, but she gives no steady, enduring beams.

My connection with the editorial staff of the *Independent* is
delightful. The "poppy and the rose" join me in wishing you
and yours a happy New Year. I wish we could send you the rose
on my desk.

> Sincerely yours,
> MAURICE THOMPSON

The second edition of the *Poems* was issued on December sixteenth with a different cover, a light-green spine replacing the
gray of the first edition. Mr. Niles says:

> Boston
> *Dec* 15, 18¢

DEAR MRS TODD

I did not quite like the looks of the binding of the first E
of Miss Dickinson's poems and I have changed it on the secon

If you do not think it is an improvement we will return to th
style of the first Ed. in the third.[11]

> Yours truly
> THOˢ NILES

[11] Since the "instant and hearty recognition" seemed to assure the book
permanent place in libraries, a cover more durable than the Christmas gi
book variety of the first and second editions was needed. So a cover

So Mr. Niles was already expecting to print a third edition!

Meanwhile, Colonel Higginson's acquiescence had given way to tremulous excitement, as this letter to my mother shows:

Cambridge
Dec. 15, 1890

DEAR FRIEND

Pardon me if I bore you, but I often wish for your sympathy, because you are the only person who can feel as I do about this extraordinary thing we have done in revealing this rare genius. I feel as if we had climbed to a cloud, pulled it away, and revealed a new star behind it. I have just been going over the reviews & noting in the book who quotes each poem. Have you observed how they are *distributed*? Sooner or later each poem, it would seem, must find its one admirer. A few poems show a *consensus* of appreciation, e.g. "The Sea of Sunset" ["This is the land the sunset washes"] (on the whole the favorite), "Exclusion" ["The soul selects her own society"] and "Alter! when the hills do." Yet some of the finest are not yet picked out by anybody. I wish I could remember who suggested each title; some of the best, I now, are yours. On the whole, they help.

I have had no specially interesting letters about the book—but have unusually full notices from Spr. Repub. (*not* Sanborn), Sunday Herald (Mrs. Moulton), Beacon (A. Bates), Indpt. (prob. Maurice Thompson—this one of the best), Critic, etc. Shorter ones from B. Post & Lit. World—the latter rather unappreciative. Shall I send you any of these?

Such things as I find in her letters! "The Madonnas I see are those that pass the House to their work, carrying Saviors with them."[12] Is not that one of the take-your-breath-away thoughts? There is much that I never could print as where she writes,

---

uniform color was substituted. Though it was more practical, the editors did not wholly approve of the change. My mother wrote, "Rather unfortunately, it seems to me, the quaint silver and gray and white binding of the first edition has not been repeated in later ones, a dull gray-green, a brighter green and other variations of color taking the place of the original cool, gray tones." The design of Indian pipes was retained on them all. In some editions the white cover with green spine was used, the wavy line between white and gray straightened out. The paper on which the first edition had been printed was heavily calendered, giving the book substantial size. After the third edition thinner, uncalendered paper was used. See Appendix III.

[12] *Letters*, 1931, p. 300.

"Of our greatest acts we are ignorant. You were not aware that
you saved my life."[13] What an unique existence was hers.

Do you think she ever saw H.H. [Helen Hunt Jackson] many
times? H.H. did not know of her poems till I showed them to her
(about 1866) and was very little in Amherst after that. But she
remembered her at school.

Ever cordially
T. W. Higginson

On December twenty-sixth, we read in my mother's diary:

Snowing hard. . . . Snow too thick to see out. Nevertheless, I
ploughed over to Vinnie's, to see her letter to Mr. Higginson
Staid awhile, getting back with great difficulty.

In order to understand this entry we must retrace our steps.
Throughout December, as Sue showed increasing opposition to
Lavinia's "crusade," and as Lavinia became aware of Colonel
Higginson's wish to pacify her, the state of suspended animosity
between the two houses grew more and more vibrant. On December twenty-third Lavinia drafted a letter to Colonel Higginson.
Before quoting this now famous letter I should perhaps explain
why she took so long to compose it; why, although it was dated
December twenty-third, it was not dispatched for three days; and
why she sought my mother's advice before mailing it. The point
was this: she wished to make clear to Colonel Higginson her
attitude toward Austin's wife without saying too much. It was
hard to explain the situation to a kindly man who liked to see
genial spirit prevail. He was still trying to bring about a state of
benevolent equilibrium among the Dickinsons when Lavinia's
letter was received. The correspondence preceding the dispatch
of the letter can now speak for itself.

Cambridge
Dec. 10, 189

Dear Mrs. Todd
I was *very* sorry to be unable to see you in Boston. What sa
you as to the future vol. Also was *Mrs.* Dickinson annoyed o

[13] *Ibid.,* p. 284.

offended about the editorship or publication? I wrote a few weeks ago asking her how she liked it, & have had no reply. I addressed "Mrs. A. Dickinson"—I never can get that name right. It seems Sanborn did not write the Spr Repub article, but (he thinks) C. G. Whiting.

Ever cordially

T. W. HIGGINSON

I hv. heard nothing (except in *Critic*) of a 2ᵈ edition.

Amherst, Tuesday evening

16 *December*, 1890

MY DEAR MR. HIGGINSON: —

I was very happy to receive your letter [of December fifteenth] this morning. My thought has turned often to you in all these days when our wonderful book has been running the gauntlet of the critics, and coming through so triumphantly. It was actually out of print for a few days. The second edition appears today. I am not surprised at the success of the poems, for there is nothing like them in English. Their haunting, compelling effect upon me while I was putting the seven hundred into shape was beyond anything I can express. Only you can understand it.

Your *Nation* review was delightful. I have seen all the other reviews you speak of except the *Beacon*. I have Arlo Bates' article in the *Courier* of November 23. There was an appreciative one in *Life* for November 27th. Who is "Droch"? Doubtless you have seen, now, the notices in the *Globe* and *Transcript* for December 14 and 15. I am trying to get a complete collection of the reviews, and to that end I subscribed to Romeike's Press Cutting Bureau, but some he fails to get, although he has sent, among others, one or two unimportant ones from Philadelphia and Pittsburgh which I should not have seen otherwise.

Mr. Whiting wrote the *Republican* article. I gave a little talk to the Women's Club in Springfield last week, and had afterward a pleasant conversation with Mrs. Whiting about the poems. She was very appreciative.

The various quotations interest me greatly. The one most often verbally quoted to me as a favorite is, "The heart asks pleasure first." Oh! how *could* Emily epitomize life so perfectly and with such bitter force! With hardly a shadow of form, this poem almost breaks my heart; and it seems to appeal to many others similarly.

The *Independent* critic was wrong about the misprints. Those words are written in the original MSS unmistakably as we printed them in the book.

Some of Emily's letters *must* be published. I have just now those she wrote to Samuel Bowles;[14] and I hope to have those to Dr. Holland in a few days. I am sure we can find enough for an entire volume of prose. And equally necessary is another volume of verse. Some of the unpublished poems are fully equal to the printed ones; and in addition to those you have seen are several hundred "scraps," written on backs of envelopes or elsewhere, mere fragments, but filled with her own weird power. I am gradually arranging and copying them. I .could pick out two hundred, at once, to make a volume fully as startling as the first.

Do you not think it should be done before very long?

"H.H." saw Emily but seldom. She used occasionally to go there and have long conversations—perhaps not over three times in the last twenty years of her life.[15]

As for Mrs. Dickinson, I think it not at all unlikely that she is incensed at the publication of the volume. She is apt to be incensed. But she had the poems at her entire disposal for two years after Emily's death, with Lavinia continually urging her to do something toward publishing a volume. She at first said she would think of it, but did nothing, and finally gave it up definitely. Then Lavinia came to me; and I began what proved to be a long and intricate work. So you see Mrs. Dickinson can have no real cause of complaint at its being done.

[14] In the diary my mother writes on Dec. 1, 1890, "Mr. Dickinson for a moment with a package of Emily's letters to Mr. Bowles." It was this sample which convinced my mother that "some of Emily's letters *must* be published."

[15] This statement that "H.H." saw Emily "but seldom" was given on the authority of Austin and Lavinia in answer to Colonel Higginson's inquiry. I have recently discovered the draft of a letter in Emily's own writing which settles the matter. She says: "I never saw Mrs. Jackson but twice, but those twice are indelible, and one day more. I am deified, was the only impression she ever left on any heart (house) she entered." Austin and Lavinia knew, of course, that Mrs. Jackson had become an enthusiastic admirer of such of Emily's poems as she had seen. But as with Emily's other relationships, the timbre of her friendship with "H.H." was a matter of speculation to them. They tried to find out more about it. In the very year of Emily's death I find in my mother's diary, Dec. 26, 1886: "We looked over Saxe Holm's Stories & found a poem or two by Emily in there."

Colonel Higginson was sure that it was Mrs. Jackson who, in spite of Emily's reluctance, had sent the poem "Success" to George Parsons Lathrop editor of the anthology entitled *A Masque of Poets*, published in November 1878. At that time the poem was commonly attributed to Emerson. (Compare *Letters*, 1931, p. 299.)

Lavinia is delighted with the book, and with the numerous letters of congratulation she constantly receives from her own and Emily's friends everywhere. And Mr. Dickinson wrote you some weeks ago, I believe, of his pleasure in it. So I am sure your satisfaction and mine should be unalloyed.

I send you with this a copy of Mrs. Logan's *Home Magazine* for November, in which I put a short notice of the *Poems*, in my regular article on new books. I could not resist the temptation of introducing them to a new audience, where *some* might be appreciative.

If you can spare the *Beacon* review, I shall be very glad to have it. There was one in the Saturday Evening *Gazette* for November 22, but I have not succeeded in getting a copy.

Pray pardon the length of my letter, dear Mr. Higginson, and believe me

Very cordially
MABEL LOOMIS TODD

Camb.
Dec. 23, 1890

DEAR MRS. TODD

I send the *Beacon* notice, which I confounded with the *Courier*. This is probably by Lilian Whiting. I have at last a long letter from Mrs. Dickinson, who, it seems, was astounded by my paper in the *Chr. Union*, having no intimation of it & having planned a vol. of prose & verse for *private printing* only. She is evidently a little sore, but kind and gracious. Should another volume be planned, she should at least be consulted. But it is hard to steer safely among Dickinsons! You may keep this Beacon notice if you wish. There should ultimately be a collection of memorials of E.D. in the Amherst Town Library (or College).

Ever cordially
T. W. HIGGINSON

Xmas greetings

Mrs. Dickinson's letter to Mr. Higginson, until recently missing, is now in my possession, the gift of Dr. Barney. Though it bears no date, it must have been written between December tenth and twenty-second, as Mr. Higginson had not received it on the tenth but refers to it in his letter of the twenty-third.

My dear Col. Higginson

Thanks for your kind letter duly received. I have not answered it before, because I was so dazed, by the announcement of Emily's poems in the Xtian Union that I do not rally easily. It was my first intimation that stranger hands were preparing them for publication. I planned to give my winter, with my daughter's aid, to the arrangement of a vol. to be printed at my own expense sometime during the year, subject to your approval of course, with an introduction also by yourself, to make the setting perfect. The volume would have been rather more full, and varied, than yours as I should have used many bits of her prose—passages from early letters quite surpassing the correspondence of Gunderodi[e] with Bettine—quaint bits to my children &c &c. Of course I should have forestalled criticism by only printing them. I have been held back from arranging them to be published the past years by your verdict of "un-presentable." My own taste must be my own, but a market judgment I have none of, and shrank from going contrary to your practical opinion in the matter. I think this much is due myself—my life long intimacy with Emily, my equally long deep appreciation of her genius. I am told Miss Lavinia is saying that I *refused* to arrange them. Emily knows that is not true. You are generous enough to be patient with my exegesis even if tedious to you. "The Poems" will ever be to me marvellous whether in manuscript or type. Most of your titles are perfect—a few I don't happen to fancy. I want to thank you, for her as well as myself for the perfect way in which you have led her before the curtain—but for that, her verses would have waited a long time for the recognition your name and fame have won for them. I trust there may be no more personal detail in the newspaper articles. She hated her peculiarities and shrank from any notice of them as a nerve from the knife. I sometimes shudder when I think of the world reading her thoughts minted in deep heartbroken convictions. In her own words (after all the intoxicating fascination of creation) she as deeply realized that for her, as for all of us women not fame but "Love and home and certainty are best." I find myself always saying "poor Emily." And so I go up in the snow to-morrow to put a wreath of her own mountain laurel on her grave. I will only add that I missed many favorites among the collection which knowing your taste I wonder over.

I fear you have no time to read so long a letter, but my own self respect and regard for yourself seemed to demand just this.

Yours as ever cordially
S. H. DICKINSON

Lavinia had not yet mailed her letter when Mr. Higginson's communication of the same date—the twenty-third—was brought to her attention. Her own letter was finally posted on the twenty-sixth.

December 23rd [1890]

MY DEAR FRIEND

I trust you are aware of my deep appreciation of your most satisfactory work in presenting "the wonderful poems of Emily Dickinson" to the world.

If you knew my disappointed endeavors for 2 years before Mrs Todd & your self came to my rescue, you would realize my gratitude to you both. Mrs Dickinson was enthusiastic for a while, then indifferent & later, utterly discouraging. I naturally looked to her *first* (with you) for help, supposing 'twould be her highest pleasure, but I found my mistake. She wished the box of poems *there* constantly & was unwilling for me to borrow them for a day, as she was fond of reading them (the verses) to passing friends. Mrs Dickinson has fine ability but lacks mental energy to complete. She has many ideal plans for work worthy of her talent, but the world will (probably) not see any finished. But for Mrs Todd & your self, "the poems" would die in the box where they were found. After my brief talk with you (2 years ago last summer) I resolved (if your life was spared & your interest continued), the poems *should* be published. I have (from that time) never mentioned the subject to my neighbors, prefering the *new deal* to take their own way, satisfied in their hands the end would be success. I intented to tell Mrs Dickinson, before the "Christian Union" was printed, *how* my wish was *at last* accomplished, but the paper appeared, a month in advance of the date I expected, so I sent it to her at once (with as I thought) a fitting note. Since then I have not seen her face or received any notice of the attention. I have had a "Joan of Arc" feeling about Emilies poems from the first & their reception convinces me I was right. As all Emilies possessions were given to me, years before her death, I recognize the right to magnify her name as she deserved. When the public demand more of her, I can safely trust my kind & efficient "two friends" to continue their work untrammeled (if they are willing). I hope you are pretty well. I wish I might see you as there are many things I would prefer to say to you in person. I have written to you more than once since last May. I hope the letters found you.

Again thanking you for your beautiful labors I am

> Heartily
> LAVINIA DICKINSON

My writing (sometimes) puzzles not very familiar eyes. I trust you will be able to read every word & will tell me *in* a word if you master my language.[16]

The unforeseen demand for the *Poems* was creating no little embarrassment for the publishers, especially in view of Christmas sales. This letter from Mr. Niles is addressed to my father:

> Boston
> *December* 23^d 1890

DEAR SIR

I have yours of the 22^d & also telegram. I regret to say we cannot send the books, our 2nd Ed. being exhausted. The 3^d Ed. will

---

[16] The "utterly discouraging" attitude alluded to by Lavinia may have resulted from Sue's failure to interest magazine editors in Emily's poetry. That such an inference is not without foundation is shown by a letter in the Century Collection of the Manuscript Division of the New York Public Library. I cannot find that any poem such as the one alluded to by Mrs. Dickinson ever appeared in *The Century*.

> Amherst, Mass.
> *Dec.* 31, 1886

Mr. Gilder
DEAR SIR

I enclose a poem of Miss Emily Dickinson's on the "Wind" thinking you might like to print it in some early number of the Century. After her death in May last we found she had left a mass of manuscript poems which we shall undoubtedly publish at a suitable time. Col. Higginson, Dr. Holland, "H.H." and many other of her literary friends have long urged her to allow her poems to be printed, but she was never willing to face the world. As not only she herself, but her family were intimate with Dr. Holland [the Assistant Editor], it would be more agreeable to them to see anything she wrote in the Magazine with which he was so closely identified. Will you pardon a novice's attempt at type-writing, and return the same to me at your convenience?

> Yours very truly,
> MRS. WM. A. DICKINSON

go to binder today, and I think we shall be able to fill orders on Friday [December 26] or Saturday.

I had to print a hurried second Ed. on a balance of paper wh. we had on hand. It amounted to only about 400 copies. For the third Ed., 500 copies, we were obliged to wait for the paper to be made.

Perhaps Mr Spear [Amherst bookseller] can take orders & fill them when the books are ready.

Yrs truly
THO^s NILES

The following Monday Mr. Niles wrote again:

Boston
Dec. 29 1890

DEAR MRS TODD

Your Ck. for $26.00 rec^d and today I send you by Am. Exp. 4 copies of the 3^d Ed. Emily Dickinson's Poems just in from the binder.

I have also sent Mr M. N. Spear the 10 copies in the supposition that he would still want them.

I suggested to Mr. Higginson the other day the idea of bringing out a cheaper Ed. reducing the price to $1.00 i.e. after the 3^d Ed. has been sold. What do you think of it? It would perhaps tend to popularize it.

Yours truly
THO^s NILES[17]

[17] A few days later Mrs. Todd notified Mr. Niles that the pages in the copies of the third edition she had received were wrongly numbered.

Boston
Jan. 3^d 1891

DEAR MRS TODD

I am afraid the whole 250 copies of the 3^d Ed. all we have had bound, are bound up wrongly, a mistake of the folder in folding the title signature.

The error had not been noticed by anybody else and we have sold 180 copies of the 250.

We should put the same design & lettering on the cover of a cheap Ed.

Yrs truly
THO^s NILES

On January eighth Mr. Niles wrote that "the blunder in folding has been corrected." The wrongly bound copies have become a collector's item.

Mrs. Todd's endeavor to make the book accurate in every particular is illustrated by the following letter.

Amherst, Mass.
29 *December*, 1890

DEAR MR. HIGGINSON:—

The third edition of our volume was to appear, I believe, on Saturday last. In view of a probable fourth edition before very long, I should like to ask your opinion about one or two slight changes.

The first [in the poem beginning, "A wounded deer leaps highest"] is on page 20—of which I wrote you some time ago—in the line "In which it cautious arm," printed cautiONS, although I three times corrected it in the proof.

Had we not better have the N turned into a U, and so leave it as Emily intended and wrote it?[18]

And on page 54 [in the poem, "My river runs to thee"], in the last line, I am sure she intended it to be two lines instead,

> Say, sea,
> Take me!

and that is very piquant and like her. How does it strike you?

The third suggestion occurring to me is on page 53 [in the poem, "As if some little Arctic flower"]. Should not the "only", beginning the last line, be instead the final word in the preceding line? If it read

> What then? Why nothing, **only**
> Your inference therefrom!

would not the rhythm be better?

And do you think it best to leave the ungrammatical use of *lain* instead of laid, in "When one who died for truth was lain"? [See page 35.]

These are merely suggestions which have occurred to me from time to time, and if you think they are improvements, they can

---

[18] This word, which by printer's error appeared as "cautions" in the first three editions, was then corrected to "cautious," as Emily wrote it; now, in the current edition, it reads "caution."

Nathan Haskell Dole thought the line should read, "In which it cautious aim" (letter to Roberts Brothers, Nov. 3, 1896).

be used in a fourth edition, probably without much trouble. But I am quite sure the first one I mentioned ought to be changed, at least.

Thank you for the *Beacon* notice. Mr. Howells' in the January *Harper*, and Mr. Chadwick's in the Dec. 18 *Christian Register* are exceedingly good. Nothing seems to have appeared yet in the *Tribune*. [Notice only, November 15, 1890.]

Very sincerely
MABEL L. TODD[19]

[19] This letter to Colonel Higginson was included in a group of seventy-seven letters collected by Mr. Firuski of the Housatonuc Bookshop, Salisbury, Connecticut. With this one exception all were addressed to Roberts Brothers and were written by Mr. Dickinson, by Miss Vinnie, by Mr. Higginson, and by my mother. As most of them were replies to letters already in my possession, important links in the evidence were thus supplied. Brought to my attention in 1935, they were purchased by me in 1936. Mr. Firuski describes their discovery:

As regards the brief but romantic story of the E.D. MSS material: In the early part of 1930 one Silverberg (I think the spelling is correct), a "runner" ("runner" is a free lance buyer and seller of books, etc. Usually they are poor and live from one day to the next. Some of them are honest; but most of them are not the most ethical class of citizens), found some boxes in the Boston freight yard addressed to a paper (junk) dealer. He (Silverberg) noted the boxes had come from Bar Harbor, Maine, and had "Roberts Bros." stamped on them. He went to the paper man and bought the boxes which had been consigned for the hopper (wrapping paper, corrugated board, etc., would be the final products). Apparently part of the shipment had already been chopped up. Silverberg, having shown brilliant imagination, now proceeded to be very stupid. The shipment contained letters from all the famous writers on the Roberts Bros. list—including Hearn, Stevenson and many others. He went from bookshop to bookshop hawking a letter here, another there, etc. The result was that all the material was scattered far and wide. He had neither the knowledge nor patience to keep the subjects intact. Accordingly it took me years to pick up fugitive bits and probably a few are still in various corners. When I asked him if he had seen any duplicate files containing the firm's answers to this correspondence he said he had but considered them worthless. Rushing back to the paper man he found he was too late, they had been chopped up. These letters had remained unopened in their boxes for years. One assumes that Mr. Hardy after he left the firm [of Roberts Brothers] took the excess files to Maine and that after his death his family or heirs did not bother to open the boxes.

MAURICE FIRUSKI

Housatonuc Bookshop
Salisbury, Connecticut
June 9, 1936

Except the last, all the suggested corrections were made. "Was lain" remains to this day, as Mr. Higginson decreed.

> 25 Buckingham St.
> Cambridge, Mass.
> *Jan.* 5, 1891

I have forwarded yr corrections approved except the *lain* which I think had better stay as it is.

Mrs. Dickinson thinks "a pair of spectacles afar just stir" should be "ajar" as in her MS. [From poem beginning, "I know some lonely houses off the road."] If you approve please notify Mr. Niles.

> T.W.H.

The letter from Mrs. Dickinson to which Colonel Higginson refers was presented to me by Dr. Barney.

> Oriental Hotel
> *Jan* 4",/91

DEAR COL. HIGGINSON

I forgot in my letter to you to speak of a blunder (of the printer I suppose) in Emily's robber poem. In the verse, "An almanac's aware" &c the vol. has it "the spectacles *afar*." Emily wrote and meant it, "ajar." I wish it might be changed for her sake. Sitting up late at night long after her family had retired, I can easily see, as she came on the unclasped spectacles of her Father, how that, and the other expressions came. I meant to have told you too of a funny bit. One of our Prof's returning the Library copy of the Poems said to my son, Col. H. is a famous literary man but does not know much about typography. "I have made a correction in the poem about the approaching shower" ["A drop fell on the apple-tree," *Poems*, 1890, page 81] The book has it, "*hoisted* roads." Of course it should be *moisted*, "there is no sense in the other." Need I add that I sent for the vol. erased his "*m*," and said Prof E. is a fine geologist but no poet. I did not mean this to be so long. Do not trouble to reply.

> Very sincerely yours
> S. H. DICKINSON

Sue was right about the spectacles. But instead of calling the mistake to the attention of her neighbor, Mrs. Dickinson had

of eccentricity, do nevertheless eschew society, retire from the world, and live the life of a recluse as triumphantly as Emily Dickinson did. But analogies are not convincing. The sanction of public preference has given the legend of a broken heart such vitality that it has successfully withstood all attempts to uproot it. It still remains for most people the only plausible explanation for a life like hers. So they try to find the man. An article entitled "A Melancholy Fidelity" in the *Commercial Advertiser*, August 23, 1893, shows the extreme to which speculation can go:

> It is said that Miss Dickinson's eccentricities resulted largely from disappointment in love. While she was still a girl she became deeply interested in a young man who was pursuing his studies in Amherst College. This young man subsequently became an instructor in the college. Mr. Edward Dickinson, Miss Emily's father, disapproved of the intimacy, which gave promise of ending in marriage, and at last (being a somewhat violent man) he peremptorily forbade the young man the house. It is said that at that time Miss Emily told her father that, as he had closed the doors upon her friend, so he had closed the doors upon her, and from that day she so seldom left the house—and, for that matter, so seldom left her room—that she was for thirty years practically as much a recluse as any nun doing penance.
>
> It will be of interest to Chicago people to know that the man identified by Amherst gossips as the object of Emily Dickinson's hopeless yet loyal affection was the late George Howland.[2]

Lest, on the strength of this article, someone should be tempted to unearth George Howland as the man for whom Emily re-

[2] George Howland, who graduated from Amherst College in 1850, was a tutor in the college from 1852 to 1855, and instructor in Latin and French from 1855 to 1858. It seems that he had literary aspirations. One of his poems entitled "Angling" consists of twelve stanzas, beginning

> Just down from the house is a sweet little brook,
> Where I love in vacation to throw in my hook,
> Not because I care much for the fishes, but yet
> It gives such a thrill when a nibble I get,
> A fresh thrill each new nibble I get.

Later Mr. Howland went to Chicago where he became Superintendent of Public Schools, a post held until the year before his death in 1892. He never married.

nounced the world, a few words from a letter sent to her brother
at the Harvard Law School may clear the air.[3]

Thursday Evening [*Dec.* 1, 1853]

Austin,—George Howland has just retired from an evening's
visit here, and I gather my spent energies to write a word to you.
"Blessed are they that are persecuted for righteousness' sake,
for they shall have their reward!" Dear Austin, I don't *feel*
funny, and I hope you won't laugh at anything I say. I am thinking of you and Vinnie—what nice times you are having, sitting
and talking together, while I am lonely here, and I *wanted* to sit
and think of you, and fancy what you were saying, all the evening long, but—ordained otherwise. . . .

The emotional experience of Emily Dickinson cannot be
defined in terms of thwarted love. It cannot be limited to her
feeling toward any single individual. A broken heart is not
needed to explain her way of life. To try to understand it in
such terms is to fail to grasp its quality. She says

> That love is all there is
> Is all we know of love.

And she amplifies the statement in a poem as yet unpublished:

> Love is like life, merely longer;
> Love is like death, daring the grave;
> Love is the fellow of the resurrection,
> Scooping up the dust and chanting "Live!"

Any suspicion that she had a particular person in mind when
writing this poem is disposed of by another version of it in which
the word "love" reads "faith" throughout.

Emily's love was of the essence of creation—an enveloping
effulgence. Any object, man or earthworm, entering its sphere
of light was caught in shining words. If, now and then, it was
stimulated by the sight or the touch of another human being,
that moment was transitory, while love, "the royal infinity,"
remained.

[3] *Letters*, 1931, p. 116.

But if a broken heart is not the answer, the reader may retort that her withdrawal from the world was abnormal, a sign of morbidity. As a matter of fact, Emily was a recluse in the sense only that she withdrew from the limitations of village life in order to investigate things that interested her more. The secrets of life she knew and explored throughout her "swift career." Her understanding was based on the intensity of her own feeling which was not a vicarious experience but a very real one, deep within "that campaign inscrutable of the interior." She explained that "to live is so startling it leaves but little room for other occupations"; merely "to be alive is power." And this was said in the simplest surroundings.

Once, as Henry Thoreau and my grandfather were floating down the Concord River in a little boat, Henry's face became suddenly transfigured as he looked up into the branches of a great oak tree beneath which they were passing, and he exclaimed, "There is enough in that oak tree to occupy a man his entire life!"

To excite Emily's interest nothing was too trivial or too familiar. She took nothing for granted, ignoring it as one ignores air. Snakes and flies, grass and stones, as well as wind and rain and the rising of the moon over the Pelham hills, all were of the essence of miracle. The lowliest forms of life were as authentic, as worthy of note, as those usually celebrated in poetry. This is what she says of earthworms in a hitherto unpublished poem:

> Our little kinsmen after rain
> In plenty may be seen,
> A pink and pulpy multitude
> The tepid ground upon;
>
> A needless life, it seemed to me,
> Until a little bird
> As to a hospitality
> Advanced and breakfasted.
>
> As I of he, so God of me,
> I pondered, may have judged,
> And left the little angleworm
> With modesties enlarged.

Emily did not reach out toward abstractions in order to find universal truth. The smallest object close at hand would serve. Through the gateway of minutiae she opened mighty vistas, each one adjusted to him who is able to perceive it. Indeed, I have at times suspected that what we think of Emily's poetry is more a measure of ourselves than of her. By our changing attitude toward it we can estimate our own growth. Many of the poems I have known by heart since early childhood. But as insight deepens, sentences whose tinkle always pleased me suddenly become heavy with significance. On rereading the words, familiar through a lifetime, their truth suddenly flashes:

> For each ecstatic instant
> We must an anguish pay
> In keen and quivering ratio
> To the ecstasy.

It takes a lifetime of striving, and of failure, to comprehend that.

But to return to the critics who, my mother said,

were manifestly bewildered, and could hardly use their accustomed words in description. Practically all united in admiration of the confusing thoughts which seemed to arouse their latent response, heretofore unsuspected; although there was also practical unanimity in their regret that she *would* neglect her rhymes so flagrantly. But nearly all were more than friendly, these astonished writers. The London *Daily News* [January 2, 1891], however, was incredibly harsh and cruel in its utter lack of any appreciation or understanding of Emily's peculiar genius, and Andrew Lang—who indeed may have written the various articles in the *Daily News*—called her work "balderdash" and "mere maundering."

This article was the first British review to reach Amherst. It ran in part as follows:

Mr. Howells has been captivated by a minstrel who subdues grammar to rhyme, and puts even grammar before sense. . . . Of course the idea occurs that Mr. Howells is only bantering; that he cannot really mean to praise this farrago of illiterate and uneducated sentiment. It is as far below the level of the Poet's Corner in a country newspaper as that is usually below Shakespeare. There are no words that can say how bad poetry may be when it is divorced from meaning, from music, from grammar, from rhyme; in brief, from articulate and intelligible speech. And Mr. Howells solemnly avers that this drivel is characteristic of American life! . . . If poetry exists it is by virtue of original, or at least of agreeable thought, musically and magically expressed. . . . The verses adored by Mr. Howells are conspicuously in the worst possible words, and the thought, as far as any thought can be detected, is usually either commonplace or absurd. . . . It is, in itself, a touching thing that a lady of extremely solitary habits should have solaced herself by writing a kind of verses; but to proclaim that such verses as we have quoted are poetry, and good poetry, is to be guilty of "the pathetic fallacy" in an original manner, and is to encourage many impossible poets.

This sounds not unlike the tirades which greeted the early poetry of Shelley.

The reviewer chose the poem beginning

> I taste a liquor never brewed
> From tankards scooped in pearl,

on which to comment:

It is literally impossible to understand whether she means that she tastes a liquor never brewed at all, or a liquor never brewed "from" tankards scooped in pearl. By "from" she may mean "in." Let us give her the benefit of the doubt, and she still writes utter nonsense. It is clearly impossible to scoop a tankard from pearl. The material is inadequate.

Again, quoting the lines

> How many times these low feet staggered,
> Only the soldered mouth can tell;
> Try! can you stir the awful rivet?
> Try! can you lift the hasps of steel?

he says

We could, perhaps, if we tried, but we cannot make sense out of balderdash. What are "low feet"? The words are meaningless. This remarkable composition ends thus:

> Indolent housewife in daisies lain!

This is no more English than it is Coptic. "In Daisy's lane" might have a meaning. . . .

When Lavinia's "fury," my mother's word, aroused by this review had somewhat abated, it began to take on a characteristic form—to harden in a determination to make the poems known throughout England as widely as possible.

In America there were mild echoes of the same sort of thing. But, except for the *Daily News* article, Lavinia dismissed derogatory reviews with pitying disdain. One such from the *Commercial Advertiser*, January 6, 1891, entitled "Grim Slumber Songs," was sent by Mr. Niles to Mrs. Todd:

> Extreme hunger often causes strange visions. That this hermitess never satisfied, perhaps never could satisfy, her craving for human companionship, may have first brought her into her strangely visionary state. Upon the theme of human love she becomes absurdly, if not blasphemously, intemperate. . . . Isolated from humanity, she cannot turn the current of her thoughts toward it except in intermittent galvanic shocks. . . . Both Blake and Emerson are unique elements in literature. She is a unique composition of familiar elements.

As to that "craving for human companionship" to which the reviewer alludes: when Colonel Higginson asked Emily whether "she never felt want of employment, never going off the place, and never seeing any visitor," she replied, "I never thought of conceiving that I could ever have the slightest approach to such a want in all future time," and added, "I feel that I have not expressed myself strongly enough."[4] This she did elsewhere:

> In thy long paradise of light
> No moment will there be
> When I shall long for earthly play
> And mortal company.

[4] *Letters*, 1931, p. 286.

At the end of two months the success of the book had been not merely "a success of esteem." It was selling so fast that Mr. Niles, always punctilious, proposed to Miss Vinnie an adjustment of the contract. Although royalty checks went directly to her, she attended to none of the necessary negotiations, nor at this time to any correspondence which had to do with money matters, my mother serving as her amanuensis.

It seems that in spite of mounting sales Mr. Niles could still hardly credit the "immediate" and "emphatic" success of the book.

Boston
Jany 16, 1891

Dear Mrs Todd

The success of Emily Dickinson's Poems has been so good that we are quite willing to modify the original agreement by paying for the plates and copyright on all sold at ten per cent. This is the way it stands:

We have printed 1380 copies. Supposing 1280 copies to have been sold (100 given to the press) the copyright on these at 15 cts. per copy (10%) would amount to $192.00.

According to the original plan, first Ed. exempt, there would be copyright on 880 copies at 22½ cts. each

(15%) $198.00
less cost of plates $122.65
―――――――
$ 75.35

shewing a difference in Miss D's favor of $116.65.

Now, I want to popularize the book by putting it in a different dress & reducing the price to $1.25. I thought at first to make the price $1.00, but I can't make the book quite good enough to fix the price so low.

I have never liked the appearance of the book as it is. Well enough for a special purpose as a holiday edition, but wanting in solidity, for a permanent library book.

I send you by mail a dummy shewing the paper on which the fourth Ed. is now printing, & an English volume, shewing the way in wh. I want to bind our book, putting the same dies on it as we have on the previous Ed., but stamping all in gold.

I am sure it will please all bookbuyers who are buying for the library shelves.

> Yours very truly
> THOˢ NILES

The new Ed. will open easily because the paper is more pliable.

> Boston
> *Janʸ* 24 1891

DEAR MRS TODD

. . . . In regard to the different arrangement as to copyright on the Dickinson poems, of course Miss D. will do just as she prefers. If the book is likely to sell *more* than 2000 copies in addition to the three editions already printed (1380) it will be better for her to let the present arrangement stand.

If it does not sell 2000 more, the arrangement I proposed would be in her favor.

> Yours very truly
> THOˢ NILES

Mr. Niles's letter of January sixteenth, forwarded to Colonel Higginson, brought the following reply.

> Cambridge
> *Jan.* 26, 1891

DEAR MRS. TODD

I return this letter, which is a very kind & generous one, and confirms H.H.'s opinion that he was the only Boston publisher who knew how to treat a lady. I think Miss Lavinia should by all means accept the offer. It is no real advantage to an author to own the plates, & he will push the book more efficiently for having it wholly in his charge. I think Miss Lavinia has come well out of the enterprise; few new volumes do so well.

If you are in Boston pray let me know. I am well this winter & (now) not harassed with so much work; and I want to see you, about this curious poetic enterprise, this adopted child of ours.

> Ever cordially
> T. W. HIGGINSON

On January twenty-ninth the fourth edition of the *Poems* was issued. The same day Mr. Niles wrote to Mrs. Todd:

Jany 29 1891
Boston

MY DEAR MRS TODD

Yours enclosing ck. for $16.00 rec^d & same credited your a/c.

I send you today four copies of the 4th Ed. of "Emily Dickinson's Poems." I hope the new dress will please you. To my mind it has a more enduring appearance, as though it had come to stay.

We do not intend to put them into boxes, beyond using up a few we had on hand. . . .

Yours truly
THO^s NILES

Miss Vinnie's acknowledgment of copies of the same edition runs as follows:

February 2nd 1891
Amherst

Mr Niles
DEAR SIR

Thank you for sending "Emilies poems" in their new & tasteful dress & for the early check [$193.80] which convinces me of the reality of their cordial reception from the world. I hope the success of *our* enterprise is satisfactory to you. Believe me deeply grateful to you for the result of your work. I have added your enclosed codicil to the early contract. I am quite anxious to have these poems reach England. Will *you* encourage their introduction if you approve?

Thanking you again for your courtesy

I am gratefully
LAVINIA N. DICKINSON

In reply to Mr. Niles's assurance that the poems were already on sale in England, Miss Vinnie wrote again. Her confidence was increasing.

Amherst
February 9th [1891]

MY DEAR MR NILES

Thank you for the English tidings. I'm eager that the whole world have the opportunity to enjoy *her* genious as she was too shy in life to take her rank.

Thank you for the cutting & the assurance of continued appreciation of "the poems."

I trust you will be interested to print another volume before very long—all readers of the *first* so far as I can learn are ready for more.

Thanking you once more for the success of "our enterprise" believe me heartily

LAVINIA DICKINSON

My mother's work on the poems, which until now had been intermittent, was beginning to absorb more and more of her time.[5] Less than two months after the publication of the first volume

[5] The diary (1891) is basis for this statement:

Jan. 4 About three went to Vinnie's, and sat an hour with her, talking about the second volume of *Poems*.

Jan. 6 To Vinnie's at noon, and she had five interesting letters, and a cutting about Andrew Lang and the *Poems*.

Jan. 8 Went to Vinnie's soon after two, and had a mixed-up afternoon. She had stacks of callers.

Jan. 9 Finished Emily's scrapbook up to date.

Jan. 11 In the evening I wrote two hours at Emily's letters to Mr. Bowles. [Copying letters sent by Emily's correspondents now accompanied work on the poems.]

Jan. 14 Copied, and sent some of Emily's poems to *The Independent*. . . . At Vinnie's awhile in the afternoon.

Jan. 17 Letter from Mr. Niles. *Poems* going at once into fourth edition—and he proposes to pay for the plates. Nearly 200.—already, for Vinnie.

Jan. 18 Worked nearly all day on Emily's poems. Also found those she sent personally to me. The "humming bird" is among them. Some are so fine they took my breath away. And there are hundreds more than we are familiar with. There will yet be *ten* volumes of her poems, and one or two of prose.

Jan. 25 After tea went over to Vinnie's for an hour. . . . Reviews read, and Niles' new proposition discussed.

Jan. 27 Looked over the volumes of the "Round Table" [in Library] and found "My Sabbath," exactly as we put it in the volume, only a different title [compare p. 71]. . . . After dinner Vinnie came over. . . . I worked on the second volume a little.

Jan. 28 Sent some poems to *Life* and *St. Nicholas*.

Jan. 30 I received the new (4th) Edition of Emily's *Poems*. Very prettily bound. . . . Vinnie received $193.80 from Roberts, royalty on the volumes sold so far, at 10%. The plates are now Roberts'.

Feb. 1 Looking over further MSS of Emily's.

Feb. 3 Letter from . . . *St. Nicholas* accepting with delight two poems of Emily's. *Dial* notice of the *Poems*—for February. Yesterday I found

she and Miss Vinnie were already discussing the possibility of a second book of poems. More than enough had been copied to make such a volume.

On Thursday, February twelfth, in response to an invitation from Colonel Higginson, my parents went to Boston to attend a meeting of the Round Table—a literary society of which Colonel Higginson was president. On this visit the subject of a second volume was taken up with Mr. Niles.

February 12, 1891

Went first to see Mr. Niles. *Poems* going fast. Fourth edition already gone. Fifth in press. Wants another volume for next fall.

February 13

We found Vinnie's cousin, Miss Norcross, at last, in the [Harvard] Divinity School Library. Pleasant enough half hour; & then we went to Col. Higginson's to lunch, at one. He is very dear and lovely. We are going right ahead with another volume; and he read me some wonderful letters of Emily's—unprecedented and unparalleled.

This Miss Norcross was Frances Lavinia, better known as "Fanny," whose place of employment, though within a few minutes' walk of Mr. Higginson's house, had been discovered only after quite a search. She and her sister Louisa—Emily's "Little Cousins"—had received from her a quantity of letters

---

"The Snake.". . . Copied some of Emily's poems. . . . Wrote a brief life of Emily for an encyclopaedia. . . . Vinnie came over after tea.

Feb. 5 Called at Vinnie's to tell her about *St. Nicholas* letter.

Feb. 8 In the morning I wrote an article about Emily for the *St. Nicholas*, & picked out some more poems for them. . . . Went to Vinnie's for awhile. Heard the kitten knock!

Feb. 9 Rewrote and copied yesterday's article.

Feb. 11 Finished up the Emily scrap-book to date.

Feb. 17 I worked hard all the morning on the Emily article for *St. Nicholas.*

Feb. 18 Austin likes my *St. Nicholas* article on Emily very much.

Feb. 20 In the evening I went with Vinnie (!) . . . to an entertainment at Miss Buffum's. Series of bright tableaux. Many students, and others.

Feb. 22 I put in final shape and copied my Emily article for *St. Nicholas.*

Feb. 24 Worked again over the article, using David's suggestions, and then re-copied it all. It now reads very well, and gracefully.

Feb. 26 Finished Emily scrap-book up to date.

which Miss Vinnie was determined to see. This call was the first in a series of attempts to gain access to them.

Meanwhile, demand for the book was continuing.

Boston
Feb 17, 1891

DEAR MRS TODD

I will have copies bound as before & in full gilt edges, & put them in a box.

These will make beautiful presents and the price will be $1.50. The fourth Ed. all sold. 5th binding.

I sent a copy to Miss Rossetti, who acknowledging it says: "a very remarkable work of genius—though I cannot but deplore some of the religious, or rather irreligious pieces."

Yours truly
THO[s] NILES[6]

Mr. Niles sent Miss Rossetti's letter to Miss Vinnie, who acknowledged it as follows:

Amherst
February 24th

MY DEAR MR NILES

Thank you for fresh courtesies. Both the "letters" interest me, though I'm sorry Miss "Rossetti" fails to comprehend "Emily" faithfully.

I trust the 5th edition will hurry away to make room for the 6th.

Has the *book* been introduced in California? Would there be any harm in acquainting some book seller *there* with the news? I have heard of it (today) in Michigan & Tennessee. We want it everywhere.

Should you have any English *good* news, I would be grateful to know it. I'm greedy for every *crumb* of appreciation. Thank you again for all your kind interest in my "Joan of Arc" "crusade."

Most heartily
·LAVINIA DICKINSON

1891

[6] The copy which Mr. Niles had sent to Christina Rossetti in November came, after her death on Dec. 29, 1894, into the possession of George Herbert

Now, after three months, the critics with few exceptions agreed that the poems were works of genius. The public had paid the price in terms of sales on a scale unprecedented for a book of poetry.[7] Miss Vinnie was riding on air, urging editors and publisher to work faster—to issue more poems, and still more. Mr. Niles was eager to do so.

Colonel Higginson was absorbed in rereading Emily's letters to him, in which he kept finding new poems fully as remarkable as any which had been published. He was planning to write an article about them for *The Atlantic Monthly*.

As for my mother, she was ploughing ahead—rearranging copied poems for a second volume, as well as copying letters sent to her by Emily's correspondents. She was sending new poems to periodicals, writing Emily's biography for an encyclopaedia, and articles of which we shall hear more later.

Little has been said about business arrangements connected with the literary début of Emily Dickinson. A contract, we know, had been signed, and in accordance with its terms the first royalties had been received by Miss Vinnie. But the reader may be curious to know what compensation the editors had received. The fact is that the subject had never been alluded to until, out of her first royalties, Miss Vinnie sent—by my mother as messenger—$50 to Colonel Higginson with the following note.[8] (Later he received $50 more. My mother also received $100.)

Palmer of Harvard University. It was, my mother told me, "the first of his three volumes of first editions of Emily Dickinson's *Poems*, the others being my presentation copy to him with my own inscription and a bit of Emily's manuscript, and the other Colonel Higginson's personal copy with his autograph." These are now included in the valuable collection of first editions of English verse presented by Professor Palmer to Wellesley College in memory of his wife, Alice Freeman Palmer.

[7] Editions were issued on the following dates: First, Nov. 12, 1890; second, Dec. 16, 1890; third, Dec. 27, 1890; fourth, Jan. 29, 1891; fifth, Feb. 17, 1891; sixth, Mar. 11, 1891. Although the number of copies in each edition was supposed to be 500, only 480 were issued of the first and 400 of the second. For a partial list of subsequent editions, see Appendix III.

[8] This is the fourth and last of the letters presented to me by Dr. Barney, for whose generosity I would like to express my gratitude. See pp. 66, 86, and

1891
Amherst
February 12th

MY DEAR MR HIGGINSON

I have received my first check from "Roberts Brothers" as the result of the work of the triple combination & want to divide with my colleagues.

Will you therefore accept the enclosed in token of my grateful appreciation of your generous & chivalric part in it all.

Very sincerely
LAVINIA N. DICKINSON

Colonel Higginson's astonishment sounds as naïve as it was manifestly sincere.

25 Buckingham Street,
Cambridge, Mass.
Feb. 17, 1891

DEAR MISS DICKINSON

I was quite surprised at your note by Mrs. Todd, with its unexpected enclosure, inasmuch as nothing had been said about that side of the matter. But I recognize the justice of it and can not afford to decline what you send. Of course, I spent a good deal of time on the poems.

The result certainly indicates your foresight and judgment. I have agreed with Mrs. Todd to plan for another volume this year; and find that some of the best poems were left out. I may also write for the *Atlantic* a little account of my first acquaintance with her, with some of her first letters to me. Another year perhaps (1892) there may be a prose volume.

One thing strikes me very much in the book-notices. No two critics quote the same poems. Each finds something different. That is a much surer guarantee of permanent interest than where all fasten on one or two poems. Yes! I think your "Joan of Arc" crusade has been successful.

Ever cordially
T. W. HIGGINSON

CHAPTER VII

Flying Sparks

My friend attacks my friend,
Oh, battle picturesque!
Then I turn soldier too,
And he turns satirist.

How martial is this place!
Had I a mighty gun
I think I'd shoot the human race
And then to glory run!

NO ACCOUNT of the literary début of Emily Dickinson would be complete apart from its emotional setting. The antagonism between Lavinia Dickinson and her sister-in-law, Susan Huntington Gilbert Dickinson (Plate X) was a force to be reckoned with —"Vesuvius at home" was Emily's word for it. I have alluded to this relationship—an armed truce at best. It supplied a background of shimmering animosity for all that went on.

One incident serves as well as another to make my meaning clear. I have chosen the one which follows only because the correspondence relating to it has been preserved. It illustrates the state of tension in the midst of which the editing took place —a balance of strains so delicate that no annoyance was too slight to upset it, no episode too trivial to serve as an escape-cock for pent-up feeling. The skirmish here recorded is typical of the sisterly give and take in the Dickinson family.

Except for those in my possession, the letters in this chapter are in the Harvard College Library (to which my thanks are due for permission to print), having found their way thither by way of the manuscript collection of the late Amy Lowell. (Miss Lowell had intended, as she told my mother, to write a life of Emily Dickinson in which analysis of her relationship to the members of her family would be the central theme.) The explanatory comments were given to me by my mother in the summer of 1932. She said that Lavinia was always convinced that the poems in question had been wrongfully kept by Sue, that she had failed to return them with the box of poems which Lavinia had left with her soon after Emily's death.

On March 11, 1891, the diary refers to the arrival of "surprising proof from *The Independent*." This was proof of two of Emily's poems, "Called Back" and "The Martyrs."[1] My mother wrote to the editor by the next mail to ask what it meant and to express Lavinia's emphatic disapproval.

In this instance the one caught between the upper and nether millstone was the Editor of *The Independent* himself, Dr. William Hayes Ward, Assyriologist—a vastly learned gentleman. A graduate of Amherst College in the class of 1856, he was an old friend of the Dickinsons. Because of that fact, as well as because *The Independent* was an influential paper, Lavinia had been anxious from the first to have favorable notices appear in it. At her request, and before the book was published, my mother had written an article about Emily which was dispatched to *The Independent* on October 24, 1890. Not until December twentieth, however, was it returned with the letter which opens this correspondence. In reply to Dr. Ward's letter my mother sent him some poems, three of which appeared in his paper on February 5, 1891. And now, suddenly, a few weeks later, came this proof of two other poems which neither Lavinia nor my mother knew anything about. What could it mean?

The entire passage-at-arms, including Dr. Ward's letters to Mrs. Todd which led up to it, is self-explanatory.

The Independent
251 Broadway
New York

Dec. 20, 189(

MY DEAR MRS. TODD:—

I trust you will have seen that we have published a review o. Miss Dickinson's poems.[2] I put the book in the hands of the

---

[1] "Called Back," beginning, "Just lost, when I was saved," *Poems*, Second Series, p. 85; "The Martyrs," beginning, "Through the straight pass o suffering," *Poems*, Second Series, p. 33. Both poems were printed in *The Independent*, Mar. 12, 1891. See footnote, pp. 145-146.

[2] *The Independent*, Dec. 11, 1890.

man at the head of our literary department—Dr. Twining— and the review was written on some consultation between us. We always prefer to use our own work rather than that which comes from abroad, if we feel equal to it, and I think you your- self would prefer to have such a review come from us rather than to publish this which we return to you. I am thoroughly surprised at the excellence of the poems. I have read them over and over at my home to my sisters, and three or four of them cling in my memory. She had a real genius, and it is extraordi- nary that with her sense of poetic thought and her sense of metre too, she had absolutely no sense of rhyme. A mere closing con- sonant was enough for her. With her, rhyme was very much like the definition of comparative philology, that science in which the vowels count for nothing and the consonants for very little.

Are there other poems of hers in any large number unpub- lished? I suppose this is a selection. If there are any others that compare with the best ones in the volume, I should like much to publish them in *The Independent*.

Yours very truly,
WM HAYES WARD

"In compliance with this request," my mother said, "Lavinia and I selected four poems which I sent to Dr. Ward on January 4, 1891." They elicited an immediate reply:

The Independent
251 Broadway
New York

Jan. 15, 1891

MY DEAR MRS. TODD:—

I thank you very much for sending these four poems. Three of them I will take and print as soon as I may. They are fresh and interesting. One of them I return. It seems to me so unsatis- factory in the way the last two verses are worked up. I am afraid I fail to catch the meaning except generally. Perhaps you may come across others which you would be willing to send. What is to be done about paying for them?

Yours very truly,
WILLIAM HAYES WARD
Superintending Editor

With regard to Dr. Ward's last question [my mother told me], I may say that the payment, $15, was sent to me and given to Lavinia.

The rejected poem, if my memory does not fail me, was

> Of tribulation these are they
> Denoted by the white
>
> [*Poems*, Second Series, page 227]

Those which he accepted were printed in the issue of February 5, 1891, "The Lost Jewel," "Fringed Gentian," and "Went up a year this evening," which Mr. Higginson had called "Emigravit." They were reissued in the Second Series of *Poems* published later in the year, "I held a jewel in my fingers" [page 106], "God made a little gentian" [page 172], and "Went up a year this evening" [page 218], the title "Emigravit" having been changed to "Gone," at my request.

Four days after these poems had appeared in print Dr. Ward received the following letter:

Amherst, Mass
Feb. 8"/91

My dear Mr Ward

My husband on his return from the Alumni dinner in N.Y. spoke of your interest in Miss Dickinson's poems. I delight in such recognition of her genius as I have known and felt it since our early girl-hood intimacy. All the more am I indignant at the silly fear of the public or lack of ability to recognize the power of many that were ruled out of the volume just printed. I have many manuscripts, letters, poems, &c. which I mean to make up into a unique volume as I can command the time. Magazines and newspapers are now eager for anything of Emily's, but should prefer the Independent to them all as I rate it's literary merit most highly. I enclose the poem on the Martyrs—clear and crisp as rock crystal to me. If you will print it for a money compensation I should be glad and will reserve others for you which have never been seen. Scribners gave me $15. for "Renunciation" printed in August.[3] I do not care for barter and am no "Shylock" but some price is fair I suppose. I would like this

---

[3] See footnote, p. 149.

confidential as the sister is quite jealous of my treasures. I was to have compiled the poems—but as I moved slowly, dreading publicity for us all, she was angry and a year ago took them from me. All I have are mine, given me by my dear Emily while living so I can in honor do with them as I please. Pardon so long a letter

And believe me cordially
MRS WM A. DICKINSON

The gist of Dr. Ward's reply can be gathered from Mrs. Dickinson's next letter to him.

Amherst, Mass.
Feb. 18"/91

Mr Ward
DEAR SIR.
Thank you for spending so much time over my letter. I recognize fully all Miss Emily's lack of rhyme and rhythm, but have learned to accept it for the bold thought, and everything else so unusual about her.

I think if you do not feel that your own literary taste is compromised by it, I would rather the three verses of the "Martyrs" should be published if any. I shall not be annoyed if you decide not to publish at all. I should have said *printed*. I do not think she meant to speak of the needle as at the pole—but it's apparent struggle to it's allegiance in any air—*polar* air appealing to her imagination as making a colder figure for her passionless poem. You know "The morning stars never did sing together" or "jocund day stand tip-toe on the misty mountain top"! I enclose a poem in her own hand which you can use or not as you please and in a few days, send you several little poems which you can use or not as you care, but kindly return. Emily never wrote long poems—the longest are in her volume. The money part is of little value anyway, anything you do will be satisfactory. Mr. Dickinson thinks as Col. Higginson and Niles are to bring out another vol. of the poems, it is not best, or fair to them to print many. I do not feel in any way bound to them, but will of course defer to his wish in the matter.

Yours cordially
S. H. DICKINSON

That Mrs. Dickinson had not "deferred" to her husband's "wish" we know, as both "The Martyrs" and "Called Back" were printed in *The Independent*. They were the "Two Lyrics" sent by Mrs. Dickinson, the "surprising proof" of which was received by Mrs. Todd the day before the poems appeared in the magazine.

To Mrs. Todd's letter of inquiry written on March eleventh Dr. Ward replied as follows:

> The Independent
> 251 Broadway
> New York
>
> *March 13, 1891*
>
> Mrs. Mabel L. Todd,
> Amherst, Mass.
> MY DEAR MADAM:—
> The proofs were sent to you by mistake by the clerk, who supposed they had come from you like the other poems we printed. There was a second copy in the hands of Mrs. Dickinson, to whom Miss [Emily] Dickinson sent them and from whom I received them. Of course I did not know that there were duplicate copies, and I presume she did not. It would seem as if somehow you ought to pool your interests and not have any division over so sacred a matter. I have no doubt Mrs. Dickinson acted in perfect good faith in sending them to us as we did, and I do not see why she had not full right to do so.
>
> Yours very truly,
> Wᵐ HAYES WARD
> Superintending Editor

That Dr. Ward must have written to Mrs. Dickinson on the same date is evident from her reply to him:

> MY DEAR MR WARD.
> I am very sorry you have been annoyed in any way over an apparent "conflict of possession" in the little matter of Emily's verses. I sent them to you in great innocency of motive and as they are mine, many of them yellow and faded with time—(many too personal and adulatory ever to be printed) and as mine I shall make such use as I choose of them. When I have a little

leisure I will send you a few more—meanwhile may I remind you to return the mass of Emily's I sent you.

Yours cordially
S. H. Dickinson

Amherst, Mass.
March 14″/91

[P. S.] It just occurs to me that you may not care to print more after this sort of injunction of Miss Dickinson's.

Lavinia herself followed up her "injunction":

Amherst, Mass.
March twentieth, '91

Dr. Wm H. Ward,
Dear Sir:—

My attention was called last week to two poems of my sister's in the *Independent*, and I also was shown the letter you wrote Mrs. Todd on the subject, in reply to hers enclosing proofs which you had sent her.

I wish simply to say that my sister gave her poems to me, all of them, as I can prove, if necessary; and that although copies of them have been given at different times to different persons, they have been so given simply for private perusal, or reading to others, and not to pass the property in them, which is in me. So there will be no occasion for any pooling of interests which you suggest.

I have been urged to allow another volume of these to be prepared, and had decided in view of this not to permit more of the unpublished, unless quite occasionally, to appear either in newspapers or magazine at present. Certainly this cannot be done without my consent.

Very truly yours,
Lavinia Dickinson

The contents of Mr. Ward's rejoinder can again be inferred from the letter which follows.

Amherst, Mass.
March 23,/91

My dear Mr Ward.

I have just read your letter to my husband and regret that I so innocently have drawn you into a hornet's nest. I beg you will not be drawn into any correspondence with Miss Lavinia over the poems, or allow yourself to be troubled by her foolish fits of temper which have worn into her brother's life very deeply. She feels a little baffled by my possession of so many mss of Emily's and is very foolish in her talk of *law*, etc. I am quite used to her vagaries, and while I pity her, I shall never yield a line in my possession to her. It is an advantage to have them printed in the Independent as she well knows. I have a little article in my mind, with illustrations of her (Emily's) own, showing her witty humorous side, which has all been left out of her vol. I presume Mr Bowles will be glad of it. I thank you for your intelligent courtesy toward me in the matter. The little poem I am happy to have your sister keep, and pray do not yield it up to any one. I will send her another soon. I wish I could persuade my daughter[4] to send you an Easter poem she has just written—but she is immovable, having a most feminine horror of print.

Yours very cordially,
S. H. DICKINSON

My daughter wrote a sketch, "My Surviving Aunt" a couple of years ago which I would like to read to you sometime. I should have thanked you for the check and the papers duly rec'd.

S.H.D.

Lavinia intended to see to it that such a thing as this should not happen again. First, she asked my mother to find out what steps the publishers could take to prevent publication of Emily's poems without her knowledge or consent. Mr. Higginson's name was used as a subterfuge.

Boston,
Mar 25, 1891

Mabel Loomis Todd
DEAR MADAM

It is our opinion that persons who have received fugitive poems would have no moral or legal right to publish and receive a compensation for them. Our Mr. Niles is out of town but we

---

[4] Martha Gilbert Dickinson, later Mrs. Alexander E. Bianchi. I have been told by several persons that at this time Sue was more interested in her daughter's literary career than in Emily's poetry.

expect him home in a few days and he will then give you his opinion on the subject.

Very truly yours

Roberts Bros

E. D. HARDY

This letter was followed by one from Mr. Niles himself:

Boston

Mch 30, 1891

DEAR MRS TODD

I find your letter on my desk after my return.

It is a well settled point of law, I believe, that the receiver of letters has no right to dispose of them in any way & I presume manuscript poems would be protected in the same way.

The new copyright law covers this matter. It says, "Every person who shall print or publish any manuscript whatever without the consent of the author or proprietor first obtained shall be liable to the author or proprietor for all damages occasioned by such injury."

I suppose, however, Mʳ Higginson has a perfect right to *read* Miss D's correspondence and MS poems in public or in private.

Yours very truly

THOˢ NILES

My mother said:

This letter did not satisfy Lavinia. She was determined to take the steps necessary to preclude the possibility of further "unauthorized" printing of Emily's poems. She asked me to confer with a Boston lawyer as to what to do, and chose for the purpose Benjamin Kimball, with whom Emily had been acquainted.

St Botolph Club, Boston

April 22, '91

MY DEAR MRS. TODD:

I was sorry you did not let me know your address when in town so that I might call. I have heard from Miss Dickinson, asking me to confer with you on your next visit. With pleasure and cannot you in advance perhaps let me have a line from

[you] giving your address & perhaps a word or two about the matters upon which Miss Dickinson would ask my counsel. I go west today but shall be back very soon, a week or so.

With kind regards
BENJAMIN KIMBALL

When the letter arrived, Mr. Kimball was out of town. Before his return Vinnie had quieted down sufficiently so that no legal advice was asked of him, or of anyone, and no further trouble was encountered at that time. Sue made no more "unauthorized" attempts at publication.

CHAPTER VIII

Momentum

A man may drop a remark,
In itself a quiet thing,
That may furnish the fuse unto a spark
In dormant nature lain.

Let us deport with skill,
Let us discourse with care,
Powder exists in charcoal
Before it exists in fire.

THE "auction" had been a success. Anxiety which had oppressed both sister and editors before the poems were published had given place first to relief, then to satisfaction, and finally, after three months, to a sense of exultation.

Miss Vinnie was by this time not only aware of the benefits accruing from copyrights. She was even beginning to worry about her financial security in England and wrote to Mr. Niles to find out about it.

Boston
Mch 11, 1891

DEAR MRS TODD

The six poems were sent yesterday. The fifth Ed. is selling well, we have about 250 remaining, & the sixth Ed. is printing. We have now the *gilt edge* style in box, retail $1.50, if you want any.

The [international] copyright bill is not everything to be wished, but it is a great victory nevertheless & in time can be made more perfect. The great objection to it made by *unknown* authors is the *simultaneous* publication clause.

A *new* author could hardly expect that his book would find a publisher here ready to take hold of it before it had been tried at home, but if the right to secure copyright extended say six months after publication in England, it would secure many valuable works, which will now be pirated as usual.

Truly yours
THOˢ NILES

The critics were still busily at work. A notice in *The New York Tribune* on March 15, 1891, referred to "a wholesome comment in 'Scribner' this month on the so-called poems of Emily Dickinson." That article in "The Point of View," chiefly a defense of form in literature, was also a protest against the lack of it in her poems. And yet Emily's poetry challenged such critics. Intellectually they repudiated it. In point of fact they read it and read it again, finding it difficult to express their judgment in measured terms.

If a test of great poetry is its capacity for evoking emotion, then Emily Dickinson can meet the test. For it is as true today as it was in 1891 that no one can read it with indifference. Even those who disparage it most do so with fervor.

Nor was it critics only who felt the challenge. "The curiosity of the public with regard to Emily's life was insatiable," my mother said, "and both Colonel Higginson and myself were swamped with requests to write articles about her and to talk about her."

On March 22, 1891, Colonel Higginson gave a reading from her letters to a group of friends. Though a hypothetical wife was courteously included in the following invitation, Mr. Niles had never married.

March 17, 1891
25 Buckingham St.
Cambridge, Mass.

DEAR MR. NILES

Next Sunday at 4 P.M. I am to read to Howells, Scudder & a few others extracts from Emily Dickinson's correspondence including things never likely to be published. We should be very glad to see you and Mrs. Niles also, if you can come.

Ever cordially
T. W. HIGGINSON

Among those who were present[1] at this first reading of Emily's letters was William Roscoe Thayer, biographer and historian.

> 15 Ware Street
> Cambridge
> *March 24, 1891*

DEAR COLONEL HIGGINSON:

I have been thinking over many passages from Emily Dickinson's Letters. I regretted that I had to go before you had finished reading—and they seem to me to embody so unique and interesting a character, that I can only hope that her whole correspondence with you may be published as soon as possible. Surely our New England Calvinism never brought forth any other flower so sweet and un-Calvinistic. It's a miracle like that of young Keats coming out of the stables of London cockneydom. But then, genius is always a miracle.

Thanking you for allowing me to enjoy this foretaste of the published correspondence, I am

> Very sincerely yours,
> WM. R. THAYER

To Col. T.W.Higginson
Cambridge

I can't forget—and I don't believe anyone who understands it will forget that phrase of hers: "They pray to the *great eclipse* whom they call Our Father."

Mrs. Todd was preparing a talk to be given in Springfield, Massachusetts. I quote from her diary:

March 26, 1891

At nine o'clock beginning my Springfield paper on Emily. . . . Wrote all day, except half an hour's running out at noon, and fifteen minutes just before six—and finished it. Sixty-five pages, exclusive of the unpublished poems to be read. I think it is interesting, and in a not-deep way rather a comprehensive sketch of her life and personality and work and literary characteristics. David and I went over to the Central station instantly after

---

[1] Colonel Higginson's diary gives a list of the *invités*:
  March 22, 1891. Read from E.D.'s letters. Present Howells, S. Longfellow, Greenes (2), Osgoods (2), Mrs. Hammond, Thayer, Howes (2), J.S.M., Sylvia Scudder, Lorings (2), F. Warren, with Alice, Edw. & Steve, 20 with ourselves. Did not come, Fairchilds, Nileses, Davises, Whitmans, Santayana, Eastman [Wellesley].

dinner, and put it on the 7.26 train, to go to Boston and be type-written.

April 1

Went to Mrs. [D.] Holland's, on Maple Street, where the Women's Club met, this time. There were over sixty ladies present. I read my paper on Emily Dickinson, with selections from her unpublished poems, and many incidents which I told informally, between the graver paragraphs of the paper. It was voted a great success: they only wished it had been longer.

According to the little book in which my mother kept a record of her talks, she received for this one $10 and "expenses," *i.e.*, railroad fare. Springfield is twenty miles from Amherst.[2]

My mother described "an amusing incident" connected with the publication in *The Christian Register*, April 2, 1891, of the following poem which she had sent to the editor:

> God is a distant, stately lover,
> Woos, as He tells us, by His Son;
> Verily, a vicarious courtship,
> Miles and Priscilla were such an one.
>
> But lest the soul, like fair Priscilla,
> Choose the envoy and spurn the groom,
> Vouches, with hyperbolic archness,
> Miles and John Alden are synonym.

He accepted it at once:

> The Christian Register
> No. 141 Franklin Street
> Boston

March 26, 1891

Mrs. David P. Todd
Amherst, Mass.
MY DEAR MADAM:

Many thanks for your kindness in sending me the poem of Emily Dickinson. What a genius she was! Her resurrection surely

[2] A report of this talk before the Springfield Women's Club in *The Republican*, Apr. 2, 1891, was reprinted in the *Amherst Record*, Apr. 8, 1891.

came. Would that we might always think that genius had its Easter and was not buried in the tomb.

Cordially yours
S. J. Barrows

A month later this letter was followed by another:

Boston
April 22, 1891

My dear Mrs. Todd:

I have had two letters from readers who have been greatly shocked by the poem of Emily Dickinson which I published, and Rev. Brooke Herford who forwarded one of them says: "It is one of the most offensive bits of contemptuous Unitarianism that I have met with." (!!)[3]

I have looked over the poem and cannot see myself that it is any more irreverent or daring than the metaphors used in the Song of Solomon which the church has regarded as of divine inspiration, nor any worse than the metaphors representing the Church as the Bride of Christ in the Apocalypse. But it makes some difference whether such a poem has the stamp of traditional authority upon it or not.

Perhaps it would have been better to publish a little note with it telling people more about Emily Dickinson. I have wondered whether you have any matter about her religious life out of which you could make a brief article for the Register which might vindicate her against the charge of irreverence.

Yours very truly
S. J. Barrows

My mother did not write such an article; but someone else did. An editorial in *The Christian Register*, April 30, 1891, provided a stalwart apology for Emily by way of soothing offended subscribers. The poem was not included in the second volume, however, which appeared later that year.

Poems were continually being sent to magazines. There is a

[3] The Reverend Brooke Herford, himself a Unitarian, was pastor of the Arlington Street Church, Boston. The poem in question was published "for the first time" by Emily's niece in 1929; see p. 389. See also *Letters*, 1931, p. xxx.

slip from *Harper's Magazine* returning "It will be summer eventually" on April 23, 1891. Meanwhile, those for the new volume were being chosen, "sometimes with Vinnie, sometimes by myself," my mother said. She wanted to talk with Colonel Higginson and asked him to appoint a time for their meeting.

> 25 Buckingham Street
> Cambridge, Mass.
> *Apr.* 5, 1891

DEAR MRS. TODD

I shall be glad to see you. If you are coming down at the end of this week, cannot you come to the Round Table on Thursday eve at Rev. B. Herford's, 12 Chestnut St.? Mr. F B Sanborn will speak on "The New Nationalities of Southern Europe," & I have hopes that Mr. Stepniak will be there. If not, perhaps you can come here on Saturday morning or afternoon. I also have points on which to consult you.

It seems that the College Alumnae Club wish you & me to talk to them some afternoon about E.D. & perhaps the Misses Eastman could come then. They are going to write you.

> Ever cordially
> T. W. HIGGINSON

This is an official invitation to the R.T.[4]

The invitation to the Round Table was accepted and Mrs. Todd went to Boston on April eighth,

partly [she said] to talk over the forthcoming volume, partly to hunt for old furniture for Vinnie.

This interest in old furniture on the part of Lavinia seems strange. She might be supposed to have inherited all the old furniture she needed. But she had given away to citizens of Amherst who had worked for her many pieces of her old mahogany and had replaced them with quartered oak furniture.

[4] Mr. Frank Sanborn of Concord, friend of Emerson and Thoreau, was a writer and lecturer who "peddled culture" throughout New England. Mrs. Julia Ward Howe also spoke. Sergei Stepniak, reformer and revolutionist, was a member of the Russian nobility, trying to improve the lot of the peasant. "Mr. Stepniak," my mother told me, "was the lion of that particular winter in Boston. The Misses Eastman, . . . cultivated ladies, were enthusiasts about Emily's poetry." Colonel Higginson's diary describes this as a "good meeting," with about seventy present.

As soon as she realized her mistake she was eager to purchase some more old mahogany, and the task of finding it devolved upon me.

The diary records on April eleventh that my mother "reached Col. Higginson's house about 10.30. Discussed the new volume, and arranged the poems, a little, I had selected, looked over letters, and had a very pleasant morning." Ten days later he wrote to her enclosing some poems—a preliminary selection for the volume. His letter suggests a change of attitude toward altering the poems.

> 25 Buckingham St.
> Cambridge, Mass.
> *Apr.* 21, 1891

DEAR FRIEND

I think you may like to have these before our reading. I have classed them under the four heads, putting in such of Miss Lavinia's as seem to me best, but please don't regard it as final. Those at the beginning of each department I have considered carefully. Those of my own, which you have not, I will send or give you later.

Let us alter as little as possible, now that the public ear is opened.

One poem only I dread a little to print—that wonderful "Wild Nights,"—lest the malignant read into it more than that virgin recluse ever dreamed of putting there.[5] Has Miss Lavinia any shrinking about it? You will understand & pardon my solicitude. Yet what a loss to omit it! Indeed it is not to be omitted.

> Ever cordially
> T. W. HIGGINSON

P.S. The Amherst Lit. Monthly editors have asked me to lecture there May 5th. I can't but have offered for May 12th if they pay me $75, which they probably ought not.

While Colonel Higginson was busy preparing his article for *The Atlantic Monthly*, my mother "at jerky intervals," was writing her paper for the Boston College Alumnae Club. This meeting was held at Sleeper Hall, 12 Somerset Street, on Satur-

---

[5] *Poems*, Second Series, p. 97.

day afternoon, May second, with an audience of about two hundred. She read her paper on Emily, "with a little talk at intervals," and then Colonel Higginson "read some of her letters to him, with comments." Among others, Miss Fanny Norcross and Charles E. L. Wingate were present, and Mr. Dickinson came from Amherst for the occasion.

Mr. Wingate gave his impressions in his Boston Letter to *The Critic*, May 9, 1891:

> An astonishing statement regarding the literary activity of Emily Dickinson was made by Mrs. Mabel Loomis Todd at the College Club meeting on Saturday. The poet, whose work, published by Roberts Bros. after her death, has now entered upon its sixth edition, must have spent very much of her time in writing, as she left 800 manuscript poems complete, besides fragments of nearly as many more. That she wrote for love of writing is certain, for as one reads her poems he feels that her heart, as well as her thoughts, was in her work; but yet, as Mrs. Todd pointed out, there were indications of a hope of publication expressed both in the preludes and in the fact that, in mentioning the papers to be destroyed after her death, she did not include these poems. Col. T. W. Higginson, whose interesting preface introduces Miss Dickinson's published poems, read to the College Club several letters from the poet, his enjoyable acquaintance with whom was almost entirely by correspondence; while Mrs. Todd corrected certain impressions regarding the author's life. Those ideas, that made of Miss Dickinson a woman eccentrically dressed, an invalid, an irreverent woman, or the victim of a love tragedy, were explained away, and she was shown to have had a strong dislike for the shams and trivialities of life, which united with shyness to keep her confined to her home. Her love of children was illustrated by her lowering of gifts from her windows, while her pleasure in books and in music was marked.

The selection of poems for the second volume was nearing completion. Meanwhile, Mr. Higginson was again going over those that Emily had sent to him. He mailed a list of them to my mother:

DEAR FRIEND

I send the list.[6] Let me know which you want copied for you and I'll send them. All marked √ should go in. One verse

[6] Footnote on facing page.

I copy for the pleasure of copying it, though you may have it.

Ever cordially

T.W.H.

Camb.
May 13, 1891

[*Enclosed*]

> Lay this laurel on the one
> Too intrinsic for renown.
> Laurel! veil your deathless tree.
> Him you chasten, that is He!

---

[6] On an enclosed sheet:

List of Poems (E.D.)

    ought to have

        We play at paste
        The nearest dream } (You have)
        Your riches taught me poverty
        A Bird came down the walk
        Of tribulation these are they
        The Robin is the one
        The wind began to rock the grass
        The humming-bird (You have)
        Ample make this bed
        (The Gale) It sounded as if the streets were running
        I have no life but this
        (The Blue-Bird) "After all birds"
        (Epitaph) Step lightly on this narrow spot
        He preached upon Breadth (You have)
        A death blow is a life blow to some
        Lay this Laurel (1 verse) very fine
        The Blue-jay [No brigadier]
        South winds jostle them
        As imperceptibly as grief
        Before I got my eye put out
        The White Heat [Dare you see] (You have)
        The possibility to pass
        When I hoped I feared
        The soul unto itself
        The sea said "Come" to the brook
        Blazing in gold (You have)
        To undertake is to achieve
        Remembrance has a rear & front
        The days that we can spare
        Who were the Father & the Son?
        Faithful to the end
        Because that you are going

(I may have a few more)

[Of the poems listed, Colonel Higginson had checked all except the last six.]

She wrote it after re-reading my "Decoration." It is the condensed essence of that & so far finer.

Because this quatrain was a particular favorite of Colonel Higginson's it was used as the concluding poem of the Second Series.

Mrs. Todd replied:

> Amherst
> 18 *May*, 1891

DEAR MR. HIGGINSON:—

I find I have a good many of those whose first lines you sent me, but not all, by any means.

That exquisite "The Nearest Dream" I do not find—which you read so thrillingly in Boston. The others that I have not, are these:—

> Your riches taught me poverty
> The Robin is the one
> The wind began to rock the grass
> I have no life but this
> After all birds
> Step lightly on this narrow spot
> He preached upon breadth
> A Death-blow is a life-blow to some
> The possibility to pass
> When I hoped I feared
> The sea said 'come' to the brook
> To undertake is to achieve
> Remembrance has a rear & front
> The days that we can spare
> Who were the father & the son
> Faithful to the end
> Because that you are going

One or two of these first lines sound very familiar, but they are not with the six hundred others—that mine from which I always expect to draw unlimited riches. I do not think my "Blue Jay" is yours, either. It begins, "A bold, inspiriting bird is the jay."

And I have one beginning:

> It sounded as if the air were running,
> And then the air stood still,

hich may be identical with yours using *streets* instead of *air*.
ave you anything on the Indian Pipe? I have heard of one,
it cannot get hold of it. I think she wrote it many years ago.
The scraps, written in pencil which I have recently begun to
range and copy, are, some of them, very fine. I will put in a
w before I send the poems back to you.

I enclose a sonnet written to E.D. out of pure enthusiasm by
ie of our students here.[7] Does it not seem to you very good?
He was going to publish it in the *Literary Monthly* here—he
one of the editors—but I suggested his sending it to the
ıristian Union instead. What do you think? He was much
eased to have you see it.

Cordially
MABEL L. TODD

Though the month of June was largely taken up with college
tivities, an entry in Mrs. Todd's journal shows where her
oughts were:

iesday morning, *June* 16, 1891

It is ninety in the shade this morning. . . . I have looked over
ne more of Emily's poems, although all the selection has been
ide for the second volume. The success of the first volume is,
uppose, really phenomenal for poetry. The seventh edition is
her preparing or already out this week—I have not heard
·m Mr. Niles for two or three weeks. And separate poems
ave sent to *St. Nicholas,* the *Independent, Life, The Christian
gister,* and the *Youth's Companion,* where they have been
:epted with avidity and paid for.[8] Vinnie has reaped a harvest,
d she will have another large check July first from the pub-
her. Mr. Niles is very gentlemanly and generous. The second
lume will appear October first.

With all her delight and satisfaction in the success and

The sonnet, written by LeRoy Phillips of the class of 1892 at Amherst
lege, was published in the *Amherst Literary Monthly*, June, 1891, and
in in *The New England Magazine*, November, 1891. It is one of two
ms listed in *Emily Dickinson, a Bibliography*, The Jones Library, 1930,
having been dedicated to her in 1891. Two other poems to Emily
·eared that same year: G. E. Meredith, "The Poems of Emily Dickinson,"
e Literary World, Boston, Apr. 11, 1891; and Mary Elwell Storrs, "Emily
kinson, 1830–1886," *The Springfield Republican*, May 22, 1891.
See footnote, p. 158.

Ther. 60   FRI. JULY 31, 1891   Wea.

a perfect June day
so cool & bright —
[...] & I left at [...] 20
for Amherst — he rode
over the hills for Pea-
cocks !! & I visited
with Lavinia Dickinson
very enjoyable after-
noon — [...] the history
of Emily's poems —
& (Sue's devilstry)! —
Austin came to the
station, & visited [...]
strange [...] — originally
called at Sophy's &
[...] Maddock's [...] her
two sisters — Ella met
us at the P. station
business with her
father —

*Page from the diary of Eudocia Converse Flynt of
Monson, Massachusetts*

preciation of the book, poor Vinnie has had a great deal of
in through Susan. Neither she nor Mattie has spoken to her
ace last September when they first learned of the coming
lume. And Susan sent two poems which she had of Emily's
the *Independent*, and kept the money for them. . . . The
reat big, black Mogul" has also crowned her atrocities by
ling various people (so that it is current gossip everywhere)
at Emily bequeathed all her writings to her; that Vinnie
rrowed the poems, had them surreptitiously copied and pub-
hed—and she is trying to gain sympathy for this supposed
ong!
It is a miserable business. . . .

Lavinia's suffering at the hands of her sister-in-law was a
rmanent if intermittent state. At times she sought sympathy.
1 July 31, 1891, she received a visit from Eudocia Carter
nverse (Mrs. William N. Flynt), an old friend from Monson,
r mother's early home. That lady had been a close friend of
vely Eliza Coleman (Mrs. John Dudley) to whom both Emily
d Lavinia were devoted. Mrs. Flynt wrote in her diary a few
rds descriptive of her call.

er. 60   Fri. July 31, 1891   Wea.
perfect *June* day so *cool* & bright. Wm. & I left at 12.20 for
herst—he rode over the hills for Peacocks!! & I visited with
vinia Dickinson very enjoyable afternoon—heard the history
Emily's poems — & (*Sue's deviltry*)! — Austin came to the
tion, & visited me—strange family—original. . . .

CHAPTER IX

Preparation of *Poems*, Second Series

> *This is a blossom of the brain,*
> *A small italic seed*
> *Lodged by design or happening*
> *The spirit fructified.*

ON SEPTEMBER 20, 1891, my mother summarized in h
journal her vacation activities:

> The summer was spent in my own little red house, hard
> work. I have few vacations at best, and this year, as last,
> volume of poems was in progress. I had to get it ready, sele
> and arrange the poems, compare copies with originals, a
> write the preface to this second volume. Then the proof can
> and I had to correct it, again comparing each original.
>
> Before the proof began, however, I made a complete alph
> betical index of everything already copied, not including eith
> published volume. This list made nearly one thousand. Th
> I catalogued the original manuscripts, so that I can find any o
> at a moment's notice. David helped me a great deal about
> this work.

My mother's correspondence with Colonel Higginson a
took a good deal of time—an exchange of letters so constant
frequently to overlap. Enough of this correspondence has be
preserved not only to clarify several debatable issues, but
reveal the personalities of the editors, whose points of vi
were often widely divergent. In spite of disparity of age a
experience, however, both were considerate of attitudes th
could not understand. Even when they differed most, they ma
tained toward one another extreme courtesy. In fact, it so

nes seems as if the more their opinions differed, the politer
ey became.[1]

The first letter from Colonel Higginson was received a few
ys after Mrs. Todd had begun to prepare the manuscript for
e printer.

Dublin, N.H.
July 6, 1891

ᴇᴀʀ Mʀs. Tᴏᴅᴅ

It is long since I heard. Are you to send me the MS. again?
hought so.

I have my paper nearly ready for the Atlantic with E.D.'s
ters. I meant to print a few poems among them. Please tell if
y of the following have been printed, as I hear that some hv.
peared in the *Transcript* which I don't see.

> We play at paste
> The nearest dream
> Your riches taught me poverty
> A bird came down the walk
> Of tribulation these are they
> A resonance of emerald (Humming-bird)
> No brigadier throughout the year (Jay)

If these have not appeared please withhold them.

What was the date of Mr. [Edward] Dickinson's death & was
taken ill at the State House or at his lodgings? I think he
ᵈ in Boston. I had a very interesting talk with Miss Norcross
ᵒ is here & told me many things—I mean the one who is
brarian at Divinity Hall, Cambridge. [Without signature]

Some of Mrs. Todd's letters were placed by Colonel Higginson in his
alatea Collection," as he called it, in the Boston Public Library, together
h other documents relating to Emily Dickinson. He began to catalogue
he says, on Mar. 23, 1891. On Oct. 7, 1896, he sent a "box of books" to
s same collection. The Dickinson material may well have been included
this shipment. But whether it was or not, it has been available to the
blic for at least thirty years, Colonel Higginson having died in 1911.
quently drawn upon, this collection is well known. But when these
ters are supplemented by Colonel Higginson's replies, all of which are in
possession, the correspondence becomes source material indispensable in
paring a final edition of *The Poems of Emily Dickinson*.
n this chapter *Poems*, Second Series, 1891, and *Poems*, Third Series,
6, will be referred to as "S.S." and "T.S."

[*Post card, mailed the same day*]

Also—have "The White Heat" ["Dare you see a soul at t
white heat"] & "As imperceptibly as grief
               The summer waned away"
been printed?

T.W.H.[2]

Mrs. Todd's reply follows:

Amherst, Massachuse
9 *July*, 1891

My dear Mr. Higginson:—

I hope you will pardon my long delay in sending you the N
second volume. The unusual rush at Commencement and t
inauguration of President Gates, with a house full of gues
must be my excuse.

Now I have my time quite free again, and I will send you t
poems on Monday. Many in this volume will be far finer th
most of the first. Miss Lavinia wishes to look over the volu
once more with me, to be sure none of her especial favorites a
omitted.

None of those whose first lines you sent me, have, to n
knowledge, been printed anywhere. By with-holding them
suppose you mean from any publication before the volun
I shall take pains to have them kept out of sight until yo
article appears in the *Atlantic*. I wish that might be before t
volume is published. Am I to be so happy as to see the proof
the article?

Mr. Edward Dickinson was making a speech at the Sta
House in Boston, on June 16, 1874, upon some rail-road matt

[2] All of the poems here referred to appeared in the Second Series. T
second line of "As imperceptibly as grief" (S.S., p. 168) reads, "the summ
lapsed away," in all printed versions, and from all of them four stanzas
missing.
    In the poem beginning, "Your riches taught me poverty" (S.S., p.
the final line reads, as Emily wrote it, "While just a girl at school."
Higginson wanted to change the order of the words so that "girl" wo
rhyme with "pearl." The final stanza would then have read

> It's far, far treasure to surmise,
> And estimate the pearl
> That slipped my simple fingers through
> While just at school a girl.

believe the State management of the Hoosac Tunnel. It was
tween twelve and one o'clock of a cruelly hot day. In the
dst of his speech he felt faint, and sat down. The House
journed, and a friend accompanied him to his room at the
emont House. He walked there, and began to pack his bag
home, after sending for a physician. When the doctor came,
pronounced it apoplexy, and proceeded to give him opium
morphine, a drug which had always been poison to him.
course it killed him. These facts have just been re-told me by
r. Austin Dickinson, so I am sure of their accuracy.

The poems, all of them, which I have seen in the *Transcript*,
e merely quotations from Volume I. I have seen no others.
ope we may have all those selected, for Volume II. I counted
em up yesterday, and find about 180. But all are fine.

> Cordially
> MABEL LOOMIS TODD

In my mother's next letter to Colonel Higginson it is worth
ting that she, not he, suggests a change in wording, one which
was quick to accept.

> Amherst
> 13 *July* 1891

AR MR. HIGGINSON:—

I send you this afternoon the MS second volume of E.D.'s
ems. I think it is really better than the first.
Will you send it to me again, or right to Mr. Niles?
Do just as you prefer. I suppose you will not wish to change
e line in the "White Heat"— only as she makes *blaze* and
ge as rhymes in the last stanza, I thought it might be good
t to have them in that relation twice. Few changes seem
cessary anywhere.
Within a few days I hope to send you a few words I want to
in a preface. If anything further to say occurs to you just
d it, and we could both sign it.

> Sincerely, ever,
> MABEL L. TODD

In one version of this poem ("Dare you see a soul at the white
at?" S.S., page 28), in Emily's writing, the second line of the

second stanza reads, "It quivers from the forge," instead of, " quivering substance plays," as it reads in all published editio This is the line to which my mother referred. Also, in manuscript copy, the final word in the second line of the th stanza reads "ring" instead of "din," as in all editions.

On July fourteenth Mrs. Todd wrote the first draft of preface for the new volume and sent it off to Colonel Higginso On the sixteenth she began to select poems for a third volu which, however, was not to appear for another five years. B "classifying and copying" all the remaining poems was a p requisite to any subsequent collection.

Dublin, N.
July 16, 18

Dear Mrs. Todd

MS. arrived with letter. There is a good deal of work to done on the pronunciation [MS plain]. I like your suggest prelude. A few of your suggested alterations I have evaded a little change in order of her own words. In the verses

> I know that he exists
> Somewhere in silence[3]

the present arrangement of verses seems to me better than you It is so late now I shall send it to Niles & let you see it next print. One poem I hv. transferred to Part 2 (end) as that is t empty. ("What if I say I shall not wait?") [S.S., page 107] & sh others, if I can.

Is not "The flower must not blame the bee"[4] a little t enigmatical?

I hv. sent my MS. to Atlantic, with request for duplic proofs to be sent you. Are you at home all summer?

Ever cordially
T.W.H

Do as you think best ab't preface.

[3] S.S., p. 83. The second stanza of this poem begins, " 'Tis an insta play," and not, " 'Tis in instant's play," as in the current edition of poems.
[4] The discarded poem was published in 1935.

[*Post Card*]

Dublin, N.H.
July 16, '91

In "The Sleeping Flowers," [" 'Whose are the little beds?' I asked," S.S., page 122] "Her busy foot she plied" is subst. for 'She rocked & gently smiled." Which is E.D.'s.

T.W.H.

The following letter answers all his questions:

Amherst, *July* 18, 1891

DEAR MR. HIGGINSON:—

If "The flower must not blame the bee" seems too enigmatical, let us leave it out—there is a sufficient number certainly, although Mr. Niles said he did not in the least object to a larger number than the first volume showed, since the public certainly wants them.

In "The Sleeping Flowers"

> She rocked and gently smiled
> Humming the quaintest lullaby
> That ever soothed a child,

is the way it appeared in the June *St. Nicholas*, put so in order to have the rhyme perfect, in a child's magazine. It reads in the original, E.D.'s handwriting, thus—

> Her busy foot she plied,
> Humming the quaintest lullaby,
> That ever *rocked* a child.

What do you think about the cover design for this volume? I am painting one of witch-hazel, which is not yet in just the shape I want it; but several of Emily's friends have said they *did* hope the same indian-pipes would be used again. "So singularly appropriate," "So characteristic," etc. Do you think indian-pipes and Emily Dickinson should be, as it were, synonymous permanently?

Thank you for asking that a proof of your article be sent me. I shall be here most of the summer, probably away for a few days in early September—but too much on hand for a real vacation this year.

Cordially
MABEL L. TODD

Colonel Higginson wrote to Mrs. Todd on the same day:

> Glimpsewood
> Dublin, N.H
> *July* 18, 189

DEAR FRIEND

1. Where is that lovely poem, "She laid her docile crescent down"? [T.S., page 157] Did you not mean to have it? I never knew just what the docile crescent meant, but the rest of it is exquisite.

2. I have combined the two "Juggler of Day" poems [versions] using the otter's window of course (oriel!!) & making the juggler a woman, as is proper. [S.S., page 166][5]

---

[5] One version of this poem, "Blazing in gold and quenching in purple," called "The Juggler of Day" by Colonel Higginson, was furnished by the Reverend Perez D. Cowan whose letter follows:

> 1 Ashburton Place
> Boston, Mass.
> *June* 9, 1891

Mrs. Mabel Loomis Todd
DEAR MADAM:

Your name has been given me by Roberts Brothers as the Editress of Miss Emily Dickinson's poems. Miss D. was a highly valued cousin of mine. During my college course at Amherst [1862–1866] one of her poems on the Sunset was given me, which I have greatly enjoyed, and which I was sorry not to find in the first volume of her poems. Thinking that possibly it may not have been brought to your attention, I refer to it, with the hope that it may appear in the volume soon to be published.

As my books are at present all packed, it is impossible for me to send an exact copy. But, I should think that Mrs. Austin Dickinson who gave me my copy, could furnish another. If the second volume should not appear before Fall, I might be able to get access to my copy in time. As nearly as memory can supply the lines, I give them below but think several lines may be lacking.

> Blazing in gold, and quenching in purple,
> Leaping like leopards in the sky,
> At the feet of the old horizon
> Laying her spotted face to die,
>
> Bending low at the oriel window
> Flooding the steeple, and tinting the barn,
> Kissing her bonnet to the meadow—
> And the Juggler of Day is gone.

> Very respectfully yours,
> P. D. COWAN

Address, Falmouth Heights, Mass.

3. I think we had better leave the 2ᵈ blue-bird, "After all birds," etc., for a future volume. It is rather ponderous. But the 2ᵈ oriole is quite distinct & we might keep that. ["To hear an oriole sing," and "One of the ones that Midas touched," S.S., pages 125 and 126]

4. I hv. put titles to many of the Nature poems, wh. you can *dele* [My mother remarked at this point, "I think so!"], if you prefer. I hv. put "Mother Nature" first ["Nature, the gentlest mother," S.S., page 111], then the Dawn poems & so through the day—then spring to autumn, mingling in birds, etc., closing with "Summer's Parting" ("As imperceptibly") [S.S., page 168, title deleted in volume], "Summer's Obsequies" ("The gentian weaves") [S.S., page 170] — delicious — & closing with "The snow" ["It sifts from leaden sieves," S.S., page 174]. This is the only part I have yet all ready.

5. I demur about "The flower must not blame the bee," for though the first verse is exquisite, yet the footman from Vevay is so perplexing. She has associated bees & Vevay elsewhere, but here a bee is not a *foot* man & it is the bee who is repelled. What do you make of it.

6. In "The night was wide" [S.S., page 98], the dog's feet were like intermittent *plash* surely, not *plush* as you have it.

7. In "He put the buckle round my life" [S.S., page 105], is it "a member of the cloud," & what does it mean? "A member of the breed" would be intelligible & rhyme. (I wish we had more love poems—only 16 including "What if I say I shall not wait," which I have put at the end of this division.)

So far, so good. More anon.
T.W.H.

The diary frequently refers to being "at work with Vinnie."[6] All the poems were read aloud to her in the hope of enlightning comments.

Emily's alternative line, "Stooping as low as the otter's window," preferred by Colonel Higginson, was used in the second volume. In the current edition of the poems the line reads "kitchen window."

A week or two later, on August eighth, the Reverend Mr. Cowan came to Amherst. He called upon Mrs. Todd to talk about "poems and Emily." She says of him, "He has a lovely, pure face, and a white soul, I know."

July 18 About eight I . . . [looked] finally over the manuscripts of the poems, to see if I have omitted to copy any. Found about a dozen—in as many of the little volumes.

[*Post card to Mrs. Todd*]

Dublin, N.H.
July 21, '91

My paper on E.D.'s letters has gone to printer for Atlantic Oct. no., (appearing September 25). Proof will be sent you & returned by you to me with yr. suggestions, but it must be done very promptly, as you can understand.

T.W.H.

P.S. I assume that you & Miss Lavinia will be at Amherst for some weeks.

To Mrs. Todd, Colonel Higginson wrote again the next day, enclosing a sheet labeled "Notes" and the following letter from Miss Fanny Norcross, with whom on July fourth he had had "tea at Miss Peabody's."

Concord, Mass.
July 19, '91

Dear Mr. Higginson,

I am impelled to send to you my cousin's poem on the Mushroom ["The mushroom is the elf of plants," S.S., page 144] and also this gem about a Spider ["A spider sewed at night," S.S. page 147].

I remember that you said you had not seen the first, and as I was reading it to a friend yesterday, I was so much impressed with its weirdness and originality, that I felt that you ought to see it at once.

The other is certainly one of the daintiest she ever wrote.

Yours respectfully
Frances L. Norcross

Dublin, N.H.
July 22, 189

Dear friend

I send a real *trouvaille* & assume yr. consent to putting in both poems. Please return. But what can "fleeter than a tare" mean? Tear?

July 19 At work on the poems & at Vinnie's trying to complete my survey of all the volumes. Finished only about half—there is *such* a quantity!

July 21 I went to Miss Buffum's with Vinnie to draw a picture of a "low-boy." . . . Worked on poems in the evening.

Perhaps you already had them. You say nothing of the "docile crescent" omitted. Please answer all my points. Nothing now remains but to number sheets of copy.

T.W.H.

[*Enclosure*]

Notes[7]

(1) In "Just lost when I was saved" I prefer "Slow tramp the centuries" to yr. rearrangement. [S.S., page 86]

(2) So in "I know that he exists" I prefer the shorter lines & have kept them. [S.S., page 83]

(3) I hv. put "Of all the souls that stand create" at the head of "Love" it is so noble; & called the poem "Choice." [S.S., page 89]

(4) I like "No life can pompless pass away" better than yr. rearrangement. [S.S., page 200]

(5) It might be well for you to suggest in your preface that we never can tell to what rigorous revision these poems might have been subjected, had the author printed them herself. They are to be regarded in many cases as the mere unfinished sketches or first studies of an artist, preserved for their intrinsic value, but not presented as being in final form.

Points (1), (2), and (3) were settled in accordance with his suggestions. Under (4), however, the first line of the poem still reads in all editions, "Pompless no life can pass away," as Emily wrote it. (See Mrs. Todd's letter of July twenty-fourth.)

A reply to his previous letter was already in the mail:

Amherst
22 *July*, 1891

DEAR MR. HIGGINSON:—

I send "She laid her docile crescent down." I do not understand it, and although it is beautiful, I omitted it because there were already so many more for Vol. II than had appeared in Vol.

[7] For over half a century this page of "Notes" had been filed with a subsequent letter from Colonel Higginson and, out of context, had been the cause of much perplexity. I am indebted to Esther Nichols Clarke for discovering its proper place. For this, and for her intelligent and devoted assistance in the preparation of the manuscript of this book, I wish to record my grateful appreciation.

I. If you care to include it, I shall approve. You would be almost incredulous if I should tell you that there are over 500 more already copied, in addition to the two volumes, and in addition to a box of "scraps" in pencil, some of which are gems. Yet such is the case. One volume more? Yes, half a dozen.

I am classifying them all now, and I have made an alphabetical index of first lines.

In "The night was wide," the "dog's belated feet" *were* "like intermittent *plush*"—she wrote the word unmistakably, every letter distinct and separate.

I had put, in *Nature*, as perhaps you noticed, all the dawn and sunrise and spring poems at the beginning, then noon and summer, and sunset and autumn, & snow last. Probably your way is better—to have the *day* ones first, and the *seasons* after, as you describe.

The love poems are certainly growing less in numbers. I might find two or three more, perhaps, for this volume, but on the whole I think they will be needed more in a subsequent one—when we finally use "The flower must not blame the bee," with its rather confused metaphors!

The line in "He put the belt around my life" does read "A member of the cloud," in the original, and I suppose simply means to express the great loftiness conferred by the love given, which made her "fold up" her lifetime, "henceforth a dedicated sort."

I expect to be here through the summer—except possibly a day or two, or three, in September. I hope you received my letter in which I asked you your idea of cover-design. Please tell me, when you write next.

Your card has just come—I am *very* glad your article will come in the October *Atlantic*. I am impatient to see it.

Cordially
Mabel L. Todd

The enclosed poem, "She laid her docile crescent down," was called "Epitaph" by Emily ("The Monument," T.S., page 157). For the second line, "And this mechanic stone," there were two alternative readings, "And this subjunctive stone," or "And this confiding stone."

On July twenty-second, the diary says: "At work on preface

"About this time," my mother told me, "Lavinia received from Miss Norcross the following communication to which she asked me to reply."

MY DEAR VINNIE:

We are much pleased to have found two poems which must have been among the latest sent us. The oriole which we have missed so long and another humming bird. Also a little one written much earlier.

I send first lines on next page, and will send the wholes if you say so.

FANNY

Oriole

7 or 8	One of the ones that Midas touched
verses	Who failed to touch us all,
	Was that minute domingo
	The blissful oriole. [S.S., page 126]

* * *

2 verses	A route of evanescence
	With a revolving wheel
	A resonance of emerald
	A Rush of cochineal. [S.S., page 130]

* * *

(Signed) "Humming bird."

* * *

This is	*Speech* is a prank of *parliament*
all of this	*Tears*—the surf of the *nerve*—
	But the heart with the heaviest freight on
	Doesn't always move.

The last poem is a variant of one sent to Mr. Bowles in 1862.[10]

Colonel Higginson's diary records that the manuscript of the book, sent to him by Mrs. Todd on July thirteenth and finished by him on July twenty-second, was dispatched to Mr. Niles on July twenty-fifth.

[10] *Letters*, 1931, p. 200.

My mother's reply to Miss Norcross, also dated July twenty-fifth, asked for the complete text of the poems quoted in her letter to Lavinia. Miss Norcross wrote again as follows:

My DEAR MRS TODD,

I enclose the poems you mention at this my earliest opportunity.

The others that you do not recognize, I am quite sure I have sent you, but even if you haven't them, I believe it is no matter; they are fragments, and I am sure you would not use them.

I sent Mr. Higginson the "Mushroom," and he wishes "truffled hut" were "ruffled hut" perhaps your copy reads differently from mine. I should be glad to know.

In haste yours sincerely
FRANCES L. NORCROSS

Concord,
July 28, 1891

The words were printed "truffled hut."

After Mrs. Todd had finished the first draft of her preface to the second volume, on July twenty-fifth she sent it to Colonel Higginson with a letter.

Amherst
July 25, 1891

DEAR MR. HIGGINSON:—

I know there is too much of this Preface, but I have tried to answer, point by point, the things said of her by the critics. I have almost a complete collection of the newspaper & magazine notices of the first volume—certainly all the important ones. Most of them say she was an invalid, that she was cruelly disappointed in love, that she was irreverent,—that she never had left Amherst, that she was a recluse from childhood, and other nonsense. And then, some friends have wondered at variations in the printed poems from those she sent them—and I have been questioned about her handwriting and manuscripts; indeed there seems an endless curiosity, both printed and verbal, about her. And I thought it the proper opportunity to forestall further spreading of what is not true about her. Cut it wherever you choose. Mr. Dickinson likes it, and says if it is not too long he should like most of the points to remain. Vinnie approves.

The poem in fac-simile in the volume will be the *Renunciation*—of which I spoke to you. I told you then the reasons for it, and Mr. Niles, who was very glad to use it. I am hoping for a word from you today about the cover design.

Please, dear Mr. Higginson, criticize this little sketch freely, and write me *just* how it strikes you. My trust in your judgment, taste, and friendliness are boundless.

M.L.T.

Mr. Niles had already approved of reproducing the poem, "There came a day at summer's full," as a frontispiece to the coming volume. This was in spite of the fact that it had already appeared in the first volume, and in spite of the fact that, as he said, "it will be noted that changes have been made in the printed text."[11]

[11] The following incident, referred to on p. 59 concerns the poem, "There came a day at summer's full," entitled "Renunciation." It had been sent "without authorization" by Mrs. Austin Dickinson to *Scribner's Magazine* and was printed in the issue of August, 1890, p. 240. As it then appeared it differs from the version published in *Poems*, 1890, p. 58, in several unimportant, as well as in two essential, respects. First, it consists of six instead of seven stanzas, the fourth, which reads as follows, having been omitted:

> Each was to each the sealed church,
> Permitted to commune this time,
> Lest we too awkward show
> At supper of the Lamb.

Second, the change of a word in the second stanza altered the meaning. In Emily's manuscript it reads as follows and was so printed in *Poems*, 1890:

> The sun, as common, went abroad,
> The flowers, accustomed, blew,
> As if no soul that (the) solstice passed
> Which (that) maketh all things new.

In *Scribner's* the word "soul" was printed "sail." In *Poems*, Second Series, 1891, Emily's manuscript was reproduced in facsimile as the frontispiece *solely in order to dispel doubt on this one point.* Had it not been Sue who was guilty of misreading the word, the point might not have been made an issue.

In the edition of the poems now current, although the word "sail" has been reinstated, all seven stanzas have been used.

Boston
July 14, 1891

DEAR MRS TODD

I would suggest that the fac-simile poem be printed entire oc-
cupying 4 pages of the book, to be followed immediately by the
same poem in type.

You can allude to it in the preface by way of reference. It would
be quite unique and shew her peculiar method of writing.

It seems to me it would be better to have a distinct title to the
new volume and a different cover design, but that is a matter wh.
you & Mr Higginson can arrange I have no doubt.

Yours very truly
THO⁸ NILES

I do not think there will be too many poems. The public want
them, judging by the sale of the first

Mr. Niles also is gaining confidence. As to the "distinct title"
and "different cover design," however, he later changed his mind,
as his note of August 6, 1891, shows. What led him to do so may
appear in the following exchange of letters:

[*Post card to Mrs. Todd*]

Dublin, N.H.
July 23, 1891

I have written to ask Niles if we shld. seek a new *title* or rely
on "Part Second." If we have a title, how would "Indian Pipe
and Witch Hazel" do—they being the two *weird* flowers & hence
significant of her. It really needs both to characterize her. We
cd. then put yr. design (w.h.) on the new volume.

T.W.H.

[*Post card to Mrs. Todd*]

Dublin, N.H.
July 27, '91

I sent the MS. on Saturday not including the "docile crescent"
which we will keep. Mr. N. thinks well of "second series;" but
to test it I hv. asked him what he wd. think of "Indian Pipe &
Witch Hazel." I incline to the witch hazel for Vol. 2., lest the first
grow monotonous—but am not positive. Each flower has something in common with her.

T.W.H.

Of the latter flower Emily said, "Oh that beloved witch-hazel. . . . I never had seen it but once before, and it haunted me like childhood's Indian pipe, or ecstatic puff-balls, or that mysterious apple that sometimes comes on river pinks."[12]

Because of her own decided preference, my mother told me, her design of Indian pipes was again chosen for the cover of the second volume—to make it in a way the symbol of Emily.

[*Post card to Roberts Brothers*]

Dublin, N.H.
July 27, '91

I believe I suggested to you calling the 2^d vol. (if a new name is needed) "Indian Pipe & Witch Hazel"—but shld. personally prefer the simpler "2^d series" if you think as good for sale.

Please send duplicate proofs to Mrs. Todd & me as before— she will send hers corrected to me & I will send back but one.

Every one who has heard extracts from Vol. 2 thinks it *quite* equal to the other.

T.W.H.

Mrs. Todd's corrected preface had reached Colonel Higginson on Monday, July twenty-seventh. After giving that day and the next to revising it (according to his diary) he wrote to her as follows:

Dublin, N.H.
July 28, 1891

DEAR MRS. TODD

I like much of yr. preface,[13] but have used your generous permission to revise it, as I should a draft of my own.

The passage on p. 1 beginning, "The vague yet subtle sense" is not I think clearly enough stated as I fail to catch it definitely. Nor do I see what you mean (pp. 4-5) by saying that her earlier verses were more conventional, more punctuated, etc. Surely none are less so than those she sent me at the very beginning— "We play at paste" & "I'll tell you how the sun rose" (first letter,

---

[12] *Letters*, 1931, p. 257.
[13] This preface, together with those of the first and third volumes of poems, is reproduced in Appendix IV.

Apr. 1862). What you say of change in handwriting is wholly true, but I see no other.

In publishing this, I would suggest that your name be signed to it, as was mine to the other preface & that we equalize matters as we did then, but now by putting my name first on title-page. I do not insist at all on this, however.

Ever cordially
T. W. HIGGINSON

On July 25, 1891, Lavinia had received from Roberts Brothers a check for $179.51, acknowledged as follows:

Amherst
July 27th [1891]

MY DEAR MR NILES

Thank you for substantial appreciation of "Emilies poems," also for your clear explanation of the new "copyright act." [See his letter of March 11, 1891.]

I trust the sale of "the poems" continues satisfactory. I have seen several notices that the 8th edition was printing. I hardly believed it true but hope it is so.

I chanced upon a letter of Helen Jackson's to Emily (just now) where she urges her "to give her verses the light" & begs the liberty (if she outlives Emily) of acting as her "literary legatee & executor."[14] It may seem appropriate to add this letter to some future volume. Thanking you again for your courtesy

Believe me
Gratefully
LAVINIA DICKINSON

Later in the year, having discovered the whereabouts of the widower of "H.H.," Mr. William S. Jackson, my mother wrote to inquire whether the other side of this correspondence, Emily's letters to his wife, could be found. Here is his reply:

---

[14] On Mar. 3, 1891, an entry in my mother's diary reads: "[Vinnie] has found a lot of letters from Col. Higginson and Helen Hunt [Jackson] to Emily—thank Heaven!" But beside the entry I jotted down a comment made by my mother as we went over the diary together: "Never gave them to me." She did not tell me why, nor what became of the letters, which might have filled an important gap in this story, nor how they happened to have escaped Lavinia's first frenzy of destruction immediately following Emily's death. They seem to have been lost again as soon as found.

El Paso County Bank

W. S. Jackson, Cashier   Colorado Springs, Colo. *Oct.* 13, 1891

Mrs. David P. Todd
Care of Prof. Todd, Amherst, Mass.

DEAR MADAM:

Replying to your letter of long ago I am sorry to have to write you that so far I have been unable to find the letters of the late Emily Dickinson written to Mrs. Jackson. I have not yet given up finding them for I am quite sure they were all preserved by Mrs. Jackson. Possibly she may have sent them to Mr. Wentworth Higginson who was in correspondence with her about Emily Dickinson's writings. If by good fortune I find them I will write you.

Sincerely yours,
Wᵐ S. JACKSON

On rereading your letter I see Col. Higginson was associated with you in bringing out the volume of poems which makes it clear he does not have the letters referred to.

Not accepting this letter as final, however, Mrs. Todd made another attempt two years later to discover the much desired letters. (See page 227 *et seq.*)

[*Post card to Mrs. Todd*]

Dublin, N.H.
July 29, '91

I wish you wd. send me that passage in wh. H.H. expressed the wish to be E.D.'s literary executor & that you wd. consider the expediency of prefixing it as a sort of motto for the new vol. I shld. like to link their names. Niles writes that they will begin to print at once; he thinks that "I.P. & W.H." [Indian Pipe and Witch Hazel] wd. make a good title but is not sure that "2ᵈ series" is not the best we can adopt. So we will regard that as settled. Miss Norcross says that "fleeter than a tare" is unquestionable.

T.W.H.

After receiving from Colonel Higginson the proof of his *Atlantic* article on August first, Mrs. Todd "went over it with

Mr. Dickinson, returning it the next day with a letter suggesting one or two corrections of fact and some other changes." His reply follows:

D[ublin].
Aug 4 '91

DEAR FRIEND

Your proof just received but no note, wh. troubles me. *I thought you were to show the proof to Mr. and Miss D.* How can I print the passages about "Eclipse they call their Father" & "pure and terrible" without their permission. If a letter from you is on its way, telling me this, all right; if not, please telegraph me on receipt of this whether I can safely publish or not.

In haste
T.W.H.[15]

P.S. Thanks for yr. criticisms—all to be adopted except that about the mocking sky & steadfast honey ["The nearest dream recedes, unrealized," S.S., page 24]. In my copy it is very distinct as a second verse or detached moral. It wd. belittle it to attach it to the boy only.

The same day Mr. Higginson wrote again, "I hv. sent H.H.'s letter to Niles for a prelude. I think it goes best with the *poems.*" In accordance with his suggestion, the letter from Mrs. Jackson was embodied in the preface to the second volume.

Mr. Niles's next letter is a reply to one from Mrs. Todd which is missing:

Boston
Aug 6, 1891

DEAR MRS TODD

I do not quite agree with your friend. It is my feeling that the same cover designs should be used, with the simple addition of the words Second Series.

Then both books can be sold in uniform binding & it will suit buyers much better.

[15] My mother's letter of August second, which is missing, had evidently conveyed the desired permission from Austin and Lavinia Dickinson. Presumably the letter also mentioned Mr. Dickinson's reluctance to publish Emily's letters. (See p. 167.)

The Saturday Review man evidently did not get enthusiastic about the poems.[16]

Yours truly
THO⁵ NILES

While discussion of the preface to the new volume and of Colonel Higginson's *Atlantic* article was in progress, Mrs. Todd had been occupied with another time-consuming task—that of indexing all of Emily's original manuscripts, which she said "seemed endless." This alphabetical list of first lines, in a leather-covered notebook, contains 926 poems copied by my mother, not including those already published in the first and second volumes. It is given in full in Appendix V.[17]

On August thirteenth the preface was again dispatched to Colonel Higginson with a letter:

Amherst
August 13, 1891

DEAR MR. HIGGINSON:—

This is the Preface pruned and revised. I wish I could get it shorter yet, but I want to say every one of these things—so how can I? . . .

I see the *Poems* are just published in London by Osgood. Why doesn't the proof of the second volume come? I want to go away for a short time before the term opens, September 17, but I want to be here when the proofs come to compare them all with the originals.

[16] The note in *The Saturday Review* (London), July 18, 1891, to which Mr. Niles alludes said among other things that "*Poems*, by Emily Dickinson, (Boston, Mass.: Roberts), form a collection of verse more noteworthy for quaintness of phrase and odd unexpectedness of conceits than for the Blake-like quality which Mr. Higginson, a friendly editor, discovers. For example:—'Belshazzar had a letter.' . . ."

[17] Aug. 8 Very hot. Indexing most of the day. There will be about a thousand poems indexed in this little book, not counting those in the two Roberts volumes,—neither the scraps.

Aug. 10 Provisional index done. Contains just short of a thousand first lines. Afternoon spent on my Preface. I want to say certain things, & I want to make it short as well—a hard combination in this case, it seems.

Aug. 12 Hotter still. I must finish my Preface this morning. Did, . . . & took the Preface over to Vinnie's to read to Mr. Dickinson.

I am afraid I have discovered a rather serious error in Volume I—that the "Psalm of Day" ["A something in a summer's day," page 82], as printed, is two separate poems put together. I see exactly how it happened, and it is a curious thing. It began by Mr. Bates marking the ones he wished omitted, & then passed to you & to me—but the responsibility is of course mine, because I had the original manuscripts. The line, "Like flowers that heard the tale of dews" begins another poem, while the last stanza of the first poem, in a different metre from the rest, is left out entirely. When you come I will show you the originals, and see what you think about correcting it in some other edition.[18]

Cordially
MABEL L. TODD

Please return the Preface to me, and tell me if it is better. I think it a good idea for your name to come first on the title-page, and for me to sign the Preface as you say.

On August fourteenth Colonel Higginson received the first proof of the Second Series and sent it on to Mrs. Todd the same day. This is the final entry in his diary with regard to the poetry of Emily Dickinson. The day following he wrote to Mr. Niles:

Dublin, N.H.
Aug 15, 189

DEAR MR. NILES

I have just sent back to Mrs. Todd the final copy (revised) of her preface to the new volume of E.D.'s poems. She will sign & my name will now be put *first* on title page—thus reversing the method adopted in vol. 1.

I wish the first edition could be on as nice paper as with vol. 1. The distinction & delicacy of that made the poems appear choicer.

Yrs. ever
T. W. HIGGINSON

[18] This correction has never been made and the poem still stands originally printed. The omitted stanza reads:

> So looking on the night, the morn
> Conclude the wonder gay,
> And I meet coming through the dews
> Another summer's day.

Returning her preface on the same day, he sent with it the following note:

Dublin, N.H.
Aug. 15, 1891

I like this now very much, and my few suggestions are mainly literary, to be rejected if you think best.

T.W.H.

My mother's diary for August fifteenth records that she and my father worked over the proofs together all day, comparing each poem with the original as was their custom. The omitted portions of the following letters have to do with anxieties about delay of the proofs.

Dublin, N.H.
Aug 18, 1891

DEAR FRIEND

. . . . The most serious mistake is in printing the last verse of "God gave a loaf" [S.S., page 50] as a separate poem—this through my fault, I fear—but I have corrected it.

Also, I had altered "Like intermittent plush" to "In intermittent plash," thinking it must be plash—but as you say it is not, I have altered it back to your reading. [From "The night was wide, and furnished scant," S.S., page 98]. . . .

Ever yrs.
T.W.H.

Amherst, *August* 20, '91

DEAR MR. HIGGINSON:—

. . . . There were two serious errors besides the one you mention. The two last stanzas of "Called Back" (beginning "Next time to stay") were printed as a separate poem [from "Just lost when I was saved!" S.S., page 85]—and "The soul [unto itself] is an imperial friend," two stanzas [S.S., page 37], was made to be part of "Experiment to me" [S.S., page 51], another little poem of two stanzas. There were other minor errors, but these were the worst. [Both these mistakes were corrected before the book appeared.]

How does the division *Life* strike you in print? They are strong, but I think the two last divisions will be even better. As com-

pared with Volume I, I have not yet been able to decide which
is better.

I hope we may soon get the last half of proof.

Ever cordially
M.L.T.[19]

[19] "Earlier in the year," my mother said, "I had sent to *The Youth's
Companion* six unpublished poems from which to choose: 'Simplicity,'
'Hope,' 'Saturday,' 'Vanished,' 'The Storm,' and 'Old-fashioned.' In accepting
the poems the editors wrote, 'We hope we do not underestimate their worth
to you or to *The Youth's Companion* in enclosing its cheque for fifty dollars
($50.00) in payment for them and your sketch of Miss Dickinson's life.'
The poems had not yet appeared in the magazine when I found that all
but one, 'Saturday,' had been included in the forthcoming volume [S.S.].
I wrote at once to Mr. Niles" whose reply follows:

Boston
Augt 19, 1891

DEAR MRS TODD

I do not see any other way than to ask "The Youth's Companion" to
accept other poems in lieu of any wh. may be published in the volume
before their appearance in The Y.C. or to refund the amt. paid for such
poems.

I should make no allusion to the fact that a very few of the poems
have been printed elsewhere—so few it certainly is not necessary.

And I really do not think the index of first lines is necessary.
It would be in great measure a repetition of the Contents.

Yrs very truly
THO^s NILES

My mother told me that she never was resigned to Mr. Niles's decision
to omit an index of first lines. The lack of it was an unnecessary incon-
venience she could not countenance.

On her next visit to Boston, Sept. 30, 1891, Mrs. Todd took some more
poems to the editor of *The Youth's Companion*, Edward Stanwood. He
selected seven, including "Saturday" and "Vanished" from those originally
sent. Five of the seven were printed on the dates indicated below with titles
supplied by himself. The other two, "My Little King," ("I met a king this
afternoon"), and "Heart's Ease" ("I'm the little heart's ease"), appeared in
the issue of May 18, 1893.

The three poems here reproduced have not been included in subsequent
volumes.

A Nameless Rose [Dec. 24, 1891]

Nobody knows this little rose,
It might a pilgrim be
Did I not take it from the ways
And lift it up to thee.

Only a bee will miss it,
Only a butterfly,

Recurrent differences of opinion which seemed irreconcilable—those relating to titles and textual changes in particular—only the warm friendliness between the editors could resolve. With all the tact that she could summon Mrs. Todd tried to tell Mr. Higginson that many of his titles were "wooden."

Hastening from far journey
On its breast to lie.

Only a bird will wonder,
Only a breeze will sigh—
Ah, little rose, how easy
For such as thee to die!

"Vanished" [Aug. 25, 1892. Previously published in S.S., p. 216. First line, "She died,— this was the way she died"]

Autumn [Sept. 8, 1892]

The name of it is autumn,
The hue of it is blood,
An artery upon the hill,
A vein along the road,

Great globules in the alleys,
And oh, the shower of stain
When winds upset the basin
And spill the scarlet rain!

It sprinkles bonnets far below,
It gathers ruddy pools,
Then eddies like a rose away
And leaves me with the hills.

"Saturday" [Sept. 22, 1892. T.S., p. 34. First line, "From all the jails the boys and girls"]

In September [Sept. 29, 1892]

September's Baccalaureate
A combination is
Of crickets, crows, and retrospects,
And a dissembling breeze

That hints without assuming
An innuendo sere
That makes the heart put up its fun
And turn philosopher.

As to the sketch of Emily's life: three years later my mother wrote to the publishers about it. Mr. Stanwood replied on Oct. 24, 1894, that he did not know what could have become of it as they no longer had it in their possession. I cannot find that it was ever printed.

Amherst
23 *August* '91

DEAR FRIEND:—

I send you with this the second batch of proof. In the first, which I returned at once to the printer, I took the liberty of changing your title "A Prayer of the Lowly" to simply "A Prayer" [compare page 57], as those most interested seemed to think it represented that most unusual poem better. ["I meant to have but modest needs," S.S., page 34]

I have, in this set, left your title "Out of the Morning," although in the May *St. Nicholas* it was called "Morning," simply. ["Will there really be a morning?" S.S., page 113]

Do you not think that, after all, "One of the *ones* that Midas touched" [S.S., page 126], as she wrote it, is too characteristic of her to change? So many of her friends are familiar with that first line in its original form, that unless you care particularly to change it, I should suggest leaving it. However, if you think differently, I shall acquiesce. All of these, also, I have compared with the original MSS.

Cordially
MABEL L. TODD

As we read this letter my mother exclaimed, "Oh, yes indeed! We were wonderfully polite to each other all the way through!"

The preceding letter was followed the next day by another:

Monday, 7 P.M.
August 24

DEAR MR. HIGGINSON:—

I sent you the proof this morning; since then, in looking over a fresh box of Emily's "scraps" I have come upon this copy of "One of the ones."[20]

[20] In one version the first stanza reads,

> One of the ones that Midas touched,
> Who failed to touch us all,
> Was that confiding prodigal,
> The *reeling* oriole.

And the final stanza,

> But if there were a Jason,
> Tradition *bear with* me,
> Behold his lost *aggrandizement*
> Upon the apple tree.

I never saw it before in Emily's handwriting, as the version in our volume is taken from a copy Miss Norcross sent me. [See page 147.]

What do you think of the two in comparison? You will notice the word *attar* instead of *altar* as she [Miss Norcross] gave it.

Please return this when you have finished with it.

Cordially
M.L.T.

Mr. Higginson replied:

Dublin
Aug 26, '91

DEAR FRIEND

I find no changes of yours on anything but the *Oriole* & the two versions are indeed perplexing. With some misgiving I have substituted

> *attar* for *altar* (MS. plain)
> *lost* [emolument] for *last*
> *confiding prodigal* for *minute Domingo*

I have left *blissful* instead of *reeling* for his flight is surely very direct & swift. And we will have *one* of the *ones* as you say—perhaps it is more characteristic.

Ever yrs.
T. W. HIGGINSON

In so far as she understood them, Miss Vinnie was of course interested in editorial perplexities, but the welfare of the cats was a more immediate concern. On August twenty-second, in the midst of a day of confusing work, the diary says, "Vinnie sent for us to see a sick kitten." To meet such a summons my parents would drop whatever they were doing and go at once.

During the last few days of August and until September second—when she left for western New York to visit her cousin, Mrs. Lydia Avery Coonley—Mrs. Todd was busy with the box of "scraps" already alluded to. She says, August 25, 1891, "Very hot in the morning. I worked over the arranging & classifying of more scraps, finding interesting and unexpected duplicates, as well as fine new poems."

The two following letters were written during her absence:

Wyoming, New York
8 *September*, 1891

DEAR MR. HIGGINSON:–

This proof arrived this morning—I corrected it at once by the originals, which I brought. I took out your title "Tints," because the verses seemed to me more distinctively on "Yellow," and if I mistake not, she so calls them somewhere in the scraps. ["Nature rarer uses yellow," S.S., page 152]

The other changes are mainly merely for putting the two-page poems on two opposite pages instead of turning the leaf.

I am in a lovely place, and having a fine rest—but we shall be back in Amherst by Saturday the nineteenth.

Cordially
MABEL L. TODD

Wyoming, N.Y.
10 *September*, 1891

DEAR MR. HIGGINSON:–

More proof today. I have changed the order of some of the last "Nature" poems, so that the two on the departure of summer may not come after "November," but before, bringing "November" ["Besides the autumn poets sing," S.S., page 173] just before "Snow" ["It sifts from leaden sieves," S.S., page 174]. I have taken out a good many titles, because, except in a few instances, I know Miss Lavinia and her brother would prefer none, especially when they might seem a trifle artificial. They have both said to me at different times they saw no necessity for any. So unless you are particularly desirous of retaining them, perhaps we had better omit most. All of these I have compared with Emily's MSS., except "The Rat" ["The rat is the concisest tenant," S.S., page 156], which I have not. Your changes in "The Cricket," "The Battlefield," etc., I like very much. ["Farther in summer than the birds," S.S., page 167, and "They dropped like flakes," S.S., page 190]

How long do you stay at Dublin?

As ever
MABEL L. TODD

Colonel Higginson replied:

Dublin, N.H.
Sept. 11, 1891

DEAR FRIEND

. . . . I hv. withdrawn "Tints" & with *great* unwillingness substituted "germ" (of alibi) ["The mushroom is the elf of plants," S.S., page 144] for "joy" wh. I like far better, & which is in E.D.'s cousin's copy, plainly written. So you see I am docile.

Do come back, for saving of delay! I hv. given up my addresses at Amherst & So. Hadley, for health' sake.

Ever cordially
T. W. HIGGINSON

[*Post card*]

Dublin, N.H.
Sept. 13, 1891

Yr. proof (154-91) with note dated Sept. 10 arrived last night & will be forwarded by me today. My orders to them are, if yr. & my corrections conflict, to follow yours. Of course you must judge about the titles, but I think in some cases (as "I have not told my garden yet" [S.S., page 189] or "She sweeps with many-colored brooms" [S.S., page 162]) the poems will fail to be understood for want of them. But the wishes of kindred must be respected.

T.W.H.

I have read and sent back the *final* proof.

The second stanza of "I have not told my garden yet" reads as originally written

> I will not name it in the street,
> For shops would stare at me—
> That one so shy, so ignorant,
> Should have the face to die.

Both poems appear without titles in the Second Series, the title "Sunset," which Colonel Higginson gave to "She sweeps with many-colored brooms," having been used on the previous page for a more "enigmatical" poem beginning, "Where ships of purple gently toss."

On September 14, 1891, my mother "spent the afternoon on the final proof of the *Poems*—up to Finis—David helping me." Only the preface and table of contents remained in addition to plate proofs of the entire volume in which further corrections were found necessary. My parents had returned to Amherst when the following letters were received.

Boston
Oct 5, 1891

DEAR MRS TODD

The printers had Emily Dickinson 2^d S[eries] on the press. I have ordered them to lift it & to wait for your corrections.

We ought to be out with the book now & this will delay, I don't know how long, because the printers are very busy & may not get to press again very promptly.

Yours very truly
THO^s NILES

[*Post card*]   Dublin, N.H.
Oct 4, '91

Your preface looks capitally in print, & I hv. only called attention to two obvious typographical errors.

How does Amherst approve the Atlantic article containing letters?

T. W. HIGGINSON

Colonel Higginson's article, "Emily Dickinson's Letters," had appeared in the October number of *The Atlantic Monthly*. It is fortunate that Mrs. Todd's first letter to him about this much-talked-of paper should have been preserved.

Amherst
6 *October*, 1891

DEAR MR. HIGGINSON:—

. . . . I wanted, first, to congratulate you on the *Atlantic* article, not only on its reading even more entertainingly than in the proof, if possible, but on its great notoriety and popularity, everywhere.

I find no one who has not read it—and everyone admires it. It was a very delicate thing to write, and done in the most admirable taste.

Mr. Dickinson says of it just what he said when he saw the proof—as I wrote you at the time. Miss Lavinia is more than delighted with it, and has before this, I doubt not, written you to that effect. She intended to write on Sunday. * * *

Your card has just been brought to me. I am glad the Preface looks well to you. I have had to take out some of it, to make room for the H.H. letter—they had not allowed pages enough before the plates of the poems themselves. I think, however, it is better now—and I hope you will. We are to have "Renunciation" in fac-simile. [See footnote 11, page 149.]

I found a "Dawn" ["When night is almost done," *Poems,* 1890, page 31], in the first volume, so I had to strike the title "Dawn" out of this one—and we had two "Triumphs" in this volume—so to save cutting out the plate, I called one "Triumphant" ["Who never lost, are unprepared," S.S., page 29; "Triumph may be of several kinds," S.S., page 199]—the one about the "promoted soldier." I believe there are *no* errors now, and I hope the book can proceed to see the light soon.

I was very sorry you could not come to Amherst. I should greatly like to see you.

> Cordially
> MABEL L. TODD

After hearing the *Atlantic* article, Lavinia wrote as follows:

> *October* 7th [1891]

MY DEAR MR HIGGINSON

Thank you for giving Emilies wonderful letters to the world. I hope you are well & will sometime let me talk with you about our mutual enterprise. I believe the 2nd volume will be welcomed most eagerly. I'm sure *you* are glad I *insisted* the poems *should* be published. Aren't you?

> Gratefully
> LAVINIA DICKINSON

A long soliloquy prompted by the article appeared in *The Springfield Republican* on Sunday, September 27, 1891. My mother read it aloud to Miss Vinnie the same day. Although the author thought that "Emily Dickinson was afflicted with almost an aphasia, for no one can well deny that her words are often

hard to wrench into appositeness with her very clear thought,"
he nevertheless conceded that "altogether, this was a strange and
wonderful spirit, and her verses are a priceless legacy to a world
too full of excellent formalists."

The *Atlantic* article was commented on in *The Review of Reviews* and *The Bookbuyer* for November and in other periodicals.
Its appearance was well timed to arouse interest in the forthcoming Second Series of *Poems*. But even more it aroused interest in
the possibility of a volume of Emily's letters. A search for them
was already under way before the Second Series of *Poems* was
issued. Those she had written to Samuel Bowles had been in Mrs.
Todd's possession for several months. (See page 84.) On October
fifteenth she writes that she "spent over an hour on Emily's
lately found letters to Mrs. Holland." The uncertainty in Mrs.
Todd's mind as to the advisability of publishing the letters, however, is reflected in her journal. On October eighteenth, during
the lull preceding the publication of the second volume of poems,
she wrote:

The new volume of poems will be out in a week or so, I suppose, so that is off my mind for a time. Col. Higginson's article
with Emily's Letters in the October *Atlantic* has attracted very
wide attention. Everyone read it with interest, nearly all with
admiration, not only for the unusual quality of the letters themselves, but for the graceful way in which Mr. Higginson connected and explained them. But there is now and then a person
who thinks it was a species of sacrilege to print them. President
Seelye [of Amherst College] said to me that to publish the letters
of that "innocent and confiding child" seemed to him horrible—
that he remembered Helen Hunt Jackson once saying to him, that
Emily used to express her intense surprise that "H. H." could
consent to publish. "How can you," she would say, "Print a piece
of your soul!" This goes well with Emily's poem—

> Publication is the auction
> Of the mind of man.

Yet my own opinion is that she thought sometime her own verses
might see the light of print, only by other hands than hers. As to
the letters, that is different. Those to Mr. Higginson are not of a
private nature, and as to the "innocent and confiding" nature

of them, Austin smiles. He says Emily definitely posed in those letters, he knows her thoroughly, through and through, as no one else ever did. He tells me many things quite unsuspected by others. He did tell me when we had the proof of Mr. Higginson's article here, in the summer, that publishing those letters would be against his taste, because he thought they put Emily in a false position, but that he did not feel strongly enough about it to ask him not to print them. All of which I wrote, as he asked me, to Mr. Higginson.

Although it may have been true that Austin Dickinson knew his sister "thoroughly," I am bold enough to question whether he did entirely understand her correspondence with Colonel Higginson. May she not have made light of it in order to conceal from her brother how much it meant to her? She had always yearned to know how her poetry impressed a well-qualified judge. So, after reading an article by Mr. Higginson in *The Atlantic Monthly* in which he gave counsel to a "young contributor," she had sent him some poems.[21] (She was thirty-one at the time.) The thing Emily Dickinson despised most was pretense. And she seemed to fear dishonesty. Later she wrote to him: "Will you tell me my fault, frankly, as to yourself, for I had rather wince than die. Men do not call the surgeon to commend the bone, but to set it, sir, and fracture within is more critical." And again: "I marked a line in one verse, because I met it after I made it, and never consciously touch a paint mixed by another person."[22] If she had wanted to indulge in pleasantries, or to assume a facetious pose, does it seem likely that she would have chosen to do so before Colonel Higginson, the literary stranger to whom she had turned for advice about her "mind" because she had "experienced honor" for him? So far from being a pose, her correspondence with him seems to me poignant in its eagerness for understanding, while at the same time hesitant, almost fearful, in the search for it.

In his *Atlantic* article Mr. Higginson himself interpreted their relationship as "on my side an interest that was strong and even affectionate, but not based on any thorough comprehension; and on her side a hope, always rather baffled, that I should afford

[21] Compare p. 70 and *Letters*, 1931, p. 272.
[22] *Letters*, 1931, pp. 276, 278.

some aid in solving her abstruse problem of life." Though he became her "safest friend," Mr. Higginson's affectionate interest was tempered with caution, not to say bewilderment. And he was silenced by her austere integrity—so high, so solitary.

> I like a look of agony,
> Because I know it's true;
> Men do not sham convulsion,
> Nor simulate a throe.

There is her love of truth in mighty caricature, the product of torment long endured. Truth was the mainspring of her life, her ultimate support.

> The truth is stirless. Other force
> May be presumed to move.
> This then is best for confidence—
> When oldest cedars swerve
>
> And giant oaks unclinch their fists
> And mountains, feeble, lean,
> How excellent a body
> That stands without a bone!
>
> How vigorous a force
> That holds without a prop!
> Truth stays herself, and every man
> That trusts her, boldly up.

With the fate of her poetry at stake, it hardly seems likely that Emily Dickinson would have attitudinized in front of Colonel Higginson.

On October eighteenth Mrs. Todd received from Colonel Higginson a letter which they agreed was the most penetrating analysis of Emily Dickinson's character that either of them had seen. Although parts of it were quoted in the Introduction to the new edition of the *Letters*, 1931, it deserves to be reprinted in full, together with Colonel Higginson's letter in which it was enclosed.

> Dublin, N.H.
> *Oct* 16 '91

DEAR FRIEND

This is the most remarkable criticism yet made on E.D. Its author is Sam. G. Ward, *not* "Sam Ward" Mrs. Howe's brother but a far superior man—an early transcendentalist & writer in *Dial*, but for many years a N.Y. banker & agent of Barings—a rich man with a wife (Anna Barker of New Orleans) one of the most charming of American women—his daughters Catholics & married in Europe.

Send it when read to my sister in enclosed envelope. She agrees with Mr. Dickinson as to printing the letters. I had a very cordial letter from Miss Lavinia. Show the enclosed to Mr. D if you think best.

> Ever cordially
> T. W. HIGGINSON

> *Leaving* Narragansett Pier
> *Oct*ʳ 11 '91

MY DEAR MR. HIGGINSON,

I am, with all the world, intensely interested in Emily Dickinson. No wonder six editions have been sold, every copy, I should think to a New Englander. She may become world famous, or she may never get out of New England. She is the quintessence of that element we all have who are of Puritan descent *pur sang*. We came to this country to think our own thoughts with nobody to hinder. Ascetics of course, & this our Thebaid. We conversed with our own souls till we lost the art of communicating with other people. The typical family grew up strangers to each other, as in this case. It was *awfully* high, but awfully lonesome. Such prodigies of shyness do not exist elsewhere. We get it from the English, but the English were not alone in a corner of the world for a hundred & fifty years with no outside interest. I sate next to Jones Very for three years & he was an absolute enigma till he flashed on me with the Barberry Bush. Afterwards he sought me at my office one day, with his heart in his hands & said he had come to lay the axe at my root, to bring me to the Spiritual Life. I was deeply touched to find that he had all the time thought me good enough for the axe! Did you know Ellen Hooper (born Sturgis) & do you know her poems? If the gift of articulateness was not denied, you had Channing, Emerson, Hawthorne a stupendous example, & so many others. Mostly it was denied, & became a family fate. This is where Emily Dickinson comes in. She was the articulate inarticulate. That is why it appeals so to New England women.

You were fortunate & skillful in drawing her out.

Believe me
Sincerely yours
SAM^l G. WARD

1608 K St., N. W.
Washington, D.C.

P.S. Was it one of your family or mine that came up from Salem one day & said to a "mutual" friend, "John is dead. He died yesterday. He didn't want much said about it."

CHAPTER X

The Second "Auction"

Fame of myself to justify!
All other plaudit be
Superfluous, an incense
Beyond necessity.

Fame of myself to lack, although
My name be else supreme,
This were an honor honorless,
A futile diadem.

THOUGH announced for November fourth, *Poems by Emily Dickinson*, Second Series, actually reached the market on November, 9, 1891. The white cover was similar to that of the first edition of the first volume, except that the gray back was replaced by a light-green spine.[1] The book was greedily welcomed. A few days after publication my father received the following letter:

Boston
Nov 13, 1891

Prof D P Todd
Amherst, Mass.
DEAR SIR

The book seems to go like "Hot Cakes" here also, for our whole edition with the exception of a few in white & gold have been taken up and we are still behind hand with orders. A new Edition has just gone into the binder's hands and we hope to get some by next Wednesday [18th], probably not before that date. We send the 5 in white to help along.

Very truly yours
Roberts Bros
E. D. HARDY

[1] See Appendix III.

As I read this letter aloud, my mother exclaimed, "They were the most surprised publishers you ever saw!"

On November nineteenth Mrs. Todd went to Boston to See Mr. Niles and Colonel Higginson. One purpose of the visit was to obtain a contract for the Second Series—a detail still awaiting attention. The following characteristic letter from Miss Vinnie was received while there. Her interest in old mahogany was gaining momentum as added resources enabled her to satisfy her ambition. She was beginning to realize hungrily the value of what she had in ignorance given away.

Thursday
[*November* 19, 1891]

DEAR MABEL

I did not see my *adviser* so must delay the velvet. Should you have the time please ask at the suitable store if *new* "low boys" are made & if nòt, is there any pretty article that would be as grand in the desired spot?

I hope you are well & all will be satisfactory in your journey

Love for Mr & Mrs Andrews. I think I may make her a little call some day with you.

Lovingly
LAVINIA

A week or so later the contract for the Second Series, having been approved by Mr. Dickinson, was returned by Miss Vinnie with a letter to Mr. Niles:

1ˢᵗ *December* [1891]

MY DEAR MR NILES

I enclose the *contract* as desired. I hope you are entirely satisfied with the change. I should not have thought of it but you were so kind to allow me a choice as at first, that I will try the *new* way, if entirely agreeable to you.

I appreciate all your courtesy & am grateful for your continued interest in my enterprise. I trust the 2ⁿᵈ edition of the 2ⁿ volume is fast disappearing.

Heartily
LAVINIA DICKINSON

The changes alluded to were not specified.
After receiving the January royalty check she wrote again:

February 1st [1892]

MY DEAR MR NILES

Thank you for such satisfactory result of "Emilies poems". I know you are in sympathy with me in the great success of this enterprise. Thank you for your interest & courtesy.

I hope the supply of *both* volumes will be constantly abundant, for the demand seems not to lessen, so far as I know.

Thanking you again I am

Gratefully
LAVINIA DICKINSON

The final mention of money matters in connection with the poems is contained in her next letter to Colonel Higginson:

February 4th [1892]

MY DEAR MR HIGGINSON

Accept recognition of your interest & service in the 2nd volume of "Emilies poems." I know you are happy in *her* welcome from the world. I hope you are well. I trust I may see you again some time.

Heartily
LAVINIA DICKINSON

My mother told me that "this 'recognition' was a check for $100, and I received from Lavinia a like amount. This was the second—the first also a check for $100—and last sum of money that I received for my part in editing the poems of Emily Dickinson."

What impression had the second volume created? Had it met the expectations aroused by the first?

In general, critics kept the *parti pris* to which they had committed themselves the year before—the cautious were still cautious, the astonished still astonished, the disapproving more disapproving, while the open-minded eagerly awaited further jolts. Those who had taken an emphatic stand either for or against the poems found their feelings intensified. The belligerent became more articulate, emboldened by the discovery that others agreed with them, while reviewers like Louise Chandler Moulton, who had taken Emily to her heart after a single reading of the first volume, could with difficulty express their enthusiasm. "There was something in Emily Dickinson that transcended art and made her a law unto herself," wrote Mrs. Moulton in the *Sunday Herald*, Boston, November 22, 1891.

These various attitudes are reflected in early reviews. First, the cautious:

> We do not find the poems of this volume inferior to those of the first selection, notwithstanding a few things we would have left out. —*The Springfield Republican*, November 8, 1891

> The same qualities which marked the first volume are to be found in this, although it must be confessed that there are more of the faults and fewer of the virtues than in the other.—*Boston Courier*, November 22, 1891

Possibly the "Boston Literary Letter" in *The Springfield Republican*, December 10, 1891, should be included in this category

> This second volume of Miss Dickinson's epigrams and fragments is well enough, and is justified by the success of the first one, but it is hardly needful to print more, even if there are others left in the portfolio. Enough has now been given to the world to show what the writer was; more would not deepen the impression, and might tend to efface it.

Astonished reviewers said things like this:

> She runs over rhythm as a horse jumps a hedge, with a bracing if not smooth effect.—*The Chautauquan*, January, 1892

Another group of critics reveal in their emphatic disapproval a note of petulance if not defiance.

> The second series . . . is as exasperating as the first. . . . It is hard to understand how such a mind as Miss Dickinson's must have been in its native powers can have exhibited the intellectual

—we had almost added the moral—defects which the construction of her poems displays.—*The Congregationalist*, December 31, 1891

It is questionable if the admirers of Miss Dickinson's experimental vagaries have done wisely in spreading her posthumous crudities before the public.—*The New York World*, December 6, 1891

There are many things . . . which . . . "take away one's breath." But one does not wish to have one's breath taken away entirely. A thought may be striking, but the stroke should not be fatal. After reading two volumes of Miss Dickinson's poems one gets exhausted, and a healthy mind begins to fear paralysis. There is too much of the same thing in them—morbid feeling, jerky and disjointed writing, and occasional faults of grammar.—*The Critic*, December 19, 1891

Again we find the hardly human dumbness, the isolated and singular point of view, the neuralgic darts of feeling voiced in words that are sometimes almost inarticulate, sometimes curiously far-fetched—the rhyme, meter, and vocabulary jarring upon the artistic sense. One pities deeply the suffering of such an incommunicative spirit. . . . The best criticism of Miss Dickinson's verse is that which has set the wan Indian pipe upon her book as an emblem.—*The Literary World*, December 19, 1891

In contrast to the foregoing, some reviewers admitted genuine interest. The writer of the following notice excused his growing f reluctant admiration.

The half finished sketches of an old master, revealing where here a line was contemplated and there a line was erased, have a subtler fascination for latter day artists than have all the treasures of the Uffizi. The first rough draft of a famous tale is a treasure incomparable in its hints of changed ideals and bettered methods of work. A drama in rehearsal is full of unique entertainment. . . . Bohemia owes not a little of its flavorsome charm to the fact that it is a world of workshops.

So with Emily Dickinson's verses; their very lack of finish has in it compensation, in added nearness to the singer's personality. . . .—*Boston Transcript*, December 9, 1891

Other critics of a similar turn of mind, at a loss to explain why the rough verses fascinated and held them, tried to justify their interest. Professor Francis H. Stoddard thought there might be something more in the poems than one gets at first glance. In analyzing "I died for beauty" in "Technique in Emily Dickinson's Poems," *The Critic*, January 9, 1892, he says:

> Miss Dickinson's poems may be formless, or they may be worded to so fine and subtle a device that they seem formless, just as the spectrum of a far-off star may seem blankness until examined with a lens of especial power.

The final group of critics are frank in their admiration.

> The first volume of those unique, wonderful poems . . . thrilled the reading world with a sense of surprise, delight and critical inquiry. Diamonds in the rough they were, but preëminently diamonds and not paste. The second series needs little heralding. The bare announcement of its publication will incite the eager response of thousands of readers in both this country and England —*The Boston Budget*, November 15, 1891

> Of the quality of these poems it is difficult to give an idea by the aid of selections. Their effect is cumulative. . . . —*The Chicago Tribune*, December 12, 1891

A Boston critic, Arthur Chamberlain, wrote in *The Commonwealth*, December 26, 1891:

> Very often the form suits the sentiment with an absolute propriety, as in "Called Back" ["Just lost when I was saved!"] while in "I know that He Exists" there is an unusual play of rhyme and a rhythm which cheats the ear into a supposition of rhyme where it really does not exist. . . . But then, Miss Dickinson was evidently born to be the despair of reviewers.

Some writers suggested that Miss Dickinson threw a great deal of responsibility upon her editors, as in *The Christian Union*, June 18, 1892:

> One must also admit the many good things in the "Poems"— their unexpected quality, which renders them so readable, the

clever bits one stumbles on here and there, nuggets with the right hue and true ring. There has, however, been plenty of work for the editors to refine this metal to a presentable standard.

The attitude of the general reader was expressed in *People and Patriot*, February, 1892:

> There is no comparison to make between the first and second volumes of her poems; they are all of a piece. Whoever has read one must have the other, and the world will not rest satisfied till every scrap of her writings, letters as well as literature, has been published.

Early editions were absorbed so fast that the record-breaking sales of the first series were very nearly equaled. The voracity of the public was reflected in letters such as this:

> Huntsville, Ala.
> *Dec.* 11th 1891

Thomas Wentworth Higginson,

SIR,

Why not publish the remaining poems of Emily Dickinson for a Christmas present to the sorrowing?

Her fingers touch the chords that soothe the aching heart, then why withhold anything of hers from suffering souls?

> Respectfully
> MRS. H. C. SPEAKE

The editors were deluged with letters.

Most of the people who wrote to Colonel Higginson he referred to me for answers [my mother said]. They wanted information so they could write a paper on Emily—to know about her life, about her connection with Saxe Holm, how she "composed"; they wanted an autograph letter, a manuscript poem or a photograph; they wanted permission to include her poems in collections they were compiling; some women thought their work resembled hers; and some letters were just outpourings of the heart in admiration.

One such letter is here reproduced because a partial draft of my mother's reply, illustrating her manner of dealing with such requests, has been preserved.

231 East 14th Street
New York

Mrs. Mabel Loomis Todd,
DEAR MADAM,

It has become my duty to write a paper on the "Life and Poems of Emily Dickinson," the paper to be read before a club to which I belong, the Brooklyn Heights Seminary Club, founded by the late Mary Brigham. I find so few sources of information that I ventured to apply to Colonel Higginson, who, though personally I am quite unknown to him, has very kindly answered and directed me to a number of the Springfield Republican which I am trying to obtain. Colonel Higginson has advised me to apply to you for further information, which I do with much hesitation, knowing that you must be much occupied, and fearing to trouble you with my request. But if you could make any suggestion to me as to where to look for more light upon the life of this remarkable woman, or if you would yourself give me a few dates and facts, with regard to her, I should be deeply grateful. As I have already explained to Colonel Higginson, it is not our wish to pry into the private life of a woman of genius, but if there is anything interesting which we are not forbidden to know we should be very glad to learn it, and to study its bearing upon her poetry.

Pardon my request. You will understand my anxiety not to disappoint the hundred or more members of our club, who take a vital interest in literary matters, and especially in women of literary note. Any information or suggestion or reference will be most acceptable.

Yours very truly,
ANNIE D. HANKS.

Nov. 20th, 1891

Amherst, Massachusetts
24 *November*, 1891.

MY DEAR MISS HANKS:—

On my return from an absence of a few days, I find your letter awaiting me.

Of the life of Emily Dickinson very little has yet been made public. The only sources of reliable information yet published are Col. Higginson's preface to the first volume of her poems, and my own to the second—with her letters published in the October *Atlantic*. An article in the *Christian Union* of October 24 is also suggestive, as far as it goes. The article to which you refer in the *Springfield Republican* is probably one which appeared about the time of her death, and of which I know there is no extra copy at the *Republican* office. However, it gives very little of her personality.

Many fine literary reviews of the first volume have appeared during the last year in *Life*, for Nov. 27, 1890, the *Nation* for the same date, the *Independent* for Dec. 11, 1890, The February *Dial*, several editorials in the *Christian Register*, the January *Harper's Magazine*, Editor's Study, and others. A forthcoming article of my own in the *Youth's Companion* speaks of her girlhood; in general, articles written about her now are necessarily more literary than personal.

I however prepared a paper last year upon Emily Dickinson for Women's Clubs in Springfield, Boston and other places, which contains more of her life than anything else has done, and as much as her brother and sister are yet ready to have made public. As I am to give this several times this winter in different places, I could hardly send it to you for extracts; but I think an interesting paper may be made from the sources I have suggested. There is a fine review of the second volume in an early October *Nation*. [End of draft][2]

---

[2] From among the poems dedicated to Emily at that time, I give but one, together with the letter in which it was enclosed. It shows that Emily's touch could quicken the humblest heart to which, because of her, the heavens were opened.

Spokane, Wash[n]
May 25 1892

Mrs T. W. Higgenson
DEAR MADAM

As editress of the Poems of Miss Emily Dickenson perhaps it may interest you to read the little poem I herewith enclose written by Miss Martha Eileen Holahan of Reads Landing, Minnesota. Miss Holahan is herself a real poet—as you will discover upon reading her lines— struggling without recognition as yet, writing because she cannot help it, and yet earning a living as a telegraph operator and station agent on the Chicago, Milwaukee & St. Paul Railway. These lines I send you are just as they were struck off by her in the telegraph office upon telegraph paper, and in pencil, no copy being kept by her and the poem sent to me fresh from her hand without any intention on her part of its being seen by other person than myself who had sent her the review

During the summer of 1891, previous to the appearance of the Second Series, James R. Osgood, McIlvaine & Co., London, announced the publication of "*Poems* by Emily Dickinson, Edited by Mabel Loomis Todd and Thomas Wentworth Higginson. Crown 8vo, cloth extra, gilt top, 5s." The cover was of plain yellowish cloth without the Indian pipe design. Since those

---

of Miss Dickensons Poems in the April number of the Nineteenth Century. Miss Holahan's lines are in my judgement so good & so appreciative of your effort to rescue from oblivion the name of one so deserving of fame as Miss Dickenson that I have taken the liberty to send them to you. Trusting that I may not have imposed upon your good nature by doing so, I am

Yrs Resp^{ly}
H. W. HOLLEY

The Poet's Epitaph

Dedicated to Miss Dickinson

She sang—as wildly weirdly sweet
As ever trilled a forest bird;
She sang—but in that crowded street,
None paused, perchance, alas! none heard;
She held her hands out to the throng—
Cold, empty hands, that craved a mite!
They heeded not her vibrant song,
They thrust the songstress out of sight.

She sang—her voice as sad as Death;
Tears drenched her pallid pleading face;
She sang; but none drew quicker breath,
Or sighed, in that great market-place.
The Jews placed Mammon once, 'tis said,
Upon the shrine of David's son;
Jerusalem, alas! is dead,
The spirit of her creed lives on.

She sang—a minor strain divine,
While Charon plied his muffled oar;
It wakened slumb'rous Proserpine
A-slumber on Death's pulseless shore,
And from the gloomy Styx, the doomed
Looked up, forgetful of their pain;
Looked up, each face with joy illumed,
To listen to that minor strain.

Its echo only came to men;
It floated through their busy mart;

flowers are unknown in England, the symbol would have been meaningless.[3]

How had the poems been received in Great Britain? The publication of the volume is in itself an answer, if only a partial one. For it is a curious fact that although in England criticism had been almost uniformly unfavorable, there was nevertheless sufficient demand for the poems to justify a well-known British publishing house in issuing a small edition.

Several English reviews have already been alluded to and one, thought to have been by Andrew Lang, in the London *Daily News*, January 2, 1891, referred to by Mrs. Todd as "incredibly harsh," was quoted at length on page 100. That review seems to have sounded the keynote for subsequent criticism in England. So outraged was Mr. Lang by Emily's book that he did his best to annihilate it. But the vitality of the poetry which so offended his taste seems to have withstood his attack, for it gained rather than lost in popularity. "If fame belonged to me," as Emily said, "I could not escape her."

After two months' reflection Mr. Lang had simmered down sufficiently to admit in *The Illustrated London News*, March 7, 1891, that "one turns over Miss Dickinson's book with a puzzled feeling that there was poetry in her subconsciousness, but that it never became explicit." Though less vitriolic, this review was just as disparaging as the first. "One might as well seek for an air in the notes of a bird," he exclaims, "as for articulate and sustained poetry here."

The London *Bookseller*, May 6, 1891, ventures the opinion

It reached their thoroughfare and then
It reached—somehow—their critic's heart.
So when the poet's head is dust,
Her soul above reward, renown,
They calmly, blindly say: " 'T is just
We give to her a laurel crown."

May 1st, 1892

[3] In a letter addressed to me, Professor M. L. Fernald, Director of the Gray Herbarium of Harvard University, says: "Replying to your inquiry regarding *Monotropa uniflora*, I find that there is no evidence in the European botanical works of its occurrence anywhere in Europe. It is found outside North America in eastern Asia, from Japan and Korea to the Himalayan region."

that "it is probable that the reputation which these poems have gained in their own land will be forthcoming here in due time. The editorial preface compares them to Blake. Certainly America, generally sterile in poetical production, has produced nothing so truly poetical as these fugitive thoughts."

On May 18, 1891, Mr. Niles enclosed in a letter to Mrs. Todd a copy of one of these English reviews, observing in his moderate way, "I augur from this that the reviewers have found something more than the ordinary thing."

A writer in *The Saturday Review* (London), July 18, 1891, quoted on page 155, concluded that "on the whole, the poetry of Miss Dickinson surprises more often by singularity than charms by *naïveté* and simplicity." But that famous periodical did not dismiss the poems with one notice. On September fifth another article referred to

> . . . the uneducated and illiterate character of some of these verses, although we fully recognize in them the unmistakable touch of a true poet. . . . [She was] gifted with a far saner mind [than Blake]. . . . But in some of her roughest poems there is still an idea which forces the reader to attend to its meaning and impresses him, in spite of the irritation he may feel at the form. . . .
>
> There is much that is very striking in these poems, they reveal great depth of feeling, and the tone of them, though melancholy, is not morbid. In some there is a kind of exultation and a concentrated force of expression which is really remarkable.

In *The Graphic* (London), September 12, 1891, we read that

> the verse is not always readily intelligible; still there can be no question that the late Miss Dickinson possessed the poetic temperament and insight into some of the sorrows and mysteries of life. Nevertheless there is a sense of incompleteness about her work as if the thought were dashed off and committed to her portfolio in a hurry.

A well-known article entitled "An American Sappho" in the London *Daily News*, October 3, 1891, begins with the words:

> Queer, queer are the fortunes of books. Few fates have been stranger than those which attended the poems of the late Miss

Emily Dickinson. This lady dwelt remote, in an American village, a maid whom there were few to quote and very few to read.

The writer speaks of the great sale the book has had, of Mr. Howells' enthusiasm over the poems, though they "scorn rhyme, grammar, rhythm and sense, and lack humor," but adds that "Mr. Higginson at once conceived that the lady had a wholly new and original poetic genius, and the American public seems to agree with him."

In conclusion the reviewer wryly trusts "that her admirers will not become her imitators."

An indictment of the English attitude toward Emily's poetry came from the gifted sister of William and Henry James, who wrote in her journal on January 6, 1892, "It is reassuring to hear the English pronouncement that Emily Dickinson is fifth-rate—they have such a capacity for missing quality."[4] But Alice James was not the only one to pillory English reviewers. Frank B. Sanborn, in his column, "The Breakfast Table," in the *Boston Daily Advertiser*, October 27, 1891, voices a protest against Philistines in general and the *Daily News* tirade of October third in particular:

> . . . . One of these English Philistines—possibly Andrew Lang, who writes for the London News editorially—has devoted a column in that journal to the subject. Much that he says is indisputable,—for example: "Her verse, at its very best, has a distant echo of Blake's. Poetry is a thing of many laws—felt and understood, and sanctioned by the whole experience of humanity, rather than written. Miss Dickinson in her poetry broke every one of the natural and salutary laws of verse. Hers is the very anarchy of the Muses, and perhaps in this anarchy lies the charm which has made her popular in America, and has caused Mr. Howells to say that she alone would serve to justify American literary existence."
>
> I take exception to the word "anarchy" which is used in England to express all sorts of deviation from custom—highway robbery, mobbing the bishop of London, or refusing to wear a stove-pipe hat. But the irregularity of Miss Dickinson's verse does find more favor here than it could in England. But our Philistine goes on thus: "She seems to have been a kind of unfinished, rudimentary

[4] *Alice James, Her Brothers, Her Journal.* Edited by Anna Robeson Burr. New York, 1934, p. 248.

Brontë, and her character is so unusual and interesting, that it is a pity her rhymes should make matter for mirth. Unless all poets, from the earliest improvisers to laureate, have been wrong in their methods, Miss Dickinson cannot possibly have been right in hers. Compared with her, Walt Whitman is a sturdy poetical conservative. Her only merit is an occasional picturesque touch, and a general pathetic kind of yearning and sense of futility."

This is bad enough; but still worse is the parody that he makes, and his allusion to an English versifier, who seems to have lent an "effort" to this critic for the verdict. He says: ". . . . Most critics get odd poems from strangers, with requests for a candid opinion, which it is highly dangerous to give. For example, what can a man say to an author whose poems 'On a Gipsy Child in London' ends thus:—

> So we leave her,
> So we leave her,
> Far from where her swarthy kinsfolk roam,
> In the Scarlet Fever,
> Scarlet Fever,
> Scarlet Fever Convalescent Home.

But this, at least, though betraying a lack of humor, has rhyme and common sense to recommend it. Miss Dickinson's performances lack both of these desirable qualities." This is mere Philistinism, like that of the English coroner who read Wordsworth's verses in the house of commons, and made fun of them. . . .

An example of the small influence exerted by hostile reviews upon English readers is contained in a letter sent to Colonel Higginson and forwarded by him to Mrs. Todd with a pencil note, "Is not this curious? I have replied. Note the penny postage. T.W.H." (A British stamp was affixed to the self-addressed envelope enclosed for reply.)

SIR.

Although perfect strangers to you, we venture to write to you, as we are great admirers of Miss E. Dickinson's poetry—and having read, in the preface to the little book published, that it contained only a *selection* of her works, we are extremely anxious to know if there is any chance of our being able to enjoy some more of her delightful poetry?

The exquisite originality of her style seems to open a new world of poetry, and we cannot help grudging the idea that there may be other verses as beautiful, which we may not be privileged to read.

Our only excuse for troubling you must be our great admiration for those poems we have read.

Yours faithfully
A. M. PREVOST
KATHARINE HICKLEY

Newhaven
Walton Cliff
Clevedon
Somerset

Aug. 23ᵈ 1893

After looking through the English volume Colonel Higginson sent a post card to Mrs. Todd:

25 Buckingham Street,
Cambridge, Mass.
Dec. 6, 1891

On p. 49 of Vol. I, did you alter "will not *state* its sting" into *sate,* as in English edition? Either word is intelligible, but I always supposed it meant that the sting was vexatiously withheld, till it wd. be a relief to have it definitely "stated."

T.W.H.

Mrs. Todd replied as follows:

Amherst
7 *December,* 1891

DEAR MR. HIGGINSON:—

No, indeed, I did not change 'state' to 'sate' in the English edition.

Some over-bright reviewer, last winter, wrote that it should be 'sate,' and I immediately looked up the original, finding it unmistakably '*state*,' and I wrote him to that effect. It was the same brilliant gentleman who also wrote that she meant 'Latin races' instead of 'satin races,' in *The Hemlock*. Some people never can apprehend the way Emily Dickinson used words.

Thank you for letting me see your condensation of that horrid

English review. Why are they all so determined over there that she shall be made ridiculous?

I have just given an "Emily Dickinson talk" to an enthusiastic club of ladies in Westfield. I think the interest in her is continually growing. I have today read an interesting article about you, my friend, in *Light*, published in Worcester.

Cordially
MABEL L. TODD

The word "state" in the poem beginning, "If you were coming in the fall," had troubled others. (See page 78.) In all editions except the English, the word is "state" as Emily wrote it and as first published in 1890. In parenthesis, two stanzas of the printed version are not like a copy in Emily's handwriting which reads as follows. (Differences in the second and last stanzas are indicated in italics.)

If you were coming in the fall,
I'd brush the summer by
With half a smile and half a spurn,
As housewives do a fly.

If I could see you in a year,
I'd wind the months in balls,
And put them each in separate drawers,
For fear the numbers fuse.

If only centuries delayed,
I'd count them on my hand,
Subtracting till my fingers dropped
Into Van Dieman's land.

If certain, when this life was out,
That yours and mine should be,
I'd toss it yonder like a rind,
And take (taste) eternity.

But now, *uncertain* of the length
Of *this, that is between,*
It goads me, like the goblin bee,
That will not state its sting.

Adverse criticism in England gave encouragement to hostile commentators in this country. A much quoted unsigned review in *The Atlantic Monthly*, January, 1892, was thought by Mr. Higginson to have been written by Miss Agnes Repplier. But the author proved to be Thomas Bailey Aldrich. One fact which most critics of the nineties could not seem to grasp was that partial rhymes, for Emily, had a special function—to arrest the attention where she wanted it arrested.

In a recent letter, Martha Hale Shackford, that critic of unerring insight, characterizes Emily's rhymes as "intricately and fascinatingly and challengingly related to the subject [she] is presenting with such poignant brevity. . . . She was teased by sound echoes that were not always exact, yet were enough so as to be suggestive. . . . I think E.D. cared a great deal for assonance—in the technical sense."

Such thoughts could not have been within the range of Mr. Aldrich's experience, for his review concludes:

> Miss Dickinson's versicles have a queerness and a quaintness that have stirred a momentary curiosity in emotional bosoms. Oblivion lingers in the immediate neighborhood.

It becomes increasingly easy to understand why Emily refused to cast her "mind" upon the waters. If Keats died "a victim of critical assassination," she was justified in avoiding what she knew would be a similar fate.

CHAPTER XI

Collecting the Letters

How lovely are the wiles of words!

ANOTHER story dovetails into that of the poems, a different kind of story. It has to do with the only prose Emily is known to have written in her maturity—letters to her friends.

Although the idea of a volume of letters had been in the minds of both Miss Vinnie and my mother for over a year, although the latter had been copying groups of those which came to her attention—by-products of work on the poems—and although the idea had been given support by the acclaim with which Colonel Higginson's article in *The Atlantic Monthly* had been received, a specific event was needed in order to change the idea from a vague hope into a plan of action.

Such an event took place on December 1, 1891. I quote a few words from the diary on that day including the effort involved in reaching a town only twenty miles from Amherst in time for an eleven o'clock meeting. "Rose at 5:30. Midnight darkness and stars shining. Took the 7 train for Palmer—thence to Westfield. Went to Mrs. D. L. Gillett's, & read my paper on Emily Dickinson, also many letters & unpublished poems, to a club of ladies. They were all intensely interested, and I received quite an ovation."

In *Letters of Emily Dickinson*, 1931 (pages xv-xvi), Mrs. Todd has described what happened following the lecture.

After I had finished, a little lady in a black bonnet came up to me, told me she had been a schoolmate of Emily at Amherst Academy, that she had never forgotten her extraordinary compositions, and *where* might she read some of Emily's prose? I told her that Lavinia, . . . after searching the house, . . .

had failed to find any remnants, even, of those remarkable documents, reports of which had been reaching her ever since the poems were published. Neither had she been able to find any diaries or journals, which indeed she knew it had not been Emily's habit to write. "Keeping a diary is not familiar to me as to your sister Vinnie," Emily once wrote to her brother. Lavinia could find no prose whatever, though there were hundreds of poems and scraps of unfinished poems. But I hoped, as I told the lady in Westfield, Mrs. [A. P.] Strong, that some of her letters might be rescued. She responded eagerly that she and Emily had been the dearest and most intimate friends, that she still possessed a large number of letters written during Emily's early girlhood, and that nothing would delight her more than to send them to me—which she promptly did.

So a chance meeting was the spark which touched off a long train of events culminating in the publication of the two volumes of letters in 1894. The collection opened with those girlish messages to "dear Abiah," beginning shortly after Emily's fourteenth birthday. I used almost all of them because of the light they shed on her method of mind and its development. Furthermore, they contain even yet the most complete record known to exist of those early years.

The copying of Emily's letters was soon under way. Editorial problems were different from those connected with preparing the poems for publication. But though different, the task was no less exacting. The handwriting was still troublesome at times, although after many years' intimacy the mere deciphering of manuscripts, which in the beginning had absorbed so much time, was no longer a real obstacle. Difficulties were of another sort.

First, the letters must be found. The poems had been all ready —there, in their box, in Miss Vinnie's house—awaiting an editor. But the letters, scattered here, there, and everywhere, had to be lured from their hiding places once they had been discovered. Miss Vinnie and my mother applied themselves to this task for several years, following up any lead however slight as to where more letters could be found. Sometimes they ran afoul of tradition. When that happened, further search had to be abandoned; for in the early nineties tradition in New England had the force of a Polynesian taboo.

After recipients of letters had been located, often a long task in itself, they must in many instances be wooed before they would give up their treasured documents to anyone to read even, let alone print. Publishing private letters was considered a sacrilege. (See President Seelye's comment, page 166.) They were a sacred trust. But though never shown, neither were they destroyed. That also would verge on disloyalty. Letters were hoarded irrespective of whether or not they had intrinsic value. Indeed, that had nothing to do with the case, since a moral code was involved. Letters once hoarded were kept hoarded—inviolate—as long as life lasted. Sometimes this sense of false loyalty was coupled with false modesty, illustrated in caricature by the Norcross "girls." Furthermore, if consent to publish were obtained, the letters must first be censored. To "deal in personalities" was abhorrent, an offense to good taste. A decent person would never reveal remarks complimentary to himself. Even Colonel Higginson fell in with this attitude. (See page 81.)

In case the recipients had died, would those who inherited the letters be more likely to look with a kindly eye upon their publication? At this point the editor ran into another question of morals. My mother says:

The usual pious duty of those nearest to the departed was to destroy letters if requested to do so by him. This was the first rite performed after the funeral and was done without looking at the contents of the letters to be destroyed. This was the chief obstacle Vinnie and I encountered in trying to find Emily's letters. Over and over again survivors of their recipients wrote that they had had a great many, but that "when mother died" they had all been destroyed at her request. It was fortunate that our efforts to collect the letters came so soon after Emily's death that many of her correspondents were still alive, and in consequence, their little bundles of letters from her still intact. Had we delayed a few years before beginning, possibly the collection of enough to make a volume might have been impossible. Indeed, the originals of many of those collected by us and published in 1894 were subsequently destroyed by their recipients or their survivors in fulfilment of the traditional rite.

That there were ever any published volumes of Emily Dickinson's letters at all we owe, first, to the diplomacy of my mother as well as to her diligence and that of Lavinia Dickinson in discovering their whereabouts; and, second, to the fact that a few of Emily's correspondents could see beyond their affection and their desire to shield the object of it, to a realization however vague that the letters had literary value.

Once letters had been found and permission to publish them obtained, another routine task followed—that of finding out when they had been written, as none but the very earliest were dated. My mother says:[1]

A suggestion of the all but insurmountable difficulties I encountered in trying to piece together anything like a consecutive story from [the letters] will perhaps be glimpsed in the course of these remarks. In a life devoid of incident such as [Emily's], I could never have done it at all without the daily help of Austin and Lavinia. . . .

We soon found ourselves in a pile of manuscripts, bewildering in dimensions, equally so in lack of dates. The latter I was forced to determine in one of several ways. The handwriting was a general guide, having three distinct periods, each corresponding to a different literary style, the diffuseness of girlhood contrasting with the poignant sententiousness of middle life. . . .

The change in handwriting of which specimens are given in facsimile, was no less noticeable than Emily Dickinson's development in literary style; and this alone has been a general guide. The thoughtfulness of a few correspondents in recording the time of the letters' reception has been a further and most welcome assistance; while occasionally the kind of postage stamp and the postmark helped to indicate when they were written, although generally the envelopes had not been preserved.[2] But the larger part have been placed by searching out the dates of contemporaneous incidents mentioned—for instance, numerous births, marriages and deaths [Appendix VI]; any epoch in the life of a friend was an event to Emily Dickinson, always noticed

---

[1] These quoted passages are excerpts from Mrs. Todd's introductions to *Letters*, 1894, and *Letters*, 1931, both included in the latter volume, and two sentences from an unpublished article she wrote about the publication of the *Letters*.

[2] In determining dates it is dangerous to rely on the kind of stationery used. Emily sometimes kept her writing paper for years before using it, so that a sheet previously associated with the fine thin stroke of the early middle period of penmanship may show instead the heavy pencil script of the latest period.

by a bit of flashing verse, or a graceful, if mystically expressed, note of comfort or congratulation. . . . In this arduous task Austin Dickinson was an indispensable help, as he was an encyclopaedia of information. He had kept for many years articles relating to early Amherst days, as well as a mass of historical material which he had inherited. . . .

After months spent in collecting the letters and arranging them by dates, I at last began the engrossing task of editing them. There was something akin to dread, almost fear, as I approached them critically, lest the inner and hitherto inviolate life of Emily might be too clearly revealed. Should they indeed be published at all? Austin thought they should, and Lavinia, as always, insisted that every word Emily ever wrote should be published. So I went on with the editing which was to occupy me for the next two years. Fascinating yet exhausting labor!

Although Colonel Higginson did not assist me in editing the *Letters*—nor the Third Series of *Poems*, for that matter—he was deeply interested always, and sent me his entire correspondence with Emily except for a few letters which he thought too personal to print. . . . He agreed with me that a volume of Emily's prose should be published. So much labor was involved in the plan, however, that he was unable to take part in it, other than by vivid interest and occasional advice. . . .

So large is the number of letters to each of several correspondents, that it has seemed best to place these sets in separate chapters. The continuity is perhaps more perfectly preserved in this way than by the usual method of mere chronological succession; especially as, in a life singularly uneventful, no marked periods of travel or achievement serve otherwise to classify them.

As in the case of the poems, Emily's punctuation was conventionalized in the volume of letters, My mother tells us why:

In more recent years, dashes instead of punctuation, and capitals for all important words, together with the quaint handwriting give to the actual manuscript an individual fascination quite irresistible. But the coldness of print destroys that elusive charm, so that dashes and capitals have been restored to their conventional use.[3]

[3] One thing my mother failed to mention was Emily's habit of lapsing into poetry in the middle of a letter—another pitfall for the editor who thus might fail to detect a poem.

During the early months of 1892 the letters which occupied my mother were those written to Samuel Bowles and his wife, and to Dr. and Mrs. J. G. Holland. All the letters to these friends that have appeared in print are included in *Letters*, 1931, pages 153-213. But others could not be found as this letter from Mrs. Holland indicates.

August 30th 1893
Bonnie-Castle
Alexandria Bay, N.Y.

My dear Mrs. Todd,

Your letter of the 29th is just at hand. I am very happy to answer any questions I may be able to in order to help you in your work.

My *"little boy"* was born in 1859. The "Minnie" alluded to was my youngest sister who died about ten years ago. She was married in 1856.

"Little Katie" was dangerously ill in the summer of 1854 (and autumn). Annie was married December 7th, 1881.

If there are any other questions you would like to ask, don't hesitate to do so. I regret I had so few of the many letters dear Emily wrote me to send you. As I remember them, there were many more interesting and quaint than these I have.

I congratulate you on the able manner in which you have edited the poems, and trust the letters may be equally successful.

With kindest regards for you and your husband, I am

Yours very truly
E. C. Holland

Dictated

The following two-stanza poem was printed as prose in *Letters*, 1894, p. 335:

"And with what body do they come?"
Then they *do* come! Rejoice!
What door? What hour? Run, run, my soul!
Illuminate the house!

Although, in the 1931 edition of the *Letters*, p. 324, the first stanza still appeared as prose, the second was recognized as a quatrain:

"Body!" then real—a face and eyes!
To know that it is them!
Paul knew the Man that knew the news,
He passed through Bethlehem.

Royalty check from Roberts Brothers, publishers, to Lavinia N. Dickinson

Lavinia N. Dickinson

The missing letters were subsequently discovered.

The letters to James D. and Charles H. Clark were also received early in 1892. "Mr. Charles Clark sent them to Vinnie," my mother told me, "and she gave them to me." This group revealed in a measure Emily's attitude toward the Philadelphia clergyman, Dr. Charles Wadsworth, whom she revered. They were first published in their entirety in *Letters*, 1931, pages 342-357.

During this time my mother's talks about Emily were gaining in popularity. On February thirteenth she spoke at The Kensington, Boston, to "parlors full" of friends, and on the day following to a smaller group. An account of the first of these two talks was written by Arthur Chamberlain in *The Commonwealth*, Boston, February 20, 1892:

> Those who heard Mrs. Mabel Loomis Todd's keen, witty and sympathetic exposition of Emily Dickinson's genuine but elusive genius, . . . must have felt that the author was singularly fortunate in her interpreter. . . . As she stood there—an almost girlish figure in her black lace dress whose sole adornment was a small bunch of her favorite jonquils—every tone and gesture revealed not only the intelligent critic but the loving friend. . . .
>
> Calvinism is a somewhat gnarly tree, but its core is as sound as eternal righteousness can make it, and the recent graft of liberal thought bears some wonderfully fine olives. This may explain that real reverence which underlies the most startling of Miss Dickinson's utterances; a reverence which we need no longer question now that Mrs. Todd has set it forth with that explicit statement of one who speaks with authority. Nor will it be difficult for the discerning mind to discover in that same Calvinistic inheritance the reason for the hatred of cant and sham which is conspicuous in all of Miss Dickinson's writings.

On January twenty-ninth, Miss Vinnie had received from Roberts Brothers a check for $505.59.

Before taking up a matter which at this time was irritating her to the bursting point, it is refreshing to read a letter to Miss Vinnie from the Right Reverend Frederick Dan Huntington, Bishop of Central New York. A graduate of Amherst College in

e class of 1839, he spent his summers in Hadley, an adjoining
wn. It is good to have a glimpse of Emily Dickinson through
e eyes of that strong, saintly man.

Diocese of Central New York
210 Walnut Place
Syracuse, N.Y.
Ap. 1. '92

Y DEAR FRIEND—

The package which you were so thoughtful & so kind as to send
e has reached me safely. I had not forgotten y'r prompt offer
the precious volumes when I inquired about them. Many of
r sister's remarkable verses I had read but for lack of pains
d never owned a copy.

It was long ago that she gave me her confidence & made herself
y friend, tho' afterwards I scarcely saw her. The image that
mes before me when I think of her is hardly more terrestrial
an celestial,—a spirit with only as much of the mortal investi-
re as served to maintain her relations with this present world.
is only fair that a genius so rare & so pure should be known
yond the hiding-place where its light was veiled.

With cordial & affectionate regards & remembrance for you all,
ithfully & gratefully y'rs

F. D. HUNTINGTON

After a talk to the Literary Club of New Britain, Connecticut,
March 23, 1892, my mother sailed the day following for a
ief holiday in Bermuda. "While I was gone," she says, "Vinnie
rned that a man named Gardner Fuller said he had some
ters Emily had written to him, and threatened to publish
em unless he received from her a large sum of money."

This attempted blackmail was one more episode which Miss
nnie's sheltered life had provided no training to withstand.
 her it was an enormity. She was outraged and angered out
all proportion to the importance of the affair. My mother told
 that as the Dickinsons "had never heard of him before, Austin
ked a friend of his who knew someone in Taunton [where he
ed] to find out about the man."

The following letter, a copy in my mother's writing, is, I judge,

the reply to Mr. Dickinson's inquiry. It lacks both date an
signature.

MY DEAR FRIEND:—

I have made the inquiry and received the reply, which is a
follows:

"Gardner Fuller has *no* business, *no* reputation, *no* position i
society—I mistake; he has a reputation for *everything that is ba*
He is called "Foolish Fuller," and it is said that he has no
common sense. He boards with his brother here, who is a lawye
a smart man, and respectable—a widower. If he had a wife I d
not believe she would have Gardner there. I am not personall
acquainted with him, but I hear he is notoriously bad *every way*.

My friend would not like to have her name used, so I do n
give it.

In haste,
Yours ever
_____

Mr. Fuller had, it seems, been offering the letters for sale, bu
without success.

Emily Dickinson

Editor Nation:
DEAR SIR.

I see, by an article in the October "Atlantic" that there is
universal desire for the publication of any letters written by th
late Emily Dickinson.

I have in my possession twenty odd letters and some vers
(about 19000 words, more or less) written by this talented autho
ess during the war, (1861 to 1864) which are probably the on
letters in existence giving a clear insight into that beautiful an
secluded life. These letters are worth their weight in diamond
I know of nothing published in the English or any other langua
that will compare with them and if they were properly place
before the public would, I am sure, command a phenomenal sal
These letters touch upon almost every phase of life and chara
ter. There are discussions on Art, Religion, Politics; criticisn
on Authors and Books; Eulogies on our foremost men an
women; essays upon Nature, friendship, Ideals and the immo
tality of the soul, &c; in language so pure and lofty and yet
simple and grand,—a sublime marvel altogether, if you will,-

and with just a tinge of rosy-romance running all through, making them intensely interesting.

Faithfully yours
GARDNER FULLER

Taunton Mass. *Nov.* 23rd 1891

It would appear that, having failed in his attempt not only to interest editors but also to intimidate Emily's relatives, Mr. Fuller next tried the expedient of advertising. The correspondence is given in full because it throws light on Miss Vinnie's technique.

Amherst *April* 5th [1892]

MY DEAR MR NILES

I'm very grateful to you for the "Gardiner Fuller" information, shocking as the facts are. My Brother is in Washington—Mrs. Todd in the Bermudas—else one of these would consult you in person as to what can be done to interrupt this villain. Can you advise any course?

I shall never believe *these* letters are this man's, unless I can see the handwriting. I was never many months separated from Emily—we always knew each others friends—this mystery is all black—these letters may have been stolen.

I have never felt *easy* since you sent me "G.F.'s" first letter. I had ascertained he was *worst* of men & I feared mischief. I wanted the man seen *at once* & some comprimise effected, if he really had anything in Emilies handwriting. My Brother was sure he was a hoax & so I did not urge my conviction. Has any one any legal right to publish letters written only for one person?

Pardon my writing so at length but I'm too appalled to know what to say. Will it be asking too much to beg your advice.

Heartily
LAVINIA DICKINSON

Unable to restrain herself until her brother's return to Amherst, Miss Vinnie asked Mr. William I. Fletcher, Librarian of Amherst College, to write to Mr. Fuller for further information regarding the letters in his possession.

Before a reply to Mr. Fletcher's letter was received, however, Mr. Dickinson had returned:

April 15th [189

MY DEAR MR NILES

My Brother has returned home & says letters can be *sold* (th
is the original manuscript) but not published or reproduce

He believes the man is a *crank* & never had any of Emili
letters unless he has stolen them from some early friend lor
ago forgotten. My Brother (at present) thinks no notice of h
advertisement the wiser course. Do you approve this suggestion

There seems a peculiar desire for larceny toward Emily.

Should you see any new developments from "Gardner Fulle.
I should be glad to be informed. I hope I have not troubled yo
too much.

Gratefully
LAVINIA DICKINSON

A few days later a reply to Mr. Fletcher's inquiry came:

Taunton, Ma
19th *Ap.* 1892

W. I. Fletcher, Esq.
DR SIR.

I must beg your indulgence for my delay in replying to yo
letter.

The letters in question were written to me during the W
when I was engaged in the publishing business in Boston. Th
are purely of a literary character and of a high order of tale
such as only Miss Dickinson could have written.

I know of nothing equal to them yet published. One letter co
tains a lock of her hair. I have no price set for them, but if yo
wish to make an offer *of your own originating* it will be co
sidered and a prompt reply given.

If not sold I shall publish them in the early Autumn.

Very Respectfully
GARDNER FULLER

68 Winthrop St

On Mr. Dickinson's advice nothing further was done just the
about Gardner Fuller. A month elapsed before he was aga
heard from.

On April seventeenth my mother returned from Bermuda. Sh
was greeted by a communication addressed to "Dr. E W Donal

7 West 10th st, New York," and marked, on the back, "For Mrs. Todd."

April 16th [1892]

DEAR MABEL

Should you see "Mr Howells" please ask if my letter & book were received.

I shall rejoice to see you at home.

Faithfully
LAVINIA

In compliance with Miss Vinnie's suggestion, my mother called on Mr. Howells on April eighteenth.

A post card from Colonel Higginson was awaiting her in Amherst:

25 Buckingham Street,
Cambridge, Mass.
Apr. 18, 1892

You'll find in 19th Century for April 1892 a review of E. D. by Hamilton Aïdé attributing the 1st preface to *Mrs.* T.W.H. I dined with him at Mrs. Howe's & he probably took me for a disguised woman!

T.W.H.

At Miss Vinnie's request my mother soon embarked on another venture for the "magnification" of Emily. This time it was a "Birthday Book," a type of daily reminder then in vogue, containing a quotation for each day in the year. It is hard to think of any writer whose work would lend itself better than Emily's to selection of epigrams. My mother began with enthusiasm, and by the end of May two hundred quotations had been selected. Mr. Niles approved, writing that he thought "such a book would find purchasers." Perhaps it might have. But it was not long before Miss Vinnie changed her mind. She may have discovered that its preparation would take time and would interrupt work on the letters. Be that as it may, the book never appeared, although the idea was broached again two and a half years later.

Meanwhile, Mrs. Todd kept sending poems to magazines in

order to gain a wider public. Some were accepted, some rejected.
One poem sent to Colonel Higginson for *The Atlantic Monthl*
he returned without having shown it to the editor.

Cambridge
May 10, 189

DEAR FRIEND

I don't think Scudder would print this, for *I* should not. It ha
fine lines, especially "The Chimes may falter"—but it is in ex
ecution *more* exasperating to me than anything of Emily's fo
the haphazard mixture of rhyme & blank verse.

How about the letters? Are they to appear by and by.

Ever Cordially
T. W. HIGGINSON

On May twentieth Mrs. Todd received a letter from Mr. Nile
in answer to one from Miss Vinnie asking if there were "an
further developments in the 'Gardner Fuller' matter." He "wro
Miss D. about the Fuller letters a day or two since," he sai
adding that "Fuller says he has arranged for their publication ou
West." To this Miss Vinnie replied the very same day.

May 20th [189

MY DEAR MR NILES

Thank you for forwarding new information concerning "Gar
ner Fuller." I shall never believe *these* unseen letters are
Emilies writing until the original manuscript is seen by someor
familiar with her handwriting at that period. "G. F." might ca

---

[4] On Feb. 24, 1892, *Life* sent back "Cobwebs." On May 25, 1892, *T*
Christian Union returned five poems: "We like March," "The spider as a
artist," "It will be summer eventually," "Hope is a subtle glutton," and "
had a guinea golden." Even Mr. Howells wrote:

The Cosmopolitan Magazine
Editorial Department

June 21, 1892

DEAR MRS. TODD:

Neither of these poems seem to me of the author's best, and I cou
use only her best to justify my own applause of her.

Yours sincerely,
W. D. HOWELLS

any letters "Emilies" because she is known at present (with favor) for the sake of trying to gain fraudulent money. Of course if there is no *way* of proof, what can be done?

My brother believes still *he* is a hoax, but I don't feel easy about the thing. In your own case, what would you advise?

How is the *sale* of "Emilies poems"—it is a long time since I have known. I should not expect the holyday rush to continue.

I fear the volume of letters will not be ready for print this Fall. Would you advise another volume of *poems*?

Believe me most grateful for all your kindness.

LAVINIA DICKINSON

A note in Mr. Dickinson's handwriting dated merely "1892" states his position.

I take no stock in Gardner Fuller. I don't believe he has any of Emily's letters. At the same time he has written what he has, and I think it best to see what it means, whether he has put us on a track that leads to anything.

I suggest that Mr. Niles write him that. On reflection, if he will bring the letters he mentioned up to him, he will read them carefully, and if they seem to be genuine and of interest, worth publishing, he will endeavor to get Miss Dickinson's consent thereto. Then if there should prove to be such letters, hold onto them under the pretext of considering them further or consulting about them, or anything else, till he could telegraph me, when I would go down and decide with him (Mr. Niles) what course of action to adopt.

On May twelfth my mother had given a talk about Emily in the parlors of the First Church of Northampton, seven miles distant across the Hadley meadows. It aroused so much interest that she was asked to repeat it in Amherst on June second.

The popularity of these talks must have been coming pretty close to Miss Vinnie. Once I asked my mother if she was not jealous of them. These are the exact words of her reply:

It never occurred to me at the time that Vinnie was jealous of my talks. It might have had some effect—why [after a pause] no! She was quite interested that I went to these places. It added to her income of course. It sold the books. It is barely possible she was jealous, but she didn't let me know that.

On May 24, 1892, the diary says:

Wrote on the E.D. letters to Mrs. Strong, all the morning. . . .
Went to see Vinnie a minute at six. She is edgy about everything
—Gardner Fuller, the letters, that I don't come over enough, that
she never sees Austin, that her garden isn't attended to every
minute, that she doesn't want a "Year Book" & a dozen other
woes. It is very funny.

The Amherst talk was given in Walker Hall, one of the college buildings, President Merrill Edwards Gates introducing the
speaker. One hundred and ten people were present. The occasion
was a great success, and enthusiasm waxed high. An account of
it appeared in *The Critic*, June 11, 1892.

The effect on the local community is described in the following
letter:

Amherst College Library
Amherst, Mass.

W. I. Fletcher, Librarian   *June 3, 1892*

DEAR MRS TODD:

I couldn't attempt my expression to you of my feelings at the
close of your lecture yesterday, for under such circumstances it is
always difficult to avoid the hackneyed "praise" that is "as mere
as blame."

But I cannot let the occasion slip far into the past without
thanking you for the treat you gave us, and (which I fancy is
worth more to you than thanks or praise for yourself) expressing
the immensely increased appreciation of Emily Dickinson which
I brought away.

I had hardly thought of it before, but now I see that her
peculiar life so far from being incongruous or strange, was one
of the most simple, natural, congruous lives that were ever lived.
I profess great respect for the "conventionalities" in so far as they
embody the historic consciousness of mankind as to what is
seemly and even necessary for us poor mortals who have a "place
to fill" among our fellows. But I think nothing could be more
grateful to my sensibilities than the daring naturalness which
you so truthfully defend from the charge of irreverence. My own
thought of nature and of the charm of this world, in almost any

of its many phases of beauty, was certainly expressed, while it was also emancipated, by her bold assertion of the superfluousness of a better world. Of course this is from the Paradisiacal point of view. The tremendous "ifs" which she prefixed to the idea of the *sufficiency* of this world ought to be enough for pessimism to claim.

Mr Stedman has lately been trying to define poetry. It is a hard task. Emily Dickinson wrote poetry which embalmed and interpreted the most insignificant things in nature. J. Whitcomb Riley writes

> Without, beneath the rosebush stands
> A dripping rooster on one leg.

I suppose this is also poetry (it rhymes [i. e. his verses do] better than your friend's) but it merely helps us see the *things* without doing much to help us see *into* them.

Sincerely yours,
W. I. FLETCHER

By June, results of the long search for Emily's letters were at last beginning to show. They were pouring in. My mother copied them as they arrived. She describes the way in which the valentines sent by Emily in her early youth to "Mr. Bowdoin" came to be discovered.[5]

Anna M. Kellogg was the distinguished and brilliant sister of Rufus B. Kellogg, banker, of Green Bay, Wisconsin, a graduate of the college in 1858, the first trustee to be elected by the alumni (1875), and donor of the still active Kellogg prizes for public speaking. She had a famous school for young ladies in Paris as well as one in Washington. She was a splendid looking woman and carried things with a high hand. After the death of her brother she became afflicted with melancholia. She used to come and stay at the Amherst House.

Miss Kellogg sent the valentines to Miss Vinnie with an accompanying note.

[5] *Letters*, 1931, pp. 136-138.

June 16th '92

DEAR FRIEND—

More than a year ago our old & mutual friend Mr Bowdoin passed into my keeping the enclosed mementoes of your gifted sister, written in her early days—when she was full of "fun" & "tease." I should have sent them to you long ago, but forgot them in my great sorrow & bereavement.

Sorrowfully yours,
ANNA M. KELLOGG

Most of the summer and early fall of 1892 was given to copying and editing Emily's letters to her brother Austin when he was at the Harvard Law School. He kept finding more and more of them and it was necessary to read them all, in microscopic writing, in order to select passages for the forthcoming book.

Miss Vinnie was controlling her patience with greater and greater difficulty. The copying took too long. Failing to receive a July check from Roberts Brothers, she wrote to Mr. Niles on August tenth in her customary direct manner: "As I did not hear from you in 'July' as was last years custom I venture to ask if the *sale* of 'Emily's poems' ceased with *January*. Pardon my intrusion." The subtlety of the suggestion produced immediate results. Her next letter, written five days later, thanks Mr. Niles for a check for $159.36, explaining that "I was not in the least haste for the *finance* but feared a letter from you might have missed me & I seem uncourteous by silence." She adds in a postscript, "I am collecting remarkable letters written by 'Emily.'"

Throughout the fall my mother devoted a good deal of time to keeping the scrapbooks of clippings up to date. But by the end of October she had settled down to pretty steady work on the letters, as her diary shows. The very early group written to "Dear Abiah" beginning in February, 1845, when Emily was only fourteen, proved quite troublesome.

November 1, 1892

Wrote nearly all day on those letters of E.D. to Mrs. Strong. Some are bright & interesting, but they are immensely *wordy*— one letter often uses fifteen pages in copying, although it is usually but three foolscap pages in the original, or rather, octavo. The writing is microscopic.

November 2

Wrote on the E.D. letters two or three hours.

November 3

At work most of the day on E.D. letters. I have finished those to Mrs. Strong, and arranged them, with much study and thought, chronologically right. The earliest are dated—the latest not at all. Worked into a very hot headache. Sun came out about one, and I took a walk. Then worked until five, and went out again, about the meadow, and near by, to clear my head for dinner.

November 4

Went to see Vinnie about one. She is rampant for the "letters" to come right out—sees no necessity for chronological arrangement, or anything, indeed, except merely copying them. She is horribly ignorant.

My mother wrote to Mrs. Strong asking her many questions about dates and so on. Her replies suggest the kind of detective work required for obtaining any definite information.

> Pittsfield, Mass.
> *Nov.* 9, 1892

MY DEAR MRS TODD

Your letter was forwarded to me from Westfield and is just received.

I think that in the chapter devoted to my letters from Emily Dickinson, I prefer to have my initials used as you suggest— "Letters to Mrs. A.P.S."—and having them begin only "Dear A"

As to the dates of the letters I think you will find *somewhere* on each one of them, the year, written by me.

Those sent to me in Philadelphia were written after Jan 1st and before the middle of June, 1852.

I could not fix the dates of the other letters without looking them over, and I will do that if you will send them to me.

My impression is, that you *will* find a date, i.e. the year, somewhere in those letters for I remember thinking that it was important for you to know as nearly as possible when they were written.

You may keep the letters through the winter as you desire. I have no doubt that they will be preserved, as you say, with "scrupulous care." You need not hesitate to send me the letters you refer to, if you find no date upon them. If you send them this week you may address me *Care of Rev. Edward Strong, D.D., Pittsfield, Mass.* I will do what I can to fix upon the time they were written. I await with interest the book you are preparing, and wish you success in this effort to secure a continuous record of her experiences in her own words.

Very Sincerely Yours,
A. P. STRONG

Pittsfield
11 *November* 1892

MY DEAR MRS TODD

The letters are just received and I see I am mistaken—it was my own name that I wrote upon them, instead of the dates.

The one marked "15" was written late in August 1851.

The one marked "18" was written late in 1850 or very early in 1851. It was after the death of Mr Humphrey and I think he died in the Autumn of 1850.

The one marked "19" was written as you suppose after 1850. I am not sure whether it was in 1851 or 1853. The "Susie" to whose illness she refers was Miss Gilbert, now Mrs Austin Dickinson, and the illness was so serious I think Miss Dickinson will recall their anxiety for her and can perhaps remember the year. I may be mistaken in my impression, but I think it was written after midsummer in '51 or '52 or '53.

If you can learn the precise time in the way I have suggested, please write the date upon the letters and oblige

Yours very sincerely
ABIAH P. STRONG

After several journeys back and forth, Emily's letters were finally returned to Mrs. Strong six months later.

Westfield
May 30, '93

MY DEAR MRS TODD

I wish I felt sure of the word you could not 'translate' in No 17 of Emily Dickinson's letters.

I have hesitated between *straw* and *show*. The word looks more like straw—(she sometimes failed to cross the *t* by a separate stroke of the pen) but the vivid coloring of the Dandelion made me uncertain.

I am very sorry that I cannot help you to just the word.

I learn from the ladies that I missed a great deal in not hearing your reminiscences of Japan. They enjoyed them very much.

The letters came 'in good condition.' I should have ackowledged the receipt at once, if they had not been registered and I knew you would have a card from the P.O. I waited to make out the word if possible.

Hoping there may be no more hard words as you go on with the letters, and with every good wish

Very sincerely
Abiah P. Strong

We were still devoting much time [my mother told me] to trying to find the quantities of letters which Lavinia was sure Emily had written to Mrs. Helen Hunt Jackson. But, except for the fragment printed in *Letters*, 1894, the long search was without avail.[6]

In acknowledgment of a royalty check for $196.24, in January, 1893, Lavinia wrote to the publishers:

My Dear Mr Niles

Thank you for todays check & all your interest in "Emilies poems." I hope her *letters* will be arranged for print before very long. I'm sure you will be interested in the volume.

I'm sorry none written to Mrs Jackson can be found. Has "Gardner Fuller" appeared on the surface again?

Thanking you once more for all your courtesy

I am

Heartily
Lavinia Dickinson

Amherst
January 30th '93

After months of silence the thought of Gardner Fuller still rankled.

[6] *Letters*, 1931, pp. 413-414.

CHAPTER XII

From the Wings

> *Crumbling is not an instant's act,*
> *A fundamental pause;*
> *Dilapidation's processes*
> *Are organized decays.*
>
> *'Tis first a cobweb on the soul,*
> *A cuticle of dust,*
> *A borer in the axis,*
> *An elemental rust.*
>
> *Ruin is formal, devil's work,*
> *Consecutive and slow.*
> *Fail in an instant no man did,*
> *Slipping is crash's law.*

As I have been reading these documents—letters, journals, and diaries—I have tried to understand Miss Vinnie. Perhaps it should be repeated that this story, in so far as personal relationships are concerned, has been as great a revelation to me as to the reader. But certain facts are now plain, certain conclusions inescapable. I will try to retrace the steps by which they have been reached.

It began to dawn upon me little by little that Miss Vinnie's attitude toward my mother was changing. As I read, I sensed disloyalty—a stealthy lurking thing, showing itself by inadvertence —as early as 1891. At first it seemed to me so contemptible that I turned away in disgust and decided to give up trying to write this story. But I could not leave it there. I had to go on. If I did not try to understand, I whose life has been molded by Dickinsons, who else could be expected to do so?

The basic fact was Lavinia's adoration of Emily. "Her feeling," to use Stevenson's words, "partook of the loyalty of a clansman, the hero worship of a maiden aunt and the idolatry due to a god."

Now what was happening? Here was my mother, a young woman of undeniable magnetism and personal charm—a fact, by the way, which did not help to gain from Lavinia appreciation of services rendered—to whom people were turning more and more for information about Emily, information which Lavinia felt she alone had the right to impart. As long as my mother confined herself to copying poems and doing errands for her in Boston, she was enthusiastic in expressions of her devotion. But now that my mother was becoming an authority, to be consulted when questions concerning Emily required answers, it was different. Others might work for Emily, but she, Lavinia, was the sole proprietor when rewards of whatever nature were concerned. For Emily belonged to her. She felt that she had conferred a favor on my mother as well as on Colonel Higginson by allowing them to edit Emily's manuscripts. For that privilege they were indebted to her. In doing the work they were only parts of the machinery, automatons, and should so consider themselves. Lavinia took it for granted that the manuscripts would be handled with intelligence and discrimination, but there the editors' responsibility ended. They must hold themselves aloof from identifying themselves with their work. For anyone but herself, or Austin, to feel pride in Emily's achievements was presumptuous in the extreme, another clear case of "larceny." In her journal my mother exclaims with bewilderment, "Vinnie seems to think that the poems could have published themselves without aid from me!"

In consequence of this attitude Lavinia, while accepting an indispensable service, ignored the existence of any obligation on her own part and resented the recognition of it by others. Most of all, she resented my mother's talks. It was not so much that she objected to the "$10 and expenses" which my mother sometimes received for her lectures about Emily (not always, however, by any means, for many of them were given without pay),[1] but

[1] Talks on Emily Dickinson given by Mrs. Todd:

1891

Apr. 1	Mrs. D. Holland's, Springfield, Mass.	$10 and expenses
May 2	College Alumnae Club, Boston, Mass.	$10 and expenses
Sept. 6	"Hillside," Wyoming, N.Y.	Nothing
Dec. 1	Mrs. D. L. Gillett's, Westfield, Mass.	$10 and expenses

that my mother was somehow or other capitalizing some aspect of Emily—some emanation which she, Lavinia, could neither reach nor control. It reminds one of the hoarding by a savage

---

1892

Feb. 13	The Kensington, Boston, Mass.	$15
Mar. 18	Mrs. MacCord's, Bridgeport, Conn.	$10
Mar. 23	Mrs. Stanley's, New Britain, Conn.	$10 and expenses
May 12	The First Church, Northampton, Mass.	$10 and expenses
June 2	Amherst College, Amherst, Mass.	$10

1893

Feb. 15	Congregational Church, New London, Conn.	$15 and expenses
July 31	Mrs. L. A. Coonley's, Chicago, Ill.	Nothing

1894

Feb. 16	Mrs. D. P. Clapp's, Brooklyn, N.Y.	Nothing
Feb. 21	Mrs. W. C. Spellman's, Brooklyn, N.Y.	Nothing
Mar. 7	Amherst Woman's Club, Amherst, Mass.	Nothing
Apr. 11	Mrs. C. E. Prentiss', Brooklyn, N.Y.	Nothing
Apr. 14	Vassar Students' Aid, Brooklyn, N.Y.	$10 and expenses
Apr. 16	Mrs. Blanche Wilder Bellamy's, Brooklyn, N.Y.	Nothing

1895

Jan. 23	Memorial Hall, Worcester, Mass.	$10
Feb. 4	Unity Art Club, Boston, Mass.	Nothing
Mar. 20	Starr Club, Lynn, Mass.	$10
Apr. 26	Mrs. Lawrence's, Fitchburg, Mass.	$13.50
May 28	Woman's Club, Sunderland, Mass.	$13
Nov. 20	Miss Silsbee's, Salem, Mass.	$16
Dec. 10	Normal School, Salem, Mass.	$20

1896

May 22	President Dole's [Sanford B. Dole, President, Republic of Hawaii, 1896], Honolulu	Nothing

1898

Mar. 24	Mrs. M. W. Sewall's, Indianapolis, Ind.	Nothing
Nov. 19	University of Chicago, Chicago, Ill.	$25

The total amount received by Mrs. Todd for her talks about Emily Dickinson up to and including the talk at the University of Chicago on Nov. 19, 1898, was $217.50. For several years after that date she gave no more talks on the subject. From 1905 until her death in 1932 she gave seventeen lectures about Emily, all of them without compensation except for the one at Mount Holyoke College, Nov. 8, 1930, at the celebration of the hundredth anniversary of Emily's birth. For that lecture she received $50.

of the clipped hair or fingernails of his nearest dead relative. As no one had approached Emily in life except by way of her, so this new life, which was Emily in almost as real a sense, this was now to be touched only when and as she, Lavinia, wished. "Jealousy" is too simple a word to apply to her feelings.

To put it differently: there was no question that Emily was coming into her own. But to her sister's mind the intermediary in the process was a menial. So long as her activities remained impersonal, all was well. Accepting any reflected glory, however, was taking a liberty, presuming on a relationship to which no one but herself was entitled. Vulgarly speaking, my mother seemed to be cashing in on Emily in so far as reputation was concerned, and Lavinia's resentment smoldered hot.

Of course Colonel Higginson was benefiting also, in a way. But Lavinia did not know him well. She did not see him every day. She did not hear about the fame with which Emily was endowing him. Besides, he was a personage, one moreover to whom Emily herself had turned for guidance. That alone invested him with a right to share, if only a little, in the glory which association with her name conferred.

I must say I have a good deal of sympathy for Lavinia's attitude as far as glory is concerned. But after all, the expenditure of years of hard work involving literary sensitivity and skill did deserve acknowledgment as well as financial compensation. In her youthful strength and buoyancy my mother continued to go right ahead with the work, unaware of the rancor eating into Lavinia's soul.

> Not to discover weakness is
> The mystery of strength,

as Emily said. To the end of my mother's life she was bewildered by Lavinia's behavior and at a loss to ascribe motives for it. She never understood why she should in all sorts of secret ways have sought to undermine her, her best friend, the one who had given years of her life to the "magnification" of Emily and to the satisfying of her sister's ambition. And this, my mother's point of view, was the one from which I started when, after her death, I set out to try to comprehend Miss Vinnie's behavior.

There was in 1893 yet another thing which exasperated Miss Vinnie. My mother was giving part of her time to writing a book on astronomy in spite of the fact that she must very well know that bringing out Emily's letters was the only matter of importance. This division of interests on the part of my parents I took for granted as pertaining to the essential puzzle of the universe. To Miss Vinnie, states of mystification doubtless meant as little as the necessity for writing books on astronomy. I trust that in this connection a brief digression into my own childhood may not seem too remote from the course of events.

For me as a child two things were always unconsciously linked together—astronomy and Emily Dickinson. As early as I can remember I knew that they belonged. The association was inherent in all the activities of our household. Sometimes my father's astronomical research was subordinated to the reading of Emily's proof; sometimes my mother left her editing of manuscripts long enough to help with the preparation of an astronomical treatise. My father was well known as an observer of total eclipses of the sun, having already at the age of thirty-five had charge of three expeditions financed by the Government of the United States to observe the phenomenon—in Dallas, Texas, July 29, 1878; in Shirakawa, Japan, August 19, 1887; and in Angola, Portuguese West Africa, December 22, 1889.

In the fall of 1892 a book about eclipses on which he was working was turned over to my mother to rewrite in popular style. After she had finished, he decided that it was her book, not his any longer, although the material for it had been prepared by him. That is how *Total Eclipses of the Sun*, by Mabel Loomis Todd, in its William Morris cover, came to be published by Roberts Brothers in 1894. For many years it was the standard work on the subject.

To me, as a child, just how Emily's "Tyrian light" was connected with being roused from sound sleep to help thaw out my father's hands when he came down from the observatory on a bitter cold night I did not try to analyze. Emily was of course curious about things celestial from "the cube of the rainbow" to "Mercury's affair." She watched the sun from early morning when the day sprang before the hills like "hindered rubies" or "breadths of topaz," to sunset when "the juggler of day," "blazing in gold and quenching in purple," "kissed her bonnet to the meadow" and was gone. But to a sedate, astronomically orthodox child the poem beginning

> Arcturus is his other name,
> I'd rather call him star!

was vaguely disquieting, particularly the stanza beginning

> What if the poles should frisk about
> And stand upon their heads!

Taking liberties with God was one thing. But to chuck the cosmos under the chin was quite another. Of course Emily was doing neither. It was merely that God, the cosmos, and Emily were one. She has told us that.

> Nature and God I neither knew,
> Yet both so well knew me
> They startled, like executors
> Of my identity.[2]

The two poles of my existence—the starry universe and Emily Dickinson's poetry—remained fixed. As was my habit, I lived with the apparently unrelated facts in silence and never asked a question. It must have been difficult, at times, keeping my balance. But as I look back upon it now, it seems as if I accepted it all as passively as a tree takes the rain.

[2] In *Letters*, 1931, p. 201, the last line reads, "Of an identity."

CHAPTER XIII

Doubts and Difficulties

> *Somewhat to hope for,*
> *Be it ne'er so far,*
> *Is capital against*
>   *Despair.*
>
> *Somewhat to suffer,*
> *Be it ne'er so keen,*
> *If terminable, may*
>   *Be borne.*

IN THE spring of 1893 my mother's two interests, eclipses of
the sun and Emily Dickinson, were struggling for ascendancy.
On her return to Amherst after giving a talk about Emily in New
London, Connecticut, on February fifteenth, she found a letter
from Mr. Niles requesting the manuscript of her book on total
eclipses "in a week or two at farthest." This she accepted as an
emergency summons and applied herself to the task of finishing
it in a frenzy of work which was to last, however, not two weeks
but nearly two months.

Although by late spring work upon the letters had been resumed, the solar corona in abeyance, Lavinia's impatience was
getting out of hand. The delay had worked havoc. Tenseness was
increasing—sinews stiffening.

Even the elements collaborated to heighten the strain. On the
night of May third a severe storm, "wind and rain increasing to a
gale," filled Lavinia with terror. The diary refers to it:

We were all up from four to five this morning—a great hurricane. Water beating in at every east window and some north
ones. The Marshs' east bay window splintered with a crash, and
their fence blew down. Our storm porch fell flat and we hear of
great prostrate elms up town. It sounds like a storm at sea. It is
perfectly wild.

Pouring all day. I worked with David hard. Short call in the evening . . . from Vinnie. She and Maggie thought the end of the world was coming last night, and sat up in a dark passageway for hours.

Lavinia's nerves were stretched to the snapping point—what Emily called "the glittering retinue of nerves" in one of the greatest of her unpublished poems. Lavinia had to find an outlet somewhere. First, she turned toward Boston.

On the fourteenth of May my mother received a letter from Colonel Higginson enclosing one from Lavinia which he did not understand. She seemed to be trying to persuade *him* to finish the book of letters, he thought, and to get it out at once.

Lavinia's letter was returned to Colonel Higginson as he requested and has not been preserved, but the drift of it can be inferred from what it prompted him to write to my mother:

Cambridge
May 13, 1893

DEAR FRIEND

I have been wishing to see you (not that this is anything exceptional or unusual) to ask you if you did not wish for Emily Dickinson's other letters to me, to look over. Now comes this from Miss Lavinia, about which I must consult you, before answering it. I had expected to leave the letters entirely to you & at any rate the *work* of them & the profit, if any—hoping that you would agree with Miss L. to put this last on a business basis, as was not the case with her. I did not see why you should not have the whole profit of the book, since few of the letters were to her sister; but perhaps Miss L's unworldliness might take the form of thinking them all hers.

I do not now wish to do any of the editing or to read the proofs; but if *you* think that my name would help the book or that Miss L. should be indulged, I would do whatever you think best about it. Perhaps it might be well to put in my Atlantic paper just as it was, by way of *setting* for those particular letters —or did you mean to print them without the setting? If the article were reprinted, that might justify the use of my name as co-editor. But please understand that I had not thought of doing this & should not now think of it except to please Miss L. *So tell me precisely how it stands in your mind*—or better still, tell me when you come to Boston (or Cambridge) & let us talk it over.

Ever cordially

T. W. HIGGINSON

Please return the letter.

Of course if my name were used, I should expect some small share in the profits, though it might be very small,—otherwise not.

Two days after receiving this letter my mother went to Boston. She explained the situation to Colonel Higginson—that the book on eclipses had had to be finished before work on the letters could be resumed and that the consequent delay was responsible for Lavinia's mounting impatience. As a result, he refused to "indulge" Lavinia and work went on as before.

Why did Lavinia turn to Colonel Higginson at this time? The answer is simple. There was nowhere else to turn. For Sue, who had always pretended to understand Emily better than anyone else—an impertinence for which among other things Lavinia could not forgive her—was by this time alienated once and for all. Lavinia had contempt for her pretentiousness. She feared her, too, because of her ingenious cruelties. One could never tell what to expect—what Sue might say or do next. To ask her help would have been unthinkable. It would not be too much to say that, rather than do so, Lavinia would have preferred to let the book go, to allow the editing of Emily's manuscripts to remain unfinished—an impasse actually arrived at later on as we shall see.

From the few allusions to Austin's wife made thus far, the reader may not have gained a very clear impression of her. It is not for me to dissect Sue's character, but her relationship to Emily is an essential part of our story. In view of their fundamentally opposite attitudes toward life, the lifelong intimacy depicted by Sue's daughter is hard to believe.

Sue was a product of the Connecticut Valley. Her father, Thomas Gilbert, presided successively over hostelries in Greenfield, in Deerfield, and for a few years in Amherst where, in 1832, he leased The Mansion House, a tavern and livery-stable not far from the Dickinson property. For the next five years he and his family lived in Amherst where his convivial habits were well known. Sue, the youngest of his seven children, thus spent her early childhood in Amherst. She was still a child at the time of his death, December 23, 1841. Thereafter she divided her time between her aunt, Mrs. William A. Van Vranken, of Geneva, New York, her mother's younger sister, and her own sister Harriet who, a few months after their father's death, had married William Cutler of Amherst. At the time of Sue's marriage to Austin Dickinson, July 1, 1856, presumably in the Van Vranken home, for she was married in Geneva, her residence was recorded as Greenfield, Massachusetts.

As a girl Sue had a lush personality which charmed Emily and Vinnie. They were enthusiastic over her marriage to their brother, deluging her with expressions of affection. But not long after her marriage to the catch of the town she began to take on the airs of a great lady, or, in local parlance, to "put on the lugs." She assumed an attitude of lofty aloofness scarcely deigning, as she drove about town in her barouche, to acknowledge the greetings of her former schoolmates. As pretense and pose came to be her most noticeable characteristics, it is difficult to see how the girlhood intimacy with Emily, the cornerstone of whose life was love of truth, could long endure. However that may be, it was not many years before Emily could write

> That distance was between us
> That is not of mile or main;
> The will it is that situates,
> Equator never can.

Emily grieved. For of all her friends Sue had the liveliest mind—one which gave promise of real and lasting companionship and understanding. But she seemed to care only for appearances. While Emily was plumbing the depths of creation, Sue next door was "busy with scintillation" at the expense of her friends. As these traits gradually solidified, the gulf between them must have widened, straining loyalty at times until it almost snapped—but not quite. For as Emily wrote to Sue, "The tie between us is very fine, but a hair never dissolves."

Emily summed up an estrangement in five compact stanzas. So apt is the poem that I quote it all.

Now I knew I lost her—
Not that she was gone,
But remoteness travelled
On her face and tongue.

Alien, though adjoining,
As a foreign race,
Traversed she though pausing
Latitudeless place.

Elements unaltered,
Universe the same,
But love's transmigration—
Somehow this had come.

Henceforth to remember
Nature took the day
I had paid so much for.
His is penury

Not who toils for freedom
Or for family,
But the restitution
Of idolatry.

It was on my mother's May visit to Boston that the question of a contract for the forthcoming volume was first discussed. Colonel Higginson, Mr. Dickinson, and my father all agreed that the earlier arrangement by which my mother did all the work and Miss Vinnie received all the profits should be handled differently this time. That she thought otherwise is not surprising. An extra check received in May from Roberts Brothers quieted her for the moment—but not for long. In her letter of May twenty-seventh to Mr. Niles acknowledging the check she continues in another vein.

My Dear Mr Niles
   Thank you for my unexpected wealth! I realize "Emilys" mind is in honest & honorable hands & I'm deeply grateful.
   I hoped to have been in Boston in May as I was anxious to see you but I have been detained at home.
   I suppose Mrs Todd is arranging "Emilys" letters. It has been a great pleasure to collect these letters, all of them possessed by our mutual friends. The correspondence concerning these letters has been interesting & almost brought Emily back to me.
   Thanking you again for all your courtesy I am

                                        Heartily
                                   Lavinia Dickinson

Amherst
May 27th '93

My mother explained that "Vinnie wished to give Mr. Niles the impression that all the letters had been collected by her." Colonel Higginson in turn tried to make it clear to Mr. Niles that most of the letters had been given by their recipients to Mrs. Todd for use in the book. In any event, he said, they did not belong to Miss Lavinia as she imagined. Mr. Higginson thought the royalties should be shared. That she disapproved of his suggestions is implied in his next letter to Mrs. Todd written a day or two later.

Cambridge, Mass.
May 30, 1893

DEAR FRIEND

I have a letter of eight pp. from Miss D. and do not think that I hv. done the least good or ought to interfere any farther. She says nothing unkind of you, but says that nothing would induce her to "give the copyright of Emily's mind to any one but" herself & that *she* collected all the letters that will be contained in the volume "save one package."

She says that *she* selected every poem in the 2d vol. which certainly does not accord with my remembrance. And that she left the compensation for you entirely to her brother & supposed you satisfied.

It would hardly be fair to send you her letter, without authority, but the above are the essential points. It was postmarked yesterday.

Ever cordially
T. W. HIGGINSON

Always generous and kindly, Colonel Higginson had done his best to smooth ruffled feathers but, failing, now turned his attention to other things. First, he got out all the letters he had ever received from Emily.

[*To Mrs. Todd*]

The Round Table
June 7, 1893

DEAR FRIEND

I have selected a dozen or more letters, besides those printed in the Atlantic, but must sift them a little, before sending to you. Should you be in these parts let me know. I should be glad of celestial phenomena that might make your presence at the Observatory essential. We go away about June 16.

Ever affectionately
T. W. HIGGINSON

My mother replied, asking to see all the letters. He responded by sending them.

[*To Mrs. Todd*]

25 Buckingham Street
Cambridge, Mass.
June 10, 1893

DEAR FRIEND

Here are the MSS and printed letters, arranged as best I can in date. If you think there are too many, leave out some. I hate to have you copy so many.

Cordially and affectionately
T.W.H.

I am perfectly willing to have you print these as they are, after copying; & you can have proof of that chapter sent me at Dublin, N.H. We expect to go on Friday.

A few more letters were exchanged between them during the next month.

[*To Mrs. Todd*]

Cambridge
June 11, 1893

DEAR FRIEND

. . . . Could you not have your Boston function on Wednesday evening & come out here Thursday A.M.? I am sure my "copy" will offer conundrums for us. I mailed it this morning.

Yrs. as ever,
T. W. HIGGINSON

Glimpsewood
Dublin, N.H.
June 21, 1893

DEAR FRIEND

I was disappointed at not seeing you again, though I hardly expected it. Will my arrangement of E.D.'s letters do? Criticize freely.

Where are you to be this summer?

Ever cordially
T. W. HIGGINSON

Glimpsewood
Dublin, N.H.
July 9, 1893

DEAR FRIEND

I don't like not to know more about you & the book too. Do you think my chapter will go in as it is, or do you wish for change; & will you send me proofs? I wish you were coming up here, as your sister astronomeress, Mrs. Pickering, did last year. I am sure there is plenty to consult about. Shall you be in Amherst?

Ever cordially
T. W. HIGGINSON

A question which had been baffling them all for some time—editor, publisher, brother, and sister—was the matter of a picture for the book of letters. How was a satisfactory likeness of Emily Dickinson to be contrived? "I had no portrait, now," she wrote Colonel Higginson. "It often alarms father. He says death might occur, and he has molds of all the rest, but has no mold of me."[1]

This statement was not, however, strictly true. There was, first, a painting of the three Dickinson children—Austin, Emily, and Lavinia—at an early age. It had been painted by an itinerant artist—a "limner" so-called—who came to the house, and it bears striking resemblance to portraits of other children at about the same time. It was in reality more the artist's idea of what children should look like than a portrait of the three little Dickinsons—"a generic portrait of child about 1840," someone has called it. (Plate XIII.)

There was also the now well-known daguerreotype (Plate XV) of Emily at eighteen, first published by my mother in 1931. In 1893, it belonged to Maggie Maher, Miss Vinnie's servant. It was unsatisfactory to both Austin and Lavinia. It was too solemn, too heavy. It had none of the play of light and shade in Emily's face, they thought. To capture the flow of movement and grace in a single photograph of the dance is no more difficult than it was to produce by any means then known a

[1] *Letters*, 1931, p. 276.

satisfactory likeness of Emily Dickinson. Many devices have been used at different times to attain the desired end, all equally unsuccessful. The earliest attempt was in 1893 (Plate XII).

The first mention of the subject occurs in the diary on April second:

The cabinet photograph of Emily taken from Maggie's daguerreotype is dreadful—the original is far better. Vinnie is wildly impatient for the volume of letters. At present a solar corona is in the foreground.

Miss Vinnie wrote to Mr. Niles the following day:

April 3rd [1893]

MY DEAR MR NILES

I can not report any thing very favorable about Emily's picture quite yet but I hope a likeness may be secured by the suggestion of a child portrait & the picture at sixteen [eighteen]. You would not be interested in either (as they are) for your purpose.

Emily had a most interesting & startling face but neither of these pictures represent her truthfully. How early would the likeness be required for the double volume? I have not thought to ask Mrs. Todd *what* month in the Fall you prefer to print "the letters" or how early you would like them. They are collected and mostly copied I suppose.

I expect "the letters" will attract even more interest than the poems, for there is such a wide spread desire to read them. Where is "Gardner Fuller"?

Sincerely
LAVINIA DICKINSON

In reply to another letter from Mr. Niles about the picture, one in which he also asked Miss Vinnie whether she approved of his idea of combining the *Poems*—first and second series—binding them together in a single volume,[2] she wrote:

[2] The volume containing both series of poems, published in 1893, had a cover similar to that of the first edition of the first volume, a curious choice in view of Mr. Niles's objection to it. (See his letter of Dec. 15, 1890, p. 80.)

[*May* 1893]

My Dear Mr Niles

Combining the *two* volumes pleases me but a *portrait* of Emily will not be so easy I fear, though I shall try for it with all my might. The only picture of Emily was taken when she was 16 [18]. It is possible a genious with crayon might create a likeness, with the help of this early picture & family suggestions—can *you* mention a skillful artist?

Mrs Todd has been so busy with her own work that I have hardly seen her this winter but after her last visit in Boston she told me you thought Fall better than spring to present "the letters" so I hope nothing will prevent this plan.

I'm very anxious "Emilys letters" should be published while *she* is so fresh in the interest of the world. I presume only *one* volume will be printed *this* Fall.

I'm sure you will be charmed with these letters.

Heartily
Lavinia Dickinson

For several weeks they went on trying to concoct an acceptable picture. First, they sent the daguerreotype already mentioned to Mr. Niles together with another daguerreotype of a cousin whose hair was arranged as Austin and Lavinia wished to have Emily's hair arranged. The two pictures were to be combined.

Boston
July 3, 1893

Dear Mrs Todd

The artist has made a sketch of Emily Dickinson merely to shew the proposed arrangement of the hair. If this is satisfactory he will go to work on the likeness.

The hair is not puffed out so much as the hair of her cousin in the daguerreotype, but I imagine that lady had a more bountiful supply than Emily had.

Yours truly
T. Niles

The sketch (Plate XII) was not returned for ten days because, on the last day of June, my parents had left Amherst for a month in the West. The trip had two objectives; first, a visit to the

World's Columbian Exposition in Chicago where my father had charge of arranging the exhibit of Amherst College. That task accomplished, their second objective was Colorado, where they went in the hope of finding some of Emily's letters to Helen Hunt Jackson, a search long under way. Her widower was then living in Colorado Springs. During my parents' absence Miss Vinnie was obliged to possess her soul in patience, concerning herself largely with affairs of a practical nature.

> Amherst
> *July* 17ᵗʰ [1893]

MY DEAR MR NILES

I'm interested to know if the new "Copyright Act" is of *value* to American Authors & publishers. I don't quite understand it & know of no one to ask, so I take the liberty of troubling you.

Pardon my intrusion & answer at your own convenience if you please.

> Gratefully
> LAVINIA DICKINSON

Before my mother had reached a decision about the sketch sent by Mr. Niles, she received another letter from the publishers inquiring whether she had "got to the point" where she could "make up a title page for the Dickinson *Letters*." She replied from Chicago:

DEAR Mʳ NILES,

I waited before sending back this sketch of Emily Dickinson to show it to her brother, whom we expected a day or two here in Chicago. He came, and we showed it to him. He says the hair and dress are not unlike her, but he says the face has not a trace of her expression; (I see by re-reading your letter that the artist has not yet tried to get that) and hardly suggests her to him. But he says the daguerreotype itself is not like her. There is an old oil painting, done when she was a little girl, which he says is far better, and when he gets back next week he will have it photographed and send you. Perhaps with the two her real expression may be evolved.

The title-page of the "Letters" should read something like this:

Letters of
Emily Dickinson
from 1847 to 1886
Edited by Mabel Loomis Todd

The title of the picture of the old house is "Emily Dickinson's home; built by her grandfather, Samuel Fowler Dickinson, in 1813." We shall be back in Amherst about August first.

Very truly
MABEL L. TODD

620 Division Street
Chicago, Illinois
13 *July*, 1893

Mrs. Todd reached home on August fifth. On August ninth, she was again at work.

August 9
Worked on Emily's letters to Austin until six.

August 10
Worked over six hours on E's letters to Austin and finished them.

August 11
Up town for errands, and back to work all day on Emily's letters to the Norcross girls. Endless work, and no dates, & Miss Norcross has still further complicated matters by a loose way of copying, and no chronology suggested by their order. People are dreadfully slovenly.[3]

August 12
Hard work on the letters. Finished Norcross ones, and began on Clark letters. Some sentences very fine. Other parts too personal to use. [These parts, omitted in 1894, were published in

[3] On this day Lavinia wrote to Mr. Niles, the length of her letter adjusted to the size of the check just received—$46.87.

Amherst
August 11th '93

MY DEAR MR NILES
Thank you for another check.

Heartily
LAVINIA DICKINSON

the new edition of the *Letters*, 1931.] . . . Trying to fix some dates, but it is hard work.

August 15

Work on Clark letters—eliminating.

August 17

I worked on the letters to Maria Whitney.

August 18

I fixed Chapter I of the letters for the printer. . . . Worked on my proof (Ch. VII) all the afternoon, and finished arranging Ch. I of Letters.

August 19

Working on proof of Ch. VIII (Eclipses) and arranging Ch. II (Letters) for printer.

August 20

Worked four hours in the morning on the miscellaneous letters. There must be two chapters of those, one of relatives, one of general friends. I have already arranged twelve chapters, and not yet any to H.H., except one scrap. Mr. Jackson may yet find them.

August 21

Worked on letters—then up town finding more proof, and spent the rest of the morning on that, the final pages of Eclipses, Ch. VIII.

August 22

Worked all the afternoon on the letters—T.W.H. chapter.

Letters were exchanged with Mr. Niles:

Amherst,
21 *August*, 1893

DEAR Mr NILES,

The Emily Dickinson Letters are coming on bravely—I hope to be able to send you Chapters I, II and III in a few days— a week at most. It will make a most unusual book, worth coming home from Chicago and Colorado to put in shape—as I did. I find the photograph of the old oil painting of E.D. had not been made in my absence, as I expected, but I will see to it myself today. It may not help much, but we can try.

Mr Jackson, whom I saw in Colorado Springs, thinks E.D.'s letters to H.H. are still in his house, and promised me to look thoroughly, once more.

Can you tell me what poem was enclosed to you with this letter [Emily to Mr. Niles] I send you, which she refers to as a "pebble"? There was no poem with it, and I am wondering if it could be that lovely one, included in Volume II, beginning

How happy is the little stone—

Do you remember? And may I have the letter again, if you do not want it yet? Please excuse the block.

> Very truly
> MABEL LOOMIS TODD

Mr. Niles replied at once:

> Boston
> *Aug 22,* 1893

DEAR MRS TODD

I think that was the poem but I am not positive. I sent you all the poems I had & if that was one of them, it must have been.[4]

I am afraid it will be unwise to publish the new volume this year. Business is in altogether too depressed a state.

> Truly yours
> THO^s NILES

Though the decision of Mr. Niles not to publish the *Letters* in 1893 was disappointing to my mother, it did not change her course. Preparation of the book and search for more letters went on as usual. But with Miss Vinnie it was otherwise. To her the excuse of economic caution was merely a subterfuge.

The following letter was addressed to Colonel Higginson:

[4] The poem in question was indeed "How happy is the little stone." Of the six poems sent by Emily to Mr. Niles (*Letters*, 1931, pp. 406-407), that is the only one which she could have referred to as a "pebble." The others were, "A route of evanescence," "The wind begun to rock the grass," "Farther in summer than the birds," "It sifts from leaden sieves," and "Ample make this bed," all of them named by Emily with the titles under which they appeared in *Poems*, Second Series, 1891.

Amherst
23 *August*, 1893

My dear friend,

I hope you had a word from me from Chicago. Later we went to Colorado for two or three weeks. At Colorado Springs I met Mr Jackson most pleasantly. He says he is confident that Emily Dickinson's letters to his wife were never destroyed. If she did not send them to you—which he had supposed she did—then they are in his house, and he will make an absolutely thorough search, which I am devoutly hoping he is doing this month. I told him Mrs Jackson never sent them to you, or if she did they must have been lost in the mail. I hope he will find them.

I send you these two unfinished fragments, hoping you can find a beginning for the one and an ending for the other. I have copied all your original letters from E.D., but I will keep them a little longer, if I may, sending them to you at Cambridge, later. The volume is nearly ready for the printer, and I have nearly made myself ill—I work from eight to ten hours a day on it.

I hope your summer is happy and fruitful. The August light on the Pelham hills goes to my heart like wine—or unrecognized pain.

Your friend, always,
Mabel L. Todd

On the very day this letter was written, Mrs. Todd was summoned to Lynn, Massachusetts, by the death of her grandmother, Mrs. Wilder, at the age of ninety-two, after a lingering illness.

Deeply saddened by her grandmother's death, my mother returned to Amherst immediately after the funeral. Her thoughts were turning toward the past. She talked a good deal with Austin and Lavinia about the far-off days of their youth.

On August twenty-sixth she writes:

Went to Vinnie's to tea, and had an interesting talk with her & Austin on the peculiarities of their bringing up. It must have been a stiff, Puritanical and trying home. Some of Vinnie's stories were appalling—of the way they were watched and guarded for fear some young man might wish to marry one of them. It made me indignant.

Those unacquainted with New England tradition are apt to confuse the Pilgrim Fathers with the Puritans. The former had little of the uncompromising austerity of the latter. Edward Dickinson was a Puritan. Punctilious about the observance of Sunday and all religious conventions, he had at heart little Christian charity. Looking after a departing figure, he is said to have mused, "There goes another fool that thinks he can make something of himself."

Once he was persuaded to sit for his photograph. Bolt upright, his head was clamped rigidly in place from behind. His jaw was set—his eye steady. The photographer, taking a step toward him, faltered, "Squire Dickinson, could you—smile a little?" To which the Squire thundered back, "I *yam* smiling." This depicts the man—held fast by an invisible brace of iron. (Plate XI.)

My mother often referred to the indignation she felt because of the strict supervision Emily and Lavinia had been subjected to in their youth. She resented all the "sharp-edged" people. Once, while we were reading the poems aloud together, she came to the one beginning, "Before the ice is in the pools."[5] As she finished the final stanza,

> That which sings so, speaks so,
> When there's no one here—
> Will the frock I wept in
> Answer me to wear?

she looked up with tears in her eyes, exclaiming, "Oh, the poor, poor little thing!" Then she went on to tell me about those early years which Austin and Lavinia had described to her. As she spoke, I took a few notes and quote them word for word as I wrote them down.

Their mother was a meek little thing. She didn't know what to do for them. She was not important enough to be included in the family feuds. The father was terrific. If he had married a different woman, he wouldn't have been such an overbearing man. He kept the girls down in a little valley in his mind. He became quite admiring of Austin and said he would give him a house and anything he wanted if he would only stay in Amherst.

[5] *Poems*, Third Series, p. 183.

He did not like to have students come to see the girls.

Everybody was invited to the Dickinsons' Commencement reception. Emily stayed away, seated in the library. If the gay company wanted to come in there, they might see her.

Vinnie went away to school,[6] though there was no inspiration of intellect to take her. Emily did as she wanted to. She heard that Miss Lyon's was a different kind of school from any that she had been to before.

To disappear was like Emily. She was repressed, and had nothing to do with young men. Vinnie was pert and flirted if she wanted to. The father and mother would not let young men come [to the house] for fear they would marry. They [Mr. Dickinson and Austin] were men that could manage the world if they wanted to, and wouldn't have any foreigners in their family. They didn't want a strange young man in the family.

Austin always admired his father very much, but he'd bang you if anything went wrong. The father never knew fine intellectual women. He needed to know about them.

I asked a friend of Miss Vinnie's, Mary Lee Hall, what Austin's attitude toward his father was. In a letter of August 5, 1933, she replied: "Mrs. [A. B. H.] Davis was at the home when the body of Mr. Edward Dickinson was brought from the station, and after the undertaker and his assistant left, Austin leaned over his father's face, kissed his forehead and said, 'There, father, I never dared do that while you were living.' "

Emily's universal sympathy and understanding were matched by her family's equally universal contempt for humanity. The Dickinsons despised most people. They never discovered that such feelings destroy those who entertain them. From Emily they might have learned the profoundest truths. But genius is incommunicable. They lived in one world, she in another. In spite of her almost consecrated loyalty to her family, it seems nevertheless as though she winced when she thought

[6] In 1850, at the age of seventeen, Lavinia was sent to the Ipswich Female Seminary. Two considerations would seem to have determined the choice of that school. First, it was near Salem, the home of Judge Otis P. Lord, Mr. Edward Dickinson's friend. Mrs. Lord was Miss Elizabeth W. Farley of Ipswich, before her marriage on Oct. 9, 1843. Second, the school was recommended to Emily by Mary Lyon, who had been assistant to the principal, Zilpah Polly Grant, before founding Mount Holyoke Seminary in 1836.

about congenial home life. She has described "the bleakness" of her lot:

> 'Tis true they shut me in the cold,
> But then, themselves were warm
> And could not know the feeling 'twas—
> Forget it, Lord, of them!
>
> Let not my witness hinder them
> In heavenly esteem,
> No paradise could be conferred
> Through their belovéd blame.
>
> The harm they did was short, and since
> Myself who owe it do,
> Forgive them even as myself,
> Or else forgive not me.

And again:

> I was the slightest in the house,
> I took the smallest room,
> At night, my little lamp and book
> And one geranium,
>
> So stationed I could catch the mint
> That never ceased to fall,
> And just my basket—let me think—
> I'm sure that this was all.
>
> I never spoke unless addressed,
> And then 'twas brief and low,
> I could not bear to live aloud
> The racket shamed me so.
>
> And if it had not been so far
> And anyone I knew
> Were going, I had often thought
> How noteless I could die!

It might have been her father's return after an absence that was welcomed in these words:

I think the longest hour of all
Is when the cars have come
And we are waiting for the coach;
It seems as though the time,

Affronted that the joy was come,
Did block the gilded hands
And would not let the seconds by—
But slowest instant ends.

The pendulum begins to count
Like little scholars, loud,
The steps grow thicker in the hall,
The heart begins to crowd,

Then I, my timid service done,
Though service 'twas of love,
Take up my little violin
And further north remove.

An eloquent communication in the writing of the sixties suggests Emily's relationship to her father. At the top of a blank sheet of letter paper is written "Dear Father," and, at the bottom, "Emily." Nothing more.

Her family lived as remote from Emily Dickinson as though they spoke another language. Even her brother, who, my mother told me, was closer to her and understood her better than anyone else, actually thought that sensitiveness about her appearance was the reason for her retirement, that she withdrew because she knew "how plain she was." Austin was not only devoted to her; he deeply admired her, and yet misunderstanding as utter as this shows how far even he was from grasping the mainsprings of her life. Nor could Lavinia understand, "under terrific headway" as she always was with domestic duties. She knew nothing of her sister's real interests. "Emily has fed you on thin air," she once wrote to Austin.

As for Amherst, Emily met an unbroken front of blinking bewilderment wherever she turned. The community was gentle, but unresponsive. The same static incomprehension met her everywhere. This she had accepted when scarcely more than a child, living thenceforth, as she has told us, in other company.

My best acquaintances are those
With whom I spoke no word;
The stars that stated come to town
Esteemed me never rude

Although to their celestial call
I failed to make reply,
My constant reverential face
Sufficient courtesy.

My mother's diary indicates that work on the book of letters was resumed on the day following her return from Lynn.

August 27, 1893

In the evening I finished Volume II of the Emily Scrap Book, up to date.

August 28

Work on the letters awhile.

August 29

Worked all day hard on Norcross chapter of E.D. letters. Note from Col. Higginson. To tea at Vinnie's.

Mr. Higginson's "note" was a reply to my mother's letter of August twenty-third.

> Glimpsewood
> Dublin, N.H.
> *Aug. 27, 1893*

DEAR FRIEND

I have done the only thing in my power by sending to Cambridge for E.D.'s letters & then I will report to you.

H.H.'s correspondence with her was after she had gone to Colorado & so the letters were never sent me. I do not believe they were preserved; in our Newport life together [when Colonel Higginson and Mrs. Hunt were both living there], I was always under a pledge to burn all her letters to & from everyone should she die; and have no doubt she did all this before her second marriage & not without reason, for she lived in the moment & was a most hazardous correspondent. She may have transformed herself in that, as she did in everything else she could, after her second marriage, & have kept her letters.

I feel half sorry to hear that the book is so nearly ready; it will be the last, I suppose, & will not only yield the final news of E.D. but take from me a living companionship I shall miss.

> Your friend, always
> T. W. HIGGINSON

I expect to be in Chicago Sept. 17–25.

The wistful note sounded by Mr. Higginson was echoed in another direction, though this was a note not so much of calm regret as of tremulous apprehension. I have in mind the Norcross "girls" of Concord, Massachusetts. One wonders of what they were afraid, inasmuch as they not only had deleted from Emily's letters all passages bordering on what they called "the intimate" but had never allowed anyone even to see them.

For the benefit of those who are not in our tradition it is well to repeat that the bashful attitude characteristic of these sisters was not thought strange. Indeed, diffidence was considered such good form that those to whom it did not come naturally would sometimes assume it.

I asked my mother what the "little cousins" were like. These are the emphatic words of her reply, jotted down as she spoke:

They had the most intimate letters from Emily, but they wouldn't let anybody put their eyes on them. They copied them all. They would not send the originals. They made up their minds to destroy all they had of Emily's [which they did]. They thought that they were the great patrons of Emily, but they were nothing of the kind. Louisa pretended to be a reticent person, out of the world like Emily. They adored her like a god. Vinnie wasn't devoted to the Norcrosses. They were such geese.

Had the Norcross sisters been of a different temperament, had they been willing to have their letters from Emily published, complete, as she wrote them, the correspondence might have settled many a question to which now we shall never know the answer.

A letter from Miss Fanny follows:

Concord, *Aug* 21, 1893

MY DEAR MRS. TODD

Is it possible that Emily's letters are so nearly ready for the public. I am glad and yet it makes me shudder.

The date of the letter containing the poem you speak of must be 1873. It is in pencil, so after the trouble with her eyes. It was when my uncle her father was in the legislature, and in the fall of the year, and the letter speaks of sending a plant to us by him "the legislator." My mother died in 1860 (April) and the death of my uncle's wife Mira was in 1861 or 1862 probably the latter. Of course, I can get the year *exactly* from my cousin if you need it. I think we have nothing from my cousin earlier than 1859. I think you have a letter in which she speaks of my mother's delicate health & of Vinnie being with us at that time, that may have been 1858, but probably some time in the winter of 1859.

It is most unfortunate that so many of the letters can not be dated excepting approximately. I am most impatient to know how the letters have been arranged and how many are to be published—and all about it, but I must not bother you with questions, for you must have enough work for all your spare time in this direction.

If I can be of any further service to you please tell me.

Yours sincerely
Fanny L. Norcross

The photograph of the oil painting (Plate XIII) of the three Dickinson children, first promised in July, was finally dispatched to the publishers two months later with this letter:

Dear Mr Niles:

I send you with this a photograph of an old oil painting of Emily Dickinson, taken in a group with her brother and sister, when she was perhaps seven or eight years old. You will see that the proof of this photograph—in the yellow envelope—is a good deal softer and prettier, on its own dark background, than in the finished one where the background has been taken away. Shall I have any attempt made by the photographer here to preserve the dark background and yet dispense with the oval around it—or can some artist touch it up better in Boston?

The little picture is so pretty that I think it would be well to put it in the volume of Letters as it is, and then see what can be done with the later daguerreotype by itself. I send also three letters, written by E.D. at three distinct stages of her penmanship, which I think will be interesting to all readers, in facsimile. The first is to Mrs J. G. Holland, the second to Mr Samuel Bowles, and the third to Mr Clark, a friend in Brooklyn. I have indicated on each what part should be reproduced. Please have the engraver treat the originals as carefully as possible, for they must be returned to their owners.

I have not heard yet from Mr Jackson as to that bundle of letters to H.H. which he felt pretty sure were in this house, but I expect a letter in a few days. Otherwise the MS of the "Letters" volume is all ready—at any time—to show you.

Very truly
MABEL L. TODD

Amherst
13 *September*, 1893

The expected letter came a few days later from Mr. Jackson's second wife, the niece of "H.H.," and reads as follows in so far as it is pertinent:

Colorado Springs
Colorado
Sept. 16, 1893

MY DEAR MRS TODD:
In the press of business and of getting his little family settled my husband has neglected to answer your note. I am just as sorry as you are that the correspondence between Emily Dickinson and my Aunt Helen cannot be found. I have given the trunks, containing many old, interesting letters, a thorough search and fail to discover what you so earnestly request. . . .

Sincerely yours,
HELEN BANFIELD JACKSON

This was a great disappointment, but there seemed to be nothing further to do about finding this important group of Emily's letters.

During the summer Mr. Niles's new expedient for popularizing the poems—the two volumes bound together in the original gray and white cover—finally materialized. The device met with Miss Vinnie's approval:

September [*October*]^rd '93

MY DEAR MR NILES
You were very kind to send the new volume of Emily's poems so promptly—the combination pleases me entirely.
I hope you will feel like publishing Emily's letters, this Fall.

Her friends & mine are very anxious to see the book. Is there any success with her picture and do you like the child picture?

Sincerely
LAVINIA DICKINSON

October 3rd

My mother, meanwhile, had thrown out another line of inquiry. A description of Emily in her youth was needed to supplement the memories of Austin and Lavinia and to make up for lack of a picture. So she had written to various schoolmates of Emily's, even to far-off Abby Root who lived in Beirut, Syria, the wife of the Reverend Daniel Bliss. These efforts met with small success until, in reply to some questions about letters sent for publication, the following note from Emily Ellsworth Fowler (Mrs. Gordon L. Ford) seemed to promise help.

[Post card addressed to Miss Lavinia Dickinson; postmarked September 8, 1893]

Easthampton
Long Island

Yours just forwarded here, and shall not be at home to answer for a week, so answer as well as I can. Dates of letters from 1848 to 1853. The word is *"lock"* of hair—other words must guess y'rself as the letters are in pencil and much rubbed. The typewriter couldn't make them out, nor I. The two later letters are one about my book, the other about her father's death.[7] I will hunt them up when I return home, but doubt if you could use them. I had some of her poems but all were in the book, the one about the robin—but they have vanished. The other things which I wish I could put my hands on were *funny*, sparkling with fun, and that is a new phase to the public, but she certainly began as a humorist. I do wish I could recall them. I am staying at my daughter Mabel's.

Affy,
E.E.F.F.

My mother followed up the lead. She called on Mrs. Ford in Brooklyn on October 19, 1893, to ask her to write down her

[7] *Letters,* 1931, p. 395.

memories of Emily. A day or two after the visit Mrs. Ford sent the following post card:

There may be some little delay in receiving what I promised you. I have written to Mrs. Stockbridge of Baltimore to see if she [can] add anything of interest to what I have to say, and also to see if my memory is aright in some particulars. I hope to send it to you by the end of the coming week—if I do not, it [is] because I wait for answers. How sorry I am to realize that while but three of the group of ten girls who were much together are dead—*all* the men, except Mr. Alden, are gone and he is so grave and silent now that I doubt if he would say anything of those days.

E.E.F.F.

97 Clark St.
Brooklyn, *Oct.* 19th

Mrs. Ford's sketch was received about two weeks later.[8] On November thirtieth the diary says, "Read him [Austin] Mrs. Ford's account of Emily's youth. It must be cut a good deal, but will be used in my book. Mrs. Ford died a week or two ago [November 23, 1893]—shortly after she sent it to me."

In reply to Mrs. Todd's letter of September thirteenth telling him that the manuscript was ready, Mr. Niles wrote that there was no hurry about sending it. It would be better to wait until business had picked up a little.

Boston
*Sep*ᵗ 26, 1893

DEAR MRS TODD

The photograph of the painting with the background will make the best picture. I suppose the negative can be had for that purpose from the Andover [Amherst] photographer when it is wanted.

We can, of course, begin work on the "Letters" at any time but it will be unwise to bring out the book in this depressed & uncertain state of business.

Yours truly
THOˢ NILES

[8] This sketch was published in abbreviated form in *Letters*, 1894, pp. 126-132, and complete in *Letters*, 1931, pp. 123-132.

They took advantage of the further delay to add to the number of letters in the volume, writing to other friends of Emily's in the hope of finding still more. But Miss Vinnie's impatience was steadily increasing. She wrote to Mr. Niles at shorter and shorter intervals. On October third she had written, "I hope you will feel like publishing Emily's letters this Fall." On October nineteenth she wrote again:

My Dear Mr Niles

In a letter to you some days ago I asked if you would publish "Emily's letters" *this season*. As no reply has come I venture the question again thinking maybe, *that* letter failed to find you.

Pardon my intrusion but Emilys friends are constantly enquiring *when* they can read *the letters* & I dont know what answer to make.

Cordially
Lavinia Dickinson

Amherst
October 19th '93

Once more she wrote:

28th *November* [1893]

My Dear Mr Niles

I was greatly disappointed that the *times* prevented the publishing of "Emilys letters" & I venture to ask if there's any hope that "Easter" will welcome the volume? I have never heard whether the efforts to secure a picture of "Emily" were [a] success.

Pardon my intrusion & believe me

Heartily
Lavinia Dickinson

On receipt of this letter Mr. Niles wrote to Mrs. Todd. The burden of decision as to when the *Letters* would be published appears to have shifted.

Boston
Nov 29, 1893

My dear Mrs Todd

Miss Dickinson has written about the volume of "Letters" & I have replied that we are quite ready to go on with it whenever you will furnish the copy.

She also wants to know what has been done about the portrait & I have told her that we are still waiting for the photograph of the oil painting.

Truly yours
Thos Niles

This letter was followed by a card of the same date.

I want to correct my statement as to the photograph of the oil painting. We have it safely & the letters from wh. facsimiles are to be made.

Truly yours
T. Niles

Nov 29, 1893

What Mr. Niles had said to Miss Vinnie is implied in her next letter to him:

My Dear Mr Niles
    Thank you for the certainty of expecting to see "Emilys letters" in print for "Easter."
    Mrs. Todd assured me they were all ready for your call last September so I suppose they can go to you at once.
    Will you be so kind as to send *one* volume of "Emilys poems" to me, the combined variety & believe me gratefully

Lavinia Dickinson

December 11th '93

[P. S.] Is the "Xmas" demand for "Emilys poems" at all satisfactory?

I spoke of efforts to find other letters during the enforced delay. The following is characteristic of the replies received. It is from Miss Currier, the stepdaughter of Emily's aunt, Mrs. Elizabeth Dickinson Currier, her father's youngest sister.

4 Harvard S^t
[Worcester, Mass.]
Nov. 18th [1893]

My Dear Miss Dickinson
    I inclose a copy of the only letter of your sister's that I have.

And this was in a package of letters written to Mother at the time of her engagement to my Father—so I presume was intended for a congratulatory letter.

I regret exceedingly that I burned *all* Mother's letters after her death—but it was done at her request and sanction.

I am sure many of your sister's letters were thus lost—as Mother never destroyed any during her life time, but it was only the fulfilment of our promise to her that made *us* destroy them.

We have enjoyed the "Poems" as have so many, all over the world—and am glad to be able to rescue this one little note for your sake. Aunt Mary has told me you would be glad of it.

> Yours sincerely,
> ANNIE DICKINSON CURRIER[9]

Miss Vinnie was outraged by this letter, because she "thought every word of Emily's was sacred and could not comprehend how anybody could destroy anything she had written."

During December, work on the letters was going forward—this time in collaboration with Mr. Dickinson who told my mother, as they read them together, "intensely interesting things." On December twelfth she writes:

> Austin came toward four, and we read a lot of Emily's letters, which I have prepared for publication. He did not take much exception to any sentence anywhere.
> He also came in the evening and we finished the set to himself, which interested him surprisingly. He stayed until ten o'clock. We shall go through the letters again, in detail.

The entry in the diary for the day before Christmas reads: "Took some presents over to Vinnie. She gave me a broken blue plate." This was one of the set in her dining-room, decorated with a picture of the landing of Lafayette.

On December twenty-ninth Mrs. Todd conferred with Mr. Niles about the *Letters*. She had at the time two other books in

---

[9] Thirty-seven years later, when Mrs. Todd asked to see this note again in order to include the omitted parts in her new edition of the *Letters*, Annie Dickinson Currier, then Mrs. Arthur Newton Brown, admitted with reluctance that it could not be found. Emily's letter appears as originally printed in 1894 on p. 428 of the 1931 volume.

press—*Total Eclipses of the Sun* and *Wayside Sketches*, the latter a volume of nature studies by my grandfather. On the same day she also paid a visit to "dear Colonel Higginson. He has just had his 70th birthday."

The year 1894 was to witness a speeding up of work by my mother. As she says, she "worked like a soldier." It was the home stretch as far as the *Letters* were concerned. She had put on such pressure that shortly after the book was published she was ill in bed—a most exceptional occurrence for her. But the fatigue soon vanished and her strength and spirit were restored.

The story of the year 1894 is so fully documented that it can be told for the most part in the words of the principal characters.

But first let us make the acquaintance of some of Emily's correspondents—actual persons to whom she addressed herself.

CHAPTER XIV

Emily's Correspondents

Finding is the first act;
The second, loss;
Third, expedition for
The golden fleece;

Fourth, no discovery;
Fifth, no crew;
Finally, no golden fleece—
Jason sham too.

EMILY'S contemporaries had an aversion to publishing private correspondence. The search for her letters, which had been going on intermittently for at least two years, presented problems in human relationships rather than perplexities of a literary nature. Frequently more ingenuity than insight was required to inveigle persons who had received letters into parting with them even for a short time. And to secure their reluctant permission to publish demanded not only tact and persuasiveness but a great deal of patience. It was not that these people were secretive or prudish, exactly, but reserved. They abhorred publicity even concerning matters of general interest. And of course "purely personal" parts of their correspondence must not appear in print on any account. Even the son of Samuel Bowles fell in with tradition, although he had been brought up with the printed page. Some correspondents went further, refusing to permit their identity to be known even after they had themselves expurgated the text.

In the case of the now familiar Norcross sisters reluctance went beyond the reach of persuasion. As we know, they would not allow Miss Vinnie or my mother to look at their letters. Instead, they themselves copied such excerpts as they could consent to have published. Fanny, the younger and less crotchety of the two, the one who "went out to meet the world"—Emily's characterization of her employment in the library of the Harvard Divinity School, not, one would think, the most venturesome of careers—died of pneumonia shortly after the book was published. Louisa, the "invalid," my mother wrote in 1893, had "become a recluse after the manner of Emily, but she hasn't any ability as Emily had." This Louisa lived to be a cantankerous old lady of seventy-seven. She kept Emily's letters always beside her, inviolate to the end. When she died in 1919, at the Home for the Aged, Concord, Massachusetts, they were burned at her request, the superintendent told me, either just before or just after her death. The Norcross sisters have occupied a place among Emily's correspondents out of proportion to their importance and solely because all of her letters to them had been preserved.

A never-ending problem was how to determine when the letters had been written. Only the earliest were dated. So the recipients were asked to supply dates for events alluded to or, if dates could not be recalled, to suggest collateral ways in which to get at the facts.

The letters in this chapter were written by Emily's correspondents or by their next of kin. The reader will be impressed, I think, by the gulf between the outlook of some of these individuals and the mind of Emily Dickinson. He will be shocked by the incongruity of their receiving her notice, even, let alone her affection. Could it have been of them that she said,[1] "My friends are my 'estate.' Forgive me then the avarice to hoard them"?

A few of these letters were written during the autumn of 1894 after galley proofs of the book had been returned. For while a chance remained to put in yet another fragment of Emily's writing, the search went on. It continued, together with verification of dates and other facts, until the plates were cast and no possibility of further change remained.

These letters from Emily's acquaintances, a heterogeneous group, can now speak for themselves.

Concord
Feb. 1, '94

My dear Mrs Todd.

Mr. Higginson's date of 1863 cannot be right. Emily was not in

[1] *Letters*, 1931, p. 182.

Boston for her eyes, till she came to us in Cambridge, and that was in the summer of 1864, or possibly 1865. Certainly not 1863, for we did not go to C. till Nov. 1863. We were in C. from Nov. 1863 till about Nov. 1865[2]; so Emily's two visits to us (for she came twice about her eyes) must have been between those dates.

May not Mr. H's date read 5 instead of 3; they are often made very much alike you know.

We shall be intensely interested in the book when it does come.

Thank you for telling me how it is arranged. You ask how long Emily was with us. The first time, for many weeks, and in the summer, the second time a shorter time, probably the next winter. It may be just the reverse, that is, the longer summer time, may have been after the shorter winter time. For this reason, I think the time "since April" may have been 1865 and the *first* winter trip in the season of 1863 & 64. Altho, as I remember, there was not a long time between the visits. I should think however the letters would show this. I think I have copied them for you, in which she speaks of coming a second time, and also of the result of the first trip.

Yours very truly
F. L. NORCROSS.

I am glad to be of any service to you.[3]

Colonel Higginson helped as much as he could in affixing dates to his own letters from Emily. But his memory was not always dependable.

[*To Mrs. Todd*]

25 Buckingham St.
Cambridge, Mass.
Feb. 3, 1894

DEAR FRIEND

All good little editresses should keep a cyclopaedia close at hand. "The army broke out" as Riley says, in the spring of 1861 and Bull Run and Ball's Bluff with smaller battles occurred that year, before Christmas—not "decisive" battles & not so "bloody" as later ones, but seeming more important because of the novelty. Davis was captured May 10, 1865.

[2] *Letters*, 1931, p. 280.
[3] Emily's letters to the Misses Norcross are printed in *Letters*, 1931, Chap. VII, pp. 214-270.

I will enclose her letter, with the address she gave (I think it is in her brother's hand) showing where she was. Please return. I think it must have been that year because I was not "hurt" at any other time & did not have illnesses. It is in my memory, too, as belonging to that time & the handwriting may help to fix the time. It must be possible to fix the year when she was at that address, too [Miss Norcross']. Note too that it was while Carlo lived. Perhaps she only staid a month in Cambridge.

As ever
T. W. HIGGINSON.

Another letter from him soon followed.

25 Buckingham St.
Cambridge, Mass.
Feb. 7, 1894

DEAR FRIEND

You are right and I wrong. I supposed her letter was written soon after I was wounded, while I was in S.C., but I see now that it must have been written during the following summer (1864) when I was invalided at Pigeon Cove—the remote result of the same trouble. It is to this that she refers in the subsequent letter, speaking of "the after, slower days."

Ever affectionately
T. W. HIGGINSON

[No date]

MY DEAR MRS TODD,

I certainly thought I could write you before this that we were settled in our domestic affairs, but alas, nothing has come to help us yet.

When we are not doing housework, we are searching for some [one] else to do it for us, are have [and have been] subjected to delays and then disappointments for almost two months.

When it will all end I cannot tell, perhaps not till we are brought to our own end.

Pardon this torn sheet, which I did not discover till I turned the page.

I trust you will be able to wait for me a little longer.

I will write again.

Yours sincerely
FANNY L. NORCROSS.

Emily's friend, Samuel Bowles, editor of *The Springfield Republican*—to whom, with his wife, she wrote the letters contained in Chapter VI of *Letters*, 1931—had a son of the same name, the sixth "Samuel of Samuel," from whom the following communications were received.

Springfield, Mass.
February 3, 1894

DEAR MRS. TODD:–
I am glad to help you in regard to the letters, so far as I can. The three children, to whom Miss Dickinson refers in her earlier letters to my parents, Sallie, Sam and Mamie, were the only ones living until 1861. Charlie was born December 19 of that year.

My father made his first trip to Europe in 1862, sailing early in the spring.

I cannot give you the date of the visit at Washington, to which you refer. There were very many of them; in fact, my father went there almost every year.

My father died January 16, 1878, and my impression is that he had few letters from Miss Dickinson during the last years of his life.

My sisters found other letters from Miss Dickinson among those that were left in my mother's house. I think they were all preserved and that they are in a tin box now in my possession. If you want them, I will look for them and send what remain.

I had a few letters myself from Miss Dickinson during the later years of her life, but they were brief and I presume would not be of value to you. If, however, you care for them, I will look those up also.

Very truly yours,
SAML. BOWLES

Mrs. David P. Todd
Amherst, Mass.

On February seventh he sent the letters addressed to himself and his wife and, the day following those to his father and mother.

Springfield, Mass.
February 8, 1894

MY DEAR MRS. TODD:–
I now send you the remaining letters from Miss Dickinson, found among my mother's papers. You will see that they are

extremely personal, but that they contain many beautiful passages.

I take it that the names of the persons, to whom the letters that appear in the book were written, will not be printed. I should not wish to have my mother given publicity in connection with letters so personal and private as these.

Yours very truly,

SAML. BOWLES

Mrs. David P. Todd,
Amherst, Mass.

Springfield, Mass.
Feb. 10, 1894

DEAR MRS. TODD:—

The note about the engagement must have been written in October or early November, 1883; the one about the marriage in May or June, 1884, and the one about the birth of my boy in August, 1885.

I should like to see the proofs of the doubtful letters, as you kindly suggest.

Yours very truly,

SAML. BOWLES.

Mrs. David P. Todd
Amherst, Mass.

My mother sent proof of their own letters to all of Emily's correspondents who wished to see it—a courtesy sometimes resulting in considerable delay.

Springfield, Mass.
April 26, 1894

DEAR MRS. TODD:—

I have read the proofs with deep interest and return them herewith. I have ventured to make only a few changes. One of them is the striking out of a paragraph which you had yourself queried; another is the use of the impersonal "son" in place of my brother's name; and the others are in the name of my sister, who used to be called "Mamie," and not "Meme."

I infer there are other proofs of the Bowles letters still to be received by you, and I shall be glad to read them over, if you will allow it.

Yours very truly

SAML. BOWLES

Mrs. David P. Todd,
Amherst, Mass.

With regard to the next correspondent my mother said:

We were always hoping for a stray composition or an early letter, or a bit of fresh, novel reminiscence. We wrote to all the friends of Emily's girlhood that Austin or Lavinia could think of. The results were usually nil. . . . The only one of Emily's teachers in Amherst Academy then living whom Austin could remember was D. T. Fiske, now a very old man.[4] I wrote to him.

In a trembling but touching hand he sent the following tribute.

Newburyport
Feb. 6, 1894

Mrs. M. L. Todd
DEAR MADAM

In reply to yours of the 3ᵈ inst. I would say that I have very distinct and pleasant impressions of Emily Dickinson, who was a pupil of mine in Amherst Academy in 1842–43. I remember her as a very bright, but rather delicate and frail looking girl; an excellent scholar; of exemplary deportment, faithful in all school duties; but somewhat shy and nervous. Her compositions were strikingly original; and in both thought and style seemed beyond her years, and always attracted much attention in the school and, I am afraid, excited not a little envy. Am sorry to say that I cannot furnish you any copies of either her compositions or letters.

The new volume from her pen which you are editing will, I doubt not, find many readers, and reveal new phases of her unique genius.

Very sincerely yours

D. T. FISKE

[4] D. T. Fiske, a graduate of Amherst College, 1842, was Principal of Amherst Academy, 1842–43. Later he went to Andover Theological Seminary, was ordained to the ministry in 1847, and became pastor of the Belleville Congregational Church of Newburyport, Massachusetts, a post held throughout the rest of his life.

Another early friend of Emily's was Benjamin F. Newton of Vermont, later of Worcester, Massachusetts.[5] Although he was no longer living in 1894, my mother tried to discover the letters which Austin was sure Emily had written to him, with what success the following correspondence will show.

Though Mrs. Newton survived her husband "by nearly half a century," she apparently could not be found in 1894. It seems probable that Mr. Dickinson knew that Emily had written to the Reverend Edward Everett Hale asking for news of Mr. Newton, since it was to him that Mrs. Todd first turned for information.

39 Highland St.
Roxbury, Mass.
Feb. 1, 1894

My dear Mrs. Todd,—

We do not seem to get any light about Benjamin Newton. This is the reply to a note which I finally wrote to Mrs. Wetherell, who was Miss Hester Newton. When you spoke to me I thought it was Lincoln Newton, who was my classmate and friend. If you can give us any farther clew I will gladly follow it up among my Worcester friends.

Truly yours,
Edw. E. Hale

Not content with this discouraging report Mrs. Todd next wrote to the Reverend George H. Gould then living in Worcester.

Worcester
Feb. 8/94

My dear Madam:

Mr Benjamin Newton died some more than 35 years ago. He had no family but a wife. Whether she is living I am unable to say. I have wholly lost track of her for many years.

I had quite a cherished batch of Emily's letters myself kept sacredly in a small trunk—with other valuable papers—which some 15 years ago mysteriously disappeared in the overturnings incident to various removals.

[5] B. F. Newton was resuscitated by Professor George F. Whicher in an article entitled, "Emily Dickinson's Earliest Friend," *American Literature*, Vol. VI (March and May, 1934). Mr. Newton was given further prominence in Mr. Whicher's book, *This Was a Poet*.

I have searched far & near for that trunk—& its valuables—but thus far it remains unfound.

I wish I could help you. May I ask you to convey my most kindly regards to Lavinia & Austin, & wishing you all success in your most worthy undertaking

I am sincerely yours,
GEO. H. GOULD.

Of Dr. Gould my mother said:

He was a nice-looking old minister. He was a classmate, a fraternity-mate, and close friend of Austin. In fact he was Austin's most intimate friend in college, and so I had a respect for him. For many years he had been a pastor in Worcester and was still living there.

In this letter from George Gould there is a hint regarding his own relationship to Emily. Genevieve Taggard wove her story of Emily's "Life and Mind" around the importance of that relationship.[6] But that it was merely casual is implied, if not proved, by the sentence, "I had quite a cherished batch of Emily's letters myself," as though that fact might surprise Emily's brother, whose "most intimate" college friend he had been. My mother told me that "if George Gould had had more than a pleasant acquaintance with Emily, Austin never knew it."

In the meantime Dr. Hale had written again.

39 Highland St.
Roxbury, Mass.
Feb. 7, 1894

MY DEAR MRS TODD,

Do not let me interfere with what is none of my business, but I think your man is named not Benjamin *Newton*, but Benjamin *Lincoln*, and if there is a probability of that, I think I can find him.

Truly yours,
EDW. E. HALE

[6] Genevieve Taggard, *The Life and Mind of Emily Dickinson*. New York: Alfred A. Knopf, 1930.

Since they knew that their man was not Benjamin Lincoln, Dr. Hale's suggestion would seem to have discouraged the search for further information about Benjamin Franklin Newton. At any rate, that is the point at which it ended in 1894.

One further fact may explain why the widow was so difficult to find that, although she was living at the time within a few miles of Worcester, no one discovered her whereabouts. In reply to a rejoinder of mine in the same journal, Professor Whicher wrote as follows:[7]

Emily Dickinson's friend had no children and no sister named Hester. His wife died at Lancaster, Mass., on Dec. 2, 1899 (E.N. Leonard, *Newton Genealogy*, p. 133; I have verified the date from the town records). The following paragraph from the *Clinton Courant* for Dec. 9, 1899, gives all that I know of her story after her husband's death:

> Mrs. Sarah Newton died at the town farm on Saturday, aged 90 years and two months. Funeral services were held on Monday afternoon, conducted by Rev. Dr. Bartol, of whose church Mrs. Newton was a member. The interment was in the South Lancaster cemetery. [Another depositary of Emily's letters who died in the poorhouse!]

The circumstances of Mrs. Newton's death make it unlikely that any letters written to her husband between 1850 and 1853 could have remained in her keeping to the end.

From the poorhouse it is a far cry to Maria Whitney, one of the distinguished family of Josiah Dwight Whitney, President of the Northampton Bank during Emily's girlhood. Two of her brothers—Josiah Dwight Whitney (1819–1896), Harvard geologist, for whom Mount Whitney, the highest peak in the United States, was named, and William Dwight Whitney (1827–1894), Yale philologist, among the foremost Sanskrit scholars of his time—had an international reputation. Their sister Maria, who taught French and German at Smith College in the first years after its establishment in 1875, was both a scholar and a culti-

[7] *American Literature*, May, 1934, p. 193.

vated, cosmopolitan woman. Her drawing-room was a meeting place for the brilliant men and women of the vicinity, Samuel Bowles among them.

My mother wrote to Miss Whitney (then living in Cambridge, Massachusetts, with her unmarried brother James, Chief of the Catalogue Department and later Librarian of the Boston Public Library) to ask the usual questions—when her letters already in my mother's hands had been written, and whether there were passages she wished to omit.

In many of the published letters the very passages which made them most revealing of Emily, who always dealt with the life-germ of a situation, were the ones which the recipients would not permit the editor to use. By way of illustration I refer the reader to the letters to James and Charles Clark,[8] in which the most direct passages, those relating to the Reverend Dr. Charles Wadsworth, omitted in 1894, were printed in full for the first time in 1931. When all existing originals become available, restorations can be made in other groups of letters.

In the case of Miss Whitney the omitted paragraphs referred to a warmth of admiration for her on the part of Samuel Bowles. Emily always respected real emotion. But her recognition of this friendship did not look decorous in print.[9]

When I am tempted to feel exasperated at the reticence and false modesty which suppressed the vital essence of a letter or left it out altogether if the omission of an objectionable passage made the context meaningless, when I am tempted to call it hypocrisy, I have only to recall my own girlhood when, as Emily said in another connection, to "speak of hallowed things aloud" was not merely offensive; it was unthinkable.

Cambridge
July 30 [1894]

DEAR MRS TODD,

I should be able to answer your question as to the date of Emily Dickinson's letters to me with more certainty, perhaps,

[8] *Letters*, 1931, pp. 342-357, 428, 429.
[9] Those parts of Miss Whitney's correspondence which she was willing to print are found on pp. 324-335 of *Letters*, 1931.

if I could look at them again. Yet I feel quite confident that these were written after 1877. Before that time I think [I] rarely had a letter of any length from her. I am sorry I cannot give you any more exact information.

Yours truly
MARIA WHITNEY

Cambridge
Aug. 5, [1894]

DEAR MRS TODD,

I should be very glad to see the proof, if it will not then be too late to make any change,—I mean, if by showing it to me you intend to grant me the right of protest against the inclusion of any passages that may seem to me undesirable. Probably I shall be perfectly satisfied with your choice, as to what should be printed, but I cannot be absolutely sure, in advance.

Yours sincerely
M. WHITNEY.

Cambridge
Sept. 20 [1894]
21 Berkeley St.

DEAR MRS. TODD,

I return the proof, today. There was some delay in its reaching me, as it was not addressed to the above-mentioned street and number.

I have indicated on the galley the probable dates of the letters, for which you asked. If I am right—and I think I am,—then the sequence of the last letter on the 2nd galley is not correct.

The only error I notice is the spelling of the word Northampton,—which is usually spelled with one *h,*—and is so also in Miss Dickinson's letter.—

I do not know that I have any reason to object to what is extracted from the letters for publication, tho some of it, divorced from its context, seems to me to have lost its chief value and significance. My inclination would have been to suppress the whole, in such a case.

Yours sincerely
MARIA WHITNEY.

Post card addressed to Mrs. M. L. Todd, Amherst, Mass.]

Cambridge
Oct. 6 [1894]

Your note is just received. The word in the letter is very distinctly written "division."[10] I took it to *mean* separation, as that would give a not improbable meaning to the sentence.

Yours,

M.W.

Although my mother had met the Reverend Perez D. Cowan in August, 1891 (page 140), it was Miss Vinnie who wrote asking for some desired information. He was a "favorite cousin" to whom she enjoyed writing. His reply follows:

Pastor's Study
Presbyterian Church
Canastota, N.Y.
Jan. 22, 1894

DEAR COUSIN LAVINIA–

Two weeks of special meetings have kept me very busy; but we trust good has been done by the efforts put forth; and today, I have a little breathing space again, and I am able to answer your inquiry as to the time of the death of our little Margie. The date is Nov. 8, 1879. But my impression is that the letter of Cousin Emily in regard to her was written at a later date, on receipt of the little Memorial of the Child, which was within a few months from the little one's passage home.[11]

I trust you are well, these changeable days.—I thank you for the address of Cousin Harriet M[ontague].

The tea bell has rung. Will not you walk in and take a cup of the beverage "that cheers but not inebriates"?

Yours very affy
P. D. COWAN

The dates supplied by Mr. Cowan were definite enough to be useful in other connections. They were inserted in a list[12] which my mother always kept beside her, adding as they came to light

[10] *Letters,* 1931, p. 330.
[11] *Letters,* 1931, pp. 322-324.
[12] Appendix VI.

dates of events which may or may not have had anything to do with Emily, but which served to identify other events to which she did refer. This illustrates one step in the process of assigning dates to Emily's letters. If there was any doubt whatever my mother added a question mark to the date given.

Clifton Springs, N.Y
Aug. 4, 1894

DEAR MRS. TODD:—

The answer to your letter of the twenty-seventh ultimo has been delayed on account of my absence from home. I am pleased to learn that the Volume of letters is to appear at an early day and I await the event with much interest. It is a pleasure, also to know that the sale of the volumes of poems has been large. The date of our little Margie's death, as given by you, (Nov. 8 1879,) is correct. The date of my marriage to Miss Margaret Elizabeth Rhea, was Oct. 26, 1870. My sister, Mrs. Margaret Cowan McClung, died Nov. 17, 1883.

I regret the delay,—but hope that this will yet be in time for your purpose.

Very Sincerely
P. D. COWAN

The next group of correspondents were not favorite cousins not even intimate friends. The Reverend Forrest F. Emerson was for a brief time minister of the First Congregational Church of Amherst. He was installed on June 12, 1879, and "dismissed" —the term used at the end of an incumbency—on February 21 1883.

[*Post card addressed to Mrs. Mabel Loomis Todd*]

Worcester Mass
July 7th 94

DEAR MADAME:

Your note rec'd. When the letters are received in return and can look them over I shall be able to write you something but fear the dates cannot be remembered

Hastily yrs
F. F. EMERSON

Worcester, Mass.
Sept. 15th 94

My dear Miss Dickinson

Your postal card of inquiry was received. I received the letters while in Gloucester.

I wrote Mrs. Todd, I think, that I would write some comments on the letters; but on second thoughts, I considered my acquaintance with your sister so slight, and the *occasion* of the letters of so little public interest that I decided that I could say little that would give any new lustre to the charm of the letters, or add anything which would be in the nature of an explanation of their contents. Most of these notes explain themselves. They refer to the illness of your mother and the death of Gibbie, and the shorter notes were usually the accompaniment of fruit or flowers.

I think the note in regard to the "precious package of papers" refers to some accounts which I lent her of the death of "H.H." for whom she seemed to have such a strong affection.

We finally decided not to come to Amherst on our vacation, but went to the Gloucester coast with its fishy smells and picturesque scenery where we spent the month of August.

Very sincerely yours
F. F. Emerson

A note of September twentieth from Mr. Bowles acknowledges plate proofs of the letters to his father and mother. His delay in returning them was one of many, all of which postponed the date of publication.

Springfield, Mass.
October 1, 1894

My dear Mrs. Todd:—

Forgive me for keeping these proofs so long. I have been very busy.

There is a mistake in the letter which you give as having been addressed to Mrs. Bowles at the time of our engagement. Part of it, as it appears in the proof, I am quite sure was in a letter to me. On the whole I think it would be well to omit this letter; also the one to Mr. and Mrs. Hoar and the one to me of September 28, 1885, at the time of my brother's engagement.

Please also omit "Miss Hoar's" name from the introduction

to the letter to me of October, 1883, and change the introduction
to the letter about the birth of our boy, as I have indicated on
the proof.

Yours cordially,

SAML. BOWLES

Mrs. David P. Todd
Amherst, Mass.

"Charlie" Montague was a cousin living in Amherst. Though
Emily's letters were written to his father[13] and to his niece
Eugenia Hall,[14] I am including this communication from him
because of the phrasing of the final sentence from which one
might infer that he had access to a secret fund of information
which would be of value to the editor of Emily's book if she
could only get at it. This sort of tactics is characteristic of the
rustic Yankee who wishes to give an impression that he is possessed of important facts, while divulging neither their substance
nor their source.

Amherst
July 29, 189.

DEAR MRS. TODD:—

It affords me much pleasure to furnish you with the information requested in your letter of the 27th inst.

My niece Eugenia Hall was married Oct. 20, 1885. My aunt
Miss Harriet Montague met with the accident which broke her
hip, March 28th, 1872.

My father received a great many notes from Miss Emily Dickinson and I remember that he was very particular to keep them
all, but cannot say what became of them all during the changes
of the past two years in our family. You can depend upon the
dates I have given you as being *correct* as I do not depend upon
memory.

Very truly Yours

CHAS. C. MONTAGUE

On April 17, 1894, while my mother was in Brooklyn, Mrs
Ellen E. Dickinson called upon her. The only comment about

---

[13] *Letters*, 1931, pp. 395-396.
[14] *Ibid.*, pp. 415-416.

her in my mother's diary is, "A funny old thing." She was the widow of the "Cousin Willie" to whom Emily had addressed herself. After Mrs. Todd's return to Amherst she received a letter from "Willie's wife."

Pierrepont House
Brooklyn Heights
April 21ˢᵗ [1894]

DEAR MRS TODD,

I think I would prefer you should not ask Vinnie to send me a copy of Emily's Verses. If she had sent them of her own volition they would have been greatly prized.

The articles I have written concerning Emily are among some papers packed away, and I cannot get at them without a good deal of trouble. Let me here correct my statement as to the number of letters we received from Emily. I said "a hundred"—but in reflecting upon the matter I feel sure that we did not get so many. Still there was a considerable number, all of which after my Husband's death I destroyed. I hope you will pardon the egoism of my talk the other day about Emily, as it was in connection with her, and to show her personality. She was a woman of brilliant conversational power—of keen and subtle wit, and poetical conceptions, and I treasure all my remembrances of her. My Husband had an ardent admiration for her, and she loved her "cousin Willie." The romance of Emily's life was given me by one whose word I cannot dispute. It made her a poetess.

I may go abroad this season or to California—but if you will address me in care of Mr Henry Pike, 39 Broad St., New York City, it will always find me. I am happy to have met you and am

Cordially yours
ELLEN E. DICKINSON

The episode outlined in the following correspondence "furnished amusement to us all," my mother told me, "with the exception of Vinnie who wanted to take the lady's head off, chiefly I think because she invented a love-affair for Emily to suit herself."

Mrs. Ellen E. Dickinson had literary ambitions and had written several books, among them *New Light on Mormonism*, 1885, and *The King's Daughters, A Fascinating Romance*, 1888. The enclosure to which she refers in the following letter was an article

in the *Boston Transcript*. A copy of it had already been sent to
Mrs. Todd by Bishop Huntington. It seems to have touched up a
somewhat somber situation. From the "umbrageous trees" to the
"virginal sheets of paper" on which Emily was accustomed to
write her poetry, the article was hilarious. It was reprinted in
newspapers throughout the country. I have a copy of it from the
daily *Inter Ocean*, Chicago, December 1, 1894. Such was the
author's pride in her work that she sent the clipping to my mother
with an accompanying letter.

> Dorchester, Mass
> *Oct* 4th [1894]

Mrs. M. L. Todd
DEAR MADAME,

While visiting here, so many people have asked me about
Emily Dickinson that I have written the enclosed, which I trust
will please her sister, and yourself.

It has been suggested that I should write a magazine article
about Emily. To do so, it would be necessary to have some data
which I do not possess, but am quite willing to write the article
if it is furnished to me. Perhaps you could supply all I would
so desire, and if you signify a willingness in that direction, I will
ask certain questions, to accomplish such a task. After tomorrow
my address will be care Mr Henry Pike, 39 Broad St., New York
City.

> Cordially yours,
> ELLEN E. DICKINSON

Far from being pleased by the attention, however, Miss Vinnie
was outraged. To my mother was allotted the task of tempering
the blast of her invective until it was fit for the ear of Willie's
widow. In answer to Miss Vinnie's charges the lady replied:

> 122 Montague St
> Brooklyn
> *Oct.* 20th, 1894

DEAR MRS TODD,

Yours of Oct. 6th is received. Certainly you can believe I had no
intention to offend Miss Lavinia in what I wrote of Emily, or in
sending you the *Transcript* containing the article alluded to. The
most charitable construction to be given to the message sent to

e by Miss Lavinia is that her memory is defective. I can, if
ecessary, prove the story of the cat's tail being sent to me by
mily.[15]

A literary gentleman of Boston has written thanking me for the
admirable article on Emily Dickinson published in the
'ranscript."

As to whether I will write further of Emily, I am undecided,
ut I have quite enough material for a short paper. It is to be
emembered that when the writings of an author are given to the
orld, anyone has the privilege of making known any incident,
r fact, in connection with that author's life or environment,
> the public.

I have only the very pleasantest memories in connection with
mily, and her Father and Mother, neither of whom I feel quite
ire would, if they were living, be anything but hospitable and
indly to "Willie's wife."

> With regards
> Yours cordially,
> ELLEN E. DICKINSON

Once a person had earned Lavinia's disapproval, he was ex-
ommunicated. If ever occasion offered to remind him of his
isgrace, however, she seized it, as in the present instance.

> Brooklyn
> *Feb.* 6th, 1895

EAR MRS TODD,
Enclosed is a letter from Lavinia Dickinson which I cannot
take out, save in part—cannot read altogether, although I have
ied to do so several times. Presuming that you are aware of her
nding it, and the gist of its contents, will you kindly copy it,
id send it to me, and greatly oblige

> Yours cordially,
> ELLEN E. DICKINSON

ddress
are Mr Henry Pike
) Broad St
ew York City

[15] "Her large yellow pet cat lost its long fluffy tail by some accident, which
e sent in playful humor by express to the present scribe. There was a
nk ribbon tied round this disconnected appendage, with a verse accom-
anying it that unfortunately is lost."—*Boston Transcript,* Sept. 28, 1894.

Just what Lavinia may have written I do not know, but m
mother said that her rejoinder on hearing this communicatio
was merely, "Keep your pen to yourself."

Ellen E. Dickinson was not yet snuffed out, however. She wro
another article about Emily, also printed in the *Boston Tra*
script, October 12, 1895—a mild sort of rehash containing litt
that was new. It seems to have been concocted with one end i
view, namely, to mollify Lavinia, for the final sentence read
"The lovers of beautiful verses are indebted to her sister, Mi
Lavinia Dickinson, for giving them the effusions of the poetess
Amherst."

In so far as further injunctions from Lavinia were concerne
the lady was successful. But no *rapprochement* resulted. Ther
after Ellen E. Dickinson was consigned to oblivion.

CHAPTER XV

The *Letters* in Press

To make routine a stimulus,
Remember it can cease.[1]

AT THE close of the year 1893, although the manuscript of the *Letters of Emily Dickinson* had been for some time in the hands of Roberts Brothers, its publication had been postponed because of the business depression. Work on the book was not interrupted, however. Many practical details were needing attention, such as choice of type and set-up. Nine days after specimen pages were submitted, on January 9, 1894, proof reading was under way. And the search for material went on as usual.

The first point to be settled was this: should the letters be arranged by dates or by correspondents? Instead of the customary chronological order it seemed better to place Emily's letters in groups by correspondents for two reasons. First, time for her was not so important as her relationship to a person. That demanded continuity. Second, none of the letters being dated, even if an attempt were made to arrange them in order, it would often have to be a matter of guesswork, and that might result in distortion of facts. Either of these reasons would seem to have been conclusive. And yet, to the last, Mrs. Todd questioned the wisdom of her decision. As late as April 2, 1894, she writes, "I continually have grave doubts about my plan of arranging Emily's letters in chapters by *people*, but always, on thinking, it seems best."

A second question was: should there be one volume, or two; and if two, where could the contents be divided so that the volumes would be equal in size? Work of a different character had to do with the preparation of a preface and an index. The

[1] Only the first stanza of this poem was published in *Further Poems*, 1929.

former was a delicate piece of writing which must be approved by Austin and Lavinia at every step. The latter, though more or less routine work, was even more time-consuming. Articles, too, must be written to pave the way for the new volume and talks about Emily prepared and delivered in response to growing interest.

Another matter, long under discussion but not yet settled, was awaiting a final decision—what to do about a likeness of Emily? One must be produced somehow. To this they all agreed. But why the oil painting made in childhood should have been the only picture of her in the book of letters is in itself a quaint story—one in which false loyalty and Victorian prejudice struggled with a half-hesitant wish that a picture labeled with her name should bear some resemblance to her. Most weight appears to have been given to things other than resemblance. The arrangement of the hair is a case in point. Mrs. Ford had said that it "lay in rings . . . all over her head." That was the way Mrs. Ford remembered it. And since Miss Vinnie preferred it that way, the description was left as written in spite of the fact that other friends of Emily's youth maintained that her hair was straight. In support of their contention is the fact that in the only picture taken from life Emily Dickinson's hair is straight. One of those early friends, Mrs. E. P. Crowell, took emphatic exception to several of Mrs. Ford's remarks. In her diary my mother wrote:

January 29, 1894

I worked on E.D. proof, and in reading to Mrs Crowell, who was a schoolmate of Emily's, all the morning. Then Austin came at two, & we went over the first 60 pages of proof—Strong letters —and Mrs Ford's little article. Mrs Crowell says most of that was either the effect of a mind losing its grasp, or else wilful confusion as to times, ages, dates. So I had to leave out about half.

This matter of verifying information culled by Emily's friends from memories of half a century was not only difficult; it was exasperating. My mother told me of her despair when the elderly ladies disagreed among themselves. Any information they provided must be checked and rechecked before it could be used.

Throughout all these discussions Mr. Niles was patient as well as thoughtful in small unexpected ways, a trait which endeared him even to business associates. A letter from Mrs. Todd on January 1, 1894, bears little resemblance to the usual correspondence between publisher and author.

DEAR Mr NILES,

I was quite overcome when I reached home Saturday evening, and found your most welcome and graceful gift to me—the leather-bound *Poems*.

I had given a copy away—a little grudgingly, I am afraid, as I wanted to keep it so much—and now see how virtue has been rewarded by your kindness!

Thank you *very* much—I am more glad to have it again than I can tell you.

> Gratefully and cordially
> MABEL LOOMIS TODD

Amherst,
New Year's Day, 1894

The various strands of activity in bringing the book to completion were so interwoven that no one of them can be disentangled from the unfolding of the pattern as a whole. The correspondence is given in chronological order in the hope of reproducing thereby a little of the atmosphere of the strange tense year—1894.

During January, a month of "solid work" on the letters, there was much talk about a picture. No progress had been made since the previous summer. Then, as now, the only bona fide picture of Emily was the daguerreotype reproduced as Plate XV. Both brother and sister objected to it on the ground that it made her look too plain. On the other hand, the artist's composite sketch did not please them because it did not look like her at all, as indeed how could it have? And Mr. Niles objected with good reason to the child oil portrait on the same ground.

Lavinia favored the sketch in preference to the raw daguerreotype, but Austin would not allow a manifestly doctored picture to go into the book. And the child portrait, though both considered it more "good looking" than the other two, had as my mother said, "nothing to do with Emily's real appearance."

In parenthesis: Miss Vinnie never gave up her determination to achieve a satisfactory likeness of Emily—to contrive one somehow. Three years later a photograph of this same daguerreotype was taken at her request to Miss Laura C. Hills, the well-known miniature painter of Boston. Miss Vinnie's intermediary was a friend of Miss Hills, Gertrude Graves, daughter of the Dickinsons' cousin, John L. Graves. Miss Hills told me that she never saw Miss Vinnie, but that at her request she retouched the photograph. She softened the appearance of the hair and "rearranged the neckline of the dress." This Miss Hills did, and it was all she did. *She did not touch the face.* Nor, she told me, did she ever paint a miniature as we are led to believe, by implication, in a book by Emily's niece.[2] If Lavinia subsequently achieved a miniature of Emily, it was painted by someone else. That the retouched photograph met with Lavinia's approval her letter to Miss Graves will testify.

My Dear Gertrude

The picture is beyond my highest expectation. It really seems as if Emily was here. I will make these suggestions—I can not indulge in the *painted miniature*, just now, though I wish I could —perhaps *later* in the year I may be able for the luxury. I would like the picture a *little enlarged* if it *can* be & *only* the head & shoulders in sight. I'm sorry there is nothing in the way of *lace* to send you. I think the artist can create some fluffy finish for the neck. Perhaps a ruffle half as high & not quite so full as "Mrs Rogers's" would be the thing [Mrs. Henry M. Rogers, "Clara Doria"]. I'm sure the artist can *try* & if not at *first* a success, we can try again. I feel perfectly *sure now* Emily will be faithfully represented. I am grateful to tears for your endeavors & the wonderful result. I was faithful to "orders" & didn't venture a look till your words were all read. You can trust my *honor* in the dark! My home is a dream of beauty, today. I wish you were all here.

Love for you all.

Affectionately

2   1

Lavinia Cousin.

May 11th [1897][3]

[2] Martha Dickinson Bianchi, *Emily Dickinson Face to Face.* Boston: Houghton Mifflin Company, 1932, p. 18.

[3] This letter is used with the kind permission of Gertrude Graves's sister, Miss Louise B. Graves of Boston.

What became of this retouched photograph I do not know. But the grotesque picture used as Emily's likeness in the current edition of her collected poems was not the work of Laura Hills, on her own authority.

We now return to 1894:

> Amherst College Observatory
> Amherst, Mass.
> 17 *January*, 1894

DEAR Mʳ NILES,

I sent you the negative today of the Emily Dickinson [child] portrait; and a print from it. The photographer has apparently cut out a piece of paper to surround the head, in order to make a dark background. The dark background is all right, but it looks stiff and inartistic as he has done it. The little face, however, is very pretty, and worth giving. Don't you think so? At least if an artist can soften the edges in some way.

What about the old daguerreotype? Are you going to try to do anything with it? You showed me a pencil sketch once, in which the hair and dress were good, and the face was to be tried later. It seems an experiment worth attempting.

> Very truly
> MABEL L. TODD

> Boston
> Janʸ 19, 1894

DEAR MRS TODD

About the proposed portrait of Emily Dickinson. You know we have been waiting for you to say if we should go ahead. The "Sketch" was merely to shew the arrangement of the hair [Plate XII]. Now, if her brother thinks the daguerreotype is not like her I don't see how an artist can be supposed to make a picture wh. would resemble her. The juvenile picture [oil painting] is totally unlike the daguerreotype & as one is from life and the other from a painting certainly the daguerreotype would seem to be the one to copy.

What shall we do?

> Yours truly
> THOˢ NILES

DEAR Mʳ NILES,

I think the child portrait of E.D. is very pretty, and would be exceedingly interesting in the book. Her brother thinks it gives her expression quite strongly, and there are not now many persons who remember her at that age well enough to dispute it. If it were artistically reproduced—without that harsh outline, and altogether softened—I think I should be glad to see it in the volume. As to the other, I do not know. It certainly should be re-drawn, and the artist *might* hit just the expression. But I suppose you would hardly like to have an artist spend his time on it when it might not be used. There will be the three facsimiles of letters, and the picture of the house, in any event, and I am much inclined to use the child portrait, of which I have written. I will send a design of witch-hazel for the cover.

Very sincerely
MABEL L. TODD

Amherst
20 *Jan.* 1894

This letter with a pencil query, "Do you care to make the attempt?" by Mr. Niles, was forwarded to the artist who had made the preliminary sketch. The reply was enclosed in Mr. Niles's next letter.

A. W. Elson & Co., Photogravure
146 Oliver, corner Purchase St.
Telephone 2565

Boston
23rd *Jan.*, 1894

Thos. Niles, Esq.
3 Somerset St.
Boston

DEAR MR. NILES:—

In regard to enclosed letter would say, that if the photograph of Emily Dickinson which you have furnished me is satisfactory, I will go ahead and guarantee that the painting *shall be as satisfactory as is the photograph*. I also understand that the hair as sketched is just what they want, as well as the arrangement of the dress around the neck. Under these conditions I would be very glad to go ahead and make the drawing. Please let me hear from you if I shall do it, and oblige.

Yours very truly,
A. W. ELSON

Boston
Jany 24, 1893[4]

DEAR MRS TODD

Of course we shall make the child picture of Emily D. but what shall we do about the mature portrait?

I enclose Mr Elson's letter about it.

The cost of making the drawing will be considerable & I should hardly wish to have it done dependent upon an uncertainty.

Truly yours
THO^s NILES

It was finally agreed that the chance of obtaining a likeness in this way was too remote to justify the expense. And that is why the only picture of Emily Dickinson's face taken from life was discarded, and the reproduction of an oil painting of her as a child, which both brother and sister admitted did not resemble her, was the only one used in the volume of letters (Plate XIII).

One last word about Emily's appearance. In an unpublished poem, "Again his voice is at the door," she says

> I take a flower as I go
> My face to justify,
> He never saw me in this life,
> I might surprise his eye.

Emily had, as a matter of fact, a somewhat quizzical attitude toward what she called her "gypsy face." That the word fits is revealed by a silhouette made of her at the age of fourteen. It was never even considered for the book of letters. One glance at its quaint little upturned nose, prominent mouth, and long upper lip shows why. Austin and Lavinia did not want to think that it resembled her. It was too plain. The silhouette is here reproduced for the first time (Plate I).

Attention now turned to other things.

One detail which should have been quickly disposed of led to friction and disagreement instead. A tale difficult to understand and full of heartache, it has to do only with the writing of a contract.

This question, including that of the name in which the copyright should be issued, had been allowed to smolder for almost a year. On February twenty-third Mr. Niles reopened the perilous subject.

Boston
Feb 23 1894

MY DEAR MRS TODD
Who are we to treat with in regard to the "Letters of Emily Dickinson"?

We should like to make out the contracts. If it is to be Miss D. will she pay for the plates & receive 15 per cent copyright, or shall we pay for them & pay 10 per cent. Will you kindly inform me.

Yrs truly
THO⁸ NILES

DEAR Mʳ NILES,
I have just been two weeks in New York, and on my return I find two letters from you. About the copyright, per cent and so forth, of the E.D. *Letters* I will write you later. I have not had time to arrange it with Miss Lavinia yet.

The *Letters* are going to be a good deal larger than we thought. I have taken out, and taken out, and everything is so good I greatly dislike to cut any more. It takes up more in print than I had supposed possible, and besides, a lot of unknown and unsuspected letters have turned up at the eleventh hour. They are all falling finely into shape, and it will be a most remarkable book. I have just given two talks and readings from them in Brooklyn and they created a profound sensation.

I am to give two more there in April. Now, it has occurred to me to ask whether it would not do to have two small volumes, say of 250 pages each, instead of one with the 500 which it seems to be growing into. The pages are about the size of your beautiful Jane Austen edition. *Her Letters*, I notice, take about 325 pages, but I doubt very much if these could be compressed into that space. It is difficult to estimate my MS, but I do not believe it can make less than 500 pages—and if you should read all the *Letters* I think you would agree with me that they are too striking to leave out many. I have had the judgment of several literary people on that point. This is merely a suggestion, and of course you know much better than I as to the relative merits of one volume or two.

Another thing—I do not think it possible to get it out by Easter, or even late spring. I have had proofs of three chapters (there will be nine) and I am still one chapter ahead of the printers. But Mr. Dickinson, of course, wants to see them all, and he never judges satisfactorily what he wants in or out until he sees them in print; and I must confess that some things *I* thought quite safe to go in, look very startling in the cold impartiality of type, and have to come out. Besides, this is a peculiarly delicate piece of literary work for many reasons, and takes an endless amount of thought and tact. I am very well along with my part, but still it should be a good while before they appear. I am ready to send down two more chapters today or tomorrow. But I should think it would be two or three months before they could come out. Marie Bashkirtseff herself is not more unusual than what is revealed by these strange *Letters*.

The photogravure of the child face is very good. If the artist thinks the softening would improve it, by all means have it done.

I am very sorry to inflict such a length of letter upon you, but I had all these things to say.

Probably Mʳ Todd will be in Boston for a day or two toward the end of the week. I hope it will not annoy you to have the *Letters* appear later than we had anticipated.

Very sincerely
MABEL LOOMIS TODD

Amherst, Massᵗᵗˢ
26 *February*, 1894

Boston
Feb 27, 1894

DEAR MRS TODD

The delay in publication of the Dickinson Letters will not injure it. Business matters are not at all promising & we are destined to see dull times for a good while yet.

If your matter will occupy 500 pages we shall have to make 2 volumes and retail them for $1.00 each.

The printer is waiting for "copy" which is to be inserted & cannot go on till he gets it.

We may as well settle it that publication must be postponed till autumn.

Yrs truly
THOˢ NILES

My mother seems to have spoken to Miss Vinnie about the contract on the same day, as Mr. Niles heard from her on the day following:

MY DEAR MR NILES

I could not consent to give the "copyright" of any of "Emilys" writings to any other than myself. If you choose to pay for the *plates*, I shall be entirely satisfied or if you prefer the other way, it is for you to decide.

I am quite anxious to know if the "child picture of Emily" pleases you.

Heartily
LAVINIA DICKINSON

Amherst
February 27th '94

The subject was not broached again for another two weeks. In the interim, Mrs. Todd gave a talk before the recently established Amherst Woman's Club. The diary says:

March 7

Miss Jordan gave a charmingly analytical talk on E.D., comparing her to Henleigh [Henley], Gale & Bridges in England. Then I followed with advance sheets from my volume of the *Letters*, some talk, & some unpublished poems. Over 160 were present, and they said the afternoon was worth getting up the club for.

Two proofs of the child portrait, sent to Mr. Niles by the engraver, Mr. Elson, on March tenth, "one in a light black ink and the other in a brown," were forwarded to Mrs. Todd, who replied at once:

DEAR Mr NILES:—

The E.D. child-picture is charming. We all think the brown one rather softer and prettier than the black; and I think it entirely satisfactory. Shall I try to find an autograph, Emily Dickinson, in the late, strange writing? You know for years she signed only E. Dickinson, but I think Mr Bowles has just *one* with the Emily written out. It is the only one I know of since her girlhood. Would it be desirable to put such a facsimile

Amherst
27 *April*, 1894

DEAR Mr HARDY,

. . . . The Emily Dickinson *Letters* move along. I have sent proofs of the Bowles chapter to Mr Samuel Bowles, but he has not yet returned them. I send you with this three original letters from E.D. in the three styles of her writing, the early, middle and later periods, for the facsimiles to be made from.[5] There seems always great interest in her changing methods, particularly in that most peculiar latest hand. I am writing an article for some magazine upon her letters in general, giving examples of her growth of style, and I wish you would send me as soon as they are made, copies of these facsimiles; and also will you please send me a copy or print of the child picture, and of the old family home, all to accompany the article, which I hope some editor will like well enough to print before the volume of *Letters* appears next fall. It would be apt to attract attention to the book.

Very truly
MABEL L. TODD

Mrs. Todd's article about the evolution of Emily's handwriting was finished on May sixth and sent to *The Century*. In a letter of May 17, 1894, to Robert Underwood Johnson, later Editor-in-Chief, she says:

Emily Dickinson's sister tells me that for some years before her death she was accustomed to send off many letters and packages addressed to "Roswell Smith, Century Company." What they were no one knew, but she and her maid remember distinctly mailing such packages very often. If she were writing letters to Mr. Smith, is there a chance that they would have been preserved? The fact interested me.

Forty years later, on May 3, 1934, I had a talk about this matter with Mr. Johnson. He said:

[5] Evidently the three letters to be used in facsimile, sent to Mr. Niles on Sept. 13, 1893, receipt of which he acknowledged Nov. 29, 1893, had been returned to Mrs. Todd when, for the second time, the date of publication was postponed. These facsimiles appeared in *Letters*, 1894, on pp. 159, 218, and 355.

Roswell Smith was a delightful fellow, but why Emily should have sent poetry to him is a mystery, as he knew nothing about poetry and cared less. If she did, he doubtless handed it over to [Richard Watson] Gilder to pass on.

I inquired of living relatives of both Mr. Smith and Mr. Gilder regarding Emily's "letters and packages" but without result.

Mrs. Todd's article, refused by *The Century*, was published a year later in a fugitive magazine edited by J. S. Wood.[6]

On May seventeenth Mrs. Todd received the following letter from Mr. Hardy. It was the first time anything had gone wrong at Roberts Brothers. She felt it to be an ill omen.

> Boston
> *May* 16, 1894

DEAR MRS TODD

I send the Picture of Emily Dickinson, the House and the three facsimile letters. Also the originals of *two* of the letters. The engraver tells me that the other letter has been lost in their shop and a search of four days does not bring it to light, and no one in the place will acknowledge being the one to blame. What is to be done? Is it so very valuable that the facsimile will not take the place of it?

It's a terrible piece of ill luck and the worst of it is that I cautioned the man about keeping them safe for us. I have told him that he *must* find the letter but it's hopeless I fear. It's the first time in all my experience that such a thing has happened. If by any good luck it turns up I will write you.

> Very truly yours
> E. D. HARDY

Of the three letters—to Dr. and Mrs. Holland in 1853, to Mr. Bowles in the middle sixties, and to Mr. J. D. Clark in the autumn of 1882—the early letter to the Hollands could least easily have been spared. But that was the one which disappeared. After the proof of a group of letters had been compared with the originals, they were returned to the owners, as we know. Mrs. Todd was particularly disturbed at this loss since Mrs. Holland was the

---

[6] *Bachelor of Arts*, Vol. I, No. 1, May, 1895, pp. 39-66.

only one of the three recipients still living. The missing letter was never found.

An omen of misfortune Mr. Hardy's letter proved indeed to be. A day later, on May 18, 1894, Thomas Niles of Roberts Brothers, who had recently returned from England, died at his estate on the Mystic River in Arlington, just outside of Boston. His death was a blow to authors and publishers alike. Nobody could take his place.

On May twenty-eighth Mrs. Todd went to Boston, and writes:

Went first to Roberts' Brothers. Dear Mr Niles is dreadfully missed. Mr Hardy[7] thinks they will keep on, that is not sell out to any other firm, but Mr Roberts is very different from Mr Niles.

Proof of the Higginson and Norcross chapters was being revised during June and July. Mrs. Todd was still hoping for an opportunity to compare the Norcross letters with the originals. But the importance of a correct printed version did not impress the Norcross sisters. They were adamant. No eyes but their own should ever look upon Emily's letters. Knowing the resoluteness, not to say stubbornness, of such ladies, I am surprised, not at the stand they took, but that any excerpts, even, from Emily's letters to them should have appeared in print.

The following letters from Fanny Norcross together with the entries in Mrs. Todd's diary picture the final effort, as futile as earlier ones, to have these letters fully and accurately reproduced.

Concord
June 24, 1894

MY DEAR MRS. TODD,

I should like very much indeed to go to Amherst in July and have had the plan in my mind all winter, but now I am not sure that I can leave home at all.

We are in serious trouble over the loss of our maid servant,

[7] E. D. Hardy was now in command. I have tried to discover something about him, searching the records in Boston, in Cambridge, and in Bar Harbor, Maine, where he is thought to have lived after his retirement. But no trace of him can be found, not even the date of his death which seems to have created as little impression as his life. He was, my mother used to say, an easily overlooked person.

and for a month past have been trying to find a suitable successor. When that is accomplished I can get away probably, but I believe not before the third week in July.

You are very kind to ask me to visit you, that we will see about later. If I go to Amherst I shall also go to Monson which is not far away and perhaps it will be best to have only the day in Amherst. I shall not be in Cambridge after this month except at odd times till the middle of August. I am very sorry not to be able to ask you to visit our home in Concord, if I cannot go to Amherst, but my sister's health, a small, hot house and a new servant or none at all, will preclude all hospitality this summer, I fear.

I will write again when I see my way clear to make some arrangement for meeting you in Amherst or Boston or Concord.

Yours most cordially
FANNY L. NORCROSS

During the time which elapsed before Miss Norcross actually came to Amherst my mother was occupied with the final miscellaneous chapters.

July 29

I worked pretty hard . . . on the last chapters of E.D. *Letters.* I have come now to VIII, IX, and X. They trouble me a good deal, there are so many people represented, so few dates given me, so much confusion in every way.

July 30

To Mrs Cooper's, to get, if possible, some dates on the letters Emily wrote her. They could remember a few. . . . As I found she [Miss Pemberton] owned both volumes of Emily's *Poems* I took her over to see Vinnie, who was, as usual, encased in an old waterproof skirt, with a napkin around her neck & rubbers, gardening.

The visit of Miss Norcross was heralded as follows:

Concord
Aug. 1, 1894

MY DEAR MRS. TODD,

I will go to Amherst some day next week and spend one night, which I regret to say will be as long as I can be away from home I think at present.

You will please appoint the day, when the proof will be ready.

I cannot send the letters, not because I fear they will be lost, but because my sister and I are not willing that any one even Vinnie should have the free reading of them; many of them have whole sentences which were intended for no eyes but ours, and on our account as well as Emily's no one else will ever read them.

This we consider our right, and we must insist upon it.

I shall bring the letters which I copied almost as they are, and also those from which I made extracts, but I must retain the privilege of reading them to you. Of course the handwriting of the several periods of time will be open for your inspection.

I shall write Vinnie of my plan for going to Amherst, and may I ask you to tell her the day you appoint for me.

Yours very truly
FANNY L. NORCROSS

Miss Norcross was entertained by Miss Vinnie during her overnight stay in Amherst. Here are my mother's impressions of the visit:

August 8   .

Miss Norcross came at noon and I called on her, and soon after two she came over, and we verified Emily's letters to her all the afternoon.

August 9

Miss Norcross here about 9:30, and we finished up the letters. She is alarmed at seeing her name in print, and thinks it will annihilate her sister—who is evidently attempting to copy Emily —and succeeding weakly. She has given me more fuss & trouble & silliness than all the rest of the book together.

The day after Miss Norcross returned to Concord my mother received the following letter:

[*August* 10, 1894]

DEAR MRS TODD,

I enclose the poem, and also tell you that I found the other poem before I reached Belchertown; it is just as you printed it, even the spelling of the words "drest" and "dressed."

I have found all the letters which I did not take to Amherst and have compared them with the proof. I have made most of the corrections on the enclosed sheet, but a few I ventured to make upon the proof. You will notice these.

Now about our names. I found my sister felt just as strongly as I expected she would and after sleeping upon it, and reading all the proof and thinking of it all the time, she cannot consent to have the names appear.

Can you not call them Letters to her cousins, or letters to two cousins, or what will you do? I realize that to make this exception in your contents and headings and elsewhere hurts your harmony, but your scheme hurts us more. If you could say in some pretty way that we were intimate cousins, almost like sisters, the public would respect our shyness perhaps. What will you do?

Of course leaving out the surname, means also the continual "Lou" and "Fanny." L— & F— is enough. I am sorry to make you the trouble, this feeling of ours involves.

The volume I left with Vinnie. By the time I reached the house I realized that it would be better not to take it. She has returned it before this I presume.

The letter I told you of reads

    Little cousins
      "Called back"

                      Emily

Trusting all will reach you safely

                  I am yours sincerely
                      FANNY L. NORCROSS

Have you this anywhere?
      Thank you dear for the passage.
      How long to live the truth is.

          A word is dead, when it is said
          Some say—
          I say it just begins to live
          That day.

The diary continues:

August 11

At work on my miscellaneous chapter of E.D. . . . The chapter came back from that dull, uninteresting, commonplace Miss Norcross. How Emily could have cared one particle for her I cannot imagine. She cannot see the sacred name of Norcross in print, so I take it out (very gladly) & put "The Misses ———" in its place. I certainly have no wish to glorify them.

August 12

A fine day, and I worked like a soldier. I finished up all the endless corrections in that bothersome Norcross chapter, I put the Whitney chapter (VIII) and the miscellaneous chapter (IX) into fine & finished shape for printing; and by that time, six o'clock, having worked steadily since 9, except dinner, I was tired, & took a walk with David.

August 13

Warm day. Work in the morning & doing up horrid old Norcross chapter in proof, & Chapters VIII & IX to go by express to the printers.

Mrs. Todd finished the preface to the volume "satisfactorily except some verbal changes" on August fourteenth. Next, she tried to get an unprejudiced opinion of it—a visionary objective for any document connected with the name "Dickinson."

August 14

Pretty hot & very dusty. . . . After tea I read my Preface to President Seelye & Anna, feeling the absolute need of neutral criticism. They *said* they admired it.

August 17

Tried to begin my Index to the *Letters*, but had to give it up.

August 18

At 2:30 I went up to the Donalds to ask Mr Donald his honest criticisms of my preface to E.D. *Letters*. People are so vague, "Yes, charming," they always say—"very interesting." A detailed opinion is rare. Dr Donald read it carefully and gave me just what I wanted, an opinion on certain points and expressions.

Meanwhile an important ceremony was in the offing—the signing of the contract. After the preliminary discussion between

Mr. Dickinson and Mr. Niles in March, the subject had again been dropped when Mr. Niles left for England. As he died soon after his return, it had been allowed to hang fire—quiescent now for several months.

The contract was of secondary importance to my mother. The book came first, as the relative amount of space devoted to it in her letters bears witness. But to Miss Vinnie it was the other way around. In her opinion the book both as to appearance and as to substance could take care of itself. That it would be remarkable irrespective of how it was handled went without saying.

To call Miss Vinnie unreasonable is not enough to explain her behavior; her motives were so involved. She was jealous for Emily, but more jealous of her own rights as Emily's representative. In addition to this, she was so unused to business that she was ignorant of its practices, even of its language. So she grasped in the dark, but she grasped with determination.

The more insistent Miss Vinnie became, the more impatient was my mother, and the more dogged Mr. Dickinson's determination not to give in to his sister's demands.

While my mother was on the home stretch of work on the *Letters,* Miss Vinnie had reopened the subject of the contract with Mr. Hardy.

Mr Hardy
DEAR FRIEND

I'm sorry of the effort on Mrs Todds part to *force* me to give up the copyright to herself. This I shall never do. If Mrs Todd wanted such ownership she should have told me at the outset & then give up the work if my answer was not satisfactory. Collecting the letters was my own idea endorsed by all my friends. Not one letter would have been entrusted to anybody but Emilys sister. I have asked & received every letter that will be in the volume save *one* package to my Brother found in his attic. Emily would be indignant at any attempt to rob her sister. You may not know that Emily & I were peculiarly devoted sisters & all her possessions were given to me (legally) years before her death. Mrs Todd wished to cluster the letters together but never alluded to the contract. As she was under great personal obligations to me & had (as I supposed) found me honorable, I'm surprised at her demand. I could not do any act that Emily would not endorse. Pardon my long talk. Will you please tell me if you have any choice *who* pays for the *plates* & what the *price* will be?

Heartily

LAVINIA DICKINSON

Amherst
July 25th '94

The bewilderment of the innocent Mr. Hardy can be imagined. Following the receipt of this letter, he wrote to Mr. Dickinson, who at this point takes the center of the stage. On July twenty-seventh he went to Boston to see Mr. Hardy. The day following his call, Mr. Hardy wrote to Miss Vinnie. His letter has disappeared. He might have spared himself the trouble of writing it, however, because she took no notice of it.

Mr. Dickinson was finding it increasingly difficult to be patient with his sister's assertive self-importance. The best way, it seemed, was to leave her alone. As time passed, he sat in her dining-room less frequently than before. Her home was no longer a refuge from his own.

At our house Mr. Dickinson was always welcome. My father and mother revered him. And they were able to help him with many routine details of his work as Treasurer of Amherst College—sending out notices, addressing envelopes, making out deeds, writing up trustee records, and similar duties. This they did so habitually and so gladly that he came to spend more and more of his time with us. His harassed face would relax as he settled down beside the open fire in the little back parlor where he found the peace denied him at home.

A note in his handwriting expresses his concern over some fresh demand on my mother's time and his desire to shield her from an unnecessary drain on her energies.

[*Envelope addressed to Mrs. Todd*]

Sunday morning

DEAR FRIEND

I have been thinking over the Tuesday evening plan, and I am clear that you should be clear of any part in it.

You cannot play the host even without more drain upon your strength than you have a right to permit, and you cannot do justice to your speech without more vigor, and more time for preparation. Call this settled—on the score of health—and let D P start at once to look up an alternative.

Sterrett—at Walker Hall—Prof Montague. I have no doubt he would be complimented to be asked to read a paper on parisian life, and would read a good one—really more entertaining than anything we often have at one of those gatherings. Then there is Elwell rich in philological information, and Genung who can tell us more about Job in a familiar way than any living man, or perhaps something about King Solomon who was a most picturesque and interesting character, or some other of the old saint and sinner combined.

John Tyler—one of his bug or wild animal stories.

Fletcher—on finance, Frink—on independence in thought and action, and plenty more.

Anyhow, you get out of anything for next Tuesday. It can be done—and not to do it is a wrong to yourself, and your friends, and these are everybody,

of whom the subscriber
is one of the chief.

W A D

On August twelfth Mrs. Todd wrote to Mr. Hardy. The first part of the letter has to do with the visit of Miss Norcross to Amherst and the chapter containing her letters, a repetition of facts with which the reader is familiar.

Amherst
12 *August*, 1894

DEAR Mʳ HARDY,

. . . . I do not know if Miss Lavinia has written you yet. She spoke in an off-hand way of having heard from you, and said you rather wanted her to pay for the plates, which would be about $400.00. That seemed a good deal, to her, and she wanted to think of it. She said she had decided to give me half the proceeds of the book, the copyright, *of course,* in her name, and she saw no reason why in the contract there should be any mention of half going to me—she could hand it to me. I told her it *must* be in the contract, and she said she would speak to her brother, as to what he thought. She has not done so. But he says the con-

Letter from William Austin Dickinson to Mabel Loomis Todd
in the early 1880's

Paine and Damon Combined.

John Tyler. one of his
long or well aimed letters,
Sketches on finance,
Funk. on independence in
thought and action.
and plenty more.

Anyhow. you get out
of anything you try to
Tuesday. It can be
done. and not do it
is a wrong to yourself.
and your family.
and thus an Everybody,
of whom the Subscriber
is one of the Chief.

tract *shall* read that half comes to me, with an entire reversion to me at her death. If she does not write you pretty soon, I think you had better write to him about it. Then he will settle it at once. But the contract is to be worded in that way.

If the printers go ahead rapidly now, I do not see why the book may not come out by the middle of October.

Very truly
M. L. Todd

Mr. Hardy replied:

Boston
Aug 14, 1894

Dear Mrs Todd

. . . . Miss Dickinson has not answered my letter of July 28th in which I told her just what Mr. D. asked me to. I also said it was better to make some amicable arrangements as we should not care to give a contract to one party and be liable for a claim by the other party, and that you ought to have something for doing all the work of Editing, etc. If Miss Dickinson does not wish to pay for the plates we will make them at our expense but would prefer her to do it. The better way would be to make out the contract to Miss D. and you as joint owners of the copy't. We often do that way. Then she can transfer her rights in it to you at any time. And we should pay her half and you half when we settle. Very likely she will talk with her brother before writing me. I can draw up the contract and send it to her if that will do. . . .

Very truly yours
E. D. Hardy
for Roberts Bros.

On August twenty-first Mr. Hardy again wrote to my mother, saying that "Miss Dickinson has not written to us yet so we will drop a note to Mr. D. and ask him if it has been settled yet." And he added, "You better get his final answer regarding the Picture."

The note to Mr. Dickinson elicited an immediate reply:

Amherst College
Treasurer's Office

Mr E. D. Hardy
MY DEAR SIR

I have yours of 21ˢᵗ. The contract for publishing the letters will undoubtedly be joint, the royalty to be divided between Mrs Todd and my sister. She has not mentioned the matter to me as yet, not even that she has heard from you, although I handed her your letter, and I know that she has had a talk with one of her lady friends and got her to inquire of Mr Sanborn in a quiet way whether such an arrangement, as proposed, is proper and just.

Before answering your letter to her she will undoubtedly lay the matter before me, and then it will be settled. She doesnt know that time is an element in the transaction of business, or that there is any business of importance except hers, or that editing letters amounts to anything. She thinks all Mrs Todd has had to do has been to copy Emily's letters, and then send them in a heap to you. She doesnt understand.

Wait a little longer and it will come out all right.

Very truly
Wᵐ A DICKINSON

August 22ᵈ '94

Presumably Miss Vinnie's "lady friend" was Fanny Norcross, who could easily have asked Mr. Sanborn the question, being his near neighbor in Concord. As soon as Mr. Dickinson got wind of the fact that his sister had made such a *démarche*, he decided to check up on the result. So my mother wrote to Mr. Sanborn, a not unnatural thing for her to do since he was an old friend of her father and mother. Here is his reply:

American Social Science Association

Concord, *Aug* 16, 1894

DEAR MRS TODD:

I have just returned from Plymouth and Sandwich, to find your letter here.

I think it is customary, when letters are published, to give the copyright to the heirs of the writer; but this is rather a custom than a right, I fancy; because in fact, either the writer or the person to whom they were written can *legally* forbid their publication; since the ownership in them is a joint one.

When the editor is not one of the heirs, either of the writer or recipient, it is also quite customary for him to have the copyright; for example, I believe Mr. C. E. Norton holds the copyright of the Emerson-Carlyle correspondence.

In your case, why not have a joint interest of yourself and Miss Lavinia, with the stipulation that a certain part of the profits shall go *first* to yourself as editor, for the expense and trouble of editing? I should suppose all parties would be satisfied with that, and it would guard you against any future disagreements.

Yours very truly,
F. B. SANBORN

Mrs D. P. Todd
Amherst, Mass.

But my mother was more interested in other things.

Amherst
27 *August*, 1894

DEAR MR HARDY,

I owe you an apology for not answering your letter of August 21st before, but I had to wait for two reasons.

Mr Dickinson will not hear of that portrait [daguerreotype] of Emily being used anywhere—in the volume, or the *Book Buyer*[8] or anywhere else, on any account. So we must give it up for the present, as I seem unable to persuade him. The child one he does not object to. I think the November number would be better for the article. I waited before writing chiefly to hear from the editor of a new magazine [*Bachelor of Arts*] who wanted an article from me, & I sent him one on E.D. with copious extracts from her letters & with the facsimiles, the house and the child-portrait. I called it "The Evolution of a Style." . . . [This] mag-

---

[8] An advance article, "Emily Dickinson's Letters," appeared in *The Book-buyer*, Vol. XI, November, 1894, pp. 485-486, with only the child portrait. It contains the following sentences: "If these volumes were to be read simply for the disclosure of her inner life, too sacredly enshrined for even these friends of her lonely soul to gaze upon, they would be a disappointment indeed. Happily, the letters are, for the most part, so refreshingly original and quaint that . . . they can and will be enjoyed for themselves alone."

azine will be in the interests of Universities generally, and the first number will be sent very largely to college graduates and faculties. . . .

I do think the *Letters* needs an Index, and I am making it now. The printers have everything but that and the final chapter.

Miss Lavinia is still "mulling" over your letter. Her brother says the contract will be as we want it—the half profits and reverting to me later—but he lets her think she is doing it all, & says she will speak to him, undoubtedly, soon. That is the way it will read, however.

Very sincerely
MABEL L. TODD

Galley proofs continued to pour in throughout the month of September. On the twenty-fifth my mother comments upon another flare-up of the contract discussion.

I worked all day over proof. . . . More disgusting treachery from Vinnie—after having arranged the whole matter of my having half the proceeds of the *Letters* with Austin, she writes to Mr Hardy that the contract is to be just the same as the *Poems*—in which I have nothing. Mr Hardy promptly sends the letter to Austin, as he told him the right way. Vinnie is an awful snake, but all the same it hurts me very much. Austin is going to tell her he knows all about it tomorrow.

Miss Vinnie's letter to Mr. Hardy, forwarded by him to Mr. Dickinson who then returned it, is missing. But Mr. Dickinson's replies leave no doubt as to its contents.

Amherst, *Sep* 25th 94

Mr E. D. Hardy
MY DEAR SIR.

I have yours of 22d. I am surprised at my sister's letter to you, to put it mildly. The contract will not be made in the way she proposed. I will speak to her about it tomorrow, and she will probably then write you to make it as we had talked, royalty divided between her and Mrs Todd, which I understood her to say would be entirely satisfactory to her. It will be that or no book.

I return her letter to you. When she writes again please send that to me too.

This may all seem very queer to you, and it is. We are a queer lot, or all but me, as the children would say, but some of us know the difference between right and wrong, and possibly one or two other things.

Yours very truly
Wᵐ A DICKINSON

Amherst, *Sep* 26, 94

Mr E. D. Hardy
DEAR SIR

I have had a talk with my sister today. She had accepted the idea that Mrs Todd had done a little something about the letters—though I think she believes the main work was in copying them into an intelligible hand, and that she did this for love (as she did) and so it would be base to offer to pay for it.

She now agrees as follows. The copyright to be in her name. The plates to be paid for from first sales of the book. The royalty after this to be equally and regularly divided. Check for one half to be sent to her, and check for the other half to Mrs Todd, from you. I think the contract should state that the one half sent to Mrs Todd is in consideration of her services in preparing the book, and by agreement.

If you will send the contract to me I will look it over and see if I have any suggestions to make before offering it for signature.

Very truly
Wᵐ A DICKINSON

On the very day of this newest agreement between her brother and herself Miss Vinnie followed it up with a letter to Mr. Hardy.

Mr Hardy
DEAR SIR

My Brother assures me you are not satisfied with my platform. As I'm not under guardianship & Mrs Todd (only this morning) professed endorsement of *my way* of sharing the result of the letters (if there is any) with her I can not quite understand the continued & determined hostile attitude towards me. I prefer the pleasure of extending to her *myself* an equal share in the spoils (if there is any) as the letters & the work concern only us two.

I think she can trust my honor.

Sincerely

LAVINIA DICKINSON

Amherst
September 26th '94

This sounds as if it was not so much "an equal share in the spoils" Miss Vinnie objected to, as that the editor should receive payment direct from the publisher. She wanted to be the dispenser of bounty—to pay Mrs. Todd herself.

Before concluding the parable of the contract may I draw attention to the fact that personal traits, already well established, were becoming more and more intensified. My mother, a blithe young person of many resources and many interests among which the book of *Letters* was but one, was just beginning to feel her ability to sway an audience. It was to her an exciting discovery —a new sense of power. Miss Vinnie, on the other hand, was growing old. She was waging a brave fight, she thought, in defense of Emily. To her it constituted life. There was nothing else.

Had I been able to find a picture of Miss Vinnie as she appeared during the last few years of her life, one look would, I think, have made my point clear. But since my efforts have been fruitless, a description of her appearance at this time must serve. I asked my mother to tell me what Miss Vinnie looked like and more about her characteristics. Here are my rambling notes of her replies to my questions:

Vinnie's mouth was perfectly hideous and full of false teeth. Some were false teeth and some her own. Her skin was very white and wrinkled. Her face was repulsive—no half-beauty left in it. Her eyes were gray and her hair was long and thick and it had a tinge of red in the brown. She was very small. Her hands had grown-out joints and were always dirty. She did her hair in a loop behind and parted and down over her ears.

She dressed in quaint queer clothes. Her very best dress was a dark blue flannel. . . . The dress was made in pleats with a loose waist and a belt and had a jacket effect. The skirt had an overskirt with much knife-pleating. She never had a new dress except the blue flannel.

She had the weirdest errands for people to do. She was always sending me to Boston to buy white cotton stockings when everybody wore black stockings. She thought the dye in black stockings would poison her feet. I went into store after store to ask for white cotton stockings and they said they hadn't had any for years. I finally bought her some unbleached cotton stockings.

Vinnie had a great many callers. She went to the door herself and took them into the library. Her more intimate friends she took right through into the dining-room and kitchen. If she had more than one caller at a time, each was put in a different room to be entertained separately. People enjoyed hearing her swearing at her friends in most picturesque language.

Professor Joseph K. Chickering paid a tribute to Miss Vinnie's language:[9]

> . . . . She never said things as other people said them. . . . Her views of life were those of an onlooker, not a participator. . . . Her fiercest denunciations were reserved for those who ventured to oppose or even call in question, the opinions of her father and brother on matters of public concern. No other opinions were either conceivable or allowable.

"A virulent use of words," my mother told me, "was Vinnie's only talent," and she showed me a little book in which she had written down some of Miss Vinnie's remarks about her neighbors. Here are a few of them:

"Indigestion is responsible for more things than anything except Providence."

"He was a runaway corpse."

"She is always poulticed from head to foot. . . . Her shoulders are as high as gallows—and with sleeves."

"Her voice was sharp—it needed oiling."

"Has he a baby? Well, his wife partly had one, but it decided not to breathe when it entered this world."

Of a minister of the gospel: "He preached one of his cancerous sermons. It would be well to have a little chlorate of lime sprinkled down the aisles, there is so much 'sewer' in his sermons."

[9] *The Springfield Republican*, Nov. 30, 1899.

One morning, having been kept awake most of the night by profane drunken roistering in front of her house, she remarked, "Well, at least it shows that they have heard of our Redeemer."

Miss Vinnie was very proud of her command of language and well aware of her powers of persuasion, maintaining that she could make anybody believe anything she chose—a competence later exploited to the full, as we shall see.

In the matter of the contract Austin treated his sister like a child because he regarded her as such. Without Emily's understanding, which tempered his devotion to her with awe, Lavinia was equally unacquainted with business dealings. Lacking experience as Emily did, she lacked genius also. But though "unworldly" she was canny, a combination of traits which exasperated him. Tension was increasing hour by hour.

How unnecessary it all was! In a few years Austin was dead; Lavinia was dead; and there was never any income from the *Letters.* Could Austin have foreseen that thirty years later the work for which he was then endeavoring to insure adequate compensation would be republished by his daughter as her own, the final drop then lacking to make his cup of bitterness overflow would have been supplied.

Before the contract was actually signed a few more letters were exchanged.

DEAR MR HARDY:—

. . . . Could I see, before long, some samples of the coarse linen we had thought of for the cover? And on the whole, we are rather inclined to have entirely plain covers, except on the back, the gold lettering. Would it not be pretty to have *one* little Indian pipe on the back for the first volume, and *two* for the second? Instead of figures.

I have been of course somewhat annoyed, and also amused, at Miss Lavinia's evasion of the contract matter, but Mr Dickinson says it is all settled now, and as we wish. He will have her sign it as soon as it comes, as he wrote you. It has annoyed him a great deal.

Very truly
MABEL L. TODD

Amherst
September 28, 1894

The omitted parts of the foregoing letter had to do with the division of the book into two volumes, a subject covered by Mr. Hardy's reply.

Boston
Oct 2, 1894

DEAR MRS TODD,

I would rather have the book divided at Chap. VI for convenience in making it. If divided at VII it necessitates two weights of paper instead of one if divided at VI. If you wish the Vol. 2 to commence [with] Col. Higginson, I shall not object. I have only 296 pages cast so far, (see note from Mr. Wilson). End of Chap. VI. I have sent the book of cloths by mail today. The Indian Pipe idea can be done for the back. We will try it. Please decide about the division so I can order the paper made. I should say the same paper that we used on Dickinson Poems Vol. 1 & 2 would be about right. That will make the books about $\frac{1}{4}$ thicker than the Poem single vols. are now. This would be all we could afford for the Price, $1.00 per vol. After consulting with the printer I think it better to retain "In Two Volumes" and omit the dates, see revise proof title. Contracts were sent to *Mr.* Dickinson a day or two ago. Have not heard from him yet. I don't think *Miss* D. intends to sign them.

Very truly yours
(Roberts Bros.)
E. D. HARDY

On the same day, October second, Colonel Higginson returned the proof of his chapter which "reads very well & only required the few corrections I gave. The book will be most interesting."

The contracts which Mr. Hardy mentions having sent to Mr. Dickinson on October second elicited the following acknowledgment:

Amherst
Octo 4, 94

Mr E. D. Hardy
DEAR SIR

I duly received the forms of contract and think they are all right. Shall expect to return them to you signed tomorrow. I wanted the Todds to look them over first, and then handed them to my sister to struggle over in her own way. I think she will be delivered of her signature in a few hours more. She has great trouble in understanding how I should have any interest or part in the matter, and is disturbed by the feeling that somehow her glory and magnificence are dimmed by any other than her supreme self being recognized in correspondence.

She will have to put up with this much however, all the rest she can have for herself.

> Very truly
> W^m A Dickinson

Before this letter was mailed, however, the contracts had been signed and were enclosed with a note:

At last,
   and at length.
When you have signed, return one of the duplicates directly to her. She will feel better to see her name on the outside of the big envelope covering it.

> W^m A D

Octo 6, 94

I have in my possession a rough draft of the contract in Mr. Hardy's hand. Written on the reverse of a paper-manufacturer's acknowledgment of an order for stock, it reads as follows:

The party of the first part agrees to pay the Parties of 2^d Part the cost of making the electro plates of said work, by allowing the necessary amount to be deducted from the copyright proceeds, and as such payment being made the said electro plates shall be the property of the party of the first part. The party of 2^d Part also agrees that after the electro plates are paid for in full, the copyright proceeds shall be shared equally, with Mrs Mabel Loomis Todd in consideration of service done in preparing the MS and editing the said work

This matter of Lavinia's signature—the difficulty of obtaining it, her reluctance to sign any document, whatever its nature—was later to assume considerable importance. Giving her signature seemed to her to imply that she bestowed along with it something more than her consent—that in writing her name she was permitting some unknown hostile force to obtain ascendancy over her, another primitive flareback. Once having signed her name, moreover, she never was willing to call it a signature. It was always her "autograph."

The next day Mrs. Todd wrote to the publishers:

Amherst
7 *October*, 1894

DEAR MR HARDY

The great act has actually been consummated, the signature produced. I think we are all to be congratulated. I believe it was sent you yesterday.

I am entirely willing to divide the *Letters* as seems best to you —five chapters in each volume. After all, it may not make much difference which correspondent opens the second volume. And the paper like the *Poems* will be entirely satisfactory. [Here follows a paragraph about illustrations and title-page.]

Of the cloth, I like green the best, partly because Emily Dickinson says in one of her letters, "Why did you bind it in green and gold—the immortal colors?" And we like *equally* the "Linen 11," and "Buckram D."

We cannot really decide which we should like better. If you have any personal choice will you not tell me? As between these two. These linens and buckrams are very attractive to me.

I have galleys of the last half of VIII, IX, and X, which I mean to send down tomorrow. Then I can finish my Index as soon as they send them cast.

I believe this was all I wanted to speak about especially.

Very sincerely
MABEL L. TODD

And again on the day following:

[8 *October* 1894]

DEAR MR HARDY—

. . . . I have got all the entries for the Index as far as I have cast proofs, viz; through to VIII, but I shall have to turn it over to Mr Fletcher. It is a tremendous piece of work, and he is a professional indexer, and will do it finely. He will do it the last of this week. The preface has got to come to me once more before casting. It is rather a delicate piece of writing, and needs much study. . . .

Very truly
M. L. TODD

On October eleventh Mr. Hardy wrote that "the contracts were all executed and signed the other day."

Work at high pressure filled the final weeks preceding publication of the *Letters* late in November, 1894. My mother's diary gives the story day by day. On October ninth she finished the manuscript of the final chapter.

Hope to get off Chapter X proof today. * * * That went, also the Introduction, which David helped me with a great deal. Everything is now off my hands except the great Index, and a few plate corrections.

The next few days were devoted to the index with the help of Mr. William I. Fletcher, the librarian. A man of wide outlook and sympathies, he was well known in his field, editor of Poole's Index, and author of *Public Libraries in America* in the Columbian Knowledge Series.

On October thirteenth Mrs. Todd received word from Mr. Hardy that he had ordered "Emily" Vol. I on the press and desired all remaining copy.

The diary continues:

October 14

Work on preface—it bothers me a good deal—all the afternoon.

October 15

Worked all the morning with David on *beating* my preface into shape. Have left out a good deal. At eleven took it over to read to Vinnie. She apparently heard nothing of it except the first sentence, in which *she* was mentioned. Did not think it sufficiently prominent.

October 16

Vinnie sent for me—having lain awake all night thinking she was not given sufficient prominence in my preface, and in composing a sentence to be inserted at the beginning, in which she might flourish. . . . Then I was sent for again to go to Vinnie's, and by that time it was dinner.

October 17

Worked on my Index & a lot of proof.

October 19

A perfect whirl—had some final work to do on Chapter X and the Introduction, with David, which kept me very long.

October 20

A rare day. I forgot proofs, housekeeping, annoyances and tragedies, and basked in the day.

October 22

[Austin] is not well, I think completely tired out—no vacations, no let-ups ever. . . . The whole situation is tragic.

The reader knows Miss Vinnie well enough by now to understand why she lay awake all night after reading proof of the preface, the opening paragraph of which was this:

> The lovers of Emily Dickinson's poems have been so eager for some of her prose that her sister has asked me to prepare these volumes of her letters.

The paragraph so reads in all but a few copies of the book in which we find instead:

> The lovers of Emily Dickinson's poems have been so eager for her prose that her sister has gathered these letters, and committed their preparation to me.

No one appears to have noticed this discrepancy which, if recognized, would have given an added collector's value to the few differing copies, the exact number of which I have been unable to verify.

What is the explanation?

In her letter of May 27, 1893, to Mr. Niles, Miss Vinnie wrote: "It has been a great pleasure to collect these letters, all of them possessed by our mutual friends." Colonel Higginson, writing to Mrs. Todd on May 30, 1893, quotes a letter from Miss Vinnie in which she said that "*she* collected all the letters that will be contained in the volume 'save one package' "—those to her brother. She made the same statement in a letter of July 25, 1894, to Mr. Hardy. Facts aside, that was what Miss Vinnie preferred to believe. And so, if the preface merely stated that she had asked my mother to prepare the volume of letters, she herself would not be given sufficient credit. The reader is well aware that Miss Vinnie had not collected all the letters. But she had nursed the illusion, or the wish, so long, bolstered by the fact that she had written to a good many old friends inquiring about letters from Emily, that by now she had forgotten that she had not collected them all. Mr. Dickinson, on the other hand, was unwilling to endorse the false statement that his sister had collected all the letters contained in the book.

My mother was in a dilemma. It was a taut moment. Something had to give way. It was she who did. The proof was corrected to read as Miss Vinnie wished and was sent off.

But that did not end the matter. When Mr. Dickinson heard about it, he would not allow the proof to stand as corrected. A telegram was dispatched to Mr. Hardy instructing him to print ten copies of the book in which the first paragraph of the preface should state that Miss Vinnie had collected the letters, all subsequent copies to read as originally written.

It was a childish performance. But in many ways Miss Vinnie was a child. My mother explained that it seemed at the time the only way to deal with her. Probably so. I must admit, though, that my sympathy goes to Miss Vinnie, not because she was not given in the preface all the credit she deserved, for she was; but because her brother thought it necessary to deceive her. So far as I know the ruse was successful because she could not see to read. Having examined, by proxy, the first paragraph in an early copy of the book, she would have been satisfied once and for all that it was to her liking.

At this time my father was helping a good deal. The cover design, for instance, seems to have been his choice.

> Amherst College Observatory
> Amherst, Mass.

DEAR Mʳ HARDY

Thanks for the new illustration—proofs received this morning. About the enclosed sketch—Mʳˢ Todd and myself both would prefer the little pipes which I have encircled; but will not at all object to plain I and II, if for any reason that shd be your choice.

Of course perfectly plain cloth covers are all the rage now— but I think them rather *too* severe; and believe in a slight ornament as a median course, for the long run. The new Sherman letters (Scribners) are perfectly to my notion—it seems to me that the interlacing wreaths add greatly, & will make the book *always* in good taste & acceptable, whatever the temporary fashion. So I wd suggest a reduction (nearly 1/2) of the pipes on the front cover of E D *Poems*—to be put right in the centre of *front* page of cover. *Fourth* page of cover to be perfectly plain. Stamped in burnished gold.

But of course it will be very handsome in the Buckram D, without this; still there wd be the same appropriateness in the pipes as in the *poems*; & Mrs. Todd mentions this in her last chapter of the *Letters*. . . .

Very truly yours

DAVID P. TODD

19th *October* 1894

On October twenty-third Mr. Hardy wrote that they would "bind the book in Buckram D and have the Pipes on the side, also on the back for I & II."

The index was dispatched on October thirtieth. Complete plate proofs of both volumes were received on November fifth. My mother spent the next afternoon "sending announcements of the *Letters* to various newspaper and magazine friends. . . . Proof of Index came." On November seventh she wrote that

David and I sat up until half past twelve, correcting and verifying Index proof; and we were up this morning at six, and at it again. We sent for Mr Fletcher after breakfast, and all worked until noon. . . . Then more Index until nearly three.

Mr. Fletcher had a graceful way of handling any situation. For him the thing of importance seemed to be not that he should be paid for his work, but that each transaction should add to his store of friendly relationships.

DEAR MRS. TODD:–

I enclose my bill for services on the E.D. index. I shall gladly accept this amount, in addition to a copy of the book as I suggested, as an equivalent for my work, and am pleased to have had a share in the undertaking.

Sincerely yours,
W. I. FLETCHER

Amherst
Nov. 9, 1894

The amount of the bill was $20, a sum paid by Mr. Dickinson.

The time for publication of the *Letters* had arrived. Interest focused upon it. There is but one disturbing note—a little entry in my mother's diary for November eighteenth:

Austin . . . seems to me very tired and run down. The pitilessness of circumstances is very depressing.

CHAPTER XVI

Publication of the *Letters*

Fame is the tint that scholars leave
Upon their setting names—
The iris not of occident
That disappears as comes.

LETTERS of *Emily Dickinson* was published on November 21, 1894. In her diary my mother wrote, "The E.D. *Letters* came today —bound in light green buckram, & very pretty, the two volumes in a box.[1] I am so glad they are done."

Her six complimentary sets were acknowledged in a letter to the publisher:

Amherst, Mass^tts
23 *November*, 1894

DEAR Mr HARDY,

Many thanks for the copies of the *Letters* which came safely, and are very handsome and satisfactory. I hope they will sell finely, for the greatest interest and expectation seem to be awaiting them. We are hard at work now in finishing *Stars and Telescopes*. . . . I suppose Miss Lavinia has written you about the *Letters*—she seemed much pleased with the appearance, inside and out.

Very sincerely
MABEL LOOMIS TODD

Miss Vinnie's acknowledgment was dispatched three days later.

MY DEAR MR HARDY

Thank you for sending the books so promptly. They are quite satisfactory & are all sent away today. I regret Mr Niles is not

[1] Appendix III.

here to witness the completion of a work I believe he was interested in. I shall miss my most agreeable acquaintance with him. His considerate & gallant manner will always be remembered. I would like 6 more copies of the letters, at your earliest convenience.

Prof. Todd tells me there is only *one* thousand copies printed. I should have suggested 2 thousand as the "Holiday days" are near & what remains unsold at that time I feel *sure* will be wanted later.

Cordially
LAVINIA DICKINSON

Amherst
November 26th '94

This first edition of one thousand copies was reported "all sold" on November twenty-seventh. Expectation ran high. On November twenty-eighth my parents were already at work upon a list of corrections for the second edition. These were sent to the publisher on the twenty-ninth with a letter in which my mother said, "I hope there may be a dozen editions before Christmas." and she added:

Would it not be well in advertising the *Letters* to say "Edited, with Introduction and Notes" by M.L.T.? I notice that seems to be the general way if there *are* an Introduction and Notes by the Editor. The notes mean a good deal in these volumes, as many of the letters could not be understood without them.

A letter from Colonel Higginson reached Mrs. Todd a few days later:

25 Buckingham St.
Cambridge, Mass.
Nov. 29, 1894

DEAR FRIEND

Emilie has arrived. They sent her to Sever's bookstore where I rarely go & where she might have laid forever in a cupboard. The ghostflowers are very effective. All the editing so far seems admirable; I only doubted whether there were not a little too much of the earlier letters—not of those to Austin which are infinitely valuable with their wealth of heart—still more shown in the letters to the Hollands. But it is extraordinary how the mystic and bizarre Emily is born at once between two pages (p. 146)—as Thoreau says summer passes to autumn in an instant. All after that is the E.D. I knew. But how is it possible to reconcile her accounts of early bookreading (p. 38, etc.) with the yarns (O! irreverence) she told me about their first books, concealed from her father in the great bush at the door, or under the piano cover?* Well! What an encyclopedia of strange gifts she was.

Yours affectionately
T. W. HIGGINSON

* You told me that her brother could not recall that.

One of her first six sets was dispatched to Mr. Howells by Mrs. Todd. His acknowledgment follows:

40 West 59th St.
Dec. 2, 1894

DEAR MRS. TODD:

I shall be glad of the Emily Dickinson letters, I am sure, when they come, and I thank you for thinking of me. What a rare and strange spirit she was! Any revelations of personality that her letters may make will be most welcome to those who now love her afar.—What was the name of her sister who wrote me? I should like to write to her when I have read the letters.

We have got our girl back from Paris, and are all very happy together—except the boy, who is still away.

My wife and daughter join me in regards to Professor Todd and yourself, and with love to Millicent, I am

Yours sincerely,
W. D. HOWELLS

Mrs. Todd's next letter to Mr. Hardy mentioned an idea new to him:

Amherst
3 *December*, 1894

DEAR Mr HARDY:

The notices of the *Letters* are coming pretty fast now—some paper called it "the book of the year," and certainly it is the most noticeable one—I had almost said sensational, but it is hardly that. Yesterday's *Republican* gave it a column and a half, besides half a column more of quotations from the verses enclosed in letters.

Of course I have unpublished poems enough for at least six more volumes like the first Series and Second, and sometime we may want them—but in the meantime how does the idea of an "Emily Dickinson Year Book" strike you?[2] I talked with Mr Niles over a year ago about it, and he thought it a fine idea, and seemed to think it would sell largely. My thought is that with isolated lines from the already published poems, many of which are perfect comets of thought, and some of these wonderful epigrams from the *Letters*, together with a mass of *unpublished* lines which I should take from poems which could never be used entire, I could make the most brilliant year-book ever issued. Think of reading, against some day in March "House is being cleaned: I prefer pestilence." Or "Spring's first conviction is a wealth beyond its whole experience," or a dozen others I could quote in as many minutes, all specially appropriate to some time or season. And to have this ready for a holiday book just a year from now, daintily bound for Christmas 1895, and yet each day dated, *not* by days of the week so that it could only be used one year, but by days of the month so it could be used always—is to my mind a good idea. If I do not do it, some one else will want to, because E.D. abounds so in epigrams—and I suggest it a year in advance that if you regard it favorably I can be gradually collecting my 365 flashes, and looking over the unpublished manuscripts for some superb bits that I know are there.

The books I asked for arrived safely Saturday evening. Regard from Mr Todd.

Very sincerely
MABEL LOOMIS TODD

Boston
Dec 11, 1894

DEAR MRS TODD

I have been very busy since your letter of the 3^d came to hand. It's very likely that your idea of a Dickinson Year-Book is a good one, still I should rather wait until the first of next year and see how the "Letters" come out. So far we have not sold all of the

---

[2] Mrs. Todd and Mr. Niles had discussed the possibility of a yearbook in the spring of 1892 (p. 201).

1st Edition but they may go this week. The second Edition will be ready in a few days.

I will see what I can do with Mr R[oberts] later on.

Very truly yours
E. D. HARDY

The earlier report that the entire first edition had been sold within a week was apparently incorrect.

Meantime, Miss Vinnie's mind seems to have been running in other channels:

MY DEAR MR HARDY

Thank you for the 2nd promptness of books. Will you add 6 more copies to my account & *one* combined volume of "the poems," when convenient. I rejoice "the letters" are finding favor in the world. I expected success but one never *knows* the result of any enterprise.

In a July letter you estimated the cost of the plates possibly 400 dollars. Do you find it more or less as the work goes on? I'm grateful that you will have a 2nd thousand copies of the letters right away.

Sincerely
LAVINIA DICKINSON

December 5th '94

On the fifth of December Mrs. Todd was taken ill, the result, it was said, of fatigue. She was in bed for three weeks, an unprecedented experience for her. But she was somewhat cheered by the fact that, as she wrote in her diary, December eighteenth, "Everybody who comes is enthusiastic over the *Letters,* and most persons like best Chapter II—those written to Austin; they are so tender, and witty too."

While confined to her bed, she was devising ways in which to increase the sales of the book. I wrote to the publishers for her, suggesting how this might be accomplished. The letters in my childish handwriting have recently come to light.

Mr. Hardy acknowledged to my father my letter of December twenty-second:

Boston
Dec 24, 1894

DEAR MR. TODD.

Letter from Millicent to hand and I will have circulars sent to the names on the list. Am sorry to hear of Mrs Todd's illness and hope it will be of short duration. Kindly give my regards to her and accept the same for yourself with Merry Xmas.

Very truly yours
E. D. HARDY

On Christmas Day my mother had recovered sufficiently to sit up. She spent part of the day reading notices about the book and pasting them into her scrapbook which she had begun two days after publication and finished up to date on December thirtieth. During her convalescence she was cheered by many letters of appreciation.

"Hedgecote"
Glen Road
Jamaica Plain
Nov. 26, 1894

MY DEAR MRS. TODD:

. . . . I don't know what I have done to deserve those letters: many of them are just as dear to me as if they had been written to me. She had no business to have special friends: the world was her friend: that portion of the world who not knowing her would have known her if they had known her. That is rather awkwardly orphic. What bubbling letters: like little springs in woodland recesses full of glints and mysterious shadows: like the fountains in Maeterlinck! I like her prose better than her poetry for much of it is poetry. Did ever poet approach her art more awesomely! That second letter to Col Higginson touches the salt springs of the heart. I love it: I have read and re-read it. To be called master by such a soul! Ye Gods. . . .

But thank you for the Letters!

Yours faithfully
N. H. DOLE

Miss Eastman of Dana Hall wrote to Miss Vinnie, "There have never been letters like these printed in America. They are

Charles Lamb, Disraeli, Macauley, Dr. John Brown, Christopher
North and Mrs. Hare combined. I shall hoard mine like gold."

Dr. Donald wrote in some detail:

Trinity Church
In the City of Boston

DEAR MRS TODD:

I have just noticed that the copy of *Emily Dickinson's Letters*
you sent us is inscribed to myself as well as to Mrs Donald & I
hasten at once to thank you for my equity in the books. I do so
heartily.

Of course I have read them with very great interest—a mixture of admiration, pleasure, exasperation & amusement. The
early ones are quite human; that is to say, a good deal like
other people's letters, exceptional only in this, that they are written by a young girl. Young girls—at least those who write me—
don't write that sort of letter. The later ones are, so to speak,
exposed. What I mean is, that when a deep personal emotion
seizes—obsesses—the writer, as for example when Dr Holland's
death is announced, the phrasing becomes human again. Take
the four written after that death: the first is the simplest and
truest—the fourth shows the writer is recovering her grasp on her
style. And when Annie is married, it is recovered entirely. What is
thrown off, what is written to convey what letters were meant to
convey, is all thoroughly self-expressive, natural, what you will.

Though no one saw her in her garden, she seems never to have
been without one spectator. One eye on flower, bee, grass, tree,
heaven, the other steadily upon herself. I can't fancy her using
the mirror as we do, she had seen herself too often. Not that she
was a *poseuse*; that implies an audience—but she did attitudinize
for her own pleasure.

But no one else has done it, could do it. Her success is unique.
That makes the history, as half naïvely recorded in her letters,
interesting, amazing, fascinating. Frankly, I turned from the
Letters to the Poems to escape & recover the sense of unmixed
happiness. Poetry is public, letters are—well, private. "As
imperceptibly as grief" is worth the two volumes: that is to say,
to me.

I rather think the above is pretty brutal—one dislikes to speak
so of the helpless dead—and she a woman; but the letters are
published. I wish they hadn't been. Still, I am glad you brought

them out, for, by them, new readers may be led to the Poems, which justifies anything of this nature.

This letter illustrates what the *Evening Post* predicted of the Letters' readers. But I thank you for our copy & assure you that you "keep out of the way," in the editing, splendidly.

Yours very sincerely

E. Winchester Donald

Dec 29, 1894

Colonel Higginson paid us a brief visit at about this time. In the following letter he mentions certain lecture engagements which he hoped to secure for my mother.

Cambridge

Jan. 7, 1895

Dear friend

Here are the pictures for you and Millicent. I got home safely, though disappointed of my wish to stay over night beneath your roof. Nevertheless I had a happy visit & unexpectedly long. I have written to the Cantabrigia Club. Shall I write to Eva Channing Sec'y of the Woman's Club? They pay nothing, as you know, but are a good advertisement.

I send you a note to add to the Dickinsoniana. Since I owe to Emily the possession of your friendship, I consider that all relating to her should go to you.

Father Tabb is the new Maryland poet. He wished me to read & criticize his poems & I turned them over to Chadwick, of Brooklyn.[3]

Let me know when you come hereabouts.

Yours affectionately

T. W. Higginson

Enclosed was a letter from Father Tabb.

St Charles College

Ellicott City, Md.

Dec. 31st 1894

My dear Mr Chadwick:

Among my Xmas presents came a copy of Miss Dickinson's Poems, one or two only of which I had seen. I began at first

---

[3] J. W. Chadwick's criticism of John B. Tabb's *Poems* appeared in *The Christian Register*, Jan. 10, 1895.

to mark the thoughts "that take one's breath away" & found I had "italicized as 'twere" one half the volume. I know not where so much before is said in such a compass. The thoughts project beyond the lines & leave the jagged ends. No wonder rhymes are missing.

In saying that this author would have liked my little book, you have paid me my best compliment.

That the New Year be brimful of blessing for you, is the prayer of

Yours faithfully,

JOHN B. TABB.

A few days later Mr. Higginson wrote to my mother again:

Cambridge
Jan 13, 1895

DEAR FRIEND

I think you may like to see this notice, if you haven't—probably by Richard Burton. The "bald" is funny. [In the review "bold" was printed "bald"—in Emily's description of her hair as "bold, like the chestnut burr."]

At some time when I see you, I will tell you more about my chief interview with E.D.—some things I never put in print. It was all a most curious experience.

Perhaps I may hear you before the Woman's Club. I wish I could.

In haste

T.W.H.

P.S. A lady who used to live in Amherst & left there about 1852 is quite confident that the valentine to Howland [dated 1852] was written some years *before* that time (she had a copy given her then) & wishes you to look & see if he did not graduate earlier.[4]

Reviews had been coming in for a month or more. W. F. Whetcho, in the *Boston Daily Advertiser*, November 23, 1894, rated the literary quality of the letters high:

> There may be extravagance in these letters, over statement, but there is thought, high, subtle, delicate. These letters will be read,

---

[4] *Letters*, 1931, pp. 138-141. William Howland graduated in 1846.

quoted, will find their place in books of selections. They will comfort bereaved ones; they will help, they will stimulate. These two volumes are among the books of the year.

But most reviewers indulged chiefly in speculation about Emily's life. Here are a few excerpts:

It was well to publish these letters as a companion to her poetry. They help us to interpret this strangely realistic and impassioned woman. . . . She was entirely out of place in the religious society in which she moved. . . . There is very little biography in these letters, but throughout they are revelations of her spiritual and emotional life. . . . A personality is here revealed which has, perhaps, no counterpart in our literary history. . . . The strange and exceptional life which is here revealed will be studied by the psychologist with quite as much interest as by the person interested in literature, and it will be difficult for many to believe that so strange a personality could exist in a simple New England village and give hardly any sign of itself until death had finally completed her message to the world. . . . Her life was in many respects a protest against social and religious conditions, and as an impressionist she had a remarkably distinct and impressive career.—*Boston Herald*, November 27, 1894

It is nevertheless somewhat painful to read these two volumes. . . . For while we have no doubt that Emily Dickinson cherished the hope that her verses would be given to the world,—knowing, as she must, how precious they were for the spirit,—and even caring to leave behind her little address of greeting,—it is certain that she never meant a line of these letters to be printed. Now that they are between covers, in plain print, which the vulgar may read, we feel that the shy and elusive creature is intruded upon, and for our part, we are inclined humbly to beg pardon. . . . —*The Springfield Republican*, December 2, 1894

In Chicago the *Letters* made quite a stir. On December first two contradictory reviews appeared, in *The Inter Ocean* and in *The Chicago Tribune*. Equally divergent views were dogmatically expressed in Philadelphia:

This seclusion was due partly to the circumstances of Miss Dickinson's single life and partly to the extreme sensitiveness of her

delicate and spiritual nature, a sensitiveness that eventually developed into morbid aversion to society and finally into eccentricity bordering on insanity. [The reviewer admits, however, that] . . . the two volumes of letters are mines of jewels, among which may be found gems of priceless lustre. They do not give much biographic information, and indeed there was apparently pathetically little to give, but they add to the poet's production already published a thesaurus of verse of rare quality and permanent worth.—*The Telegraph*, Philadelphia, December 8, 1894.

Transcendentalism should claim Emily Dickinson for its own, as her prose and verse alike fulfill the intention with absolute simplicity, and complete independence of the fetters of rhyme.—*The Public Ledger*, Philadelphia, December 7, 1894

In contrast to this "absolute simplicity," *The Congregationalist*, December 27, 1894, avers that "it is probable that she deliberately cultivated eccentricity."

A review in *The Nation*, December 13, 1894, reprinted in *The Evening Post*, December 18, 1894, speaks of

notes, whose structure reminds the reader of sheet-lightning when they are most connected, of nothing in literature when they are disconnected. . . . It has been a task, too, calling for exceptional powers of interpretation and sympathy. . . . The style of a recluse is as definite and legitimate an object of investigation as the conditions that make the writer seclude herself. . . . Miss Dickinson defines genius as the ignition of the affections, and the definition seems likely in her case to have been true. . . . The pathos of her recurring, short-lived revivals of the effort to live life whole instead of by spasms is extreme. . . .

Opinion will probably swing between the conviction that these letters are a precious legacy of genius for which we have to thank the scrupulous industry of Mrs. Todd and the generosity of Miss Lavinia Dickinson, and the equally strong feeling that they are the abnormal expression of a woman abnormal to the point of disease, and that their publication by a friend and a sister is not the least abnormal thing about them. . . . The tendency, however, of Miss Dickinson's prose to fall into the favorite rhythm of her poems is, whenever observable (and it occurs constantly), the best evidence of the naturalness of her orphic outpourings.

From Washington, D.C., Mrs. Caroline Healey Dall sent an article to the *Boston Transcript,* December 22, 1894, entitled "Two Women's Books"—Emily Dickinson's *Letters,* and Mary Putnam Jacobi's *Common Sense,* a juxtaposition worth nothing. Mrs. Dall offers an explanation of Emily's retirement which is a variant of any version current at that time.

> Some years ago a relative of Emily's came to see me. . . . "It was in Washington," said her friend to me, "that Emily met her fate. Her father absolutely refused his consent to her marriage for no reason that was ever given." It was probably, as he once said, when she wanted to go away and make a visit, because "he was used to her and did not wish to part with her!" When such a motive was urged, Emily could not resist. She would wait, hoping, once, as we see in that pathetic little poem, "Almost" ["Within my reach!"]. The lover came to see her and just missed her. His "soft, sauntering step" did not overtake hers. "Hope," she once wrote, had never "asked a crumb of her." It needed no sustenance, so immortal was her love, so elastic her spirit. And this answered until death came. In a few years her friend passed out of sight. I think from various indications that she never knew where his body lay, only he had gone after she had given her heart to him, and before her father would consent to ratify the contract.

Even the magazines succumbed to speculation about the enigma of Emily's personality.

> As a recluse, a solitary, she left Thoreau far in the shade; by comparison, that much abused walker and hunter after the secret of nature was a man of the world. . . . In large measure the letters show the caprice, and mystical, symbolical language of the poems, the curious mingling of heart skepticism with intellectual piety; but they show other sides of the writer's nature, the humorous and the sympathetic in particular, and reveal the development of her mental traits from girlhood onward.—*The Review of Reviews,* January, 1895

From St. Paul, Mrs. Mary J. Reid wrote in *The Midland Monthly,* June, 1895, an article entitled "Julia C. R. Dorr and some of her Poet Contemporaries," of whom Emily was one. The others were Helen Hunt Jackson, "one of the most popular authors in America," Celia Thaxter, Ina D. Coolbrith, Edith M. Thomas, Louise Imogen Guiney, Harriet Monroe, and "that shy, unobtrusive writer of verses," Mary Thacher Higginson (Mrs. Thomas Wentworth Higginson).

Mrs. Reid called Emily "the apostle of condensation, the blameless spirit who lived apart from the world, viewing life with absolute sincerity."

One paragraph of the article contains the following excerpt from a letter written to Mrs. Reid by Lavinia Dickinson:

> Emily never knew "H.H." till she was Mrs. Hunt. Major Hunt and herself were a part of a delightful reception at our house. Emily was charmed with them both, and their mutual interest began from that event. They met rarely, but on paper "H.H." addressed Emily and urged her in the most earnest way to let the world know of her genius. After she became Mrs. Jackson the visits were repeated and the entreaties continued, but for some shy reason Emily did not seem willing to publish the poems. Emily considered Mrs. Jackson's intellect very rare. I don't remember Emily's opinion of her poems, but my sister often spoke in praise of "Ramona." Helen Hunt Jackson was a brilliant, dashing woman of the world, fearless and brave, while Emily was timid and refined, always shrinking from publicity.

Enough of the early notices have been quoted to show that curiosity about the life of Emily Dickinson aroused by the appearance of her poems was only heightened by the publication of her letters; and further, that interest in the letters themselves was subordinated to preoccupation with the personality of the writer. This was a disappointment to my mother. She had thought that the letters were great enough, as she said, "to absorb the reader in the sentiments expressed"—great enough to lift him above inquisitiveness about the facts of Emily's life. She thought that Emily had been sufficiently revealed in her poems, "every one of her phrases a distinct reflection of her personality." All of her life that can be put in words is in her poetry. She herself has told us that.

> I found the phrase to every thought
> I ever had, but one.

As to the outward events of her life, had there been more to say about them, had any explanation been required other than the mere statement that it pleased her to live as she did, her brother and sister would have asked the editor to indicate at least the nature of the explanation. In particular, had they believed in a clandestine love-affair, for there had been no open attachment, the fact would have been intimated if for no other reason than to dismiss it in a manner of which they could both approve. On this point my mother made a definite statement.

We all agreed that no "life" of Emily could be written. I felt that an attempt to obtrude another personality would be not only inappropriate in the extreme, but that it should be eliminated, made invisible, in the presence of radiance such as Emily's.

No small part of her life was her fervent attachments to several persons. She invested commonplace persons with her own magic, attributing to them qualities they did not possess. As time went on, however, her choice of those she loved became more and more discriminating.

Such *outward* events and attachments as there were were of course known to Austin and Lavinia. But in them the secret of her life did not lie. So we felt that in publishing her letters all comment except what was absolutely necessary should be avoided.

Emily's withdrawal was merely a normal blossoming of her own untouched spirit.

She lived in the presence of God and Immortality.

But the reader may not be satisfied. If there was no one man who broke her heart, how can her love poetry be explained? To attempt to explain is like trying to describe the quality of a friend's voice. Words do not help. A different level of perception is needed. I can only suggest the direction in which to look, although I realize "how few suggestions germinate."

If you grasp the significance which a stranger's face can assume, seen through a half-closed blind—the release of imagination in a single glimpse, the surge of feeling it unlooses—you will understand why an experience which for most of us must be mutual to be complete could be carried through by Emily to the end, alone, with an intensity which may have been as genuine as though fulfillment had been reached. Poets know this. Goethe said, "To understand that the sky is everywhere blue we need not go around the world." And Robert Frost: "A poet does not need to see Niagara in order to write about the force of falling water."

For Emily, I venture to think, a hint was enough to launch a flight of ecstasy no less real because it was deprived of outward expression. Some of the gentlemen—and there were several at different times who occasioned such a response—would no doubt have been startled could they have known the havoc they were creating. They could not have recognized themselves as objects of her panegyric. What, for instance, could a prosaic acquaintance have made of this?

> We met as sparks—diverging flints
> Sent various scattered ways;
> We parted as the central flint
> Were cloven with an adze,
>
> Subsisting on the light we bore
> Before we felt the dark,
> A flint unto this day perhaps
> But for that single spark.

Emily was more engrossed in the feeling she experienced in a realm which to her was of the essence of mystery—in her own response to a stimulus, if you will, with or without a specific object—than in any one person. My mother expressed the idea in simple words: "Emily was more interested in her poems than in any man." I am tempted to step on dangerous ground and to suggest further that from the very incompleteness of her experience may have sprung her love poems. Without questioning either the reality or the intensity of Emily's rapture, is it not conceivable that satisfaction for her may have been found in its poetic symbols? Successful expression of intense feeling does bring a sense of triumph, in itself a kind of bleak consummation. However this may be, one thing is sure: it is not necessary to assume a lover who broke her heart.

No explanation of why Emily Dickinson lived her life in retirement can satisfy everybody. It is, I suppose, too much to expect that those who try to account for her way of life by a specific event, a measurable cause—one which they could imagine applicable to themselves—would ever accept the mere fact of it as they would accept the fact that the Indian pipe does not grow on lawns nor the hermit thrush nest in city parks. Not all things can be understood by all people. We all have areas of unblemished ignorance which we do well not to enter. But no one, I think, should question that what Emily valued most was a chance to explore the reaches of her own spirit—a feat which could be accomplished only in seclusion or close to the elemental certainties of nature. Her poetry could spring only from the gradual expanding of a soul which functioned where it found peace—in solitude.

CHAPTER XVII

Interlude

Crisis is a hair
Toward which forces creep,
Past which forces retrograde.
If it come in sleep

To suspend the breath
Is the most we can,
Ignorant is it life or death
Nicely balancing.

Let an instant push,
Or an atom press,
Or a circle hesitate
In circumference,

It may jolt the hand
That adjusts the hair
That secures eternity
From presenting here.

THE year 1895 marked the end of an era.

There are losses which prostrate; there are bereavements which stupefy; and there are Acts of God which smite and paralyze. In August, 1895, an event befell which combined all three.

The year began quietly enough. Unpublished poems were being copied and edited as usual. Miss Vinnie was more or less quiescent, having received in January from Roberts Brothers her semiannual check:

Will the honored firm accept my thanks for their prompt and most satisfactory notice.

Gratefully
LAVINIA DICKINSON

Amherst
January 31st '95

On January twenty-third my mother gave a talk about Emily
Memorial Hall, Worcester, Massachusetts, to a club of two
undred ladies. On February twenty-fifth she gave another talk
Worcester. Among those who congratulated her was "Austin's
d classmate, George Gould, who spoke delightfully to me."
e gave four other lectures about Emily during the winter and
ring: in Boston on February fourth; in Lynn on March twen-
eth; in Fitchburg on April twenty-sixth; and in Sunderland on
ay twenty-eighth.

On February fourth there were two lectures in Boston. At three
clock she described to the New England Woman's Club her
cent of Fuji-san, the sacred mountain of Japan, which she
imbed on foot—the first foreign woman to do so. Of this meet-
g she says: "Mrs [Julia Ward] Howe presided charmingly, and
thawed out all the stiff old members who have turned to dry
st, so they enthused vivaciously." Though far from well,
olonel Higginson made an effort to attend this talk.

> 25 Buckingham St.,
> Cambridge, Mass.
> *Feb.* 6, 1895

EAR FRIEND

The fates & my own blunders are against me as to seeing (&
earing) you. I went to Boston yesterday going out for the first
me after an illness & on the coldest day of the winter, ex-
ressly to hear you at the Woman's Club—& found I was a day
o late! I *was* provoked—& the new [Public] Library building
ily partially comforted me. When are you coming again? My
ster in law, Mrs. Lathe, a very fine woman, enjoyed your Emily
ickinson very much in Worcester & was very complimentary
the lecturer.

Perhaps you had not seen this enclosed notice of the Letters.

> Affectionately
> T. W. HIGGINSON

Emily Dickinson was the subject of the evening lecture on
ebruary fourth at the Unity Art Club.

On the occasion of this Boston visit my mother stayed as she
ften did with Dr. and Mrs. Donald at the Trinity Church rec-
ry, 233 Clarendon Street.

A laconic entry in the diary reads: "I talked with Mrs Donal]
—who told me of the blackest treachery on Vinnie's part." Ju
what this might have been is not specified. But something sh
had said or done continued to weigh on Miss Vinnie's min
throughout the spring—the "late, shy, reticent New Englan
spring" my mother called it. In an attempt to cover her track
she finally wrote to Mrs. Donald who, being my mother's friend
forwarded the letter to her. Except for signature and date th
letter is typewritten—in itself a mystery.

My Dear Mrs Donald

Do you remember a confidential talk we had last summe
concerning a mutual acquaintance? A suggestion startled m
today lest our words had fallen by the way.

I hope you received a letter from me some weeks ago. I thin
of you all so warmly that I wanted to tell you so. My lettuce
getting ready for you, though I don't know *if* you are to be m
neighbors.

Please send me a word and accept my love for you all. I hav
changed my handwriting, you see, so not to puzzle my friend

> Heartily
> Lavinia Dickinson

Amherst
May 28th '95

On June second I find this entry: "Then Vinnie [came over
with some peonies. She is evidently worried, as I should think sh
had better be, over the fact that Austin & I know of her treachery
She said nothing, but is much concerned, I can see, to know jus
how much has got back to us."

The reader may have guessed that Miss Vinnie resented he
brother's insistence on adequate compensation to my mothe
for her years of work on Emily's manuscripts. She had finall
agreed to divide the royalties from the *Letters*. But now, in add
tion, he had decided to give my mother a strip of land fifty
three feet wide adjacent to our property at the western end o
his meadow. This luxuriant field, sloping gently toward th
venerable maple tree overshadowing the dell, was Mr. Dickin
son's solace and delight. He scoured the countryside for youn
trees of just the right size and shape to plant in special places

Put it either way you prefer.

2) I only put the longer lines [the two first as one] in "I know that he exists" [S.S., page 83]—because it seemed to give a more dignified resonance to the noble words, and because it seemed to show somewhat more of connection between the rather far-apart rhymes. It is nothing that I have set my heart on, at all.

3) "Of all the souls that stand create" [S.S., page 89] is superb —it was found only among the rough and penciled scraps—that box is a mine of wealth.

4) "Pompless no life can pass away" [S.S., page 200] is not my change—Miss Vinnie says it is the right way according to the original—and I am going over there now to verify. * * * She cannot find the original, but she is sure "Pompless no life," etc. is right, and wants it so. [A copy in Emily's writing so correct it.][9]

5) Your suggestion about artist sketches is good. I will use it and will send you what I have written very soon.

Your friend, cordially

MABEL L. TODD

P.S. I think "fleeter than a *tare*" is what she meant [S.S., page 144]. Tares are supposed to grow very fast—faster than wheat or anything else useful; but the mushroom comes quicker yet— "fleeter" as she says, and lives an even shorter time.

Might it not mean this?

M.L.T.

> Next time to stay!
> Next time the things to see
> By ear unheard,
> Unscrutinized by eye!
> Next time to tarry
> While the ages steal,
> Tramp the slow centuries
> And the cycles wheel!

[9] Regarding Miss Vinnie's familiarity with her sister's poems, Mrs. Edward Robinson, widow of the Director of the Metropolitan Museum of Art, New York, told me that when she asked Miss Vinnie whether she had not studied Emily's poems extensively, she replied, "Certainly not. I never looked at Emily's poems except those she showed me." Mrs. Robinson gained the impression that Miss Vinnie felt it would be disloyal to do so.

In reply to a letter announcing the appearance of this book Mrs. Robinson wrote me: "Your letter has set me remembering Miss Lavinia who, I feel, was the important character of the family. A *dire* person! Perhaps she partly explains her sister."

nd poems. Worked all day, and twisted my brain up into a
not."

Mrs. Todd's answer to Colonel Higginson's letter of the same
ate follows:

Amherst,
24 *July,* 1891

)EAR MR. HIGGINSON:—

On my return from a drive early in the evening yesterday, I
und your letter with enclosures from Miss Norcross. The mush-
om I had—in the form which I send you with this. I think Miss
orcross' version better. "Iscariot" is more picturesque than
apostate" and "outcast" than "supple". The last word of the
ird line I had always read *hat,* instead of *hut;* but the middle
tter is not enclosed at the top, and does look more like a *u* than
—although I think "truffled hat" more to the point than
truffled hut." However—she probably meant *hut.* I did not send
with the rest, because I thought we had about as many "gems"
lready as the book could well hold, but I shall be glad to put
in if you like. The spider poem is fine. I have one or two more
bout spiders, so perhaps this had better go in, also. ["A spider
wed at night," S.S., page 147]

Now, to answer your points in order.—

1) The line, "Tramp the slow centuries" ["Just lost when I
as saved," S.S., page 85] is not my emendation, but probably
nother version of her own, as you will see by the enclosed proof
om the *Independent*—these being the two published there
ithout authority by Mrs. D. last winter—of which very mixed
p performance you know.[8]

[8] The version of the poem, "Called Back," printed in *The Independent,*
ar. 12, 1891, is given below. (See p. 112.) It differs slightly from the version
the Second Series which is the one used in the current edition of
e poems.

> Just lost, when I was saved!
> Just heard the world go by!
> Just girt me for the onset with eternity,
> When breath drew back,
> And on the other side
> I heard recede the disappointed tide.
>
> Therefore, as one returned, I feel,
> Odd secrets of "the Line" to tell!
> Some sailor skirting novel shores!
> Some pale "reporter" from the awful doors
> Before the Seal!

blocked publication of a large part of the poetry of Emily Dick-inson. If Austin had outlived Lavinia, all of Emily's poems would have been published during the early part of the century, one little volume following another at intervals. By the end of the first decade all would have appeared. But because he preceded his sister in death by the narrow margin of four years, further publication stopped, Lavinia's hopes were ended, and the stalemate ensued which for nearly half a century has held unbroken.

The soul has bandaged moments
When too appalled to stir.

The death of Austin Dickinson was an all-engulfing disaster. The difficulties he had had to contend with in trying to keep order, if not peace, in his family had been all but insuperable. His wife and daughter were not on speaking terms with his sister Lavinia. At best there was armed neutrality. More often a state of war prevailed—not so much medieval as primitive— waging fiercest among the women. Now, without his controlling presence, they were all unleashed.

It might seem as if mere helplessness should have brought them together, for they had all been carried by Austin, single-handed. But as a matter of fact no one bent an inch. Relationships remained as fixed as if carved in stone.

Lavinia had had a blow from which she never recovered. When, soon after her brother's death, a friend asked her to look at the light on the Pelham hills, she turned her eyes away, saying, "There is no landscape since Austin died." But though stricken she did not turn to his family. The breach only widened.

To add to the difficulties, Austin's wife, daughter, and son— the son a semi-invalid who died three years later and who may be disregarded in so far as this story is concerned—were not on speaking terms with my parents. How did Lavinia feel toward them, she who had been accustomed to depend on them in so many practical ways? I have spoken of a change in her attitude toward my mother. Did this shattering blow bring them closer? It did not. Lavinia's feelings remained the same. Why *could* she not have seen that only by standing together could this grief— unbearable for them all—be endured?

Pitiful and incredible as this may be, much as we may wish to linger in an attempt to weigh the effect of Austin's death upon those nearest to him, we must turn away and look in a different direction.

For the significance of his death—the essential catastrophe of it—lay not in the realm of personal emotion, however poignant, but in the fact that it brought about a stalemate which

New Salem, a small town on a high hilltop, was within drivin
distance of Amherst. On August 15, 1895, my mother write

We went to New Salem today, where David was asked to re)
resent the College at the hundredth anniversary of the Academ
Samuel Fowler Dickinson, [Austin's] grandfather, taught ther
his first year out of college, and [was] their first teacher. It w
a curious assembly, out under a maple grove, with speeches an
the "Farmers' Band," and then supper at the Academy boardin
house. In the evening a concert in the old church with its hig
pews.

August 16

A beautiful, clear, hill-top morning. . . . David made his speec
this forenoon, and talked of Austin's grandfather, and his fathe
and gave a beautiful little sentence or two about Austin. . .
We drove back in the afternoon. . . . When we got back we four
he had had a sick day. He passed away almost instantaneous
at twenty minutes after seven.

r the little paper about everything from reading newspapers
July wildflowers. During July she also wrote a life of the
l master-photographer of Amherst, J. L. Lovell, for the
otographic Annual.[1]

Throughout July Mr. Dickinson had not seemed well. "His
rves are worn out from overwork and never a vacation," was
e verdict on July seventh. A week later the diary says, "The
ctors cannot find anything wrong, but he cannot eat, he sleeps
ver over one or two hours at night, and his breathing is so
pressed that life is a burden. What *can* it be?"

July twenty-first was "excessively hot—no breeze, no comfort."
1 the twenty-third a nurse was engaged.

On July twenty-sixth Miss Vinnie acknowledged her cus-
mary check:

>berts Brothers
ONORED GENTLEMEN
Accept my thanks for your courtesy & believe me

> Gratefully
> LAVINIA DICKINSON

nherst
ly 26th '95

On July thirtieth Dr. Knight of Boston, a heart specialist, was
1t for. He saw Mr. Dickinson the next day and was "not very
couraging." My mother went to Miss Vinnie's house where the
ctor gave them his verdict:

ly 31

He has an acute attack of trouble with his heart—the outer
lls are very thin, and it cannot send the blood properly, even
rough his lungs. He says if he has no sudden, unexpected
anges he can be quietly about the house, perhaps in two weeks.
second nurse has been set for.

Sometimes Mr. Dickinson felt better, "sleeping well and
eathing comfortably," then, "not as well today," or "greatly
hausted," or "a very bad night."

Mr. Lovell, a pet of my father's, had accompanied him to Mount Hamil-
1, California, in 1882, to take pictures of the Transit of Venus.

manship, he thought, but because of mastery of it that the exterior
of many poems was "harsh"—a bold statement which subjected
him to ridicule. (The proof of this article, sent to Mrs. Todd in
October, had been approved by Mr. Dickinson and Miss Vinnie.)

> Terribly unsparing many of these strange poems are [he wrote],
> but true as the grave and certain as mortality. . . .
> Few of the poems in the book are long, but none of the short,
> quick impulses of intense feeling or poignant thought can be
> called fragments. They are each a compassed whole, a sharply
> finished point, and there is evidence, circumstantial and direct,
> that the author spared no pains in the perfect expression of
> her ideals. . . .
> Occasionally, the outside of the poem, so to speak, is left so
> rough, so rude, that the art seems to have faltered. But there is
> apparent to reflection the fact that the artist meant just this harsh
> exterior to remain, and that no grace of smoothness could have
> imparted her intention as it does. . . . If nothing else had come
> out of our life but this strange poetry we should feel that in the
> work of Emily Dickinson America, or New England, rather, had
> made a distinctive addition to the literature of the world, and
> could not be left out of any record of it.

Regarding the central enigma of Emily's life, the inspiration of
her love poems, Mr. Howells again manifests his sure touch.

> There is no hint of what turned her life in upon itself, and
> probably this was its natural evolution, or involution, from tend-
> encies inherent in the New England, or the Puritan, spirit.

Emily's seclusion, the dominant theme in every study of her
life, will doubtless continue to be a stumbling block as it was to
reviewers in 1890. My mother used every opportunity—in everything she wrote, in every lecture she gave—to explain that it was
"a perfectly normal blossoming" of Emily's spirit. But mere statement of the fact could not silence mounting curiosity. I should
like to add to the statement, emphasized by Mr. Dickinson and
Miss Vinnie, one thing more—that among my friends in New
England at the present time are several spinsters whose hearts
were never broken, who, without the apology of genius or even

CHAPTER VI

The "Auction"—*Continued*

> The first we knew of him was death,
> The second was renown;
> Except the first had justified
> The second had not been.

THE popularity of the poems did not wane with the passing of the holiday season. At the opening of the new year the third edition was selling fast. Reviewers continued to pour forth their bewilderment in monthly periodicals. It is interesting to compare notices in two leading magazines, *The Atlantic Monthly* and *Harper's Magazine*, both for January, 1891.[1]

First a paragraph from the *Atlantic* notice by an unknown writer:

> Whether or no Miss Dickinson ever would have struck out a lyric satisfying to soul and ear we have not the temerity to say; but the impression made upon the reader, who interprets her life by her verse and her verse by her life, is that there could not well be any poetic wholes in her work. Nevertheless, such is the fragmentary richness that one who enters upon the book at any point, and discovers, as he surely will, a phrase which is not to be called felicitous, but rather a shaft of light sunk instantaneously into the dark abysm, will inevitably search the book through eagerly for the perfect poem which seems just beyond his grasp.

Emily's shimmering mysteries trailed no clouds of glory here! What a contrast is the oft-quoted review in *Harper's Magazine* by William Dean Howells, attuned because of his own stature to that of Emily Dickinson. It was not because of lack of crafts-

---

[1] *The Atlantic Monthly*, January, 1891, p. 128, "Comment on New Books." *Harper's Magazine*, January, 1891, p. 316, "Editor's Study," William Dean Howells.

CHAPTER XVIII

Poems, Third Series

> *The whole of it came not at once,*
> *'Twas murder by degrees,*
> *A thrust—and then for life a chance*
> *The bliss to cauterize.*

EVER since the publication of *Poems,* Second Series, in 1891, editing of unpublished manuscripts had been going on intermittently. From the copied poems enough for a third volume had already been selected. Mrs. Todd took the first step toward publication on September 24, 1895—a preliminary talk with Colonel Higginson. Had he been well enough, he might perhaps have consented to take part in launching the book. But at the time he could promise nothing. Some weeks later she went to see him again, writing on December third, "Out to Cambridge for half an hour with dear old Col. Higginson who is ill in bed, and has been for three weeks." Assistance from him was out of the question. But as Miss Vinnie was impatient for another volume and as Roberts Brothers had agreed to publish it, my mother went on preparing the manuscript without waiting for Colonel Higginson's recovery.[1]

In the fall of 1895, my mother gave two talks about Emily Dickinson in Salem, Massachusetts—one on November twentieth at the home of Miss Silsbee on Washington Square, the other on December tenth at the Normal School. Passing through Boston

[1] Mrs. Todd still kept sending poems to magazines. I have her record of some of them: an unidentified poem to Horace E. Scudder, editor of *The Atlantic Monthly,* on Oct. 30, 1895; "'Tis little I could care for pearls" and "We learn in the retreating" to *The Outlook,* Nov. 29, 1895; and on the same day, to *The Independent,* "The past is such a curious creature," "They say that time assuages," and "This world is not conclusion." In December, "Hope is a subtle glutton" was sent to *The Independent,* and "Superiority to Fate" to *The Century.*

on the latter date, she discussed the forthcoming book with Mr. Hardy. The manuscript was sent to him three weeks later.

DEAR Mʳ HARDY,

I send you today by express the MS of a Third Series of Emily Dickinson's *Poems*. There are many here which I consider just as fine as any we have already published, and one or two better ones. I am sure they will sell, since so many of her admirers are continually asking for more of her poems. I suppose it ought to come out for next Christmas. We leave for Japan probably in March. If you could let me read galley proofs pretty soon, and then page proofs before I go, you might take a good deal of time for making plate proofs, and then send the whole volume to me, cast, to my Japan address in July or August. I could then return it, wholly corrected—to be put to press in the fall. Would that do? . . .

Very sincerely
MABEL LOOMIS TODD

Amherst
31 *Decʳ* 1895

The occasion of the coming absence was another total eclipse of the sun on August 9, 1896.

Mrs. Todd's next letter implies that Mr. Hardy fell in with her suggestion:

DEAR Mʳ HARDY,

I am glad to hear that the E.D. *Poems* can go right through at once. I hope no Preface will be necessary, but I could write a few words if you thought best, to the effect that her admirers want continually more of her verses, which is the reason for a new volume—; I have said nothing to Lavinia about contracts. I will see her soon—but of course she will want everything, as usual. The next time I am in Boston I will come in to see you about it. . . .

Very truly
MABEL LOOMIS TODD

Amherst
7 *January*, 1896

Tucked away beneath a pile of rubbish, in a dusty carton which I was about to throw away, I recently found my mother's manuscript of the Third Series. Judging by the inky finger marks, this pile of manuscript was the printer's copy. Why it had not been destroyed after the book was published I cannot imagine. But there it was. This manuscript is important because, by comparing it with Emily's originals, one fact is made clear—that my mother copied the poems exactly. The fact should be emphasized that *in copying* my mother did not alter anything Emily had written. The copies differ from the originals only in the elimination of alternatives. Any corrections were made subsequently on my mother's own copies and are plainly indicated. This will eventually make it possible to restore to their original form those poems in which changes occur. I had known, both from the editors' correspondence and from an occasional discrepancy with such originals as I had, that editorial changes had been made in some of the poems in the first two volumes. But until I found the manuscript of the Third Series I did not know how often it had been done. The changes are in my mother's handwriting—most of them in order to make a rhyme, which in itself poses a problem. Whether or not it was done in deference to Colonel Higginson, whose objection to faulty rhymes has been frequently expressed, I do not know. I am the more inclined to believe that such was the case as my mother did capitulate in the matter of titles. In spite of her own dislike, more than half of the poems in the Third Series appeared with titles, many of them suggested in Mr. Higginson's handwriting on this printer's copy. I have speculated a good deal as to why my mother should have waived her emphatic preference on both these points, and as a result I have a query rather than an explanation. As long as she and Colonel Higginson were co-editors, on equal terms, she weighed his opinions even if she did not defer to his judgment. But after he was disqualified through illness from upholding his position, did she herself assume it, defending it for him? It sometimes happens that one yields, after pressure to do so has been removed. But whatever her motive may have been, this manuscript shows that my mother did alter the wording of some of the poems.

A few illustrations will serve. The following stanzas are given not as printed, but as first copied by her, before any changes had been made.

> Remembrance has a rear and front—
> 'Tis something like a house;
> It has a garret also
> For refuse and the mouse,
>
> Besides the deepest cellar
> That ever mason laid;
> Look to it, by its fathoms
> Ourselves be not pursued.

In *Poems*, Third Series, page 56, "laid" was changed to "hewed" to rhyme with "pursued." (In the current edition of the poems "hewed" remains, but "refuse" reads "refuge.")

In the next example meaning was sacrificed in order to achieve a rhyme. The opening stanza of a well-known poem reads as originally written:

> How the old mountains drip with sunset,
> How the hemlocks burn!
> How the dun brake is tipped in tinsel (draped in cinder)
> By the wizard sun!

As printed (T.S., page 134), the stanza reads:

> How the old mountains drip with sunset,
> And the brake of dun!
> How the hemlocks are tipped in tinsel
> By the wizard sun!

The next poem is first presented as Emily wrote it:

> I heard a fly buzz when I died;
> The stillness in the room
> Was like the stillness in the air
> Between the heaves of storm.
>
> The eyes around had wrung them dry,
> And breaths were gathering firm
> For that last onset, when the king
> Be witnessed in the room.

I willed my keepsakes, signed away
What portion of me be
Assignable—and then it was
There interposed a fly,

With blue, uncertain, stumbling buzz,
Between the light and me;
And then the windows failed, and then
I could not see to see.

As printed (T.S., page 184), "in the room" reads "round my
orm"; "around" reads "beside"; "firm" reads "sure"; "the
oom" reads "his power"; and the third stanza:

I willed my keepsakes, signed away
What portion of me I
Could make assignable—and then
There interposed a fly, . . .

Sometimes a stanza was deleted, as in the case of "What
mystery pervades a well" (T.S., page 117). The second stanza
f that six-stanza poem is here given for the first time:

What mystery pervades a well!
The water lives so far,
Like neighbor from another world
Residing in a jar

Whose limit none have ever seen,
But just his lid of glass,
Like looking every time you please
In an abyss's face.

In my mother's defense I should repeat that she did these
hings to protect Emily. The dose must not be too strong.
ven after the smoothing-off process the waywardness of the
oems was still offensive to many readers.

All of the poems which my mother had copied, but which
ad not yet been published, were to be included in subsequent
olumes. When she left for Japan, preludes for the Fourth

Series, "I've nothing else to bring, you know," and for the
final series, "If I should cease to bring a rose," had already been
chosen. All her papers were put in a chest and locked in the fire-
proof vault of one of the college buildings to await her return.
Many of the manuscripts are still in the same brown envelopes in
which they were placed in 1896.

The reader may be curious about royalties from the *Letters*
and whether Mrs. Todd had received any payment for her
editorial work on those volumes. She had not. Since receipts
from sales had amounted to little more than enough to pay for
the plates, the equal division of royalties between sister and
editor had been an empty compact. No income from that book
ever materialized for either of them. Mr. Dickinson's wishes regarding compensation to my mother have been made clear.
She had in her possession the unsigned deed to the strip of land
he had given her. In the diary on October 6, 1895, I find surprising evidence that Mr. Dickinson, wishing "to make things
a little more even" between her and Miss Vinnie, had decided
to go even further in the way of remuneration.

I went to see Vinnie in the morning and I find she is going to
ignore Austin's request to her—that she shall give to me his
share of his father's estate. She is, as he always told me, utterly
slippery and treacherous, but he did not think she would fail
to do as he stipulated in this. . . .

Although this is the only reference in either journals or diaries
to such a request on the part of Mr. Dickinson, a note in his
handwriting enclosed in an envelope addressed to Mrs. Todd
corroborates the statement:

I have made the will—not just as I wanted it but best for now.
I have left all my share of my father's estate to Vin with the
request that she shall turn it over to you. She has promised to do
this, so you are protected in any case.
I will see you tomorrow.

W^m A DICKINSON[2]

[2] By the terms of his will Mr. Dickinson bequeathed to Mrs. Todd two
large framed pictures, an oil painting of a landscape near Dresden, by
Johann Gottfried Pulian, and an engraving of lions at the ruins of Persepolis,
both in my possession.

Two days before the end of the old year, two days before Mrs. Todd sent to the publisher the manuscript of *Poems, Third Series*, there is one happier note in the diary.

December 29, 1895

I went to see Vinnie just before tea—and had a talk with her. She is going to do one lovely thing.

The "lovely thing" was this: Miss Vinnie had finally decided to sign the deed to the strip of land, the deed which had been made out according to Mr. Dickinson's instructions before he died. Arrangements were made, and it was signed before a notary on February 7, 1896. The diary describes the occasion.

At 6:30 Mr. Spaulding came and we went to see Vinnie—and she signed the deed before him for the piece of land 53 feet wide, and as deep as mine, adjoining mine on the east.

A great weight is off my mind, to have even that, which Austin had given me, but had not finished the deed.

Timothy G. Spaulding was a Northampton lawyer. "Vinnie preferred not to have an Amherst lawyer as she never wanted to have her private affairs known to her neighbors."

Although the contract for *Poems*, Third Series, had been drafted when Mrs. Todd went to Boston on January twenty-eighth, it was not signed for nearly two months, *i.e.*, on March twenty-fourth.[3]

Proof had begun to come on January fifteenth. Except for the preface it had all been read and returned to the printer by February nineteenth, on which day my mother "wrote *Preface* to E.D., Third Series, and sent off proof, plates, and Contents proof."

The preface consisted of three paragraphs from which I quote:

[3] MY DEAR MR HARDY

I hope to be in Boston in May & then I shall hope to see you. I have signed the paper enclosed.

Cordially
LAVINIA N. DICKINSON

March 24th [1896]

There is internal evidence that many of the poems were simply spontaneous flashes of insight, apparently unrelated to outward circumstance. Others, however, had an obvious personal origin; for example, the verses, "I had a Guinea golden," which seem to have been sent to some friend travelling in Europe, as a dainty reminder of letter-writing delinquencies.

Mrs. Todd had already explained the circumstances of this poem in a footnote following the text on page 33 of the forthcoming book. When she incorporated the same sentence in the preface, she wrote to Mr. Hardy on March twenty-second, "Please ask them to be sure to take out the note at the bottom of page 33." This was not done, however, and the repetitious note appeared in all subsequent editions of the Third Series.

In this, her final letter to Mr. Hardy before leaving for Japan, was enclosed a list of periodicals and of individuals to whom copies of the book should be sent for review. "The plate proofs of E.D. came today," she writes, indicating a few other minor corrections. "A period at the end of the fourth line on page 177 spoils the sense. It must come out." This poem was printed in *Poems*, Third Series, wrongly punctuated after all, and still appears today with the same error which Mrs. Todd tried to correct in 1896. It should read:

> The soul should always stand ajar
> That if the heaven inquire,
> He will not be obliged to wait,
> Or shy of troubling her
>
> Depart, before the host has slid
> The bolt upon the door,
> To seek for the accomplished guest—
> Her visitor no more.

The letter continues: "On page 48 in the third verse the word 'despair' is in quotation marks, which include the semi-colon— but the semi-colon ought to be outside the quotation mark." This refers to the poem beginning

> I measure every grief I meet
> With analytic eyes.

The correction was not made at that time.
    Again: "On page 139 these two lines

        Invisible as music
        But positive as sound.

There should be no comma after *invisible*, nor after *positive*."
These lines occur in the poem, "This world is not conclusion."
The commas still stand.

    As Mrs. Todd was to be gone for more than six months, an
interval during which the book was to be published, she had no
opportunity to check final corrections. Except for the semi-colon,
all the mistakes are still incorporated in the current edition of the
poems.[4]

    On April second my mother went to Boston, made a final
call on Mr. Hardy, and on April fourth left Amherst on the
first lap of the journey to Japan.[5] Her diary describes the
departure:

---

[4] Most of the poems in the current edition read as printed in 1896. A few,
however, have been altered. "Could mortal lip divine" (T.S., p. 25) reads
"Could any mortal lip divine"; "It will be summer eventually" (T.S., p. 101)
now contains the opening stanza omitted in 1896. (See p. 389.) Again, in the
poem (T.S., p. 119)

        To make a prairie it takes a clover and one bee—
        One clover, and a bee,
        And revery.
        The revery alone will do
        If bees are few,

the second line is omitted.
    The following quatrain is as Emily wrote it:

        The stimulus, beyond the grave
        His countenance to see,
        Supports me like imperial drams
        Afforded day by day.

In search of a rhyme Mrs. Todd substituted "royally" for "day by day"
(T.S., p. 144). In the current edition "royally" reads "royalty." One important printer's mistake still appears in the current volume: "If tolling bell I
ask the cause" (T.S., p. 181) should read "Of tolling bell I ask the cause."

[5] The expedition, in the nature of a fairy-tale as well as a scientific undertaking, has been described in Mrs. Todd's book, *Corona and Coronet*. Boston: Houghton, Mifflin and Company, 1898.

April 4

Up very early, and over to my little house. Finished nearly everything there, and back to the Hills' for breakfast. Then goodbye to Vinnie. Then up town for more errands, caught the carriage and rode back and had trunks put on, and got to the station for 10:30 train.

These insignificant details suggest the wear and tear attendant in Amherst at that time upon the simplest acts. In 1896 we used to walk. If we took a train and had luggage, we sent for the "hack"—the village station wagon—a means of conveyance which usually sufficed for the requirements of the town. In that equipage Mrs. Todd departed.

On reaching New York she went to the house of Mr. and Mrs. D. Willis James, 40 East 39th Street, parents of Arthur Curtiss James on whose yacht the expedition was to sail. Monday morning, April sixth, they left at 9:30 A.M. from the Grand Central "Depot." In the great vaulted shed many people assembled to bid them good-bye, including "President Gates—and the entire Glee & Banjo Clubs, who gave us the Amherst yell as a send off."

Miss Vinnie wrote to my grandparents on the very day that my mother bade her good-bye. Her departure caused an emptiness which this letter to her parents unconsciously reveals. For consolation Lavinia was grasping at a distant straw.

[*Envelope addressed to Mrs. Loomis, 1613 Florida Avenue, Washington, D.C. Postmarked Amherst, Mass., April 4, 1896*]

April 4th

MY DEAR MRS LOOMIS

Mrs Todd thought you had seen a *sideboard* that would suit me (this was some weeks ago). She was so *sure* of going to Washington before leaving the country that I waited without writing to you myself. If you could in any of your rambles find anything handsome in *Mahogany*, 5½ feet long with carved legs, I should be very grateful to know about it and to see a rough sketch. Mrs Todd thought you had seen one that the owner was not anxious to sell. Mabel left Amherst this morning in good heart. I shall miss her very much but rejoice for her sake that the attractive experience is before her.

I hope you and Mr Loomis are well. Perhaps some of your friends would know where a sideboard could be found. Pardon intrusion and believe I shall be grateful for your aid.

Love for you both.

Affectionately
LAVINIA DICKINSON

A second letter was dispatched ten days later:

[*Envelope addressed to Mrs. Loomis, 1613 Florida Avenue, Washington, D.C., postmarked Amherst, April 14, 1896*]

MY DEAR MRS LOOMIS

Thank you for all your efforts in my behalf. I had not thought of having a sideboard *built* for me. Mrs. Todd felt sure a desirable one could be found (perhaps when changes were near & tenants going away) but if that plan failed, suggested a new one. I should take it *of course* if it was made *for me* but I think it would be a little risk lest it (I mean the wood) have a newer look and not correspond with my older furniture. I am very grateful for the knowledge that a *new one* is possible & I may come to it *later* if nothing older comes to light. I hope I have not troubled you too much. I supposed you were somewhat at leisure or I should not have ventured to take your time. I am glad for you that you will be in a *real* home again. Is it your former home? I will keep the 2 designs till I decide to use them. Do you wonder that I hesitate a little in a venture of this kind? Sometime, perhaps you will tell me if the price was 1 hundred dollars or more, also *where* to *direct* to your new home. I hope the Todd friends are safe & glad. I have always felt personally afflicted for the loss [by fire] of your beautiful furniture. Love for you & Mr Loomis.

Gratefully
LAVINIA DICKINSON

Should I decide to *build* I will write at once.

On April first the deed of conveyance of the strip of land which Miss Vinnie had given to my mother was recorded. Notice of the transaction appeared in a Boston business sheet called *Banker and Tradesman,* on April 8, 1896. Forty years later I went to the office of the paper to verify the date. A white-haired man climbed up to a set of old files on a remote shelf, remarking as he lifted down the volume containing the desired item, "Afraid I'll have to blow the dust off a bit." It has sometimes seemed to me that his words symbolize the interest attaching to this part of our story.

After Mr. Dickinson's death Miss Vinnie's adviser on matters of business was their neighbor, Mr. Leonard Dwight Hills, President of the First National Bank of Amherst, a gentleman of about her own age, and unmarried. She not only depended upon his business sagacity; she was personally fond of him. When Mr. Hills came across the notice above referred to, he was indignant. He himself will explain the reason why. I quote a few sentences from a deposition made by him on October 30, 1897.

I was consulted by [Lavinia Dickinson] as to her business affairs in 1895, from about the middle of August to the end of the year. She first spoke to me on the evening of her brother's death. . . . I think it was in the very next conversation I had with her that she said, "Austin has for a long time wished me to do something for the Todds; he wanted they should have the meadow." I asked her if she had signed any agreement to do anything of that kind. She answered no. . . . I told her that I should have to ask her not to sign any paper, or agreement, without my knowledge, or examination, and she said, "most assuredly I shall not." . . . She spoke of the conveyance of this meadow land to the Todds a good number of times, for three or four months. I can't tell how many. I remember once of telling her, if she had decided to give them a deed I would attend to it and get the papers made and bring the justice or witness. The lot in controversy is a part of the meadow, and a small part.

These words of Mr. Hills contain, I think, the key to ensuing developments. He was Miss Vinnie's adviser. She had promised him not to sign "any paper or agreement" without his "knowledge or examination." She had broken her promise and had failed to tell him that she had done so. He had discovered the fact by chance as he was looking over some trade journals. The effect of the news upon him can be judged from his statement that "I stopped advising her as soon as possible when I saw the notice of the deed in the *Banker and Tradesman*."

To use the vernacular, Lavinia was in a jam. She must at all costs re-establish herself in the good opinion of Mr. Hills. He was her mainstay. Her friendship with him must not be sacrificed, come what might. How could this be done? What stand could she take—what course of action pursue?

Though the preface is dated "October, 1896," *Poems*, Third Series, was actually published on September 1, 1896. It did not make a great stir. In so far as Emily Dickinson's poetry was concerned, the risks had been taken six years earlier. Her place in American literature was by this time assured. As one critic said at the time, "The essence of her soul was decanted in that first memorable volume." After a preliminary flurry the Third Series settled down, taking its place in the steady stream of demand for the two earlier volumes.

I do not wish to imply that on the part of the critics there were not rumblings still, as for instance in *The New York Tribune*, August 23, 1896:

> Mrs. Mabel Loomis Todd has a heavy responsibility to answer for. First, she printed a collection of poems by her friend, Emily Dickinson. Then we had more poems from the same source and a lot of letters. Now, incredible as it may seem, there is in preparation under Mrs. Todd's editorship "Emily Dickinson's Poems; Third Series." This is really too much. . . . While this may have some weight with "the admirers of her peculiar genius" who have asked for "more," we do not think it will appeal to a sober critic. . . . It is incredible, we repeat, that Mrs. Todd could have brought together enough good verse to make a new collection. What she has really done, we suspect, has been to collect fragments or even complete poems which belong, as nine-tenths of Emily Dickinson's verses belong, to the sphere of casual, moody writing, to a class of verse which most poets, whether they have genius or not, regard as mere trifles or experiments. Sometimes the genius, the great genius, can afford to print these trifles, once he has made his position secure; but a poet like Emily Dickinson could never safely do any such thing. Her vogue has passed—it was a temporary affair in its highest estate—and now such reputation as she has among minor lyrists is imperilled by the indiscretion of her executors. Poor misunderstood authorship! How it must hunger in its grave to be protected from its friends!

At the other extreme was the same extravagant admiration as for the first and second volumes. In the Chicago *Inter Ocean*, September 26, 1896, Lilian Whiting wrote:

There are books that are desirable, and a few that are indispensable, and it is perhaps among the latter that the lovers of poetic insight and philosophic thought will come to class the poems of Emily Dickinson.

On the same day an article in the *Chicago Journal* summed up in one sentence the general estimate:

Altogether, the first impression of Emily Dickinson's writings is repeated and emphasized by this latest comer of the three gray sisters.

Mrs. Todd returned to Amherst on October 24, 1896 (Plate XIV). She had spent three months in a sailing yacht on the Pacific Ocean, one month in the Sandwich Islands, ten weeks in Japan, mostly on the shores of the Sea of Okhotsk among the hairy Ainu, and for full measure had taken a cruise on a French man-of-war in Japanese waters.

A "whirl of things" awaited her attention, among others, forty requests for lectures. On October twenty-sixth the diary says: "Ran over to Vinnie's. . . . Many persons speak of . . . E.D. III." Referring to this visit on the second day after her return, my mother told me that Miss Vinnie seemed just as usual, receiving her with acclaim and high enthusiasm over her gift of some blue china from Japan.

But my mother soon discovered that sinister plans had been brewing during her absence. Within a few days she found out what they were. Lavinia was going to bring suit to recover the strip of land she had given her. It was a different home-coming from any she could have anticipated. She was astounded and nonplused enough. But how would she have felt could she have known that, because of what was to follow, no more little volumes of Emily's poems would ever be published by her—that the Third Series was the last—that as far as she was concerned the literary début of Emily Dickinson was at an end?

The story of the lawsuit is not drama; it is melodrama. On the face of it, it is incredible. To the end of her life my mother never understood it. And the not least incredible fact about it is that I should now be the one to sit down and write about this thing which for thirty-four years was never mentioned by either of us. It was there of course always, a clinging if intangible disgrace of some sort. I knew the date of its beginning and that it had no end. But what or why it was, I did not inquire. It was by a strange trick of destiny that after my mother was gone I, who knew least about it, should have had to try to discover the facts in order to set them down on paper. Throughout half a lifetime I could so easily have asked her all about it! I might have had an explanation of every step, an answer to every question.

I brought up the subject of the lawsuit for the first time

shortly before she died, when we were reading her diaries together as she lay in her hammock in the sweet-smelling balsam woods of her island in Maine. But when I asked her to tell me what Miss Vinnie's motives were, how she could have done what she did, all my mother said was, "Oh! Must we talk of that? I have been trying for more than thirty years to forget it," with an expression of such wistful appeal that I dropped the subject. That I should be in possession of all the facts was of small importance if it sacrificed her peace of mind.

On second thought, I wonder whether she could have answered every question. For her attitude was one of incredulity. She never could quite accept the fact. Why had Lavinia behaved as she did? To my mother it was "blackest treachery," an act of unparalleled disloyalty. "The cruelty of the persecution," she wrote in her journal at the time, "no one can ever fully apprehend."

Now it has all simmered down into a historical issue. So it may be better that I should now, alone, be forced to be objective, to put aside feeling, and to become for a while someone else—some detached being who can impartially weigh facts and appraise motives for purposes of historicity.[6]

[6] In spite of his reluctance to allow his name to be mentioned, and in spite of his refusal to allow me to give him any prominence, I have persuaded my husband, Walter Van Dyke Bingham, to permit me to say that without his constant support, and without his insistence on the necessity for detachment and objectivity in treatment of the subject matter, the writing of this book would have been impossible.

CHAPTER XIX

The Lawsuit

The station of the parties
Forbids publicity,
But justice is sublimer
Than arms or pedigree.

THE opening of ancient wounds is seldom justified—never, perhaps, unless falsehood has been sealed over in the process of healing. In itself the lawsuit is a trivial incident shrouded in a long-forgotten "past that is safer closed." It could be ignored —allowed to stay buried as it has been buried for nearly half a century and as my mother asked to have it remain—but for its effect on American letters. Because, incongruous though it may seem, it was this suit to recover a strip of land fifty-three feet wide which put a stop to further publication of the poetry of Emily Dickinson. It furnishes the explanation of why the bulk of her unpublished poems, far from having been "withheld by her sister," were merely clogged at the source. Work on them was dropped because of circumstances which had nothing whatever to do with literature, but only with the character of Lavinia Dickinson. For the fact is that, although she wanted to have the poems published, *all* of them, as fast as possible, as the reader is well aware, her desire was frustrated and made impossible of realization by personal traits which cut off the only avenue then open by which the poems could reach the printer.

Of course Lavinia did not weigh decisions. Of course she did not put first things first, or think through to the ultimate outcome the result of her acts. If she had, she would not have gone to the extreme of suing the one person who was in process of fulfilling her dearest wish and, as will appear, suing her in order to regain a strip of land she did not even want.

When I first began to try to puzzle out an explanation of

how such things could be, Lavinia's behavior seemed as preposterous to me as it had to my mother. What possible motive could she have had? And what had the lawsuit to do with literary activities anyway? Why take it into account? What I had to find out boiled down to this: Publication of the poems stopped after 1896. Why did my mother cease collaborating with Lavinia at that time? She had betrayed her, but how? And why? My mother did not talk about it. Throughout the years something had always made it impossible for me to mention the subject.

After my mother's death I changed my tactics. If the mystery was to be solved, I must first find out what had caused the deadlock—intangible yet unbreakable and shrouded in silence. This meant that I must throw off the reserve of a lifetime and investigate the lawsuit—the untouchable lawsuit. So, from external evidence, I began to build up the narrative step by step. There was no other way since it is the only important episode in my mother's life about which, although featured in the newspapers, she kept no scrapbook. I read all the legal documents relating to the case. I explored all sources of information, talking to persons who had been present at the trial and to the only member of the prosecution still living when my search began, Judge Henry P. Field[1] of Northampton. The facts I have gathered have, I think, resulted in a solution of the mystery. The motives for Lavinia's behavior have become clear. But before analyzing them let me outline the course of events.

On November 16, 1896, Lavinia N. Dickinson filed a Bill of Complaint against Mabel Loomis Todd and David P. Todd in which she maintained that she had not understood that the paper she had signed "purporting to be a deed" was in fact "a deed and conveyance of real estate," but that she supposed she was signing an agreement "that no house should be built on the plaintiff's land next adjoining the land of the defendants." She alleged that her signature had thus been obtained by misrepresentation and fraud; that the value of the land was $2000; that no payment whatever had been made for it, and she therefore prayed for relief—to have the deed "adjudged to be null and void."

[1] Died, Sept. 30, 1937.

The week after the filing of the bill my mother went to Boston to consult Judge E. C. Bumpus, my parents' attorney and friend. I quote from the diary:

November 24

Met Mr Bumpus at Parker's and had a long legal conversation. He says I have almost an absolute certainty of winning the case which Vinnie has brought against me about this strip of land, and strongly urges me to countersuit for services on the poems.

The Defendants' Answer was filed by Mr. Bumpus on December 14, 1896. A denial of the charges was made, followed by an outline of the services rendered to the plaintiff by the defendants for which the land could be considered part payment.

The most important fact brought out during the next few months has been mentioned, namely, that Mr. Hills, Lavinia's adviser, upheld the defendants, flatly contradicting the contentions put forward in the Bill of Complaint. In his deposition he stated not only that Miss Dickinson had talked to him "a good number of times" regarding the transfer of the land to the Todds, and that he told her that if she desired to give them a deed he would attend to it; he also stated that "at no time prior to February 7th, 1896, did plaintiff ever say anything to me about an agreement, written or oral, that no buildings should be put on the lot next to Mrs. Todd's home lot." Mr. Hills concluded, "In my opinion the value of the lot in controversy is five or six hundred dollars, I think six hundred dollars rather high."

The matter dragged along for more than a year without coming to a trial. In September, 1897, Mr. Bumpus had engaged a local representative, Wolcott Hamlin, Esq., of Amherst. That gentleman was seventy-four years old,[2] the oldest practitioner at the Hampshire Bar. Mr. Bumpus was doubtless unaware that Mr. Hamlin was already suffering from what proved to be, later in the year, his fatal illness.

If the report of the lawsuit is to be complete, one further aspect of the situation must be reckoned with. For by this time the area of the feud had spread. The town had taken sides.

[2] Born, Nov. 4, 1823; died, Oct. 23, 1898.

Though under cover, a state of discord—mixed with anticipation—was sweeping Amherst. Certain persons contended in whispers that there was more to it than met the eye. They had in mind personal relationships. Partisans took their stand; on one side, those who held that the elderly Squire Dickinson had been too fond of Mrs. Todd—for had they not been seen more than once buggy-riding through the autumn woods together?—and, on the other side, those who maintained with equal vehemence that the close relations known to exist had been purely platonic. Excitement was growing day by day. Loyalties were intensified. Families were divided. Nearly everyone in town was caught in the cross fire. Mrs. Dickinson's vanity, of course, had been so offended by all the talk that a haughty scorn was added to a general attitude of condescension. She gathered her skirts about her and held herself aloof as though she knew nothing about it, although in some quarters it was intimated that Lavinia had gone to law because Sue had put her up to it. This aspect of the situation was skirted in cross-examination during the trial but was dropped without explanation as we shall see.

As time for the trial approached, insinuation focused to a point. Innuendoes need neither logic nor evidence to drive them home. The gossips were licking their chops for, as Emily once remarked, "Contention loves a shining mark."

The case came up on the first day of March, 1898, before Judge John Hopkins, in the Courthouse at Northampton. As Mr. Bumpus was in Washington, the aged Mr. Hamlin took his place.

Lavinia Dickinson's testimony was a repetitious fabric of misrepresentations and contradictions. Among others she made the following statements, quoted from her testimony and from the cross-examination as given in the printed record.

. . . I never had any talk with Mrs. Todd subsequent to the death of my brother which referred to the land near her house. . . . Mrs. Todd asked me in August, 1895, to give her that piece of land adjoining her own as a protection against possible future building. I should think that was the second week after my brother Austin's death. . . . I never had in mind an intention to deed this lot to Mrs. Todd. Until I was informed of a deed upon the record I did not know that she claimed to have any such deed. . . .

This property came to me one third by will of my brother, one third by will of my sister, and one third by descent from my father. . . .

Asked whether she had ever requested Mrs. Todd to call upon her, she said:

I was not accustomed to send notes to her to come and call on me. I never sent them. [Recalled by the defendant and shown several such requests:] I don't remember sending any note, but it is my handwriting. All those (showing) are in my handwriting.

Two witnesses were called for the plaintiff, Dwight W. Palmer, an Amherst businessman, and Lavinia's servant, Margaret Maher. Mr. Palmer testified only as to the value of the land which he thought might be worth $600 to $650. Margaret Maher gave "no material testimony." It thus appears that, of the two witnesses for the plaintiff, one failed to uphold her contention regarding the value of the land—the only point upon which his opinion was asked—and the testimony of the other was ruled out. Lavinia Dickinson stood alone, without support from any quarter.

On the other hand, my mother was supported not only by my father, but by three other witnesses whose statements corroborated her own testimony—a narrative of events with which the reader is already familiar. First, my father described Lavinia's visit to inspect the boundaries of the land:

I saw Miss Dickinson, the plaintiff, come on to the land that is included in this deed that is presented here in the month of December, 1895. I saw her first on the strip of land which is under dispute, which adjoins my lot, my house lot. I did not see her come there, but I saw her first on that land walking back and forth in several different directions upon that strip, in the month of December, at night and by moonlight. She came after this into our house, this same evening. I should say within—well, about nine o'clock, with a probable error of half an hour. She remarked that she had been all over the strip of land, and that she understood about it, what its boundaries, in a general way, were, and that she was prepared to complete the deed at any time. I do not recall anything further relating to this matter at that time. I should say there was talk about other matters. She stayed at my house possibly ten minutes, possibly half an hour. I think she did not go home alone. I almost always went home with her myself. She used to come there alone, but I went back with her from my house. She had visited my house before that frequently. Half a dozen times a month. That continued for years before.

Regarding this visit Lavinia had already testified:

I never went there at any other time, and did not go into Mr. Todd's house after, on any moonlight evening when I was down there. [Recalled in rebuttal, she enlarged upon this statement.] I did not go upon that lot at any time in the month of December. I never, in the evening or at any time, examined the bounds of that lot by walking back and forth upon the land. I never at any time went out anywhere alone at nine o'clock in the evening.

Timothy Gridley Spaulding, the attorney before whom the deed had been acknowledged, February 7, 1896, next testified that before asking for a signature on that evening he had turned to the plaintiff and said:

"Miss Dickinson, this appears to be a deed of land, a deed of a piece of land adjoining where Mrs. Todd lives, from you to Mrs. Todd," and I then took the deed and gave the side lines, the distances in the deed, and the width, as appeared in the deed. . . . And she said, "Yes, we have talked that over before." . . . And I said, "If you are ready to do it, and willing, and thoroughly understand it, there is no reason why it should not be done now as well as at any time." She said, "O, I understand it all right, we have talked it over before. Where am I to sign?" I put my finger on the line, and said, "On the line beside the seal," putting my finger there. She sat at the table and signed the deed, and I asked her if she acknowledged this as her free act and deed, and she said yes, and I took up the pen she laid down and wrote my name as witness.

Previously, when asked whether the paper presented for her signature had been properly described to her by Mr. Spaulding, Lavinia had testified:

I supposed it was merely a description of the lay of the land, where it was bounded. . . . I, supposing it was the promise I had made that no buildings should be put on that particular spot of ground, said I would sign it, and I did. I did not read it. . . . I do not remember his speaking. He did not say anything to me at all. I did not see him take the paper at all. I do not remember he made any remark about it. . . . He did not point out the place against the seal where I should sign.

As to registration of the deed, the following passage occurs in "re-direct examination" of Mr. Spaulding:

Mrs. Todd gave a reason for delaying registration. We were going toward her house from Miss Dickinson's. There was some conversation; something was said to me as to whether I heard what Miss Dickinson said. It began from that. I could give the reason that she gave, perhaps, without going into it. She said this, that she wanted it delayed, the recording of it held back, because Mrs. Austin Dickinson and she were estranged, there was a good deal of feeling between them, and Mrs. Austin Dickinson would make it very uncomfortable for Lavinia; that is the word she used; and that on that account she wanted it, the record of it, delayed. I asked her what good that would do. I didn't see what advantage that was. Mrs. Austin Dickinson would make it unpleasant. I don't know as you want me to say anything more about it. She didn't say that Miss Dickinson assigned that reason. She said Miss Dickinson didn't want to have her record it; asked me if I heard it, and I said no, and then she gave that reason why she didn't want it herself. I understood it to be her reason. "If Mrs. Austin Dickinson discovered it was deeded to me, she would make trouble, there would be a row, she wouldn't like it."

This aspect of the controversy was not again referred to during the course of the trial.

The third witness for the defendants was Miss Frances E. Seelye, Mr. Hills's housekeeper, a white-haired lady who was a first cousin of the President of Amherst College. She testified that after Mr. Dickinson's death Miss Dickinson talked with me about Prof. Todd and his wife with reference to land. I remember the first talk I had with her when she mentioned any land in connection with Prof. Todd and his wife. It was soon after Mr. Dickinson's death. . . . She was feeling very much broken down, and I began to talk about some things, and she said it had always been Austin's wish that the Todds, as she expressed it, should have that land. I said, "What land?" She said, "The meadow." . . . I said, "Why?" She said, "For what they have always done for him." I think at that same conversation, I am quite sure she said what a great help they had always been to them about the books. That is, the poems. I couldn't tell when I had the next conversation with her, for she introduced the subject so many times. . . . I don't think there was a week passed but she spoke of this land. . . . I told her I was sick and tired of the whole thing. It was in substance what she always said. . . . Something was said with reference to the poems, that they never would have been published without Mrs. Todd's help, never could have been published without her. That was said in connection with what she said about giving the land. . . . She said, "I have decided to let them have the land"—the land next to their house, and with the trees and everything anyone in looking at the land would see it was intended to go with the house; that Austin always felt it was too narrow a frontage; that the trees had been set out with reference to its being added to that place, anyone could see, and she had decided to do that.

In her original testimony as to conversations with Miss Seelye about the land Lavinia had said:

I do not remember ever saying to Miss Seelye this same thing as to what my brother wanted done. I might have said it in her presence, but not that my brother wanted it, because he never asked me to do anything. I never said to her that my brother wanted me to deed that meadow to the Todds, and I never thought of it. I never said anything to Miss Seelye about doing it. I never thought of doing it. [Called in rebuttal she emphasized the point:] I have no recollection of ever speaking to Miss Seelye of any such thing as that I had decided to let the Todds have the land next their house, for I never intended to do it. I never have said that I had decided to give them that lot. No, sir, I did not. I don't recall ever talking with Miss Seelye alone about it.

After Miss Seelye had finished, Mr. Hills's deposition was read—to the effect that Miss Dickinson had repeatedly talked over with him the matter of deeding the land to the Todds, in fact, that these conversations "lasted several months."

In her opening testimony Lavinia had said with regard to her conversations with Mr. Hills:

On my brother's death I asked Mr. L. D. Hills to look after my affairs. . . . I never stated to him that my brother had for a long time wanted me to do something for the Todds. . . . No such statement was made by me. There was never any conversation at any time.

Both parties testified regarding Mrs. Todd's work on Emily's poems and letters. Miss Dickinson said:

I intended to have them published. . . . I did not make application to any one. Not to my niece nor to any person. Mrs. Todd asked the privilege of doing it. The handwriting was peculiar, but very legible to most persons, not difficult to read, easy to read. We should not think of sending the original poems to the printer because they would be soiled, perhaps lost. No other reason,—they might be soiled or lost in the printer's hands. I wished them copied. Mrs. Todd copied them. She copied all the little volumes—what we called little volumes, of perhaps six sheets. . . . There was no family consultation at all. The poems belonged to me. I had put them in the hands of Mrs. Todd to prepare them for publication. . . . I think it was three years after my sister's death before I decided to have her do it. I waited three years before taking action. . . . [The first] volume proved a success. I had the copyright. Another volume was called for. Mrs. Todd overlooked the publication, correction of the volume as it went through the press, and did the proof-reading. We decided among ourselves the drawing for the cover. I do not know who executed it. O, Mrs. Todd had given my sister a little painting of the Indian pipe-flower, that my sister was very fond of; she had given her a little study of it, and we had that copied. Mrs. Todd originated that.

. . . . In addition to these [poems] there were published letters of my sister. Mr. Niles was very anxious to have them published, and I did have them published. Mr. Niles was our publisher, who has since died. I do not know what time was occupied in the preparation of these letters. I had nothing to do with that, only to collect all the letters from her different friends and give them into Mrs. Todd's hands. . . .

Question. Will you tell us, if you please, how much money you have received from the royalty on these books?
(Objected to. Excluded.)

Mrs. Todd asked to do it. I knew that she thought it would be for her literary reputation to do it, and it made her reputation. I furnished the letters. I was interested to have it done. I should think it might have occupied a year. I don't know. But of course all the time was not spent on it. It might have been as much as a year that it was going on, but I don't think all the hours in a year were spent on it.

In her testimony regarding the editing of the poems and letters, Mrs. Todd went into enough detail to give the Court an idea of the amount of time and effort she had put into it. Her diary describes the trial in these words:

March 1, 1898

My equity case came on in the Superior Court today. Vinnie appeared and was the first witness. She perjured herself right along for an hour. It was appalling to see a person lie so composedly. Early in the afternoon I took the stand. I told my straight story, and was cross-examined for nearly three hours. It was terribly exhausting, but everybody, even the lawyers on the other side, said I was a splendid witness. The papers said my evidence was not shaken in the least.

M^rs [W. F.] Stearns came over in the evening to hear about it.

March 2

Mrs Stearns went over to court with me, but a tiresome jury case was on for all day, about a laborer tumbling off a scaffolding and suing his employer for five thousand dollars damages. All day it dragged along, some of the witnesses having to have an interpreter for their Canadian French. I received many compliments on my yesterday's evidence. Mrs [G. W.] Cable came down to the Court House and sat with me all day.

March 3

My case came on again today, and was finished. Up to noontime it was all my way. Mr Spaulding testified, Miss Seelye, and

Mr. Hills's deposition was read. In the afternoon my lawyer made his plea to the Court, and then theirs. As mine had all the law points, theirs took it out in personal abuse of me, and for an hour I was hit in the face and pounded. It exhausted me terribly. The little judge looked rather tired of it all, and I came away feeling black and blue. Decision reserved. . . .

Professor Mary A. Jordan of Smith College, who was present, gave me an account of the trial. "Lavinia Dickinson sat there," she said, "dressed in a blue flannel dress, yellow shoes and a long black mourning veil. Her extraordinary appearance confirmed the impression of what Colonel Higginson referred to as her 'unworldliness.' Beside her on one side sat Miss Buffum, Principal of a Girls' School in Amherst, on the other her servant, Margaret Maher."

Miss Jordan described the general impression created by Lavinia's testimony:

Question. Miss Dickinson, did you know that this paper was a release?

Answer. Isn't that business? I know nothing of business.

Question. Did you not know that this was a contract?

Answer. Isn't that business too? Father always attended to business.

Question. Miss Dickinson, did you ever employ labor?

Answer. No.

Question. Do you mean that you never hired any servants?

Answer. (With lifted inquiring eye-brows) Does he mean Maggie?

The judge controlled himself with difficulty.

It was generally recognized [continued this eyewitness] that Lavinia was putting up a ludicrous testimony. But the onlookers enjoyed it. It was very amusing. It was in fact *opéra bouffe.* For instance, when the question was raised as to whether she had signed the deed, and she was asked, "Is not this your signature?" she replied, "Yes, that is to say, that is my autograph. I understood that someone in Boston wanted my autograph. I thought that was what I was doing when I wrote it."

No one supposed for an instant that Mrs. Todd had deceived Lavinia about that strip of land. Although they all knew that Lavinia was lying—and she was a complicated and adroit liar

—they thought, being what she was, that she ought to be allowed to change her mind. They agreed with her allegation as expressed in her testimony that she had made a mistake in giving away the land. It was, after all, ancestral land which should be kept in the family.

To the onlooker it may have been *opéra bouffe*. But to my mother it was tragedy, for it was slander—slander from a friend to whom she had rendered an unrequitable service.

Six weeks later the decision was filed. The defendant was ordered to give back the land. My mother wrote in her diary:

April 15–16, 1898

The Judge has given his decision against me in the law-suit. It seems incredible, in the face of five witnesses on my side, and none but herself on Vinnie's. The whole town is amazed, and aroused, and it has brought out many expressions of sympathy from heretofore neutral people.

Nothing but the Spanish war equals it in their minds for interest. . . .

It is too outrageous to think of—I must not think of it.

April 26

Colonel Higginson . . . left at 2:30, dear old man. [On April twenty-fifth he had given a talk at our house entitled "England Twenty Years After."] He says he wishes he might have gone on the stand for me, to testify to my labor on the poems, and give his opinion of Vinnie!

Almost coincident with the filing of Judge Hopkins' decision, Edward Dickinson, son of Austin and Sue, was taken ill. On May 3, 1898, he died at the age of thirty-five.[3]

My parents decided to carry the case to the Supreme Court of Massachusetts. Before presenting the appeal, however, I should like to look at the situation from another angle.

To my mother the whole affair was past comprehension, as I have said. After the trial she did not mention Lavinia's name. When, shortly before my mother died, I asked her point-blank

[3] His gravestone in Wildwood Cemetery, Amherst, gives the date of Edward Dickinson's death as "3 May 1897."

why Miss Vinnie sued her, she replied, "I haven't the slightest idea. She must have been intimidated by Sue. But I never could understand it because she despised Sue so."

Sue did influence the situation, I think, to this extent: Both Miss Vinnie and my mother knew what a scene she would make if she found out that Lavinia had deeded the land to my mother. Both wanted to avoid being involved in it. But, although on that account my mother did not want to have the deed recorded any more than Lavinia did, she did not think that in itself registration was of enough importance to make it an issue. So, when Mr. Spaulding insisted, she acquiesced. However, she did ask him to delay registration, since she was soon to leave the country for a protracted absence and would not be on hand if Sue should discover what had been done and make trouble. The delay, as Mr. Spaulding foresaw, would in the end do no good. But if my mother had stood her ground on this one point, namely, that registration of the deed should be put off at least until after her return from Japan, neither Mr. Hills nor Mrs. Dickinson might have found out the facts until after she had returned to Amherst, and the whole subsequent course of events might have been different. Mr. Spaulding did wait nearly two months but, without my mother's knowledge, arranged to have the deed recorded the very week she left Amherst.

While it was doubtless true that, after she heard about the land, Sue did all she could to annoy Lavinia, there were, I think, for Lavinia stronger goads to action than trying to appease Sue. Miss Buffum, who had sat with her throughout the trial, agreed with me that although Lavinia wanted to quiet Sue, she wanted much more to placate Mr. Hills. He was in the midst of straightening out her affairs. Besides, she was fond of him. She must reinstate herself in his good opinion whatever the cost. Both of these motives are simple enough.

But the underlying basic cause of the suit as well as of the ensuing deadlock—the clue to a solution of the entire mystery—was, I think, a fundamental incompatibility between my mother and Miss Vinnie. I will try to retrace the path which has led me to this conclusion. In the nature of the case it was an avenue of understanding closed to my mother.

To begin with, I tried to put myself in Miss Vinnie's place.

Knowing the dilemma in which she found herself when Sue discovered the gift of the land—for her a trump card—and when Mr. Hills caught her in deception, I would agree with her that her plight was desperate. Realizing her frantic resolve to extricate herself somehow, I should be inclined to agree with her further that one course of action, and one only, might offer a way out. The question was, would she be willing to follow that course to its logical outcome? For it involved further deception. It meant assuming a pose, namely, that she had been tricked into signing her name, that she had not known what she was doing when she signed the deed. It meant perjury. Would the decision to commit that crime have been difficult for her to make? I think I am safe in saying no, and for this reason: she would not have thought of it as perjury. She never felt the need of justifying any course of action which necessity required. She was not in the habit of doing so. She lived in a world of imagination. When she was brought up short, publicly, as in this case, by a plain statement of fact, any instinctive method of handling the situation which would re-establish her in her illusory domain would be appropriate. She merely had to take her stand—play the part, if you will; and she was adroit enough to play it well, so well that the judge was persuaded that she was in reality the gullible simpleton she intended to have him think she was. There is no doubt that he received the impression she sought to convey.

And I have come to another conclusion—that my mother may actually have helped Lavinia to assume her pose of aggrieved victim. For not only did she assent to the recording of the deed, although she knew that it would enrage Sue when she found it out—and no knowing what ways she would find in which to wreak her vengeance—but my mother was well aware of Lavinia's habit of keeping everything dark. It was one of her outstanding idiosyncrasies. That she never wanted her affairs talked about my mother very well knew. She once told me that "Vinnie always wished to do everything in secret. The checks she received from Roberts Brothers she always asked her brother to cash in Boston so that the Amherst bank might not know how much she was getting for the poems." (See facsimile, page 194.) But in spite of knowing all this, my mother agreed to a delayed recording of the deed and then left for parts unknown. Lavinia felt herself abandoned even before what she had done was made public. Thereafter, left to fend for herself, how much more alone must she have felt, with months in which to fulminate and brood over her plight while Sue sat gloating next door!

Though Lavinia doubtless did not and could not have reasoned it through, she was outraged because the deed had been registered without her knowledge when my mother knew she wanted it kept quiet. That was to her the heinous, unforgivable act. As a result she had lost the services of Mr. Hills. That she had signed the deed without asking his advice after having expressly promised him not to sign any paper without consulting him probably did not trouble her so much as that she had been caught. Her own deceptions never bothered her until they were discovered. Now, she must either try to justify what she had done, a most distasteful and unnecessary predicament for which my mother was responsible, or she must deny that she ever intended to make such a gift. So she took her stand, and accused my mother of fraud.

Although drives such as these may have precipitated the suit, even they might perhaps have come to nothing but for the clash of personalities—that underlying lack of understanding for which immediate causes were only a vent.

We have watched Lavinia's resentment smoldering for a long time. She tried to conceal it from my mother and hitherto had been able to keep it under cover because she realized that my mother was indispensable. Publication of the poems depended upon her. But this offense hit Lavinia at the core. She was driven to desperation, even to forget—for the moment—Emily's poems.

Here was Lavinia, unpractical though shrewd, a very Dickinsonian Lavinia. She belonged to the race which produced the aunt of Ralph Waldo Emerson—that lady who traditionally went about dressed in her shroud, riding on a donkey through the streets of Concord. Miss Emerson had more intellect than Lavinia Dickinson. But they both belonged to that crop of "queer" spinsters who were an integral part of New England society two generations ago. Such women were always allowed "the largest scope to their peculiarities," as William James said. To use current phraseology, a woman's deviation from a norm, however undefinable, was the trait guarded with pride and allowed to run riot. A tendency to queerness in youth later developed into an eccentricity accepted as the essence of her. Cherished by the community in which she lived, it might be labeled insanity by an outsider, but to her own town she would remain just "Miss Jane" or "Miss Eliza"—her own unmitigated self.

After Austin's death, in her loneliness, in her defenselessness —for his death had left her at the mercy of Sue who was not slow to recognize her power—and with her feverish anxiety to publish more of the poems as fast as possible, could Lavinia have helped resenting the fact that my mother had departed on a glamorous trip to the antipodes instead of attending to poems? Her blithe gayety, too, must have bred in Lavinia a certain hostility. And when we recall that in addition my mother was running away with something that belonged to Lavinia—the prestige with which, as editor of Emily's poems, she had been endowed—it is plain that that was an injury which could not be forgiven. In the last analysis, that resentment, I think, more than any other one thing supplied the drive that transformed anger and a sense of outrage into action.

One further point. At the trial my mother unwittingly may have been of assistance to Lavinia in establishing the point she wished to make—that she had been tricked. Lavinia was determined to have things go the way she wanted them to go— to have the facts in the case proved to be what she would have preferred that they should be. My mother, on the other hand, knew that the facts supported her in every particular. She knew further that, in telling the truth about the transfer of the land, she was upheld by the testimony of four other persons, three of them entirely disinterested. But there was one thing she may not have realized. Aware as she was not only of the transparent clarity of her intent and of the integrity of her behavior toward Lavinia in the matter of the deed, but also of the legality of her conduct in carrying out their prearranged agreement, my mother may have appeared too sure of herself. She may have exhibited the overconfidence which such a sense of security gave. If so, she certainly helped the plaintiff more than she helped herself. Had she realized the effect such assurance would have on the Court, she might perhaps have been tempted to compete as an actor with Lavinia Dickinson.

I wonder whether, if such an explanation had been offered to my mother, she would have understood, or could have believed, that the very strength of her case may have been what turned the decision against her.

In the Plaintiff's Brief submitted to the Supreme Judicial Court of Massachusetts in the September Law Sitting, 1898, the fact was stressed that

the judge who heard this case had all the parties before him in person, testifying orally with only the single exception of one Hills, is of especial significance and importance. The degree of thoughtfulness and care exercised by each witness could be seen and weighed by him. And such questions can only be given due weight by the presiding justice who sees and hears the witnesses.

In support of this contention a list of precedents follows, "a large number of decided cases," wherein the appearance of the witnesses determined the decision. The Brief continues:

The case at bar is pre-eminently a case in which the general appearance, manner and attitude of the witnesses should have been taken into consideration by the presiding justice.

The Plaintiff's Brief for the appeal thus upholds the justice of the decision on the ground that only the judge who saw both Miss Dickinson and Mrs. Todd on the stand could form an opinion as to the rights in the case.

The Defendants' Brief, on the other hand, after a general denial and after pointing out the contradiction of Miss Dickinson's testimony not only by Professor and Mrs. Todd, but also by Mr. Spaulding, Mr. Hills, and Miss Seelye, emphasizes the point that these witnesses for the defendants were of "such accredited standing and responsibility that they need not be seen to be believed."

The concluding paragraph of the Defendants' Brief contains the following sentences:

The plaintiff . . . asks the court to believe that a long-time professor of Amherst College, known and distinguished throughout the scientific world for his attainments as an astronomer, and his wife, almost as widely known as himself, have conspired together to defraud this plaintiff . . . in order to obtain this paltry strip of land worth five or six hundred dollars. This imputation wounds more deeply than any pecuniary loss could do.

The appeal was argued at the Sitting of the Supreme Court in Northampton on September 20, 1898, and was, my mother wrote, "finely presented." Soon afterwards she left for a lecture trip in the West. On November nineteenth she spoke in Kelly Hall at the University of Chicago. It was a historic lecture, I am told, the presentation of Emily Dickinson by her editor to an audience in that youthful university.

Two days later, on November twenty-first, the decision of the Supreme Court was handed down. The finding of the lower court was sustained. It was conceded that

the judge who sees and hears the witnesses has a great advantage in the search for truth over those who can only read their written or printed words. . . . The judge of the Superior Court saw the witnesses, observed their manner of testifying, formed his opinions about them, not merely in regard to their credibility in the ordinary sense, but in the case of the plaintiff and the female defendant in regard to everything in their temperament, experience, and habits of life which would help him in discovering the truth. Seldom is there a case in which the reasons for the rule that weight should be given to the impressions produced by seeing and hearing the witnesses are so strong as in this case. From reading the printed testimony a majority of the court is unable to say that the judge who presided at the trial, and had opportunities for ascertaining facts which we cannot have, was wrong in his conclusions.

Decree affirmed.[4]

In the category of cases decided on similar grounds—on personalities, that is, more than on evidence—I am told that this is

[4] Supreme Judicial Court, Massachusetts Reports, Vol. 172, August 1898—March 1899, p. 183. It is worth noting that Chief Justice Field of Boston, a friend of our family, did not sit, although he was in Northampton and sat on other cases presented at that session.

still referred to by members of the legal profession as a classic example.

Had my parents known of the self-imposed limitation on the powers of the Supreme Court of Massachusetts to weigh evidence, they might not have appealed; but it is fortunate that they did not know and did appeal. For otherwise the court stenographer's notes would not have been transcribed. After a few months the notebook would have been destroyed or lost, and the account of the trial would not have been perpetuated by printed record filed in the Massachusetts archives.[5]

On November 29, 1898, the day on which the decision of the Supreme Court was made public, my mother wrote in her diary:

My heart is broken. . . . The Supreme Court sustains the lower court verdict, and it seems as if I could not live. *How* can a lie be endorsed and reëndorsed, and the real truth put in the wrong! I am perfectly crushed.

So much for the effect of the verdict on the loser.
What was its effect upon the winner?

[5] It is probably only a coincidence that some years later Lavinia Dickinson's niece repeated, but without success, her aunt's performance by claiming in a *New York* court that a deed which she had executed, conveying some of the Amherst inherited land, was induced by duress and abuse of process (138 N.Y. App. Div. Reports, p. 215).

CHAPTER XX

A Pyrrhic Victory

We lose because we win.

LAVINIA DICKINSON had won her case. She had regained the strip of land which she had given to my mother, land intended by her brother to be part payment for editing the poems and letters of Emily Dickinson. But now that she had it, what did she do with it—that land which, with the rest of the meadow, was to remain a permanent legacy in the Dickinson family?

The week before the trial we had moved to the other end of town, to the new Observatory House, thus leaving the Dickinson zone of influence. On August 19, 1898, our little house in the meadow was sold. Within a year, on July 1, 1899, the purchaser bought from Lavinia the additional strip restored to her by legal decree.[1] Clearly it was not the land that Lavinia wanted. What then did she want? As we know, she had hoped by winning the suit to reinstate herself in the good opinion of Mr. Hills, of whose advice and friendship she was sorely in need. Had that objective been reached?

At this time Miss Vinnie had two close friends. The first of these, Miss Vryling Wilder Buffum,[2] went with her to the trial. I had a talk with Miss Buffum on November 2, 1934, in the course of which she said of the lawsuit: "I can't understand it. I never did. I can't to this day. I knew Vinnie had not a particle of truth on her side. But I went to the trial with her because she asked me to and was entirely alone. I sat on one side of her

---

[1] Within five years, on Dec. 4, 1903, all that remained of the meadow on our side of Fowler Place—as Austin Dickinson called the street which bisected his land—had also been sold. The strip in dispute blended once more with the meadow as a whole, as it passed forever from ownership of the Dickinson family.

[2] Died, Jan. 28, 1944.

and Maggie on the other. Ned and Mattie were behind." And Miss Buffum added, "I would do it again." Edward and Martha Dickinson to whom Miss Buffum refers were not accompanied by their mother.

In reply to my inquiry about a photograph of Miss Vinnie, Miss Buffum sent me the following letter:

80 Roxbury Street
Keene, N.H.
Nov. 16, 1938

MY DEAR MRS. BINGHAM:—

By a strange coincidence I was going to write you at my first moment of leisure when your note came.

I have now I think looked over all the numerous boxes and trunks that we have stored away, a work that I have been doing gradually for two years for there were many family belongings that I could give away now to the remaining members of the family and what would not interest them I've been giving to the Morgan Memorial. I regret to say that a large number of family photographs, among them baby pictures of Jane and Lucy Dickinson, cannot be found and too that dear picture of Miss Vinnie with a checked shawl and holding "Pussy." A few years ago when my sister was living someone who had no clear idea between meum and tuum cleared up the place over the garage where were stored many boxes. The only things that we knew disappeared were a box of bed linen and my handloom box. Probably he threw away or burned a box of photographs, a great loss.

The other thing I wish to bring to your attention was a true statement in regard to Miss Vinnie bringing the suit against your mother. Mr. Hill[s] had charge of Miss Vinnie's affairs and she had promised she would never sign anything without his knowledge and when he found she had he threw up her affairs. The rest of this is conjecture. I think he did not believe her when she denied that she had not realized that she was signing a deed and suggested that in that case she should bring suit. I do not know but I do not think that he thought she would do so, but it seems probable to me that he had no faith in her plea of ignorance, for we know he never had anything more to do with her. Of course I do not know the facts, but I felt that in justice to Mr. Hill[s] I should state my opinion.

Perhaps I fail in loyalty to Miss Vinnie in writing this for I was very fond of her. I only know that till after the death of

Austin Dickinson she never had control of a single cent, even to pay for a postage stamp except what came to her from the poems your mother edited. In a way I came to learn many things that accounted for some of her and also of Emily Dickinson's actions. I am anxious to read Professor Whicher's recent book, but I do not agree on his view of Emily's love story. From what Miss Vinnie told me and from what Aunt Aurelia Davis used to say I cannot.

If you are in Dublin again I should be glad to see you. Believe me,

Sincerely yours,
VRYLING WILDER BUFFUM

P.S. I've been constantly interrupted and when I came to re-read this I found my omissions left it without sense. I hope you will be able to find out what I meant. V.W.B.

Thus, although the case had been won and the land recovered —Lavinia's ostensible reason for having brought suit—Miss Buffum thought that her real objective had not been attained, for Mr. Hills never had anything more to do with her. It need hardly be added that regaining the land did not affect Sue's attitude in the slightest.

So much for the land and the part it has played in our story.

But what of the deeper wishes of Lavinia's heart—those great surges of desire in comparison to which the story of the lawsuit is as the tinkle of rain-drops upon the surface of the rising tide? What was the effect of her victory upon further publication of the poems? Since no more poems were published during her lifetime, did it mean that she no longer wished to have them all published? Certainly not. She wished it more fervently than ever. She wished it transcendently. Did she make any effort to achieve this end? It is fortunate that in order to answer this question I do not have to depend upon hearsay. But first, let me outline her fresh predicament.

Lavinia was more than ever alone—shut off from those on whom, since Austin's death, she had been accustomed to depend —Mr. Hills, my father, and my mother. She had won her suit but was left stranded, with hundreds of Emily's poems still unpublished. What was she to do with them? Where could someone be found to edit them and put them through the press? Where could she turn? To Sue, to whom she had turned twelve years earlier, only to be discouraged in her wish to publish? Certainly not. Did she turn to Sue's daughter, Martha Gilbert Dickinson, at the time thirty-two years of age with literary aspirations of her own? She did not. Could Miss Buffum help? No. She had closed her school that same year and had moved away from Amherst.

Such was Lavinia's determination to publish the remainder of the poems, however, that she appealed to a young lady who came frequently to see her at that time and to whom she was greatly drawn. Miss Mary Lee Hall, her other close friend, will herself tell the story of what happened next.

Not long after the publication by Martha Dickinson Bianchi of a volume entitled *Further Poems by Emily Dickinson*, my mother received a letter from Miss Hall, written on September 21, 1930, from which I quote:

Vinnie gave me the "Further" poems to copy just after Christmas of 1898, and I had them until the last of May, or first of June, 1899. When she became ill I felt that it was better that she should have the poems in the house, especially as she was having some serious battles with "the other house." She said she would hide them where prowlers could not discover them. Of course I did not ask about them after they left my hands. . . . Vinnie intended to publish the poems, but was never well enough to do so, & I did not want to have any part in such an undertaking.

After my mother's death, and before I had discovered the foregoing letter to her, I wrote to Miss Hall, asking her to tell me the story of the last few months of Miss Vinnie's life. Her reply, dated August 5, 1933, says the same thing in other words:

The manuscript of The Further Poems, in Emily's handwriting [was] given to me—confidential this—by Vinnie, after Ned's death. Vinnie asked me to copy them and help her to have them published. There were one hundred and fifty poems, and I copied many of them, and intended helping Vinnie to do as she wished me to, but there was "war between the houses," especially severe, and so much was done to cruelly hurt Vinnie that she became seriously ill, and I returned the precious manuscript after keeping same for four or five months, giving them into Vinnie's hands, & telling her to hide them well. She hid them so well that they were not discovered for—was it twenty years, or thirty?

Whether or not the poems Miss Hall copied were actually those contained in *Further Poems* is unimportant. The point worth noting is that although she had copied enough to make another volume before Lavinia died, the copying was finished only after she had become too ill to do anything with them.

The story of the last few months of Lavinia's life—for she died on August 31, 1899—is pieced together from Miss Hall's letters:

I know Vinnie's life was a tragedy after Ned's death. Sue & Mattie claimed that his heart was weakened by his determination to "stand by Vinnie" during the trial at Northampton. She had a bad adviser, and there were times when she regretted the step she took, also the publicity.

Yes, Vinnie spoke several times to me of "the suit," and I thought that she greatly regretted having been forced into it.

It must have been Sue who held a sword over Vinnie's head, ready to let it drop if she did *not* get that land back. It was not Vinnie who started the trouble, I am sure of that.

I think *in her heart* Vinnie admired & loved your mother, but dared not admit it on account of some dire threat held over her head.

Ned talked freely about the matter, but only in regard to Vinnie's appearing in court. We have thought his death was hastened by the friction at home over the suit. He felt bound by "the traditions of the family" to stand by his aunt, and he said, "If my aunt wins the case it will be fitting for Mattie and me to join the church, as that is about the only thing we *could* do"—a joke.

Ned told us that his life had been a "hell on earth" & that the early hour that he daily spent in reading really worth while things was what kept him sane and half decent.

Vinnie was not well all winter and was not up during the summer [1899]—it was "the Dickinson heart" as she called it, and

Dr Nelson Haskell was her physician.[3] The *cause* of her last illness was Sue who terrified her, and treated her shamefully. It
began in the fall of '98. Vinnie always had Emily's rose bushes
and other shrubs carefully attended to before cold weather. When
the day came for having the work done, the man told Vinnie
that all the "dressing" had been taken from under the barn, and
Maggie found out that Sue had ordered it put on her flower-
beds and shrubs. That stunned Vinnie. She sent for me, and I
found her hardly able to speak. When I learned the reason for her
condition I laughed, and said, "Miss Vinnie, just get Mr Lindsey
to bring you a load of fertilizer, and say nothing to Sue. Let her
find you equal to the battle, and *don't* let her hurt you." Her
heart was so rapidly beating that I cautioned Maggie to watch
her. Mr Lindsey came to the rescue, and then Sue began
to send "Sport" over to Vinnie's and he worried the pussies.
Finally, Vinnie could endure no more, and she went to bed.
[Miss Hall thus attributes the cause of Miss Vinnie's taking to
her bed to Sue's final cruelty—the theft of her manure pile.] She
asked me to write to Mr Copeland[4] [an early admirer] and he
wrote beautiful letters of tender sympathy, offering to come to
her if she so desired, and he wrote me, asking if "the other house"
was causing any trouble. I kept Mr C's letters, they are packed
with other things where I cannot get them. My belief is, that
after Vinnie's death I destroyed them. I do not even remember
his full name.

I saw her about every other day for months, & two months
before the end Mattie came down & told me not to go to Vinnie
any more. "By the doctor's orders no one is to see Aunt Vinnie,
so please do not try to see her again."

As soon as she disappeared round the corner I went to Vinnie's.
Dr. H. was going into the house and I told him what Mattie had
said. He said, "Miss Vinnie wants you here as often as you can
arrange to come—and so do I." Before my visit ended that morning, Mattie came in with a handful of red roses, and she was
furious when she found me there. She asked Vinnie if she was
tired, and poor Vinnie, who whispered all she had to say, man-
aged to tell her that my little visits rested and comforted her.

Vinnie made no pretense to me ever of having any affection for
Sue or Mattie. She was bitter in her denunciations of them.

[3] Dr. Haskell told me that Miss Vinnie's trouble was an "enlarged and
dilated heart."

[4] Melvin B. Copeland, President of the Middletown (Connecticut) National
Bank.

The attitude between the two houses was one of war.

She told me Sue had been cruel to Emily and herself and they each had suffered keenly from her insincerities, her insane jealousies, as well as her intentional deceit. Vinnie often said that Emily's life was shortened by at least ten years by Sue's cruel treatment.

I know that Vinnie told Mrs Stockbridge that Sue never ceased to annoy her in every possible way, and that she felt she was trying to *kill* her, as she knew her heart was weak.

When I entered the house to attend Vinnie's funeral, some-one made room for me near the door of the room on the right, opposite the parlor—the library, I think. The gray casket was in that room, with only the American Beauty roses that Mr Copeland sent, covering it. Mr Marsh, the undertaker, came & whispered to me that "the family wish you to sit with them." I declined and said, "I will stay by Miss Vinnie & her friends." Mrs Stockbridge was in this room, Maggie, and I do not recall any others, nor anything connected with the service, for I kept thinking of the tragedy of Vinnie's life, and when the service was over Mr Marsh came and asked if I would go with the family to the cemetery, and I declined.

I do hope that someone will write "The Life of Shadows," or the "House of Shadows," a book giving some of the *awful pressure* under which Austin, Emily and Vinnie lived; the stern, austere, unaffectionate character of Edward D., and the soft, yielding, rather unstable one of his wife. I shudder as I recall the stories Vinnie told me of their little deceptions in order to get a drop of joy out of their gloomy home life.

The shadows played a big part in the lives of the three I have mentioned, as long as they lived. Sue had a fearful influence over the three, as each one found her out to his and her sorrow.

What a novel could be written about the D. family—equal in tragedies to "The Forsyte Saga." Only the absolute truth need be revealed, and that would be startling & sensational enough for the most rabid devourer of novels.[5]

[5] At the time of my father's death, June 1, 1939, I received from Miss Hall a letter of sympathy, and at Christmas, 1939, a card. My acknowledgment of the card elicited the following reply:

> *May 3, 1940*
> Johnson City, Tenn.
>
> DEAR MRS. BINGHAM,
>   Your letter to Miss Hall just came to my hands. I am grieved to tell

The outcome of the lawsuit, then, would seem to have been immaterial. The land, to regain which the battle had been fought, was disposed of within a few months. Mr. Hills was permanently alienated, as well as my mother on whom depended further publication of the poems.

Nine months after the decision of the Supreme Court had been handed down, this solitary old woman died. Upheld by the majesty of the law in her contention that she had been victimized, but ill and helpless and immersed in venom, after all that she cared for most had been taken from her, Lavinia's life was blotted out, its work unfinished. For her it had been a Pyrrhic victory.

---

you dear Miss Hall left us Feb. 17—and is now happy with loved ones in the Great Beyond.

She was a wonderful soul and all who knew her loved her dearly.

Sincerely

MRS. S. S. PRESTON

I wrote at once to inquire about Miss Hall's papers, and on May 13, 1940, Mrs. Preston answered as follows:

Yes, I can tell you about them. She destroyed most of them before she passed away, and I destroyed what she left. The things (letters) she left was her late mail. But when she found her eyesight was failing so fast she went through her things and destroyed them. . . .

I am very sorry about the papers if they had any value for you but everything has been destroyed.

Mrs. Preston added, "She was the dearest soul I have ever known."

CHAPTER XXI

Aftermath

No drug for consciousness can be;
Alternative to die
Is nature's only pharmacy
For being's malady.

WHEN, in 1895, Austin Dickinson died, he left his family in a welter of turbulent emotions—a state of incessant pulling and hauling between his sister on the one hand, his wife and son and daughter on the other.

One by one the tensions were loosed by death. Less than three weeks after the decision following the trial was handed down the son, Edward Dickinson, succumbed—frail vestige of a powerful line of dominant males.

Lavinia was next. Percival Lowell, the astronomer, was living in Amherst during the winter of 1898. His comment on the trial was, "Perjury always kills." Be that as it may, Lavinia soon took to her bed and died the following year.

Left were Sue and her daughter Martha. Nothing was done about publishing further poems during Sue's lifetime. She died in 1913.

The year after her mother's death, Martha (who in 1903 had married Alexander E. Bianchi) published *The Single Hound*, a group of poems which, the preface explained, had been sent to her mother by Emily. A few had been previously published by my mother, and some are not among her copies. Also, certain poems in that volume of which I have copies differ more or less from the printed text, some by only a word or two, while others are sufficiently unlike to constitute separate versions. Some are fragments of longer poems. A few examples will illustrate the types of discrepancies.

First, poems previously published:

A quatrain on page 5 beginning, "Except the smaller size no lives are round," had been published in *Letters*, 1894, page 312. The second half of this poem is still unpublished.

Second, poems which differ to a greater or less degree from the copies in my possession:

"A prompt, executive bird is the jay" (S.H., page 71) reads in my copy

> A bold, inspiriting bird is the jay,
> Good as a Norseman's hymn;

and "I showed her heights she never saw" (S.H., page 132) by the change of a pronoun becomes a love poem, "He showed me heights I never saw," as in my copy.

Here is a quatrain as it appeared in print (S.H., page 93):

> To the staunch dust we safe commit thee;
> Tongue if it hath, inviolate to thee—
> Silence denote and sanctity enforce thee,
> Passenger of Infinity!

My copy reads:

> To the unwilling dust we soft commit thee,
> Guile if it hath inviolate to thee,
> Breezes caress and firmament salute thee,
> Nothing affront thy secrecy.

The last four lines of "Low at my problem bending" (S.H., page 86) are:

> I check my busy pencil,
> My ciphers slip away,
> Wherefore, my baffled fingers,
> Time Eternity?

In my copy the obscure ending is clarified:

> I check my busy pencil,
> My figures file away,
> Wherefore, my baffled fingers,
> Thy perplexity?

Some of the differences appear to result from misreading the manuscript, as on page 20:

> There is another loneliness
> That many die without,
> Not want or friend occasions it,
> Or circumstance or lot.

My copy reads:

> There is another loneliness
> That many die without,
> Not want *of* friend occasions it,
> Or circumstance *of* lot.

and the fourth line of "Just so, Jesus raps—He does not weary" (S.H., page 142), "Might He out-spy the lady's soul," reads in my copy, "Might he *but* spy the *hiding* soul."

In the next example (S.H., page 137) many alternatives were suggested by Emily. The following version, very different from the one published, appears to be the form she preferred.

> To see her is a picture,
> To hear her is a tune,
> To know her, a disparagement
> Of every other boon.
>
> To know her not, affliction,
> To own her for a friend
> A warmth as near as if the sun
> Were shining in your hand.

In the published version the third and fourth lines read

> To know her an intemperance
> As innocent as June.

It may be significant that among suggested alternatives Emily wrote the word "dangerous" upside down above "innocent." So much for differences.

A good many quatrains are fragments of longer poems.

> The duties of the wind are few—
> To cast the ships at sea,
> Establish March, the floods escort,
> And usher liberty.

Although this was printed not as a quatrain, but as a complete five-line poem (S.H., page 54), a copy in Emily's writing contains three additional stanzas:

> The pleasures of the wind are broad,
> To dwell extent among,
> Remain or wander, speculate,
> Or forests entertain.

> The kinsmen of the wind are peaks,
> Azof, the equinox,
> Also with bird and asteroid
> A bowing intercourse.

> The limitations of the wind,
> Do he exist or die,
> Too wise he seems for wakelessness—
> However, know not I.

Sometimes, instead of using the first stanza only, only the first was omitted. "We spy the forests and the hills" (S.H., page 47) has an opening stanza:

> Dew is the freshet in the grass,
> 'Tis many a tiny mill
> Turns unperceived beneath our feet
> And artisan lies still.

The title of *The Single Hound* was taken from the first poem in the volume—itself a fragment. The entire poem reads, in Emily's writing:

> This consciousness that is aware
> Of neighbors and the sun
> Will be the one aware of death,
> And that itself alone

Is traversing the interval
Experience between,
And most profound experiment
Appointed unto men.

How adequate unto itself
Its properties shall be,
Itself unto itself, and none
Shall make discovery.

Adventure most unto itself
The soul condemned to be,
Attended by a single hound—
Its own identity.

After *The Single Hound* nothing more was published for ten years.

In 1922, the copyright of *Letters of Emily Dickinson*, 1894, edited by Mabel Loomis Todd, expired. *The Life and Letters of Emily Dickinson* by Martha Dickinson Bianchi appeared in 1924.[1] Of the 386 pages in this book, 105 were devoted to the "life," 269 to the "letters" taken without acknowledgment from my mother's 1894 volumes. They were rearranged in chronological order instead of by correspondents, which my mother had thought preferable. (See page 267.) That they had not been compared with the originals is obvious, because mistakes were copied along with the text, mistakes corrected by my mother in her 1931 edition of the *Letters*. In this connection it is instructive to compare Emily's letters to her brother, some of which were left out, but to which none were added. These letters were reproduced even to the number of dots for textual omissions. A few examples will serve.

(1) Abbreviations: "E.C." in *Letters*, 1894, page 94, and in *Life and Letters*, page 165, reads "Eliza Coleman" in *Letters*, 1931, page 93; "Cousin J." in *Letters*, 1894, page 112, and in

[1] The jacket read in part as follows: "Mrs. Bianchi, the niece and sole survivor of the family, has undertaken to re-create the true Emily Dickinson. The result is one of the most notable contributions to recent American biography. . . . Of especial interest are her letters, each as clear cut and flawless as one of her poems, and the collection, as a whole, making a permanent addition to English prose writing."

Life and Letters, page 179, reads "Cousin John" (John Graves of Sunderland, later of Boston) in *Letters,* 1931, page 107.

(2) Omitted passages: In the letter containing the famous sentence, "Do you know of any nation about to besiege South Hadley?" (*Letters,* 1894, page 67), the omission has been restored in *Letters,* 1931, page 64, and the sentence beginning, "Miss F[iske] told me," put in a postscript where it belongs. In *Life and Letters,* page 123, the entire passage follows the 1894 text.

(3) Explanatory footnotes: On page 82 of *Letters,* 1894, a footnote referring to Emily's description of Jenny Lind's concert in "the old Edwards Church," explained that it was "evidently a slip of the pen, as Jenny Lind sang in the old First Church at Northampton on that occasion." Professor Jordan of Smith College told me that Emily was correct, that "the old Edwards church" and "the old First Church at Northampton" were the same. Relying upon my mother's accuracy, however, Mrs. Bianchi copied the footnote verbatim (*Life and Letters,* page 156).

(4) Mistakes: The date of the letter to the Norcross sisters at the time of their father's death is given as "January, 1864," in *Letters,* 1894, page 250, and also in *Life and Letters,* page 252. In *Letters,* 1931, page 228, the date was corrected to read "January 7, 1863," with a footnote explaining that Miss Fanny herself had been responsible for the error. It is only fair to say that copying mistakes was unavoidable, since in most cases my mother's book was the only source from which the letters could have been obtained. When the owners had died, the originals would have been hard, often impossible, to find. One group to which Mrs. Bianchi might have had access, however—those written to Colonel Higginson and placed by him in the Boston Public Library—she seems not to have consulted, as the omitted passages are identical and clerical mistakes in the 1894 volumes were reproduced.[2] Comparing the dates assigned to Mr. Higginson's letters in 1894 with those used by Mrs. Bianchi, we find them in every instance identical. Mrs. Todd, after further in-

[2] A paragraph is omitted on p. 309 in *Letters,* 1894, also in *Life and Letters,* p. 249. In *Letters,* 1931, p. 279, the missing paragraph, beginning, "I, too, have an 'island,' " is restored. Referring to Walt Whitman, Emily said to Colonel Higginson, "I never read his book, but was told that *it* was disgraceful" (*Letters,* 1894, p. 302; *Life and Letters,* p. 239). In *Letters,* 1931, p. 273, "it" reads "be" as in the manuscript.

vestigation, corrected several of the dates in her 1931 volume.[3]

The reader should be warned, however, that although the letters were taken from Mrs. Todd's volumes, passages were often omitted without indicating the cuts. Dates were confused, either by omitting the question mark, which my mother considered essential if a date could not be verified, or by juxtaposing letters written at different times, thus distorting the context. Facts such as these have been pointed out by scholars frequently and at length.

So much for the "letters." Now as to the "life." Although based largely on a paraphrasing of Emily's letters, the "life" was a web of mistakes and fiction or, as one critic characterized it, "a chaos of inaccuracies, falsities, obscurities." A frequent type of error was mistaken identity. A picture of Samuel Bowles was labeled "J. G. Holland." Emily's maternal grandfather was confused with his own son in the following manner: Emily's mother, born in 1804, was said to be the daughter of Alfred Norcross of Monson, when in point of fact that gentleman was her younger brother, born in 1815. Even Biblical characters were not immune: "Peter," in Emily's famous observation that he "took the marine walk at the great risk," was now robbed of his prowess by "Paul" (page 92). Emily herself was given a wrong middle name—Norcross. In later editions, though Elizabeth, the correct middle name, was added, Norcross has been retained. Thus in her niece's book Emily's name still inaccurately appears as Emily Elizabeth Norcross Dickinson.

Mistakes such as wrong dates for Emily's birth and death were later corrected. But others remain. Dates seem to have offered particular difficulties. "In the early days of the very last spring of her life" (1886) Emily was said to have sent "to Gib the characteristic lines"—and a poem follows (page 56). But little Gilbert Dickinson had died in 1883.

Bad as such factual mistakes were, at least they were obvious

---

[3] Examples of incorrect dates copied by Mrs. Bianchi from the 1894 volumes: (a) "1868" in *Letters*, 1894, p. 312, and in *Life and Letters*, p. 268, reads "1866" in *Letters*, 1931, p. 281; (b) "1868" in *Letters*, 1894, p. 313, and in *Life and Letters*, p. 270, reads "June, 1867," in *Letters*, 1931, p. 283; (c) "Winter, 1871," in *Letters*, 1894, p. 316, and in *Life and Letters*, p. 277, reads "Winter, 1872," in *Letters*, 1931, p. 290.

and would sooner or later be noticed.[4] Many of them have been rectified in a later edition. But misrepresentation of personal relationships is a different matter. Take for instance Emily's relation to Sue, her sister-in-law. It will be recalled that in the original volumes of letters all reference to Sue was omitted at her husband's request. In her daughter's book not only is she reinstated; she is pictured as Emily's closest friend and adviser, on whose literary acumen she depended as long as she lived. And yet, on page 86 of the *Life and Letters,* Mrs. Bianchi says that Emily "had never told her family of her writing and they never dared ask. She never showed what she wrote to them." Sue may not have been included in the "family" in this instance. But be that as it may, Emily's relationship to her sister-in-law will repay further investigation.

Her relation to her brother, on the other hand, is passed over. Except for an occasional mention of his name, one paragraph at the beginning of the chapter entitled "Childhood" suffices to dispose of him. And no picture of him appears anywhere in the book.

But the one irreparable misrepresentation in this "life" is her niece's version of Emily's "love story." Not only was the legend of a broken heart revived; it was fantastically embellished. It pleases many people to believe that Emily renounced the world because of a broken heart. They like to grieve over her because of it. That cannot be helped. But when a close relative declares in so many words that such was indeed the case, sanction is given to preference, substance to speculation. The fact that the niece does not understand her aunt, though regrettable, does not mat-

---

[4] Compare Genevieve Taggard, *op. cit.*; George F. Whicher, *op. cit.*; and Josephine Pollitt, *Emily Dickinson, the Human Background of Her Poetry.* New York: Harper & Brothers, 1930.

Regarding the poems quoted in *Life and Letters* one illustration serves to show that they, too, need further study. On page 78 appears a stanza, "Springs shake their sills," which is said to have been an alternative for the "second"—meaning third—stanza of "Safe in their alabaster chambers." There is another version of this stanza which reads

> Springs shake the seals but the silence stiffens,
> Frosts unhook in the northern zones,
> Icicles crawl from polar caverns,
> Midnight in marble refutes the suns.

I have copies of both versions in my mother's writing, and there is nothing to indicate that either should be considered part of any other poem.

ter. What does matter is that such a statement betrays Emily, because it is not true, as I trust I have shown. To misrepresent her in this is to do her the greatest disservice in the power of a relative to bestow.

Mrs. Bianchi's book is epitomized by its frontispiece—the fanciful picture of Emily referred to in Chapter XV.[5]

I begged my mother to allow me to refute some of the misstatements in the *Life and Letters*, arguing that a false impression may become permanent unless it is challenged at once. She refused. I drew her attention to the fact that no acknowledgment had been made to her early volumes. Mrs. Bianchi's name on the title-page implied that she herself had collected and edited the letters. Such effrontery left me aghast. That misrepresentation must not be allowed to stand. I asked my mother why she did not protest. She said, "Please do not talk about it." Not until after her death in 1932 did I discover that she had known in advance about Mrs. Bianchi's book. It seems that in the fall of 1923 the president of Little, Brown & Company, successors of Roberts Brothers, had written to my mother to notify her that application had been made to them "by a member of the Emily Dickinson family for the use of some of her published letters in a definitive Life and Letters." The letter from Little, Brown is in my possession; also my mother's reply, in which she asked only that acknowledgment to her own original volumes be included in the book. This letter from Little, Brown was merely an act of courtesy since Emily's letters were already in the public domain. As for the acknowledgment, none appeared in the *Life and Letters*, brought out by Houghton Mifflin Company the following year.

In the meantime, what had been happening to the poems? The *Life and Letters* was not the only book published by Mrs. Bianchi in 1924. At that time the three little volumes, series one, two, and three, together with *The Single Hound*, were still the only form in which Emily's poems were available. Frequent print-

---

[5] Amy Lowell wished to neutralize the effect of this book. She declared that as soon as her *Keats* was finished (1925) she would begin a life of Emily Dickinson in which the character of each member of her family would be analyzed. My mother agreed to help. But Miss Lowell died before she began. Compare S. Foster Damon, *Amy Lowell*. Boston: Houghton Mifflin Company, 1935, pp. 611-612.

ings of the first three series were required to meet the steady
demand. (See Appendix III.) Steps had been taken to supplant
those books, however, as soon as the law allowed. The copyright
on the first volume (1890) expired in 1918 and was renewed by
Martha Dickinson Bianchi. In 1919 the copyright on the Second
Series (1891) was likewise renewed by her. In 1924, when the
copyright on the Third Series (1896) ran out, the contents of
all three volumes, together with the poems in *The Single Hound*,
were republished, following the original arrangement and section headings, under the title, *The Complete Poems of Emily
Dickinson*.[6] A single copyright covered all poems in the book
which—with an introduction by Mrs. Bianchi whose name alone
appeared on the title-page—was offered as "a final complete
edition." In view of this fact, what was the astonishment of the
reading public five years later to learn that another volume of
poems was about to appear. These were said to have been just
discovered. The title-page read "Further Poems of Emily Dickinson, Withheld from Publication by her Sister Lavinia." The
book was hailed as the greatest literary discovery of the age.
The cause for surprise, however, as the reader is well aware,
should have been not that these poems had been discovered,
but that their publication had been so long delayed.

Certain reviewers implied that some of the poems might be
spurious. I went through the volume with my mother. She said
they were genuine. I wondered how she knew. I would read a
first line out loud and she, looking off into the distance, would
complete the poem verbatim. I asked her how she could remember so many. "I copied them all," she said. Later, I com-

---

[6] In *The Complete Poems* (Boston: Little, Brown & Company, 1924) a note
on p. v explained that "for the convenience of readers familiar with previous
editions of Emily Dickinson's poems, the original four divisions have here
been retained, each now including all the poems of its own group in the
three volumes of the series." A poem, "Title divine is mine," was added
(p. 176) to the division "Love" of the Third Series, though it had not
appeared in that volume. Four poems in the section entitled *The Single
Hound* were added to the contents of that volume: "Through lane it lay,
through bramble" (p. 297); "The Bible is an antique volume" (p. 299); "A
little overflowing word" (p. 311); and "Give little anguish, lives will fret"
(p. 313). Two of these, the second and third, were taken from the *Life and
Letters* (p. 91 and 80, respectively). Most of the poems first published in the
text of the "life," however, were not included in *The Complete Poems*.

pared *Further Poems* with my mother's copies and found every
one, although the text differed in certain respects, in some cases
so much as to constitute two distinct versions. As with those in
The Single Hound, not only are there textual differences and
mistakes in editing—a subject too large to be expanded here—
but many poems first published by Mrs. Bianchi are not given in
full.

Here are some examples to illustrate the types of error.

The first stanza on page 20 of *Further Poems* reads:

> A bird is of all beings
> The likest to the dawn,
> An easy breeze does put afloat
> The general heavens upon.

The change of a vowel focuses the simile, as in my copy:

> Of being is a bird
> The likest to the *down*
> An easy breeze do put afloat
> The general heavens upon.
>
> It soars and shifts and whirls
> And measures with the clouds
> In easy, even, dazzling pace.
> No different the birds,
>
> Except a wake of music
> Accompany their feet,
> As should the down emit a tune
> For ecstasy of it.

Another poem (F.P., page 93) consists of six stanzas, of which
the second and third were omitted:

> I rose because he sank.
> I thought it would be opposite,
> But when his power bent
> My soul grew straight.

I cheered my fainting prince,
I sang firm steady chants,
I stayed his film with hymn.

And when the dews drew off
That held his forehead stiff,
I gave him balm for balm.

I told him best must pass
Through this low arch of flesh,
No casque so brave
It spurn the grave.

I told him worlds I knew
Where monarchs grew
Who recollected us
If we were true.

And so with thews of hymn
And sinew from within,
And ways I knew not that I knew till then,
I lifted him.

The final stanza of "Inconceivably solemn" (F.P., page 131) reads as printed:

> Music's triumphant,
> But a fine ear
> Aches with delight
> The drums to hear.

My copy has a different emphasis:

> Music's triumphant,
> But the fine ear
> Winces with delight
> Are drums too near.

Mistakes in deciphering the manuscript sometimes confuse the meaning. Of "Doom is the house without the door" (F.P., page 17), the last line reads, "And hundreds bow to God." It should be "hemlocks" which bow to God.

The third and final stanza of

> The world feels dusty
> When we stop to die,

(F.P., page 109) reads as printed:

> Mine be the ministry
> When thy thirst comes,
> Dews of thyself to fetch
> And holy balms.

My copy reads:

> Mine be the ministry
> When thy thirst comes,
> Dews of Thessaly to fetch
> And Hybla balms.

In "Me from myself to banish" (F.P., page 123)—entitled b
Colonel Higginson "The Divided Kingdom"—the final lin
should be "Me of me," not "Me—or Me," as published.

> And since we're mutual monarch
> How this be,
> Except by abdication
> Me of me?

Another instance of misreading the manuscript appears in th
concluding stanza of "I got so I could hear his name" (F.P., pag
184). As printed, the two final lines, "Supremer than" an
"Superior to," are meaningless. Emily intended them as alterna
tives to the second line, "Not subject to." If put where the
belong they would offer the following choice:

> If any power behind it be
> Not subject to (supremer than) (superior to) despair,
> It care in some remoter way
> For so minute affair
> As misery, itself too vast
> For interrupting more.[7]

[7] An appendix to *Further Poems* has a foreword which reads:
    The poems in the Appendix have either been published in the "Lif
and Letters of Emily Dickinson"—but not in the "Complete Poems,"—

If the contents of *Further Poems* were to be available in the same volume with all others previously printed, a new comprehensive edition was required. For *The Complete Poems* was no longer complete. Such a volume was in point of fact issued the following year, in 1930. The title was changed, however, from "The Complete" to *The Poems of Emily Dickinson*.

After the publication of *Further Poems* I wanted to point

---

or they have appeared in part only in the "Complete Poems" and are here restored as originally written.

M.D.B.

These seven poems and their accompanying footnotes are worth examining.

The first, "It will be summer eventually" (F.P., p. 195), here consists of ten stanzas, though it is in reality two poems of five stanzas each, and thus appears in the current collected edition. A footnote to the first five stanzas states: "Published in the 'Complete Poems' on page 126 with the first stanza omitted; now given as originally written." But the four-stanza form here referred to, beginning, "The springtime's pallid landscape," first appeared in the Third Series, p. 101. (The opening quatrain was omitted by Mrs. Todd.) The second poem begins, "I'm sorry for the dead today." According to a footnote the final stanza, "I wonder if the sepulchre," appeared "on page 244 of the 'Complete Poems.'" It was first printed in the Third Series, p. 180.

The poem, "To disappear enhances" (F.P., p. 197), consists of five stanzas. A footnote states: "The first three stanzas have never before been published. The last two only appeared on page 266 of 'Complete Poems.'" What are the facts? The entire poem, with minor differences, sent to Colonel Higginson in 1876, was published in *Letters*, 1894, pp. 323-324. Twenty years later the last two stanzas appeared in *The Single Hound* (p. 30) as a separate poem beginning, "Of death the sharpest function." (This read "sternest" in *Letters*, 1894.) After another ten years these same two stanzas were reprinted in *The Complete Poems*, p. 266, as the footnote indicates, while the entire poem was printed on p. 303 of Mrs. Bianchi's own *Life and Letters*, five years previous to its appearance in *Further Poems* "for the first time."

Turning to the next poem in the appendix (F.P., p. 198) we find, "God is a distant, stately lover," with a footnote: "First four lines only before published in a paper by her niece." The reader may recall that this is the poem which, when it first appeared in *The Christian Register*, Apr. 2, 1891, created a storm of protest. (See pp. 124-125 of the present volume.) It is omitted from the current collected edition and "The Savior must have been a docile gentleman," taken from *Life and Letters*, p. 60, is substituted in its place.

As to the four remaining poems in the appendix: though credit for their previous appearance is in each instance given to *Life and Letters*, all four were first published in *Letters*, 1894—"A feather from the whippoorwill," p. 219; "There are two ripenings," p. 147; "The zeros taught us phosphorus," p. 200; "Just once—Oh, least request!" p. 217. These four poems, together with "The Savior must have been a docile gentleman," still remain in an appendix in the current collected edition. All five are wrongly paged in the index, the page numbers of the previous edition having been followed.

out some of its shortcomings. My mother forbade it. I wondered what she would let me do—what horn of the Dickinson dilemma I should be permitted to grasp. The turn of events could not be allowed to stand unchallenged—of that I was sure. So with the encouragement of several advisers I tried another approach. I asked her to permit me to help her bring out a new edition of the original 1894 *Letters*, the book which had already been republished in part by Mrs. Bianchi with mutilations of the text. A correct version, a new and enlarged edition of the original collection, I argued, was indispensable. She finally agreed to let me begin.

First, I read over letters and parts of letters which in 1894 had been left out for one reason or another—because they seemed trivial, or because the book was getting too large, or because they had been thought to border too much on what was called "the intimate." It should never be forgotten that in 1894 to publish Emily's letters at all was considered a very dubious venture. Was it proper, they questioned, to draw aside the veil from so shy a creature?

In 1930 we agreed that the time had come to restore not only the omitted passages but also letters hitherto withheld. Among the additional letters was a group addressed to James D. and Charles H. Clark, friends of the Reverend Dr. Charles Wadsworth. These letters had been suppressed in 1894 as too personal —as describing too candidly a relationship which, although neither Austin nor Lavinia understood it, both knew had meant a great deal to Emily. I wondered as I read them why these letters should ever have been left out. They seemed touchingly sincere and decorous against the background of innuendoes concerning Emily's "love-affair" which had been current during the intervening years.

The new edition of *Letters of Emily Dickinson* edited by Mabel Loomis Todd was published by Harper & Brothers in 1931 and was at once accepted as the standard source book on the subject.[8]

---

[8] Before my mother's new edition of the *Letters* appeared, Mrs. Bianchi's collaborator, Alfred Leete Hampson, had brought out a *Bibliography of Emily Dickinson* in 1930. The cover device, used without acknowledgment, was my mother's design of Indian pipes, which also appeared on p. 11. This

The next step was to prepare the account of Emily's literary début, a task stopped short by my mother's death in 1932.

That same year Mrs. Bianchi published *Emily Dickinson Face to Face*, a volume of reminiscences containing Emily's early notes, some letters, and poems and parts of poems, both published and unpublished. A few examples serve to characterize the book.

The stanza, "A wind that woke a lone delight" (E.D.F.F., page 256), had been published in *Letters*, 1931, page 307.

"Unable are the loved to die" (E.D.F.F., page 263) is the first stanza of a poem of which the second reads:

> Unable they that love, to die,
> For love reforms vitality
> Into divinity.

"Gratitude is not the mention" (E.D.F.F., page 227) also has an omitted second stanza, and "More prudent to assault the dawn" (page 247) has a first stanza which is missing.

A sentence in a note to Sue (E.D.F.F., page 265) is in reality the first stanza of a poem in the Third Series, 1896, page 40:

> The farthest thunder that I heard
> Was nearer than the sky,
> And rumbles still, though torrid noons
> Have lain their missiles by.

On the same page a poem beginning, "To wane without disparagement," had appeared as prose in a letter to Colonel Higginson, *Letters*, 1931, page 302.

A good many of the discrepancies in this book have to do with the name "Sue" which does not appear in my copies of the poems. For instance, two stanzas said to have been addressed to Sue (E.D.F.F., page 260), beginning, "But Susan is a stranger yet," are the last two stanzas of "What mystery pervades a well," published in the Third Series, pages 117-118, the line in question reading, "But nature is a stranger yet."

---

design had been used on the jacket of *The Complete Poems* as well as on that of the 1930 edition. But after the 1931 volume of *Letters* was published, on the cover of which my mother again used her own painting, the Indian pipes on the jacket of the collected edition were replaced by a gardenia.

Another note addressed to Sue (E.D.F.F., page 270) begin

> I could not drink it, Sue,
> Till you had tasted first.

A copy in Emily's writing begins,

> I could not drink it, Sweet,
> Till you had tasted first.

Within a year after my mother's death I returned to the tasl of assembling letters and making excerpts from her diaries an journals preliminary to writing the account of Emily's literar début. While I was so engaged, another volume entitled *Un published Poems of Emily Dickinson*, edited by Martha Dickin son Bianchi and Alfred Leete Hampson, came out in 1935, an was soon followed by another all-inclusive revised edition.

As in the case of *Further Poems*, all those included in *Unpub lished Poems* are among my mother's copies, though with familia types of differences.

"A weight with needles on the pounds" (U.P., page 18) has concluding couplet which reads:

> As manifold for anguish
> As *spices* be for name.

Emily wrote "species."

Certain stanzas differ from my copies, as on page 22:

> Bound a trouble and lives will bear it,—
> Circumspection enable woe;
> Still to conjecture were no limit,
> Who were sufficient to misery?

In an unpublished version this stanza reads:

> Bound a trouble and lives can bear it;
> Limit how deep a bleeding go,
> So many drops of vital scarlet,
> Deal with the soul as with algebra.

A good many poems in this book appeared in fragmentary form: "More life went out when he went" (page 4), final stanza omitted; "The first day's night had come" (page 13), last two stanzas omitted; "If he dissolve, then there is nothing more" (page 108), last two stanzas omitted; "Unit, like death, for whom?" (page 135), last nine lines omitted. In the case of "Her smile was shaped like other smiles" (page 123), the essential third stanza was omitted. The complete poem reads:

> Her smile was shaped like other smiles,
> The dimples ran along,
> And still it hurt you, as some bird
> Did hoist herself to sing,
>
> Then recollect a ball she got,
> And hold upon the twig
> Convulsive, while the music crashed
> Like beads among the bog.
>
> A happy lip breaks sudden,
> It doesn't state you how
> It contemplated smiling,
> Just consummated now.
>
> But this one wears its merriment
> So patient, like a pain
> Fresh gilded to elude the eyes
> Unqualified to scan.

The third and last stanza, omitted from "So much of heaven as gone from earth" (U.P., page 5), had been published in *Further Poems*, page 50, as a separate quatrain, "Too much of proof affronts belief."

Sometimes not a stanza but only a line was omitted. "No man can compass a despair" (U.P., page 141) is a poem of three stanzas. With the omitted line, "Unconscious of the width," restored, the poem would read:

> No man can compass a despair.
> As round a goalless road
> No faster than a mile at once
> The traveller proceed—

Unconscious of the width,
Unconscious that the sun
Be setting on his progress—
So accurate the one

At estimating pain
Whose own has just begun.
His ignorance the angel
That pilot him along.

Although some poems were published only in part, elsewhere
two were combined as one. "The trees, like tassels, hit and swung"
(U.P., page 51), here consisting of seven stanzas, is in reality two
poems. The first four stanzas describe a summer storm; to the last
three, beginning "A bird sat careless on the fence," Emily herself gave the title "Summer's Day."

Finally, as with Mrs. Bianchi's other books, many poems and
parts of poems in the 1935 volume had been previously published
by Mrs. Todd. "Never for society" (U.P., page 37) had first appeared, with a difference of two words, in *Letters*, 1894, page
369. "My loss by sickness—was it loss?" (U.P., page 43), printed
as the concluding stanza of the poem beginning "My first well
day since many ill," had been published in *Letters*, 1894, page
210, as

The loss of sickness—was it loss?
Or that ethereal gain
You earned by measuring the grave,
Then measuring the sun.

The final stanza of the poem (U.P., page 102) of which the first
two lines should read

It might be lonelier
Without the loneliness,

had appeared in the Third Series, page 64:

It might be easier
To fail with land in sight,
Than gain my blue peninsula
To perish of delight.

In the current collected edition this stanza appears twice; independently, as in the Third Series, and as the final stanza of "It might be lonelier."

"That after horror that was us" (U.P., page 145), which reads " 'twas us" in my copy, is a poem of four stanzas, of which the last two, beginning "The possibility to pass," had been published in *Letters*, 1894, page 312.

Enough has been said to make it apparent that until Emily's poems have received a thorough overhauling, and until each one has been compared with all the versions in her own handwriting, no definitive edition of *The Poems of Emily Dickinson* can be contemplated. Such a task cannot be undertaken, of course, until all her existing manuscripts have been made available.

Epilogue

The truth must dazzle gradually
Or every man be blind.

EMILY DICKINSON'S literary début did not end with the death of her sister Lavinia. It has not ended yet, after more than half a century. In the Prologue it was intimated that personalities might provide an explanation of the long delay—that a study of the persons closest to Emily and of their relationships one with another might furnish a clue to the mystery. Has this suggestion been supported by the facts?

At the outset one question baffled me as it has baffled others. My mother had stated in print that hundreds of poems still remained unpublished. What had happened to them? When I tried to answer the question, I was confronted with yet another deadlock—but one so charged with power that it has been called the major passage-at-arms in American literature. There seemed to be no explanation. And yet the answer is simple. Because of the lawsuit my mother was unwilling to have anything more to do with Lavinia Dickinson. After the trial they never spoke again —the "valves of their attention . . . closed like stone."

Here was the situation: my mother found herself in possession of over a thousand copied poems, the originals of which had been given to her by Lavinia to decipher, to edit, and to publish. The first stages of the work had been completed. These copies had been classified, arranged in alphabetical order, and indexed. One hundred and sixty-five of them had already been published in the Third Series (1896) in addition to those in *Letters,* 1894, and the remainder were to have appeared in subsequent volumes. But although the poems were ready for the printer, to see them through the press would have necessitated collaborating with Lavinia, and that was out of the question.

Lavinia, on the other hand, had hundreds of manuscripts.[1] And although to publish them was her "utmost goal," she could find no way of doing so. She herself could not copy them, and they were too precious to entrust to a publisher as they were, even if he had been willing to consider them. The hundreds of poems were caught in a vise. I have sometimes wondered how they could have stayed so long incognito. It seems as if they must have burst the locks that held them and leaped from their hiding places, so full of life are they.

At this point a little subsidiary story must be fitted into place —the story of that pile of copied poems which is still intact in spite of a hazardous history.

When my father retired from Amherst College in 1917, he and my mother went to live in Coconut Grove, Florida. In closing the Amherst house and disposing of our possessions I packed a bundle labeled "Copies of E.D.'s Poems." I did not open it or attach to it any importance. After all, it contained only copies. My mother took the package with her to Florida where it remained for fifteen years, not only during the winter months, but in summer while my parents were in the North. One day the storehouse in which it was kept caught fire—but the bundle of poems was rescued. Thereafter it was placed in the main house. That building was partly demolished and its contents water-soaked during the hurricane of 1926—but the poems were not harmed. In June, 1932, when my mother came north for the summer she brought the package with her and, four months before she died, placed it in my hands. She told me that it contained unpublished poems but said no more. Among them are all those in *Further Poems*, 1929, and in *Unpublished Poems*, 1935.[2] It is fortunate that in spite of my mother's varied interests she considered it worth while throughout the years to preserve this little bundle of papers by

[1] What happened to the original manuscripts, of which Miss Mary Lee Hall had copied enough for another small volume before Miss Vinnie died, where they were "hidden," when and where they were found, is still to be explained.

[2] Most of the copies are in Mrs. Todd's handwriting. A few are typewritten. The transcript of others by a copyist who found it hard to read what Emily had written is completed in Mrs. Todd's writing. There are pencil changes and a few titles in Colonel Higginson's hand.

means of which uncertainties regarding the text of many poems will eventually be straightened out.

Emily started a tradition—to leave her work for someone else to finish after her death. She gave Lavinia no instructions, knowing though she did only too well how inadequate to such a task were her sister's capabilities.

Austin, their brother, carried on the tradition. He died without suggesting how to deal with interlocking animosities—that chaos of conflicting emotions which he had for years held in leash, and which by his death were let loose, thereby blocking further publication of the poems.

Lavinia inherited both the task and the chaos. The former she could not complete. To the latter she added further elements of her own devising and died—without a will, without a word.

That was in 1899. Since then the tradition has held. Sue did nothing to break it. And while her daughter published over four hundred additional poems, she did not, if my estimate is correct, publish all of those in her possession. No one has brought the strange drama to an end, either by publishing all the poems, or by explaining why it has not been done.

The feuds are now dissolved in death. But the task remains unfinished. It has finally reached me—the last of both their houses. The dramatis personae are gone, each one who played a part in furthering, or obstructing, publication of the poetry of Emily Dickinson.

To break the tradition the first step was republication of the *Letters*.

This book is a second step.

I thought, in the beginning, that my only task was to find out why publication of the poems by the original editors stopped in 1896. Now I know why. But I know something more. I know why Emily lived as she did. For in unraveling the story of her literary début I have become acquainted with the members of her family, and in the contemplation of their personalities I have discovered one reason at least why she chose solitude.

If by telling the story I have added to an understanding of her, if as family traits have been revealed any light has been shed upon herself, then my handling of the facts in my possession will have been justified.

> The soul selects her own society,
> Then shuts the door;
> On her divine majority
> Obtrude no more.

A Contemporary Account of the Publication of the First Volume of *Poems by Emily Dickinson*, from the Journal of Mabel Loomis Todd

Amherst
Sunday morning, 30 *November*, 1890

. . . . This fall has been in many respects one of the pleasantest I have passed here—in seven or eight years. To be sure, Susan and her progeny are still outraged at me, but everything else has gone very well. Now that Emily's *Poems* are actually out, and my name on the title-page, they rage more than ever. *Why*, is a mystery to me, for they had the entire box of Emily's MSS over there for nearly two years after she died, and Vinnie urging them all the time, even with fierce insistence, to do something about getting them published.

But Susan is afflicted with an unconquerable laziness, and she kept saying she would, & she would perhaps, until Vinnie was wild. At last she announced that she thought nothing had better be done about it, they would never sell—there was not money enough to get them out—the public would not care for them, & so on—in short, she gave it up. Then Vinnie came to me. She knew I always had faith in the poems, and she begged me to copy and edit them—put them all into shape. Then she was sure Col. Higginson would write a preface, and somebody would be willing to publish them, and the desire of her heart would be accomplished.

So I took them. The outlook was appalling. Emily wrote the strangest hand ever seen, which I had to absolutely incorporate into my innermost consciousness before I could be certain of anything she wrote. Even Susan, who has credit for a complete intellectual comprehension of Emily (although Vinnie says her cruelties shortened Emily's life by at least ten years), spoiled utterly the poem "Renunciation" which she copied and sent to Scribner's. It appeared in the last August number, and read "As if no *sail* the solstice passed." That is of course meaningless; but upon consulting the original I find that to an ordinary or unaccustomed eye—or to one not in deepest inner sympathy with Emily's barely-expressed thought—the word looks somewhat like sail. But in so many hundreds of other places she writes *soul* the same way where it could not possibly be read *sail*, that I am really surprised at Susan's obtuseness. It would have been a questionable volume that she issued, if Vinnie had had her way at first!

In addition to the strange handwriting, she wrote generally on both sides of her thin paper; and she often changed poems again and again, leaving sometimes six or eight words to choose from; and then if the paper was not large enough to finish, she would run around the margin with a line or two. And of the first box submitted to me there were fully seven hundred poems!

Well, I began, and it seemed as if it were, merely mechanically, interminable. I wrote and wrote and wrote. For nearly a year I translated them into typewriter MSS. Then I had to give up the Hammond I had used, and I wrote a few on the little "World" machine, but that was rather slow. Then Vinnie began to get impatient. She could not see why it took so much time—and I knew I was doing it as fast as mortal could accomplish it, unless one devoted *all* one's time to it—and frequently I gave three and four hours a day to it.

Then I wrote them in my own hand. That was quicker. This was well into the second year; and Vinnie began to say that everybody who wanted so much to see them in print was dying—one after the other of Emily's audience. But I was not discouraged, and I kept steadfastly on.

The poems were having a wonderful effect on me, mentally and spiritually. They seemed to open the door into a wider universe than the little sphere surrounding me which so often hurt and compressed me—and they helped me nobly through a very trying time. Their sadness and hopelessness, sometimes, was so much bitterer than mine that

"I was helped
As if a Kingdom cared."

Most of them I came to know lovingly by heart, and I was strengthened and uplifted. I felt their genius, and I knew the book would succeed. No one else had faith in them—except Vinnie, & hers was a blind sort of faith, not in the least from any literary appreciation of their power.

At the same time, their carelessness of form exasperated me. I could always find the gist & meaning, and I admired her strange words and ways of using them, but the simplest laws of verse-making she ignored, and what she called rhymes grated on me. But she could not hide her wonderful power, and I knew she had genius.

About this time, trying to hasten matters for poor Vinnie, I suggested getting a copyist to help, & I would look over & correct her work. I got one, & she did perhaps a hundred poems—but I could not stand it. The absolute lack of any approach to understanding or sympathy in what she was copying, although she did mechanically well enough, made poor Miss Graves seem to me a shade worse than an insentiate [insentient] machine—and some of her mistakes in Emily's mad words were so ludicrous as to be pathetic. Besides it took more time to put her copies into fit shape than to do it all myself. And I had a queer feeling that the poems suffered in substance from such rough handling—that their dainty and veiled meanings withdrew still more into their unparall[el]ed barricade of words, and it might take years to get these meanings out again. They must be gently and understandingly wooed. So I gave that up, and sometime in the summer of '89 I copied the last one of the seven hundred.

They made an immense pile, and weighed pounds. Then came the hurry of preparation for David's expedition to Africa, and later my own going to Boston for the winter. I took the poems with me, and Col. Higginson called upon me and looked them over with me. He did not think a volume advisable—they were too crude in form, he said, and the public would not accept even fine ideas in such rough and mystical dress—so hard to elucidate.

But I read him nearly a dozen of my favorites, and he was greatly astonished—said he had no idea there were so many in passably conventional form, and said if I would classify them all into A B and C he would look them over later in the winter. So I did that very carefully, and sent them to him.

Then he was taken very ill, and for weeks nothing was heard of him except bulletins as to his illness. Vinnie was much cast down—nearly wild, in fact; said the fates seemed in every shape against her. But just before I went to Chicago I went to see him in Cambridge, and he said if I would have patience enough to let him keep them until I returned from Chicago he would certainly look them over and see what he thought of a volume.

When I came back he said he was much impressed with them—he had put about two hundred by themselves for a possible volume, & asked me to look them over, and see if it would be my selection as well.

I found that in almost every case he had chosen my *A*'s, as I should—but he put in three or four of my B's and perhaps one C.

Then I put away the rest, and I changed words here and there in the two hundred to make them smoother—he changed a very few, and put titles to them. I do not believe, myself, in naming them; and although I admire Mr. Higginson very much, I do not think many of his titles good.

For instance, he put the title,

"A World Well Lost,"

to a little poem beginning,

"I lost a world the other day.
Has anybody found?"

thereby to my mind entirely misrepresenting the thought. Also he used "At Home," as a title to

"The Bee is not afraid of me,
I know the butterfly—"

whereas the gist of that poem lies in the last two lines, which "At Home" never touched. And one more title I had to strike out because it did not apply, "In the Wood;" given to the poem beginning

> "A little road not made of man,
> Enabled of the eye,
> Accessible to thill of bee,
> Or cart of butterfly"—

for it is not a wood-road intended, but that airy highway whereon bee and butterfly pursue their invisible business.

Then we had to think of a publisher. Mr. Higginson wrote a note to Mr. Niles of Roberts Brothers, after we had decided that this firm was better than another because Mr. Niles and Emily had corresponded for years, and I took it to him. But again obstacles appeared. Mr. Niles was quite ill at his home in Arlington, and young Pratt, or Alcott as he is now called, I believe, said he would send the poems and note out to him.

After a time Mr. Niles wrote to Mr. Higginson that he had always thought it would be unwise to perpetuate Emily's work, because her poems were just as much distinguished for defects as beauties. He enclosed Arlo Bates' criticism on the MSS. In some respects it was just and discriminating—in others rather narrow—but he advised a limited edition—say of five hundred copies—and he remarked that he thought two hundred poems were too many—that he had struck out about half.

Mr. Niles then said he would print five hundred if the "surviving sister" or family would pay for the plates. After the first five hundred (if more were printed), she would have 15% of the retail price on every copy sold.

So I conferred with Vinnie (who has about as much knowledge of business as a Maltese pussycat) and I accepted the offer.

Then Mr. Higginson asked me to take the two hundred poems once more, and correct them according to Mr. Bates' suggestions. I took them and found to my dismay that he had crossed out about twenty of the very best—the cream of the volume. I looked carefully over the one hundred discarded, and calmly put back fifteen.

Among those black-marked were "How many times these low feet staggered," "I died for beauty," "Some keep the Sabbath going to church," "I shall know why when time is over," & many more equally good; but of course I retained them.

At last they were in final shape, and the printing began. Mr. Higginson and I read all the proof—and the plate-proofs also. That was some work, but very enjoyable.

Then David and I decided that indian-pipes were the flowers to have on the cover, and I took my own little painting of them to Mr. Niles which I had given Emily years before. I have a characteristic note from her in response, in which she calls them "the preferred flower of life."

Mr. Higginson thought they might be almost *too* appropriate and spectral, at first; but they were done, and are very effective.

Just here I must tell a funny little joke I have upon Vinnie. While she is constantly exasperated and outraged at Susan—as well as hurt, and wounded to death at her cruelties, she seems at times to be curiously in fear of her, and she used to wish not to offend her. Of course she knew Susan would want to kill her as soon as she found out that I had brought out the poems. So Vinnie determined that I must be kept out of sight in the matter.

When the volume was nearly ready to be issued, Vinnie wrote to Mr. Higginson that "our co-laborer must be sub-rosa." Her writing is wildly unintelligible, and Mr. Higginson knowing that I was her representative, and acting for her, sent me the letter to see if I could decipher it!

I wrote back that whatever the word was she evidently wanted the project a secret until the final minute; but I at last made out "co-laborer" to be the word. It looked like anything rather than that. However, in the meantime Mr. Higginson had written to say that my name must appear on the volume somewhere, and before his, since I had "done the hardest part of the work," and I replied that he must put it where he chose—it would please me.

When the newspapers began to announce that the book edited by myself and Mr. Higginson was coming, Vinnie was frightened to death, but she accepted the situation manfully, and plucked up a great deal of spirit. The more indignant Susan is now, the higher Vinnie holds her head. It is all immensely funny. But the book is out, and the notices are beginning to pour in. Of course there is some notice taken of the lack of form, but all agree that it is a marvelous volume, full of genius, and a legacy to the world.

And there are hundreds yet unpublished which I have here, equally as fine as those in the volume. In addition to the original seven hundred, I have also about three hundred more in scraps—written on the backs of envelopes and bits here and there which are wonderful.

I mean, also, to collect her letters gradually, and arrange them for a prose volume. They are startlingly fine.

So this, in a few words, is the general history of what has occupied me a good deal for the past two or three years. And it has been very satisfying work. I grudge no hour thus spent. The second edition will be out before Christmas.

Early Reviews of Books by Emily Dickinson
1890-1896

Emily Dickinson, A Bibliography was published in 1930 by The Jones Library, Amherst, Massachusetts. The "Biographical and Critical" sections contain references to many of the early magazine articles but few to contemporary newspaper reviews.

To supplement this bibliography I have selected the following additional items from Mrs. Todd's scrapbooks of clippings. Since newspaper reviews usually have several headlines I have, in each instance, chosen as title of the review the phrase or caption most descriptive of it. A blank indicates that there was no column heading. Volume and page have been supplied wherever possible. In the case of periodicals each issue of which begins with page 1, the page number has been omitted.

AN EDITION OF THE POEMS OF EMILY DICKINSON. "A.T." *Boston Traveller*, Nov. 22, 1890.

POEMS. [Lilian Whiting.] *Boston Budget*, Nov. 23, 1890.

MISS DICKINSON'S POEMS. [Arlo Bates.] *Boston Courier*, Nov. 23, 1890.

NEW PUBLICATIONS. *Boston Saturday Evening Gazette*, Nov. 23, 1890.

A VERY REMARKABLE BOOK. Louise Chandler Moulton. *Boston Sunday Herald*, Nov. 23, 1890.

THE POEMS OF EMILY DICKINSON. "Droch" [Robert Bridges]. *Life* [New York], Nov. 27, 1890; vol. 16, p. 304.

LITERARY TOPICS IN BOSTON. Nathan Haskell Dole. *Book Buyer* [New York], Dec., 1890; n.s., vol. 7, p. 628.

EMILY DICKINSON'S POEMS. *Beacon* [Boston], Dec. 13, 1890.

THE POEMS OF EMILY DICKINSON. *Critic* [New York], Dec. 13, 1890; vol. 17, p. 305.

SOME POWERFUL POEMS BY EMILY DICKINSON. *Boston Sunday Globe*, Dec. 14, 1890.

THE POEMS OF EMILY DICKINSON. *Boston Transcript*, Dec. 15, 1890.

POEMS BY EMILY DICKENSON [*sic*]. J. W. C[hadwick]. *Christian Register* [Boston], Dec. 18, 1890; vol. 69, p. 828.

SCRAPS OF VERSE FROM THE PEN OF EMILY DICKINSON. *Boston Herald*, Dec. 29, 1890.

COMMENT ON NEW BOOKS. *Atlantic Monthly*, Jan., 1891; vol. 67, p. 128.

THE NEWEST POET. *Daily News* [London], Jan. 2, 1891.

GRIM SLUMBER SONGS. *Commercial Advertiser* [New York], Jan. 6, 1891.

MISS DICKINSON'S POEMS. Maurice Thompson. *America* [Chicago], Jan. 8, 1891; vol. 5, p. 425.

——— *Evening Sun* [New York], Jan. 12, 1891.

EMILY DICKINSON. John W. Chadwick. *Unity* [Chicago], Jan. 22, 1891; vol. 26, p. 171.

BOOKS AND BARBARISM, BOSTON INCONGRUITIES, EMILY DICKINSON'S POEMS. *Standard Union* [Brooklyn], Jan. 31, 1891.

EMILY DICKINSON'S POEMS. *Chicago Figaro*, Feb. 12, 1891; vol. 2, p. 428.

THE POINT OF VIEW. *Scribner's Magazine*, March 1891; vol. 9, p. 395.

SOME AMERICAN POETS. Andrew Lang. *Illustrated London News*, March 7, 1891; vol. 98, p. 307.

——— *Tribune* [New York], March 15, 1891.

LITERATURE. Mary D. Cutting. *Christian Inquirer* [New York], April 9, 1891; n.s., vol. 4.

——— *San José* [California] *Mercury*, April 19, 1891.

EMILY DICKINSON'S POEMS. *Christian Register* [Boston], April 30, 1891; vol. 70, p. 274.

——— *Bookseller* [London], May 6, 1891; no. 402, p. 447.

THE READING ROOM. Denis Wortman. *Christian Intelligencer* [New York], May 27, 1891; vol. 62.

THE NEWLY DISCOVERED POET. THE LATE EMILY DICKINSON OF AMHERST, MASS. *Providence Journal*, June 14, 1891.

NEW BOOKS AND REPRINTS. *Saturday Review* [London], July 18, 1891; vol. 72, p. 94.

——— *The Graphic* [London], Sept. 12, 1891.

BOSTON LETTER. Charles E. L. Wingate. *Critic* [New York], Sept. 19, 1891; vol. 19, p. 141.

THE SIGNIFICANCE OF EMILY DICKINSON. *Hartford Courant*, Sept. 24, 1891.

THE STRANGELY ISOLATED LIFE OF EMILY DICKINSON. Lilian Whiting. *Standard Union* [Brooklyn], Sept. 26, 1891.

THE LITERARY WAYSIDE. *Springfield Republican*, Sept. 27, 1891.

AN AMERICAN SAPPHO. *Daily News* [London], Oct. 3, 1891.

EMILY DICKENSON'S [sic] RARE GENIUS. Mary Abbott. *Chicago Evening Post*, Oct. 6, 1891.

THE BREAKFAST TABLE. F. B. Sanborn. *Boston Daily Advertiser*, Oct. 27, 1891.

LITERARY AFFAIRS IN BOSTON. [Arlo Bates.] *Book Buyer*, Nov., 1891; n.s., vol. 8, p. 417.

EMILY DICKINSON. *Review of Reviews* [New York], Nov., 1891; vol. 4, p. 459.

THE LITERARY WAYSIDE. *Springfield Republican*, Nov. 8, 1891.

MORE OF MISS DICKINSON'S POEMS. *Beacon* [Boston] Nov. 14, 1891.

EMILY DICKINSON'S POEMS. *Boston Budget*, Nov. 15, 1891; vol. 21.

MISS DICKINSON'S POEMS. *Boston Courier*, Nov. 22, 1891.

EMILY DICKINSON'S "SECOND SERIES" OF "POEMS." Louise Chandler Moulton. *Boston Sunday Herald*, Nov. 22, 1891.

——— *Boston Traveller*, Nov. 28, 1891.

TALK ABOUT NEW BOOKS. *Catholic World*, Dec., 1891; vol. 54, p. 448.

THE HOME OF EMILY DICKINSON. "J.B.A." *Packer Alumna* [Brooklyn], Dec., 1891; vol. 7, p. 143.

EMILY DICKINSON'S POEMS, SECOND SERIES. *Amherst Record*, Dec. 2, 1891.

POEMS OF EMILY DICKINSON. *Light* [Worcester, Mass.], Dec. 5, 1891; vol. 4, p. 322.

POEMS FRESH FROM THE PRESS. *Cleveland Plain Dealer*, Dec. 6, 1891.

——— *New York World*, Dec. 6, 1891.

LIBRARY AND FOYER. *Boston Transcript*, Dec. 9, 1891.

BOSTON LITERARY LETTER. *Springfield Republican*, Dec. 10, 1891.

SECOND SERIES OF THE POEMS OF EMILY DICKINSON. *Chicago Tribune*, Dec. 12, 1891.

EMILY DICKINSON. *Light* [Worcester, Mass.], Dec. 12, 1891; vol. 4, p. 349.

POEMS BY EMILY DICKINSON. *Boston Transcript*, Dec. 15, 1891.

POEMS BY EMILY DICKINSON. *Literary World* [Boston], Dec. 19, 1891; vol. 22, p. 486.

THE POEMS OF EMILY DICKINSON. Arthur Chamberlain. *Commonwealth* [Boston], Dec. 26, 1891; vol. 30, p. 7.

POEMS BY EMILY DICKINSON. *Christian Register* [Boston], Dec. 31, 1891; vol. 70, p. 868.

——— *The Congregationalist*, Dec. 31, 1891; vol. 75, p. 459.

TALK ABOUT BOOKS. *Chautauquan*, Jan. 1892; vol. 14, p. 509.

POEMS BY EMILY DICKINSON. SECOND SERIES. *Christian Intelligencer* [New York], Jan. 13, 1892; vol. 63.

A PATRIOTIC CRITIC. Andrew Lang. *Illustrated News of the World* (?) [London], Jan. 16, 1892.

ONE SIDED CRITICISM. Ellen Battelle Dietrick. *Woman's Journal* [Boston], Jan. 16, 1892; vol. 23, p. 18.

EMILY DICKINSON'S POEMS. *People and Patriot* [Concord N.H.], Feb., 1892.

NOTES FROM BOSTON. Nathan Haskell Dole. *Book News* [Philadelphia], March, 1892; vol. 10, p. 307.

EMILY DICKINSON. Louise B. Edwards. *Housekeeper's Weekly*, April 9, 1892; vol. 3, p. 2.

EMILY DICKINSON'S POEMS. "W.M." *Housekeeper's Weekly*, April 9, 1892; vol. 3, p. 4.

EMILY DICKINSON. SOME REMINISCENCES OF THIS DISTINGUISHED WRITER. *Brooklyn Eagle*, April 28, 1892.

RECENT BOOKS OF VERSE. *Christian Union* [New York], June 18, 1892; vol. 45, p. 1212. (This reference is given as 1893 in bibliography of The Jones Library.)

INTELLIGENT SOCIABILITY. Florence S. Hoyt. *Congregationalist*, March 2, 1893; vol. 78, p. 337.

A MELANCHOLY FIDELITY. *Commercial Advertiser* [New York], Aug. 23, 1893.

A CONNECTICUT VALLEY POET. "G." *Homestead* [Springfield, Mass.], Oct. 6, 1894; vol. 16, p. 11.

LETTERS OF EMILY DICKINSON. [W. F. Whetcho.] *Boston Daily Advertiser*, Nov. 23, 1894.

A THOUGHT OF GOD. PRIMITIVE LINEAMENTS OF INDIVIDUALITY SHOWN IN EMILY DICKINSON'S LETTERS. *Boston Home Journal*, Nov. 24, 1894; n.s., vol. 8, p. 5.

LETTERS OF EMILY DICKINSON. *Boston Herald*, Nov. 27, 1894.

LETTERS OF EMILY DICKINSON. *Evangelist* [New York], Nov. 29, 1894; vol. 65, p. 16.

EMILY DICKINSON'S LETTERS. *Chicago Tribune*, Dec. 1, 1894.

LIFE IN BOSTON. Lilian Whiting. *Inter Ocean* [Chicago], Dec. 1, 1894.

ALONG THE LITERARY WAYSIDE. *Springfield Republican*, Dec. 2, 1894.

NEW BOOKS. *The Spy* [Worcester, Mass.], Dec. 2, 1894.

BOSTON DAYS. *Times-Democrat* [New Orleans], Dec. 2, 1894.

EMILY DICKINSON'S LETTERS. *Denver Times*, Dec. 7, 1894.

EMILY DICKINSON'S LETTERS. *Public Ledger* [Philadelphia], Dec. 7, 1894.

EMILY DICKINSON'S POEMS. Mary Abbott. *Chicago Herald*, Dec. 8, 1894.

A NEW ENGLAND NUN. *Telegraph* [Philadelphia], Dec. 8, 1894.

LETTERS OF EMILY DICKINSON. *Evening Bulletin* [Philadelphia], Dec. 15, 1894.

EMILY DICKINSON'S LETTERS. *Amherst Record*, Dec. 19, 1894.

TWO WOMEN'S BOOKS. Caroline Healey Dall. *Boston Transcript*, Dec. 22, 1894.

——— *Chicago Journal*, Dec. 22, 1894.

LETTERS OF EMILY DICKINSON. Mary D. Cutting. *Christian Inquirer* [New York], Dec. 27, 1894; n.s., vol. 7.

EMILY DICKINSON'S LETTERS. *Congregationalist*, Dec. 27, 1894; vol. 79, p. 973.

THE EMILY DICKINSON LETTERS. *Hartford Courant*, Dec. 28, 1894.

A NEW ENGLAND RECLUSE. *San Francisco Chronicle*, Dec. 30, 1894.

THE NEW BOOKS. *Review of Reviews*, January, 1895; vol. 11, p. 110.

EMILY DICKINSON'S LETTERS. Helen Marshall North. *Home Journal* [New York], Jan. 2, 1895.

EMILY DICKINSON'S LETTERS. *Beacon* [Boston], Jan. 19, 1895.

EMILY DICKINSON'S LETTERS. GLIMPSES OF A NEW-ENGLAND MUSE. *New York Tribune*, Jan. 20, 1895.

RECENT AMERICAN POETRY. *Nation*, May 23, 1895; vol. 60, p. 402.

JULIA C. R. DORR AND SOME OF HER POET CONTEMPORARIES. Mary J. Reid. *Midland Monthly* [Des Moines, Iowa], June, 1895; vol. 3, p. 499.

A FRESH READING OF EMILY DICKINSON. "W.S.K." *Boston Transcript*, July 11, 1895.

SAPPHO AND OTHER PRINCESSES OF POETRY. "Chelifer" [Rupert Hughes]. *Godey's Magazine*, Jan. 1896; vol. 132, p. 94.

——— *Boston Transcript*, Aug. 8, 1896.

LITERARY NOTES. *New York Tribune*, Aug. 23, 1896.

POEMS: EMILY DICKINSON. *Boston Courier*, Sept. 6, 1896.

ALONG THE LITERARY WAYSIDE. *Springfield Republican*, Sept. 13, 1896.

VERSE OF EMILY DICKINSON. *New York Times*, Sept. 19, 1896.

AFTERMATH OF EMILY DICKINSON'S VERSE. *Telegraph* [Philadelphia], Sept. 19, 1896.

EMILY DICKINSON. LETTERS AND POEMS OF A LONELY NEW ENGLAND WOMAN WHO BELIEVED IN "ART FOR TRUTH." Grace S. Musser. *San Francisco Call*, Sept. 20, 1896.

EMILY DICKINSON'S POEMS. Mary Abbott. *Chicago Herald*, Sept. 26, 1896.

THE THIRD OF THE GRAY SISTERS. *Chicago Journal*, Sept. 26, 1896.

LIFE IN BOSTON. EMILY DICKINSON'S POEMS. Lilian Whiting. *Inter Ocean* [Chicago], Sept. 26, 1896.

EMILY DICKINSON'S POEMS. *Book News* [Philadelphia], Oct., 1896; vol. 15, p. 56 (reprinted from *Hartford Post*).

THE THIRD SERIES OF EMILY DICKINSON'S POEMS. *Literary World* [Boston], Oct., 1896; vol. 27, p. 361.

EMILY DICKINSON'S POEMS. *Beacon* [Boston], Oct. (?), 1896.

EMILY DICKINSON AGAIN. *Chicago Tribune*, Oct. 3, 1896.

EXQUISITE VERSE. Lilian Whiting. *Inter Ocean* [Chicago], Oct. 3, 1896.

EMILY DICKINSON'S POEMS. *Commercial Advertiser* [New York], Oct. 10, 1896.

—— *New York Evening Post*, Oct. 10, 1896 (reprinted from *Nation*, Oct. 8, 1896; vol. 63, p. 275).

POEMS BY EMILY DICKINSON. *The Church* [Boston], Nov., 1896; vol. 2, p. 44.

Books by Emily Dickinson

A partial list of editions of books brought out by Mabel Loomis Todd and Thomas Wentworth Higginson, and published by Roberts Brothers, Boston, Massachusetts

POEMS BY EMILY DICKINSON, edited by two of her friends, Mabel Loomis Todd and T. W. Higginson. Preface by Thomas Wentworth Higginson. Published November 12, 1890. From publishers' announcement: "One volume. 16mo. Bound in drab and white cloth with gilt design. Gilt top. Price, $1.50." (For description of cover see page 69, xii+152 pages (discrepancy of eight pages at the beginning). 480 copies.

Second edition, December 16, 1890. Light-green and white cover (described on page 80). 400 copies.

Third edition, December 27, 1890. Similar cover. 500 copies, of which 250 were wrongly bound. (See page 89.)

Fourth edition, January 29, 1891. Cover of uniform color.

Fifth edition, February 17, 1891. Cover of uniform color.

Sixth edition, March 11, 1891. Cover of uniform color.

De Luxe edition, November, 1891. A publishers' announcement describes this holiday edition: "Gems . . . . Bound in Pure White Calf Backs and Corners, with dainty Paper Sides, gold edges, lettering and finish in gold, enclosed in fleece-lined boxes. Price $3.50 each." There were several additional printings of the "½ white calf" edition; an undetermined number of copies. (See same edition of Second Series, page 414.)

First English edition, published during the summer of 1891 by James R. Osgood, McIlvaine & Co., 45 Albemarle Street, London, W. "Crown 8vo, cloth extra, gilt top, 5s." The cover was plain, dull yellow, without the Indian-pipe design. Later, the firm of Methuen took over the English rights and issued the book with a plain green cover.[1] (See page 181.)

[1] "Of the poems of Emily Dickinson, 'an Arabic translation, made in Syria,' is said to have passed through several editions."—*The Critic*, July 18, 1891

Seventh, Eighth, Ninth, Tenth and Eleventh American editions, 1892. Covers of green and white or of uniform color, in various shades of gray and gray-green, but all with the Indian pipe design.

By 1898, the year in which the firm of Roberts Brothers was taken over by Little, Brown & Company, the number of editions of the first series had reached sixteen. The "sixteenth edition" was reissued several times. I have seen one dated 1902. The seventeenth edition, 1904, was reprinted at intervals throughout the next twenty years, some with, some without the Indian pipes on the cover. I have seen copies dated 1904, 1910, 1912, 1915, 1916, 1920.

POEMS BY EMILY DICKINSON, Second Series, edited by two of her friends, T. W. Higginson and Mabel Loomis Todd. Published November 9, 1891. From publishers' announcement: "With a preface by Mrs. Todd and an autograph letter from Helen Jackson to Miss Dickinson. 16mo. Cloth, $1.25; white and gold, $1.50." The $1.50 edition was printed on calendered paper with generous margins like the first edition of the first series. The cover was white with a light-green spine and strip instead of gray, the line between green and white straight, not wavy. Edges full gilt. The cheaper edition had a uniform dull-green binding, plain edges. Both covers had the lettering and design of Indian pipes like the first volume. 230 pages.[2]

Second edition, November 18, 1891. Uniform gray or green cover. De Luxe edition, November, 1891. Half white calf. Reissued in 1892. Third, Fourth editions, 1892. A few copies bound in all-white cloth. Fifth edition, 1893.

[2] On November fifth, three of "each kind" were sent to my parents. On the day of publication further copies were dispatched with the following letter:

Boston, *Nov* 9, 1891

Prof D P Todd
DEAR SIR
    We send the 20 copies of Emily Dickinson 2d Series also 2 in ½ white calf of the 1st Series.
    The 2d Series in ½ wh clf have not yet been sent in from binder but we hope to get them by the 15th of this month, or possibl[y] the 20th.

Very Truly Yours
Roberts Bros
E. D. HARDY

Combined edition, May, 1893. First and Second Series in one volume. 12mo. Price, $2.00. Cover similar to that of first edition of *Poems*, 1890, white with gray spine. 500 copies (page 225).

De Luxe Combined edition, 1893. In "Messrs. Roberts Brothers' Holiday Publications, 1893," "Poems by Emily Dickinson . . . . Both series in one volume, 12mo. $4.00" is described as "bound in full crushed Turkey morocco of dainty colors, and decorated in a style which fully justifies the characteristic term 'Renaissance,' being a revival of the old English bindings in vogue some seventy or eighty years ago, which were adapted from various artistic designs used in the Middle Ages. The books are hand-finished in a chaste and beautiful manner, solid gold edges, rolled on the inside and outer edges of the covers. The books are issued at extremely low prices, considering the fine quality of workmanship."[3]

By June, 1894, it was said that "twelve thousand copies of the first volume of Miss Emily Dickinson's poems have been issued and seven thousand of the second volume."—*The Independent*, June 14, 1894.

When Little, Brown took over Roberts Brothers in 1898, ten editions of the Second Series had been printed. Thereafter subsequent successive editions during the next twenty-five years were not numbered. I have seen copies dated 1901, 1904, 1913, 1916, 1923, edition not specified.

LETTERS OF EMILY DICKINSON, edited by Mabel Loomis Todd, in two volumes. Published November 21, 1894 (page 308). From publishers' announcement: "With Portrait and a view of Miss Dickinson's home in Amherst, and three facsimiles of her handwriting at different periods of her life. 2 vols. 16mo. Price, $2.00." The light-green buckram covers were plain except for the design of Indian pipes, reduced in size, stamped in gold in the center of the front cover. In accordance with Mrs. Todd's suggestion "one little Indian pipe" was used "on the back of the first volume, and two for the second," instead of figures. The same design as on the face of the cover was used on the jacket. Paged continuously, xii+454 pages. 1000 copies.[4]

[3] The wide demand was reflected in a variety of bindings, for the 1894 announcement also included "Emily Dickinson's Poems, First and Second Series, each $3.50," the "½ white calf" editions; and *Poems*, 1890, and *Poems*, Second Series, at $1.25 each, or in white and gold for $1.50 each, or "both in one volume, 12mo. Cloth. Bi-color. $2.00."

[4] In "Messrs. Roberts Brothers' Fall Publications and Announcements for 1894" an article from *The Critic*, June 11, 1892, was reproduced in full as advertisement for the forthcoming book.

Second printing, December, 1894. Also in two volumes with similar
    covers.

In 1906 Little, Brown announced a "New Edition, complete in one
volume," 12mo., brown cloth cover with paper label. Price, $1.25. This
was, however, merely a new printing of the original issue. This format
was used for all subsequent reprintings. (The *de facto* second edition
was the following:
    LETTERS OF EMILY DICKINSON, edited by Mabel Loomis
    Todd. New and enlarged edition in one volume. New York and
    London: Harper & Brothers, 1931. Price, $4.00. Green covers with
    Indian pipe design. xxxi+457 pages.)

POEMS BY EMILY DICKINSON, Third Series, edited by Mabel
    Loomis Todd. Published September 1, 1896. "16mo. Cloth. Uniform
    with First and Second Series, $1.25. White and Gold, $1.50." The
    "white and gold" cover was similar to that of the Second Series
    first edition, viii+200 pages. 1000 copies.
Second edition, 1896. Cover of uniform gray or gray-green (page 345).
    1000 copies.

After 1898 this book also was reissued by Little, Brown at intervals
during the next twenty-five years, editions not indicated. I have seen
copies dated 1914 and 1917.

Three Prefaces

Preface to *Poems by Emily Dickinson*, 1890

The verses of Emily Dickinson belong emphatically to what Emerson long since called "the Poetry of the Portfolio,"—something produced absolutely without the thought of publication, and solely by way of expression of the writer's own mind. Such verse must inevitably forfeit whatever advantage lies in the discipline of public criticism and the enforced conformity to accepted ways. On the other hand, it may often gain something through the habit of freedom and the unconventional utterance of daring thoughts. In the case of the present author, there was absolutely no choice in the matter; she must write thus, or not at all. A recluse by temperament and habit, literally spending years without setting her foot beyond the doorstep, and many more years during which her walks were strictly limited to her father's grounds, she habitually concealed her mind, like her person, from all but a very few friends; and it was with great difficulty that she was persuaded to print, during her lifetime, three or four poems. Yet she wrote verses in great abundance; and though curiously indifferent to all conventional rules, had yet a rigorous literary standard of her own, and often altered a word many times to suit an ear which had its own tenacious fastidiousness.

Miss Dickinson was born in Amherst, Mass., Dec. 10, 1830, and died there May 15, 1886. Her father, Hon. Edward Dickinson, was the leading lawyer of Amherst, and was treasurer of the well-known college there situated. It was his custom once a year to hold a large reception at his house, attended by all the families connected with the institution and by the leading people of the town. On these occasions his daughter Emily emerged from her wonted retirement and did her part as gracious hostess; nor would anyone have known from her manner, I have been told, that this was not a daily occurrence. The annual occasion once past, she withdrew again into her seclusion, and except for a very few friends was as invisible to the world as if she had dwelt in a nunnery. For myself, although I had corresponded with her for many years, I saw her but twice face to face, and brought away the impression of something as unique and remote as Undine or Mignon or Thekla.

This selection from her poems is published to meet the desire of her personal friends, and especially of her surviving sister. It is believed that the thoughtful reader will find in these pages a quality more suggestive of the poetry of William Blake than of anything to be elsewhere found,—flashes of wholly original and profound insight into nature and life; words and phrases exhibiting an extraordinary vividness of descriptive and imaginative power, yet often set in a seemingly whimsical or even rugged frame. They are here published as they were written, with very few and superficial changes; although it is fair to say that the titles have been assigned, almost invariably, by the editors. In many cases these verses will seem to the reader like poetry torn up by the roots, with rain and dew and earth still clinging to them, giving a freshness and a fragrance not otherwise to be conveyed. In other cases, as in the few poems of shipwreck or of mental conflict, we can only wonder at the gift of vivid imagination by which this recluse woman can delineate, by a few touches, the very crises of physical or mental struggle. And sometimes again we catch glimpses of a lyric strain, sustained perhaps but for a line or two at a time, and making the reader regret its sudden cessation. But the main quality of these poems is that of extraordinary grasp and insight, uttered with an uneven vigor sometimes exasperating, seemingly wayward, but really unsought and inevitable. After all, when a thought takes one's breath away, a lesson on grammar seems an impertinence. As Ruskin wrote in his earlier and better days, "No weight nor mass nor beauty of execution can outweigh one grain or fragment of thought."

THOMAS WENTWORTH HIGGINSON

Preface to *Poems*, Second Series, 1891

The eagerness with which the first volume of Emily Dickinson's poems has been read shows very clearly that all our alleged modern artificiality does not prevent a prompt appreciation of the qualities of directness and simplicity in approaching the greatest themes,—life and love and death. That "irresistible needle-touch," as one of her best critics has called it, piercing at once the very core of a thought, has found a response as wide and sympathetic as it has been unexpected even to those who knew best her compelling power. This second volume, while open to the same criticism as to form with its predecessor, shows also the same shining beauties.

Although Emily Dickinson had been in the habit of sending occasional poems to friends and correspondents, the full extent of her writing was by no means imagined by them. Her friend "H.H." must at least have suspected it, for in a letter dated 5th September, 1884, she wrote:—

My Dear Friend,—What portfolios full of verses you must have! It is a cruel wrong to your "day and generation" that you will not give them light.

If such a thing should happen as that I should outlive you, I wish you would make me your literary legatee and executor. Surely after you are what is called "dead" you will be willing that the poor ghosts you have left behind should be cheered and pleased by your verses, will you not? You ought to be. I do not think we have a right to withhold from the world a word or a thought any more than a *deed* which might help a single soul. . . .

Truly yours,
Helen Jackson

The "portfolios" were found, shortly after Emily Dickinson's death, by her sister and only surviving housemate. Most of the poems had been carefully copied on sheets of note-paper, and tied in little fascicules, each of six or eight sheets. While many of them bear evidence of having been thrown off at white heat, still more had received thoughtful revision. There is the frequent addition of rather perplexing foot-notes, affording large choice of words and phrases. And in the copies which she sent to friends, sometimes one form, sometimes another, is found to have been used. Without important exception, her friends have generously placed at the disposal of the Editors any poems they had received from her; and these have given the obvious advantage of comparison among several renderings of the same verse.

To what further rigorous pruning her verses would have been subjected had she published them herself, we cannot know. They should be regarded in many cases as merely the first strong and suggestive sketches of an artist, intended to be embodied at some time in the finished picture.

Emily Dickinson appears to have written her first poems in the winter of 1862. In a letter to one of the present Editors the April following, she says, "I made no verse, but one or two, until this winter."

The handwriting was at first somewhat like the delicate, running Italian hand of our elder gentlewomen; but as she advanced in breadth of thought, it grew bolder and more abrupt, until in her latest years each letter stood distinct and separate from its fellows. In most of her poems, particularly the later ones, everything by way of punctuation was discarded except numerous dashes; and all important words began with capitals. The effect of a page of her more recent manuscript is exceedingly quaint and strong. The fac-simile given in the present volume is from one of the earlier transition periods. Although there is nowhere a date, the handwriting makes it possible to arrange the poems with general chronologic accuracy.

As a rule, the verses were without titles; but "A Country Burial," "A Thunder-Storm," "The Humming-Bird," and a few others were named by their author, frequently at the end,—sometimes only in the accompanying note, if sent to a friend.

The variation of readings, with the fact that she often wrote in pencil and not always clearly, have at times thrown a good deal of responsibility upon her Editors. But all interference not absolutely inevitable has been avoided. The very roughness of her own rendering is part of herself, and not lightly to be touched; for it seems in many cases that she intentionally avoided the smoother and more usual rhymes.

Like impressionist pictures, or Wagner's rugged music, the very absence of conventional form challenges attention. In Emily Dickinson's exacting hands, the especial, intrinsic fitness of a particular order of words might not be sacrificed to anything virtually extrinsic; and her verses all show a strange cadence of inner rhythmical music. Lines are always daringly constructed, and the "thought-rhyme" appears frequently,—appealing, indeed, to an unrecognized sense more elusive than hearing.

Emily Dickinson scrutinized everything with clear-eyed frankness. Every subject was proper ground for legitimate study, even the sombre facts of death and burial, and the unknown life beyond. She touches these themes sometimes lightly, sometimes almost humorously, more often with weird and peculiar power; but she is never by any chance frivolous or trivial. And while, as one critic has said, she may exhibit toward God "an Emersonian self-possession," it was because she looked upon all life with a candor as unprejudiced as it is rare.

She had tried society and the world, and found them lacking. She was not an invalid, and she lived in seclusion from no love-disappointment. Her life was the normal blossoming of a nature introspective to a high degree, whose best thought could not exist in pretence.

Storm, wind, the wild March sky, sunsets and dawns; the birds and bees, butterflies and flowers of her garden, with a few trusted human friends, were sufficient companionship. The coming of the first robin was a jubilee beyond crowning of monarch or birthday of pope; the first red leaf hurrying through "the altered air," an epoch. Immortality was close about her; and while never morbid or melancholy, she lived in its presence.

MABEL LOOMIS TODD

AMHERST, MASSACHUSETTS
August, 1891

Preface to *Poems*, Third Series, 1896

The intellectual activity of Emily Dickinson was so great that a large and characteristic choice is still possible among her literary material, and this third volume of her verses is put forth in response to the repeated wish of the admirers of her peculiar genius.

Much of Emily Dickinson's prose was rhythmic,—even rhymed, though frequently not set apart in lines. Also many verses, written as such, were sent to friends in letters; these were published in 1894, in the volumes of her *Letters*. It has not been necessary, however, to include them in this Series, and all have been omitted, except three or four exceptionally strong ones, as "A Book," and "With Flowers."

There is internal evidence that many of the poems were simply spontaneous flashes of insight, apparently unrelated to outward circumstance. Others, however, had an obvious personal origin; for example, the verses "I had a Guinea golden," which seem to have been sent to some friend travelling in Europe, as a dainty reminder of letter-writing delinquencies. The surroundings in which any of Emily Dickinson's verses are known to have been written usually serve to explain them clearly; but in general the present volume is full of thoughts needing no interpretation to those who apprehend this scintillating spirit.

M.L.T.

AMHERST, *October*, 1896

First Lines of Unpublished Poems
A list compiled by Mabel Loomis Todd in July, 1891

This appendix contains Mrs. Todd's list of Emily Dickinson's poems. During the summer of 1891, after publication of the first volume in 1890, and while *Poems*, Second Series, was in press, she classified the remaining copied but still unpublished poems and entered the first lines, alphabetically arranged, in a small leather-covered notebook. (A few from the first and second series were inadvertently included.) They were grouped in three classes, "A," "B," and "C." She later indicated in the notebook in which volume the poems subsequently published in *Letters*, 1894, or in *Poems*, Third Series, 1896, could be found. The list is here reproduced without change except for some alphabetical rearrangement and the omission of a few repetitious titles. In brackets I have added notations which I trust will make clear the original place of publication of all of these poems which have appeared to date.

On the inside of the front cover of the notebook, in my father's firm, precise writing, spaced as accurately as if it were a table of figures relating to the perturbations of Jupiter's satellites, is a concise little alphabetized table, or "finding-list," for locating the poems in the notebook. It provides for every letter except X, although there are no poems beginning with Q, V, or Z. My father used to say that in science the things you leave out are as worth recording as those you discuss.

Additional poems copied by Mrs. Todd, but not entered in the notebook, are listed at the end of this appendix. I have found her copies of all the poems on both lists except the one beginning, "As so and so had been to me."

The following abbreviations are used for titles of books in which poems first appeared:

I (or Vol. I)	*Poems*, 1890
II (or Vol. II)	*Poems*, Second Series, 1891
III	*Poems*, Third Series, 1896
Letters, 1894	*Letters of Emily Dickinson*, 1894
S.H.	*The Single Hound*, 1914

L. and L.   *The Life and Letters of Emily Dickinson*, 1924
F.P.   *Further Poems of Emily Dickinson*, 1929
Letters, 1931   *Letters of Emily Dickinson*, New and Enlarged
                       Edition, 1931
E.D.F.F.   *Emily Dickinson Face to Face*, 1932
U.P.   *Unpublished Poems of Emily Dickinson*, 1935

Mrs. Todd's heading for her inventory of poems awaiting publica-
    tion reads, "Alphabetical list of Emily's poems still un-
            published in volumes, July, 1891"

Class A.   A bee his burnished carriage
           A bold, inspiriting bird is the jay ["A prompt, executive,"
               S.H.]
           A burdock twitched my gown
           A coffin is a small domain
           A dew sufficed itself   III
           A door just opened on a street   III
           A doubt if it be us
           A dying tiger moaned for drink
           A feather from the whippoorwill   *Letters* [1894, and F.P.]
           A Lady red amid the hill   III
           A light exists in spring   III
           A little East of Jordan ["A little over," S.H.]
           A loss of something ever felt   I
           A murmur in the trees to note   III
           A sepal, petal and a thorn   III
           A sickness of this world it most occasions   III
           A solemn thing within the soul
           A south wind has a pathos
           A transport one cannot contain [U.P.]
           A wife at daybreak I shall be [F.P.]
           Adrift, a little boat adrift   III
           Again his voice is at the door
           Ah! moon and star, you are very far [U.P.]
           Air has no residence, no neighbor
           All these my banners be
           Always mine! No more vacation!
           And this of all my hopes [F.P.]
           Answer July—where is the bee [U.P.]
           Apology for her
         - Are friends delight or pain   III

As far from pity as complaint [III]
As frost is best conceived
As one does sickness over
As so and so had been to me [no copy found]
As summer into autumn slips *Letters* [1894]
Ashes denote that fire was   III
Away from home are some and I *Letters* [1894]

Class B.   A bird sat careless on the fence [U.P., as part of "The trees like tassels"]
A clock stopped—Not the mantel's   III
A cloud withdrew from the sky
A day! Help! Help!
A fuzzy fellow without feet [F.P.]
A little bread, a crust, a crumb ["A modest lot," III and L. and L.]
A little dog that wags his tail
A long, long sleep   III
A man may drop a remark
A moth the hue of this
A night there lay, the days between
A pit, but heaven over it
A plated life, diversified [U.P.]
A prison gets to be a friend [F.P.]
A rat surrendered here
A science, so the savan[t]s say [F.P.]
A secret told, Ceases to be a secret [F.P.]
A shade upon the mind there passes
A single screw of flesh [U.P.]
A slash of blue, a sweep of grey [U.P.]
A solemn thing it was, I said,   III
A still volcano life [F.P.]
A toad can die of light   III
A tongue to tell him I am true
A tooth upon our peace [U.P.]
A visitor in marl [U.P.]
A weight with needles on the pounds [U.P.]
Absence disembodies, so does death
Absent place, an April day
After great pain a formal feeling comes [F.P.]
Ah! necromancy sweet! [F.P.]
All but death can be adjusted [F.P.]
All circumstances are the frame [S.H.]
All forgot for recollecting [F.P.]

All I may, if small [S.H.]
All overgrown by cunning moss   III
All the letters I can write [F.P.]
Alone I cannot be [E.D.F.F.]
Although I put away his life [F.P.]
Ambition cannot find him [S.H.]
An honest tear is durabler than bronze
An ignorance, a sunset [U.P.]
Artists wrestled here
As if I asked a common alms   *Letters* [1894]
As if the sea should part [F.P.]
As plan for noon, and plan for night
As the starved maelstrom laps the navies
At leisure is the soul [F.P.]
Aurora is the effort
Autumn overlooked my knitting [F.P.]

Class C.   A curious cloud surprised the sky
A first mute coming [U.P.]
A mien to move a queen [U.P.]
A nearness to tremendousness [U.P.]

Class A.   Baffled for just a day or two
Banish air from air
Because that you are going [G. Taggard, *Life and Mind*, 1930]
Because the bee may blameless hum
Bees are black with gilt surcingles
Before the ice is in the pools   III
Bereaved of all I went abroad   III
Best things dwell out of sight
Between my country and the others [U.P.]

Class B.   Beauty is not caused, it is [F.P.]
Because he loves her
Because my brook is fluent
Bee! I'm expecting you!
Before he comes we weigh the time   *Letters* [1894]
Behind me dips eternity [F.P.]
Besides this May we know
Better than music, for I who heard it
Bind me—I still can sing
Bloom is result—to meet a flower
Bloom upon the mountain stated [S.H.]
Bound a trouble, and lives can bear it [different version, U.P.]
But little carmine hath her face [U.P.]

By chivalries as tiny
By my window have I for scenery [F.P.]
By such and such an offering
Class C.   Be mine the doom
Because 'twas riches I could own [U.P.]
Bereavement in their death to feel [U.P.]
By a flower, by a letter [E.D.F.F.]

Class A.   Civilization spurns the leopard
Cocoon above, cocoon below [U.P.]
Could I but ride indefinite   III
Class B.   Color, caste, denomination [F.P.]
Conscious am I in my chamber [F.P.]
Could I do more for thee [F.P.]
Could live, did live—Could die, did die
Crisis is a hair
Crumbling is not an instant's act
Class C.   Conjecturing a climate [F.P.]

Class A.   Deprived of other banquet
Did our best moment last [U.P.]
Drab habitation of whom   III
Class B.   Death is potential to that man
Death leaves us homesick, who behind
Delight's despair at setting
Denial is the only fact [F.P.]
Dew is the freshet in the grass [2d and 3rd stanzas only, "We
    spy the forests," S.H.]
Did you ever stand in a cavern's mouth [U.P.]
Did we abolish frost
Distrustful of the gentian
Do people moulder equally
Don't put up my thread and needle [F.P.]
Drama's vitallest expression [F.P.]
Dropped into the ether acre [S.H.]
Dust is the only secret [S.H.]
Dying! To be afraid of thee
Class C.   Defrauded I a butterfly [F.P.]
Delight is as the flight [F.P.]
Despair's advantage is achieved [U.P.]
Did we disobey him
Doom is the house without the door [F.P.]

Dreams are well, but waking's better [U.P.]
Dying at my music
Dying! Dying in the night!

Class A.   Escaping backward to perceive
Experience is the angled road [F.P.]
Class B.   Each scar I'll keep for him
Each second is the last
Embarrassment of one another
Exhilaration is within [U.P.]
Class C.   Empty my heart of thee! [F.P.]
Ended ere it began [E.D.F.F.]
Except the smaller size   *Letters* [1894 and S.H.]
Expectation is contentment [F.P.]

Class A.   Faithful to the end [*New England Quarterly*, April, 1932]
Fame of myself to justify
Fate slew him, but he did not drop   III
Finding is the first act
Finite to fail, but infinite to venture   III
Fitter for the feet before us [U.P. as part of "Her sweet turn"]
Fitter to see him I may be [*The Poems of E.D.*, 1930]
For this accepted breath [U.P.]
Forever at his side to walk [F.P.]
Forget! the lady with the amulet [U.P.]
Four trees upon a solitary acre
Funny, to be a century [F.P.]
Class B.   Fairer through fading, as the day
Faith is the pierless bridge [F.P.]
Faithful to the end, amended [different version from that
in "A"]
Falsehood of thee, could I suppose
Fame is the tint that scholars leave
Far from love thy Heavenly Father   III
Father, I bring thee not myself   III
Flowers! Well, if anybody
For death, or rather for the things 'twould buy [S.H.]
For every bird a nest [F.P.]
Frigid and sweet her parting face
From blank to blank [F.P.]
Class C.   For largest woman's heart I knew [E.D.F.F.]
Forever is composed of nows [F.P.]

Class A.   Garlands for queens may be
             Given in marriage unto thee   III
             Glowing is her bonnet [S.H.]
             God is a distant, stately lover   *The Christian Register* [April,
                1891; F.P.; not in collected editions]
             Going to heaven, I don't know when   II
Class B.   Give little anguish, lives will fret [*The Complete Poems*, 1924]
             Good morning, midnight [F.P.]
             Good night because we must
             Good to have had them lost [U.P.]
             Good to hide and hear 'em hunt
             Gratitude is not the mention [E.D.F.F.]
             Great Caesar, condescend [E.D.F.F.]
             Growth of man like growth of nature [F.P.]
Class C.   Grief is a mouse

Class A.   Have any like myself [U.P.]
             He outstripped time with but a boat [bout]
             He parts himself like leaves [U.P.]
             He scanned it, staggered
             He touched me, so I live to know   III
             Her grace is all she has [S.H.]
             Her smile was shaped like other smiles [U.P.]
             His bill an augur is   III
             His bill is locked, his eye estranged
             Hope is a subtle glutton   III
             Houses, so the wise men tell us (me)
             How fortunate the grave
             How happy I was if I could forget
             How news must feel, when travelling
             How noteless men and Pleiads stand [F.P.]
             How sick, to wait in any place but thine
             How the old mountains drip with sunset   III
             How the waters closed above him
Class B.   Had I not this, or this, I said [U.P.]
             He forgot and I remembered
             He fought like those who've naught to lose [U.P.]
             He found my being, set it up
             He fumbles at your soul   III
             He gave away his life [U.P.]
             He told a homely tale
             He was weak and I was strong then
             He who in himself believes

Heart! We will forget him!   III
Heaven has different signs to me [F.P.]
Heaven is so far of the mind [F.P.]
Heaven is what I cannot reach   III
Her last poems poets ended [S.H.]
Her little parasol to lift
Her sweet turn to leave the homestead [U.P.]
Her sweet weight on my heart a night
Herein a blossom lies
How far is it to Heaven?
How many flowers fail in wood [F.P.]
How still the bells in steeples stand   III
How well I knew her not   *Letters* [1894]

Class C.   Had I presumed to hope [F.P.]
He showed me heights I never saw ["I showed her," S.H.]
He strained my faith
Here where the daisies fit my head

Class A.   I could not drink it, sweet [E.D.F.F.]
I could not prove the years had feet
I counted till they danced so
I dwell in possibility [F.P.]
I envy seas whereon he rides   III
I fear a man of scanty speech [F.P.]
I felt a clearing [cleaving] in my mind [III]
I felt a funeral in my brain   III
I gave myself to him   Vol. II
I had a daily bliss   III
I had a guinea golden   III
I have a king who does not speak   III
I heard a fly buzz when I died   III
I heard as if I had no ear
I knew that I had gained
I know lives I could miss [F.P.]
I learned at least what home could be
I live with him, I see his face   III
I make his crescent fill or lack [F.P.]
I meant to find her when I came   III
I measure every grief I meet   III
I met a king this afternoon
I never felt at home below [F.P.]
I play at riches to appease [U.P.]
I robbed the woods   Vol. II ["Who robbed"]

I rose, because he sank [F.P.]
I see thee better in the dark [S.H.]
I send two sunsets, day and I [S.H.]
I sing to use the waiting   III
I stole them from a bee   *Letters* [1894]
I think the longest hour of all
I think to live may be a bliss [U.P.]
I want, it pleaded all its life
I worked for chaff, and earning wheat   III
I would not paint a picture
If he were living, dare I ask [F.P.]
If pain for peace prepares [S.H.]
If she had been the mistletoe   *Letters* [1894]
If the foolish call them flowers   III
If those I loved were lost
Immortal is an ample word   III
In crashing timbers buried
In ebon box when years have flown [U.P.]
In rags mysterious as these
Inconceivably solemn! [F.P.]
It always felt to me a wrong [F.P.]
It came at last, but prompter death
It did not surprise me
It dropped so low in my regard [III]
It is an honorable thought III [" 'Tis an," in current edition]
It knew no medicine [U.P.]
It struck me every day [III]
It was a grave, yet bore no stone [U.P.]
It will be summer eventually   p. 101. Vol. III ["The spring-
     time's pallid landscape"]
It's all I have to bring today [III]
It's easy to invent a life [F.P.]
Its hour with itself [F.P.]
It's like the light   III
It's such a little thing to weep   III
I've heard an organ talk sometimes [U.P.]
Class B.   I am afraid to own a body [U.P.]
I am alive, I guess
I am ashamed, I hide [F.P.]
I breathed enough to take the trick   III
I came to buy a smile today [F.P.]
I cannot be ashamed [F.P.]
I cannot buy it, 'tis not sold

I cannot dance upon my toes [F.P.]
I cannot want it more
I cautious, scanned my little life [F.P.]
I cross, till I am weary [U.P.]
I got so I could hear his name [F.P.]
I have never seen volcanoes
I keep my pledge, I was not called
I made slow riches, but my gain
I never told the buried gold [S.H.]
I prayed at first, a little girl [F.P.]
I reckon, when I count at all [F.P.]
I saw no way, the heavens were stitched [U.P.]
I shall keep singing [U.P.]
I should not dare to be so sad [F.P.]
I stepped from plank to plank   III
I tend my flowers for thee, bright absentee [F.P.]
I think I was enchanted [U.P.]
I tie my hat, I crease my shawl [F.P.]
I took one draught of life [F.P.]
I tried to think a lonelier thing
I was a phebe, nothing more
I was the slightest in the house
I watched the moon around the house
I would die to know [U.P.]
Ideals are the fairy oil
If any sink, assure that this [U.P.]
If ever the lid gets off my head
If I could bribe them by a rose [U.P.]
If I'm lost now, that I was found
If I may have it when it's dead   III
If what we could were what we would [S.H.]
I'll tell thee all, how blank it grew
I'm sorry for the dead today [F.P., as part of "It will be
        summer eventually"]
I'm the little heart's ease [F.P.]
Impossibility, like wine
Is bliss then such abyss   III
It bloomed and dropped a single noon
It ceased to hurt me, though so slow [F.P.]
It feels a shame to be alive [F.P.]
It is a lonesome glee
It might be lonelier ["It might have been," U.P.]
It rises, passes, on our south

It troubled me as once I was
It was a quiet way [F.P.]
It was given to me by the gods
It was not saint, it was too large [F.P.]
It would have starved a gnat
It would never be common more, I said [U.P.]
It's coming, the postponeless creature [F.P.]
It's thoughts, and just one heart [U.P.]
I've dropped my brain
I've known a heaven like a tent [F.P.]
I've none to tell me to but thee

Class C. I can't tell you, but you feel it [S.H.]
I could bring you jewels
I could suffice for him, I knew [U.P.]
I cried at pity, not at pain
I felt my life with both my hands
I had not minded walls [F.P.]
I had some things that I called mine
I had the glory—that will do
I know where wells grow [U.P.]
I pay in satin cash [F.P.]
I sometimes drop it, for a quick [U.P.]
If blame be my side, forfeit me
If he dissolve, then there is nothing more [U.P.]
If nature smiles the mother must [F.P.]
If this is fading
If your nerve deny you [U.P.]
I'll clutch and clutch
I'm saying every day [U.P.]
It don't sound so terrible
It is dead—find it [F.P.]
It is easy to work
It knew no lapse nor diminution
I've nothing else to bring, you know [F.P.]

Class A. Just once, oh! least request! *Letters* [1894]
Class B. Jesus, thy crucifix
Joy to have merited the pain [F.P.]
Just as he spoke it from his hands
Just so Christ raps [S.H.]
Class C. Just to be rich, To waste my guinea [Final stanza of "Sweet, you forgot"]

Class A.   (None)
Class B.   Kill your balm and its odors bless you
           Knows how to forget [#1]
Class C.   Knows how to forget [#2, different from poem in Class B]

Class A.   Least rivers, docile to some sea
           Let me not mar that perfect dream   III
           Let us play yesterday [U.P.]
           Life and death and giants   III
           Like men and women, shadows walk [S.H.]
           Love is that later thing than death
           Love, thou art high [F.P.]
           Low at my problem bending [S.H.]
Class B.   Least bee that brew a honey's weight
           Lest this be heaven indeed
           Light is sufficient to itself
           Like her the saints retire [E.D.F.F.]
           Like some old-fashioned miracle [S.H.]
           Longing is like the seed [F.P.]
           Love is anterior to life   III
Class C.   Life is what we make it [F.P.]
           Like eyes that looked on wastes

Class A.   Make me a picture of the sun
           Mama never forgets her birds
           Me—come! My dazzled face   III
           Me from myself to banish [F.P.]
           Morning is the place for dew   III
           Morning means milking to the farmer [S.H.]
           Morns like these we parted   Vol. II
           Most she touched me by her muteness [F.P.]
           My eye is fuller than my vase [F.P.]
           My faith is larger than the hills [F.P.]
           My first well day since many ill [U.P.]
           My friend must be a bird   III
           My garden like the beach [U.P.]
           My period had come for prayer [F.P.]
Class B.   Many a phrase has the English language [U.P.]
           Midsummer was it, when they died [F.P.]
           My best acquaintances are those
           My life had stood, a loaded gun [F.P.]
           My portion is defeat, today [F.P.]
           My season's furthest flower

My triumph lasted till the drums [U.P.]
My wheel is in the dark [S.H.]
My worthiness is all my doubt   III
Myself can read the telegrams
Myself was formed, a carpenter [U.P.]

Class C. Many cross the Rhine
More life went out when he went [U.P.]
Must be a woe [U.P.]
My friend attacks my friend
My heart upon a little plate
My Maker, let me be [L. and L.]
My reward for being was this
My soul accused me, and I quailed [F.P.]

Class A. Nature and God I neither knew   *Letters* [1894]
Nature is what we see [S.H.]
Never for society He shall seek in vain (part in *Letters*) [1894 and U.P.]
No notice gave she, but a change [U.P.]
No prisoner be [E.D.F.F.]
No romance sold unto [S.H.]
No wilderness can be (part of 'For this accepted breath') *Letters* [1894]
Nobody knows this little rose [*Youth's Companion*, Dec. 24, 1891]
Not any higher stands the grave   III
Not knowing when the dawn will come   III
Not with a club the heart is broken   III

Class B. Nature sometimes sears a sapling
No bobolink reverse his singing
No crowd that has occurred [F.P.]
No matter now, sweet
None can experience stint
Noon is the hinge of day
Not any more to be lacked [F.P.]
Not so the infinite relations
Not to discover weakness is
Not what we did shall be the test [F.P.]
Now I knew I lost her

Class C. No man can compass a despair [U.P.]
No other can reduce our mortal consequence [S.H.]
Nor mountain hinder me
Not probable—the barest chance [U.P.]

Class A.   Of bronze and blaze [III]
            Of consciousness, her awful mate
            Of course I prayed [F.P.]
            Of nearness to her sundered things [F.P.]
            Of Paul and Silas it is said
            Of silken speech and specious shoe
            Of the heart that goes in and closes the door
            Oh! if remembering were forgetting *Letters* [1894 and III,
                "If recollecting"]
            On a columnar self [F.P.]
            On that dear frame the years had worn
            On this wondrous sea, sailing silently III
            One life of so much consequence [F.P.]
            Our journey had advanced [II]
            Our little kinsmen after rain
            Our lives are Swiss   III

Class B.   Of being is a bird ["A bird is of all beings," F.P.]
            Of Brussels it was not
            Of tolling bell I ask the cause III [printed "If"]
            Once more, my now bewildered dove
            One anguish in a crowd
            One blessing had I, than the rest   III
            One day is there of the series   III
            Only a shrine, but mine [F.P.]
            Ourselves were wed one summer, dear
            Over and over like a tune [F.P.]

Class C.   Of Nature I shall have enough
            One and one are one [F.P.]
            One crucifixion is recorded only
            One year ago, jots what?
            Only God detect the sorrow ["Only God possess the secret,"
                U.P.]
            Out of sight! What is that? [F.P.]
            Over the fence strawberries grow

Class A.   Pain expands the time [F.P.]
            Patience has a quiet outer
            Peace is a fiction of our faith
            Poor little heart, Did they forget thee?   III
            Portraits are to daily faces [II]
            Promise this, when you be dying [U.P.]
            Publication is the auction *Letters* (a part of it) [1894 and
                F.P.]

Class B. Pain has but one acquaintance
             Papa above, regard a mouse [S.H.]
             Partake as doth the bee
             Perception of an object costs [S.H.]
             Perhaps you think me stooping *Letters* [1894]
             Precious to me she still shall be
             Put up my lute, what of my music [U.P.]
Class C. Perhaps I asked too large

Class A. Remembrance has a rear and front III
             Reverse cannot befall [S.H.]
Class B. Rearrange a wife's affection
             "Remember me," implored the thief [S.H.]
             Removed from accident of loss [U.P.]
             Renunciation is a piercing virtue [F.P.]
             Reportless subjects, to the quick
             Rests at night the sun from shining
             Revolution is the pod [F.P.]
             Ribbons of the year
             Robbed by death, but that was easy—
Class C. Rehearsal to ourselves [F.P.]

Class A. Said death to passion
             Sang from the heart, Sire
             September's baccalaureate [*Youth's Companion*, September 29, 1892]
             She bore it till the simple veins [U.P.]
             She dealt her pretty words like blades [F.P.]
             She died at play, Gambolled away [S.H.]
             She sights a bird, she chuckles
             She slept beneath a tree III
             Shells from the coast mistaking
             So from the mould, Scarlet and gold [S.H.]
             So has a daisy vanished
             So much of heaven has gone from earth [U.P.]
             So proud she was to die III
             So the eyes accost and sunder [F.P.]
             So well that I can live without [F.P.]
             Somewhere upon the general earth
             Split the lark and you'll find the music III
             Spring comes on the world
             Springs shake the sills and the echoes stiffen [L. and L.]

Step lightly on this narrow spot   Vol. II
Struck was I, nor yet by lightning
Summer for thee grant I may be   III
Superfluous were the sun   III
Superiority to fate   III

Class B.   Safe despair it is that raves [S.H.]
Savior! I've no one else to tell [F.P.]
Severer service of myself
Sexton, my master's sleeping here [U.P.]
She hideth her the last [U.P.]
She lay as if at play [U.P.]
She rose as high as his occasion
She staked her wings and gained a bush ["her feathers," U.P.]
She's happy with a new content [U.P.]
Snow beneath whose chilly softness
So glad we are, a stranger'd deem   Letters [1894]
So large my will
So set its sun in thee [S.H.]
Some say goodnight at night [F.P.]
Some we see no more, tenements of wonder
Somehow myself survived the night [U.P.]
Somewhat to hope for
Soto, explore thyself [E.D.F.F.]
Sown in dishonor [S.H.]
Speech is a prank of parliament   Letters [1894]
Spring is the period
Such is the strength of happiness
Sunset at night is natural [F.P.]
Suspense is hostiler than death [F.P.]
Sweet mountains ye tell me no lie
Sweet, safe houses
Sweet, you forgot, but I remembered

Class C.   Satisfaction is the agent
She dwelleth in the ground
Sift her, from brow to bare foot
Size circumscribes, it has no room [U.P.]
Smiling back from coronation
So I pull my stockings off
So much summer me for showing
Some such butterfly be seen [U.P.]
Some work for immortality [F.P.]
Strong draughts of their refreshing minds [F.P.]

Class A.   Take your heaven further on [U.P.]

That first day when you praised me sweet [U.P.]

That is solemn we have ended   III

That such have died, enables us   III

The battle fought between the soul [F.P.]

The birds begun at four o'clock

The blackberry wears a thorn in his side

The bone that has no marrow   III

The brain is wider than the sky   III

The color of the grave is green [U.P.]

The cricket sang and set the sun   III

The day came slow till five o'clock   Vol. II

The day that I was crowned [U.P.]

The day undressed herself [U.P.]

The days that we can spare [*New England Quarterly*, April, 1932]

The doomed regard the sunrise [F.P.]

The dying need but little, dear   III

The face I carry with me last

The fingers of the light

The first day's night had come [U.P.]

The frost of death was on the pane

The guest is gold and crimson [E.D.F.F.]

The harm of years is on him

The Himmaleh was known to stoop [U.P.]

The hollows round his eager eyes

The judge is like the owl

The luxury to apprehend [S.H.]

The martyr poets did not tell [U.P.]

The moon was but a chin of gold [III]

The mountains stood in haze

The murmuring of bees has ceased   III

The mushroom is the elf of plants   II

The name of it is autumn [*Youth's Companion*, September 8, 1892]

The only news I know   *Letters* [3 lines only; F.P.]

The past is such a curious creature   III

The poets light but lamps

The popular heart is a cannon first [F.P.]

The props assist the house [S.H.]

The pungent atom in the air

The robin for the crumb

The robin is the one   Vol. II

The sea said "come" to the brook [S.H.]
The soul should always stand ajar III
The soul that hath a guest [S.H.]
The soul's distinct connection [F.P.]
The spider as an artist   III
The spider holds a silver ball
The spider sewed at night   Vol. II ["A spider"]
The stimulus beyond the grave   III
The sun kept stooping, stooping low
The sun went down, No man looked on [F.P.]
The test of love is death [U.P.]
The truth is stirless, outer force
The voice that stands for floods to me
The way to know the bobolink
The wind didn't come from the orchard today [E.D.F.F.]
The zeroes taught us phosphorus   Let[ters, 1894; F.P.]
There is another loneliness [S.H.]
There is a June when corn is cut
There is a languor of the life [F.P.]
There is a pain so utter [F.P.]
There is a word which bears a sword   III
There is no frigate like a book   III [and] Letters [1894]
There's been a death in the opposite house   III
There's something quieter than sleep   III
They called me to the window, for
They have not chosen me, he said   Letters [1894]
They say that time assuages   III
They shut me up in prose [U.P.]
They won't frown always   III
This chasm, sweet, upon my life
This heart that broke so long [U.P.]
This that would greet an hour ago
This was a poet. It is that [F.P.]
This was in the white of the year   III [and] Letters [1894]
Those dying then knew where they went
Three weeks passed since I had seen her   III
Tie the strings to my life, my lord   III
'Tis customary as we part
'Tis good, the looking back on grief [" 'Tis well," U.P.]
'Tis little I could care for pearls   III
'Tis opposites entice [F.P.]
'Tis so appalling it exhilarates [U.P.]

'Tis sunrise, little maid, hast thou   III
'Tis true they shut me in the cold
To disappear enhances *Letters* [1894; *The Poems of E.D.*, 1930]
To hang our head ostensibly   III
To help our bleaker parts   III
To her derided home
To interrupt his yellow plan [F.P.]
To lose one's faith surpasses   III
To make one's toilet after death [U.P.]
To make routine a stimulus [F.P.]
To my quick ear the leaves conferred   III
To one denied to drink
To put this world down like a bundle [U.P.]
To this world she returned *Letters* [1894]
To undertake is to achieve [*New England Quarterly*, April, 1932]
To whom the mornings stand for nights [U.P.]
Too scanty 'twas to die for you
Truth is as old as God *Letters* [1894]
'Twas awkward, but it fitted me [U.P.]
'Twas like a maelstrom, with a notch
'Twas my one glory
'Twas warm at first, like us [F.P.]
Two travelers perishing in snow

Class B. Taking up the fair ideal
That after horror—that 'twas us [U.P.]
That distance was between us
That odd old man is dead a year
That sacred closet when you sweep
The admirations and contempts of time [F.P.]
The angle of a landscape
The beggar lad dies early
The bird must sing to earn the crumb
The birds reported from the south [U.P.]
The chemical conviction
The color of a queen is this
The court is far away
The definition of beauty is
The duties of the wind are few [S.H.]
The feet of people walking home [S.H.]
The first we knew of him was death
The frost was never seen

The good will of a flower
The hallowing of pain
The heart has narrow banks
The heaven vests for each [U.P.]
The hills, in purple syllables
The lady feeds her little bird
The lamp burns sure, within [U.P.]
The largest fire ever known [S.H.]
The last of summer is delight [F.P.]
The lightning playeth all the while
The loneliness one dare not sound
The lonesome for they knew not what [F.P.]
The Malay took the pearl
The manner of its death
The mind lives on the heart [*New England Quarterly*, April, 1932]
The missing all prevented me [S.H.]
The months have ends, the years a knot [U.P.]
The morning after woe [U.P.]
The mountains grow unnoticed [F.P.]
The power to be true to you [F.P.]
The products of my farm are these
The province of the saved [U.P.]
The rainbow never tells me [F.P.]
The red blaze is the morning
The road to Paradise is plain
The service without hope
The soul has bandaged moments
The soul's superior instants [S.H.]
The spirit is the conscious ear
The spry arms of the wind
The sun and moon must make their haste
The sun is gay or stark
The sunrise runs for both [F.P.]
The sunset stopped on cottages
The sweetest heresy received [F.P.]
The tint I cannot take, is best [F.P.]
The veins of other flowers
The world feels dusty [F.P.]
The world stands solemner to me
There is a finished feeling
There is a morn by men unseen

There is a zone whose even years
There is an arid pleasure
Therefore we do life's labor [F.P., as part of "A still volcano"]
These are the signs to nature's inns [F.P.]
These tested our horizon
They ask but our delight
They have a little odor that to me
They leave us with the infinite
This consciousness that is aware [Last stanza only, "Adventure
    most unto itself," S.H.]
This dust and its feature
This is a blossom of the brain
This me that walks and works, must die
This quiet dust was gentlemen and ladies [S.H.]
Those fair, fictitious people ["These," F.P.]
Three times we parted, breath and I [F.P.]
Through lane it lay, through bramble [*The Complete Poems*,
    1924]
Through the dark sod as education [F.P.]
Till death is narrow loving [F.P.]
Time feels so vast, that were it not [U.P.]
'Tis anguish grander than delight
'Tis not that dying hurts us so
'Tis one by one the Father counts
To be alive is power [S.H.]
To die takes just a little while [U.P.]
To die without the dying
To fill a gap, Insert the thing that caused it [F.P.]
To love thee, year by year [S.H.]
To my small hearth his fire came [E.D.F.F.]
To offer brave assistance [F.P.]
To own the art within the soul
To wait an hour is long
Too little way the house must lie [U.P.]
Trudging to Eden, looking backward
Trust in the unexpected [U.P.]
'Twas crisis—all the length had passed
'Twas fighting for his life he was
'Twas just this time last year I died - III
'Twas love, not me, Oh! punish pray
'Twas the old road, through pain [F.P.]
Twice had summer her fair verdure
'Twould ease a butterfly

Class C. The child's faith is new [F.P.]
          The difference between despair [S.H.]
          The first day that I was a life
          The future never spoke [S.H.]
          The grace myself might not obtain [U.P.]
          The heart is the capital of the mind [F.P.]
          The love a life can show below [F.P.]
          The opening and the close
          The outer from the inner [U.P.]
          The robin's my criterion for tune [F.P.]
          The Savior must have been [L. and L. and *The Complete
              Poems*, 1924]
          The trees like tassels hit and swung [U.P.]
          The well upon the brook
          The whole of it came not at once
          The winters are so short [U.P.]
          Themself are all I have [U.P.]
          There are two ripenings *Letters* [1894 and F.P.]
          There is no silence in the earth so silent
          These saw visions [U.P.]
          They put us far apart [U.P.]
          This bauble was preferred of bees [U.P.]
          This dirty little heart
          Those who have been in the grave the longest
          Though my destiny be fustian *Letters* [1894]
          Two were immortal twice
          'Twould start them—we could tremble [unpublished part of
              "I tie my hat"]

Class A. Unable are the loved to die [E.D.F.F.]
          Uncertain lease develops lustre
          Under the light, yet under
          Unto like story trouble has enticed me [U.P.]
Class B. Unfulfilled to observation [U.P.]
          Unit, like death, for whom? [U.P.]
          Unto me? I do not know you [F.P.]
          Unto the whole, how add?
          Up life's hill with my little bundle
          Upon concluded lives

Class A. Water is taught by thirst   III
          We can but follow to the sun [2d and 3rd only, "Oh, shadow,"
              F.P.]

We cover thee, sweet face   III
We dream, it is good we are dreaming [U.P.]
We grow accustomed to the dark [U.P.]
We learn in the retreating   III
We like March, his shoes are purple   III
We met as sparks, diverging flints
We miss her not because we see
We outgrow love like other things   III
We thirst at first—'tis nature's act   III
We'll pass without a parting   *Letters* [1894]
What did they do since I saw them
What is paradise—who live there?
What soft, cherubic creatures   III
When I count the seeds
When I hoped I recollect [F.P.]
When roses cease to bloom, Sir   III
When they come back—if blossoms do [F.P.]
Which misses most
While it is alive
Who giants know, with lesser men [F.P.]
Who never wanted, maddest joy   III
Who occupies this house
Who were the Father and the Son [S.H.]
Whole gulfs of red and fleets of red
Why make it doubt—it hurts it so [F.P.]
Within my garden rides a bird [F.P.]

Class B.   "Was not" was all the statement
We, bee and I, live by the quaffing [F.P.]
We do not play on graves
We miss a kinsman more [F.P.]
We pray to heaven, we prate of heaven [F.P.]
We prove it now, whoever doubt [U.P.]
We send the wave to find the wave   *Letters* [1894]
We should not mind so small a flower [S.H.]
We talked as girls do, Fond and late [F.P.]
Were it but me that gained the height
Wert thou but ill that I might show thee
What I can do I will [F.P.]
What care the dead for chanticleer [E.D.F.F.]
What shall I do, it whimpers so—
What shall I do when the summer troubles
What twigs we held by, oh! the view [U.P.]
When bells stop ringing

When diamonds are a legend [U.P.]
When I have seen the sun emerge
When I hoped I feared Vol. II
When I see not I better see
When one has given up one's life
When the astronomer stops seeking
Where I am not afraid to go
Where I have lost, I softlier tread [E.D.F.F.]
Where thou art, that is home [F.P.]
Which is best—heaven
Which is the best, the moon or the crescent?
Who court obtain within himself [F.P.]
Who goes to dine must take his feast
Who is the East?
Who saw no sunrise cannot say
Why do I love you sir? Because [F.P.]
Why do they shut me out of heaven [F.P.]
Winter is good, his hoar delights
Without this there is naught [U.P.]
Wolfe demanded, during dying

Class C.   We don't cry, Tim and I
We learned the whole of love
We lose because we win
We see, comparatively [F.P.]
What we see we know somewhat
What would I give to see his face [F.P.]
When thrones accost my hands [part of "My reward for
    being"]
When we stand on the tops of things
Where bells no more affright the morn
With thee in the desert

Class A.   You cannot put a fire out III
You'll find it when you try to die [F.P.]
You've seen balloons set, haven't you? III
Class B.   You love the Lord you cannot see
You said that I was great, one day
You'll know her by her foot
Class C.   You constituted time
You know that portrait in the moon [U.P.]
You love me—you are sure
You see, I cannot see your lifetime [F.P.]
You taught me waiting with myself [F.P.]

You'll know it as you know 'tis noon [U.P.]
You're right, the way is narrow

Additional poems already copied but not included in the 1891 notebook

A house upon the height
A sloop of amber slips away,   III
A wind that rose though not a leaf, E.D.F.F.; 2d stanza, *Letters*, 1931
Ah, Teneriffe, receding mountain, S.H., different
And with what body do they come, *Letters*, 1894, page 335, prose
As imperceptibly as grief. This copy has four additional stanzas,   II
As subtle as tomorrow
As watchers hang upon the East
As willing lid o'er weary eye

Bliss is the sceptre of the child
By a departing light

Confirming all who analyze, E.D.F.F.
Consulting summer's clock

Declaiming waters none may dread, E.D.F.F.
Did life's penurious length
Dreams are the subtle dower

Endow the living with the tears

From all the jails the boys and girls, *Youth's Companion*, September
     22, 1892, and III

Go slow, my soul, to feed thyself, *Letters*, 1894
God is indeed a jealous God

Had I known that the first was the last
He was my host—he was my guest
Her breast was fit for pearls, *Letters*, 1894
Her face was in a bed of hair
Her spirit rose to such a height. The second stanza of this poem, "More
     prudent to assault the dawn," was published in E.D.F.F.
His oriental heresies
How spacious the wind must feel morns. First stanza reads "How lone-
     some the wind must feel nights," in Emily's writing

I often passed the village
If all the griefs I am to have
If I should cease to bring a rose
If wrecked upon the shoal of thought
Is immortality a bane

Lethe in my flower
Love can do all but raise the dead

March is the month of expectation, S.H.

No man saw awe
Not all die early, dying young,   *Letters,* 1894

Oh, honey of an hour
One crown that no one seeks

Proud of my broken heart since thou dids't break it,   III. Second stanza
    unpublished

Soft as the massacre of suns
Soul, take thy risks
Summer has two beginnings
Summer laid her simple hat. The second stanza of this poem, "Summer
    laid her supple glove," was published in *Letters,* 1894

That it will never come again
The Bible is an untold volume, *The Complete Poems,* 1924
The day grew small, surrounded tight
The day she goes or day she stays
The drop that wrestles in the sea
The incidents of love, S.H.
The joy that has no stem nor core
The mob within the heart
The moon upon her fluent route, S.H., different second stanza
The most important population
The most triumphant bird,   *Letters,* 1894
The parasol is the umbrella's daughter
The things we thought that we should do,   *Letters,* 1931
The waters chased him as he fled
The words the happy say
Their barricade against the sky
There comes an hour when begging stops

This docile one inter
Through those old grounds of memory
To the unwilling dust, "To the staunch dust," S.H.
'Twas here my summer paused

We never know how high we are,   III
What mystery pervades a well,   III
What tenements of clover, *Letters,* 1894

List of Events

Used by Mrs. Todd as an aid in affixing dates to Emily's letters

Emily stopped dating her letters at a comparatively early age. To arrange them in chronological order, therefore, required detective work of an exacting nature. One of the devices used by Mrs. Todd in order to discover when they had been written was a list of events either mentioned or indirectly alluded to by Emily, events for which exact dates could be determined. Kept always at hand, the list was written with wide spaces between the lines so that the dates of related events could be inserted as they were ascertained. It lengthened as the search continued until the book of letters was actually off the press and no further changes could be made.

The list, including several incomplete and repetitious items, is reproduced without alteration. I have not verified the subject matter.

1. Great Chicago fire 1871—November.
2. Mrs. Holland in Berlin winter 1870.
3. Dr. Holland died October, 1881.
4. "Annie" was married December 7, 1881.
5. Mrs. Holland's little boy was born 1859.
6. "Minnie" was her sister, who died about 1883, having been married in 1856.
7. "Little Katie" was very ill in the summer of 1854, and the autumn.
8. Post Office burned night of July 3 & 4, 1879.
9. Phoenix Row started to burn spring 1881, burned off roof.
10. Started again in Young's shop fall of 1883.
11. Mrs. President Hitchcock died May 26, 1863.
12. Dr. Stearns died June 8, 1876.
13. New London Northern R.R. opened April 1853. Professor Crowell, then a student, was first passenger—rode in freight car to take his examinations.
14. May 9, 1853 formal opening.
15. "New London Day," a sort of celebration of its opening early June, 1853.
16. Pelham water first introduced 1879?
17. Edward Dickinson in Legislature winter of 1873–74;

18. also for six years, beginning 1835–36.
19. Edward Dickinson in Congress 1853–54.
20. "Cousin Harriet" broke her hip M'ch 28, 1872.
21. Miss Norcross's mother died, April 1860.
22. Miss Norcross's father died 1864.
23. "Myra" was wife of an uncle [Joel W. Norcross], and died May 4, 1862.
24. Who is "Marian Earl?" In *Aurora Leigh*. (*Erle*)
25. George Eliot died in December 1880.
26. Maggie's brother was supposed to be killed in a mine, Sept. 1880.
27. Edward Dickinson died June 16, 1874; funeral June 19.
28. Commencement, about 1853, was in August.
29. The Law School term closed in July, at that time.
30. Austin Dickinson graduated at Amherst, 1850, at the Harvard Law School 1854. In between, one term (fall 1850) at Sunderland teaching, spring of 1851 and fall, teaching Endicott School in Boston, also spring of 1852 till July. Then read law in his father's office. Spring of 1853 at Harvard Law School, and winter & spring of 1854, graduating in July 1854.
31. Jenny Lind sang in Northampton July 3, 1851, at old First Church.
32. When did little 'Irish Maggie' die? July 27, 1872.
33. "The departed Humphrey" was a graduate of Amherst (1846) and valedictorian; then had charge of famous Amherst Academy, subsequently studied theology, was Tutor at A., and died 30 Nov. 1850.
34. What winter was Mr. Edward Dickinson very ill? 187 .
35. Mrs. Edward Dickinson died autumn 1882.
36. Frazer Stearns was killed March 14, 1862.
     Battle of Newbern, Mar. 14, 1862. Order of Gen. Burnside. Headqrs, Dept N. Car., Newbern, 16 March 1862—Special Order No. 52
     The Comdg. Gen. directs that the 6-pounder brass gun taken in the battery where Adjutant Stearns of the 21st Mass. Volunteers met his death, while gallantly fighting at the battle of Newbern shall be presented to his regiment, as a monument to the memory of a brave man.

             By command of Brig. Gen. A. E. Burnside
     [This explanatory note is in Professor Todd's handwriting.]
37. The Dickinsons moved from North Street house *home*, in 1855.
38. Samuel Bowles died 1878, January 16th.
39. "There is no frigate like a book," written in pencil, about 1873.
40. Emily was in Cambridge & Boston for her eyes between 1863 & 1865, Nov. Summer of 1864 first.
41. Maggie had a fever, 1880.

42. Austin had malarial fever autumn 1876.
43. Professor Tuckerman died March 15, 1886.
44. Mr. Jenkins was in Amherst 1864 to 1877.
45. Mrs. Hanson Read's little boys died Dec. 25, 1873. Wm. H. Sam. J.
46. When did some favorite sister of Mrs. E. Dickinson's die? (Answer —It was Mrs. Norcross—April, 1860.)
47. Mr. Bowles went to Europe for his health 1862, in the *China*.
48. When did the war 'break out'? Spring, 1861.
49. Kimberley's barn burned the second Saturday before Com. 1851. (This was probably late July.)
50. Mr. Dwight invited as pastor early summer 1853, entered on duty 21 August, and installed July 19, 1854.
51. *Caput mortuum et cap-a-pie* (The worthless remains, and from head to foot)
52. When was P. Cowan married? Ans. Oct. 26, 1870.
53. When did his sister Margaret die? Nov. 17, '83.
54. When did little Margie die? Nov. 8, 1879.
55. Was "Charlie" another Bowles son? Yes.
56. When was Jeff Davis captured? May 10th, 1865.
57. When were Mary, Sally and Sam Bowles born? Before 1861.
58. When was a fourth born? 1861.
59. When did Mr. Bowles go to Europe for his health in the *China*? Spring, 1862.
60. 'Charlie'—a fourth Bowles child, born December 19, 1861.
61. 'Juneating' apple, usually ripe by 20th July—North Street house.
62. Mr. Bowles's Washington trip—many.
63. Mr. Dickinson first met Samuel Bowles in 1850 at Monson.
64. Hawthorne died 19th May, 1864.
65. Jenny Lind sang in Boston, 1851 (spring).
66. Emily stayed at 86 Austin Street, Cambridgeport.
67. Fast day is   . Eugenia Hall was married Oct. 20, 1885.
68. "Cattle-show" was anywhere from September to November.
69. Samuel Bowles (IV) was engaged to Miss Hoar October, 1883.
70.   "   "   "   was married May, 1884.
71. Samuel Bowles V was born August, 1885.
72. Charlie Bowles was engaged about September, 1885.
73. Whig Convention in Baltimore June 1852, trying to nominate Webster for President; Scott got it.
74. What Governor *Bross* was in an engraving with Colfax and Mr. Bowles?
75. When did Martha Kingman and Jennie Grout die? October 30 & October 27, 1851.

76. First regular trip on Amherst & Belchertown & New London railroad was May 9th 1853.

77. "New London Day," early in June 1853, 325 New London people came up to Amherst.

78. When were Professor Adams' sons killed? Ch. Breck, Sept. 17, Sylvester Holmes Dec. 29, 1861.

79. When was the chime of bells given? & for whom? Amherst men killed in the war. Inscription, Amherst College Church:
These bells are placed here by George Howe of Boston and are to be made to chime on all suitable occasions in commemoration of the brave patriots connected with Amherst College who lost their lives in the war against the Great Rebellion of 1861. [Note in Professor Todd's handwriting.]

80. When was Rubinstein in Boston? Fall 1872 & early in 1873.

81. When did Mrs. Browning die? June 29, 1861.

82. 'Eliza' died June, 1871.

83. Norcrosses at Berkeley, Feb. '73, to Oct. '74.

84. Edward Dickinson talked of for Lieutenant-Governor,   .

85. Mr. Jameson postmaster from   to   .

86. President Garfield shot July [2], 1881.

87. 'Yellow Day' Sept. 6, 1881.

88. Article on Emily Brontë, *Galaxy*, Feb. 1873.

89. Harriet Prescott's *Circumstance*,   .

90. Mr. Bowles went to California, spring 1873.

91. Eugenia Hall was married Oct. 20, 1885.

92. Mr. Jenkins pastor from 1864 to 1877.

93. Mr. Emerson pastor from 18[79] to 188[3].

94. Professor Snell died Sept. 18, 1876.

95. Professor Chickering left here   1885.

96. Professor Root died   1881.

97. When was the volume of poems in the *No Name* series published. *Masque of Poets*, 1878.

98. 'H.H.' died August 12, 1885.

99. Emily Brontë died Tuesday, Dec. 19, 1848, aged 29.

100. 'Sounds from Home' by Gungl.

101. Did Mr. Bowles go twice to California?

102. President Lincoln assassinated April 14, 1865.

Deed to Land

KNOW ALL MEN BY THESE PRESENTS,

That I, Lavinia N. Dickinson, of Amherst, County of Hampshire and Commonwealth of Massachusetts, in consideration of the sum of one dollar and other valuable considerations paid by Mabel Loomis Todd, of said Amherst, the receipt whereof is hereby ackowledged, do hereby give, grant, bargain, sell and convey unto the said Mabel Loomis Todd a certain lot of land lying in the center of said Amherst, bounded and described as follows, viz: Beginning at the northwest corner of same, which is the northeast corner of premises already owned by said Mabel L. Todd (conveyed in deed dated June 8th, 1886, entered with Hampshire County Deeds, libro 404, folio 89), thence running south 13° west two hundred and eighty feet on premises of said Mabel L. Todd to premises of Miss Mary I. Cooper; thence south 62° 12′ east on premises of said Miss Mary I. Cooper fifty-four and one-quarter feet to a stone post which marks the more northern of the two northeastern corners of premises of said Miss Mary I. Cooper; thence northerly in a line parallel with the first mentioned line two hundred and ninety-two and one-quarter feet to the point of intersection of said Mabel L. Todd's north line extended east on the highway known as Fowler street (extension of Spring street eastward), thence fifty-three feet westerly to the point of beginning, containing fifty-five and one-half square rods, more or less.

To have and to hold the granted premises with all the privileges and appurtenances thereto belonging to the said Mabel Loomis Todd and her heir and assigns to their own use and behoof forever, and I hereby for myself and my heirs, executors and administrators, covenant with the grantee and her heirs and assigns, that I am lawfully seized in fee-simple of the granted premises, that they are free from all incumbrances; and that I have a good right to sell and convey the same as aforesaid, and that I will and my heirs, executors and administrators shall warrant and defend the same to the grantee and her heirs and assigns forever against the lawful claims and demands of all persons.

In witness whereof, I, the said Lavinia N. Dickinson, hereunto set my hand and seal, this seventh day of February, in the year one thousand eight hundred and ninety-six.

Signed, sealed and delivered in presence of

T. G. SPAULDING   LAVINIA N. DICKINSON

(Seal)

COMMONWEALTH OF MASSACHUSETTS.

HAMPSHIRE, SS.   February 7th, 1896.

Then personally appeared the above-named Lavinia N. Dickinson and acknowledged the foregoing instrument to be her free act and deed, before me.

TIMOTHY G. SPAULDING.
Justice of the Peace.

HAMPSHIRE, SS.   April 1, 1896, 3 o'clock 0 minutes, P.M.

ROBERT W. LYMAN, Register.

A true copy of record contained in Book 485, page 13.

Index

Set in Linotype Baskerville
Format by A. W. Rushmore
Manufactured by The Haddon Craftsmen
Published by HARPER & BROTHERS
New York and London